THE CODIFICATION OF JEWISH LAW

AND AN

INTRODUCTION TO THE

JURISPRUDENCE OF THE *MISHNA BERURA*

THE CODIFICATION OF JEWISH LAW

AND AN
INTRODUCTION TO THE
JURISPRUDENCE OF THE
MISHNA BERURA

Michael J. Broyde and Ira Bedzow

Boston 2014

Library of Congress Cataloging-in-Publication Data:
A catalog record for this title is available from the Library of Congress.

Cover design by Ivan Grave

ISBN 978-1-61811-278-1 (hardback)
ISBN 978-1-61811-279-8 (ebook)
ISBN 978-1-61811-451-8 (paperback)

Published by Academic Studies Press in 2014

28 Montfern Avenue
Brighton, MA 02135, USA
press@academicstudiespress.com
www.academicstudiespress.com

ACKNOWLEDGMENTS

Many people have contributed in different ways to the writing of this book and we would like to thank them:

Thank you to the Center for the Study of Law and Religion, the Law School and the Tam Institute of Jewish studies, all at Emory University, who supported us in writing this work, and the editors at *Hamline Law Review* for reviewing and publishing an earlier version of portions of this book as an article.

We particularly also want to thank Jerry and Chaya Weinberger, who supported our work in dedication to their son's, Shmuel's, bar mitzvah. Their support was a demonstration of the ideal that parents wish for their children to continue to grow and study works of Torah and Halakha, and that their learning enhances their practice and observance.

We would like to thank the many different people who helped with production of the manuscript. In particular, Sharona Vedol of Academic Studies Press helped us in many different ways. Thank you as well to Leah Levy, Judah Berger, and Avraham Lewis, who proofread various parts of this work. Many people—too many to name and thank individually—read different portions of this work, and we are grateful to each of them.

Most importantly, each of us has been privileged to be married to wonderful women without whose patience, love, affection, and kindness we would be lost, and we dedicate this book to Channah S. Broyde and Rachel Johanna Bedzow. We are both truly blessed to be married to women who have supported us in so many ways. "The heart of her husband safely trusts in her, and [therefore] he has no lack of gain."

TABLE OF CONTENTS

I

General Methodology of Codification of Jewish Law

Due to its exilic development since the beginning of the Common Era, Jewish law[1] lacks a clear method for resolving disputes. Talmudic, medieval, and contemporary debates linger, since direct, categorical rules of resolution, such as majority votes of the Supreme Court in the United States or Papal pronouncements in canon law, do not exist. The exact reason for this is beyond the scope of this introduction, yet some methodological explanation will allow the reader to have a better understanding of the relationship of the modern classical work of Jewish law, the *Mishna Berura*,[2] to other jurisprudential approaches to obedience to Jewish law.

Until about two thousand years ago, the Jewish community had a "supreme court" called the Sanhedrin,[3] a (parliamentary) joint legislative and judicial assembly that resolved disputes in matters of Jewish law by majority vote.[4] Following the destruction

---

1   For a brief note on the history of Halakha, see appendix B.

2   Though the *Mishna Berura* was written by Rabbi Israel Meir Kagan, and we provide a brief biography of the author, this article addresses the book and not the author. It is the methodology of the *Mishna Berura* as a book, not Rabbi Kagan as a jurist, that we seek to examine. See *infra* text accompanying notes 52–97 (providing more information on Rabbi Kagan, as well as on the book the *Mishna Berura*).

3   From the Greek Synedrion, the Aramaic word is commonly thought to be a translation of the Hebrew term "members of the Great Assembly," a body which derives its authority from a set of biblical verses in Exodus.

4   Maimonides, *Mishna Torah*, *Sefer Shoftim*, *Hilkhot Sanhedrin Vehaonashin Hamesurin Lahem* (Laws of the Sanhedrin and the punishments they are authorized to administer) 1:1, 3.

of the Second Temple in Jerusalem around 70 CE, this body ceased having undisputed juridical authority. Despite its temporary reconstitution in Yavneh and subsequent locations, the Sanhedrin could no longer impose uniformity of practice. The Mishna (c. 200 CE) bears witness to this phenomenon and illustrates the devolution of the Court by recounting various conflicts among the Sages without attempting to resolve them.

From the time of the disbanding of the Sanhedrin through the centuries following the redaction of the two Talmuds[5] (c. 650–700 CE), disputes as to what the Jewish law should be in any specific case were resolved by an informal, consensus-based voting process in which the ordained rabbis of the generation participated.[6] Not every dispute, however, reached a resolution, and since there was no consensus on what the normative practice should be, the law was left open.[7]

From about the year 700 CE until the modern era the process for resolving disputes further deteriorated, to the point that even informal consensus was no longer possible. Moreover, diverse halakhic opinions began to proliferate. This combination had various reasons: for example, geography made communication across communities difficult, and increased interest in Talmud study in areas with very diverse living conditions led to different ways to understand the Talmudic texts as influenced by location. Regardless of the reason, however, disagreements on points of law became common, and methods of dispute resolution became highly analytical. Support for one opinion over another rested upon which opinion was seen to be more consistent with the accepted Talmudic sources. The opinion that was shown to be a more accurate

---

5   Indeed, though the Babylonian (c. 500 CE) and Palestinian (c. 350–400 CE) Talmuds are often in accord, the very notion of two Talmuds points to a decline in any ability to develop a unified consensus authority for Jewish law.

6   Thus, for example, the Talmud sometimes concludes a dispute with the word "*vehilcheta,*" which is generally understood to mean "and this is the proper practice," denoting the consensus that is mentioned above.

7   In some instances a consensus developed, but uncertainty has since arisen as to what that consensus ruling actually was.

interpretation of Talmudic intention, given the particular social context in which it was being applied, was accepted as superior.

In many cases, the tools to evaluate various positions were insufficient in and of themselves to resolve disputes in Jewish law. Indeed, many cases exist where post-Talmudic discourse reached an impasse and was unable to provide an intellectually honest determination of which view should be considered correct. For instance, regarding a Talmudic discussion of whether the daughter of a non-Jewish man and a Jewish woman is permitted to marry a *Kohen*,[8] three equally legitimate readings (and rulings) emerge among the post-Talmudic jurists. The variances depend on whether one considers the authority of the Talmudic statements in question to be of equal weight or not. The inability to draw a single, unequivocal ruling is partially the result of the open-textual nature of the Talmud[9] which, while allowing flexibility for adaptation, may at times create ambiguity by permitting multiple positions to be seen as reasonable. Determining which of those reasonable positions ought, in fact, to be followed normatively cannot be done in many cases through the use of only first-tier principles of analytical jurisprudence.

For circumstances of this nature, commentators and codifiers developed *second*-order guidelines for decision-making, which would allow one to determine what to do when logical reasoning and close textual analysis alone cannot provide answers. These second-tier guidelines have never undergone a thorough analysis in English (and though they are quite central to Jewish law, such an analysis has never been done in Hebrew either). The second-order jurisprudential framework contains many nuanced and complex principles, prioritizing between matters of doubtful biblical or

---

8   BT, *Yevamot* 44a–45b. It is worth noting that conflicting conclusions may be reached in this case despite the appearance of the term *vehilcheta*; see *supra*, note 6.

9   See H.L.A. Hart, *The Concept of Law* (Oxford: Clarendon Press, 1961), 121-32 (describing the nature of open-textual nature of law); H.L.A. Hart, "Positivism and the Separation of Law and Morals," *Harvard Law Review* 71 (1957): 593, 607 (providing examples of what is meant by the "open-textual nature of laws").

rabbinic obligation, between ritual and financial obligation, and so on.[10] For the purpose of demonstrating the interplay among various second-order guidelines, let us provide just one example.

Jewish law mandates that when one is in doubt regarding a matter of biblical law, one should seek to be strict and fulfill it. Therefore, if people are not certain whether they have eaten *matzah* (the unleavened bread)[11] on the first night of Passover, they should eat again, since it is a biblical obligation to do so. On the other hand, Jewish law also states that, in matters of financial law, the plaintiff bears the burden of proof. The second-order framework would have to be applied when these two rules come into conflict. Consider, for example, an unfortunate fellow who is not sure if he has stolen from someone or not. Should he, due to the fact that stealing is a violation of biblical law, return that which he might have stolen, or may he decline, arguing that the potential returnee bears the burden of proof? Alternatively, consider the poor fellow who is uncertain as to whether he has already fulfilled his obligation to eat *matzah* on Passover, and sitting in front of him are *matzoth* (plural for *matzah*), which might or might not belong to him. Should he eat them, or not?

In response to these challenges, Jewish law will often invoke principles that are rooted not entirely in legal doctrine, but rather in social policy, such as "for the needs of the community,"[12] "due to the fear of dire financial loss,"[13] or permitting certain conduct "for the sake of the ill."[14] In light of the first-order and second-order principles for the purpose of analogy, Jewish law can be perceived as a box of normativity, instead of a point, whereby any action within the defined space would be deemed acceptable. The

---

10 See *Shulhan Arukh, Yoreh Deah* 242, *Shulhan Arukh, Hoshen Mishpat* 25, and *Shulhan Arukh, Yoreh Deah* 110–11, each of which codifies many of these rules. For a one-volume review of these rules, see Hayyim Hezekiah Medini, *Sedei Hemed, Klalei Ha-Poskim.*

11 See *Exodus* 12:14–20; *Deuteronomy* 16:1–8; BT *Pesahim* 120a.

12 See, e.g., *Shulhan Arukh, Orah Hayyim* 544:1; *Yoreh Deah* 228:21.

13 See, e.g., *Shulhan Arukh, Orah Hayyim* 467:11, 12; *Yoreh Deah* 23:2, 31:1.

14 See, e.g., *Shulhan Arukh, Orah Hayyim* 464:4.

variability of life necessitates that Jewish law has the flexibility to allow people to serve God properly. Yet just because the whole of the interior of the box is acceptable, it does not mean that each choice is, in fact, equally preferred. Second-order values, as manifested in the second-order principles, are promoted by limiting the *preferred* realm of desired normative action.

II

History of Codification

The ambiguity of legal decisions that the lack of a central organization engenders poses a direct hindrance to the very purpose of Jewish law, namely its adherence. Therefore, with the start of the medieval era, different approaches arose to negotiate between the first-order and second-order principles so as to develop a consistent and feasible legal practice.

One school of thought, led by Rashi,[1] his disciples, and their descendants, disregarded the priority of taking a systematic approach and creating a clearly delineated halakhic code. Rather, they focused on creating coherency throughout the Talmud. This school's major endeavor was to write commentaries and super-commentaries to explain the Talmud page by page, issue by issue, in an attempt to harmonize the diverse strands of thought found within it. Ironically, this approach gave rise to the opposite conclusion. Instead of clarity, even more confusion arose; and in the attempt to unify the Talmud, diverse theories and approaches to creating harmony developed. *Baalei HaTosafot* (or Tosafists, prominent among whom were some of Rashi's descendants) created a style of legal discourse that flourished with diverse models of analytical thought where there was only the occasional

---

1   Rabbi Shlomo Itzhaki (1040–1105) of France, author of a comprehensive commentary on both the Hebrew Bible and the Talmud. Rashi's prominence and wide acceptance has made his work the point of departure for much of Talmudic scholarship over the last nine hundred plus years.

narrowing of focus; frequently, they posited modes of analysis that, instead of contracting, vastly expanded many of the substantive disagreements in Jewish law into even greater (and irresolvable) disputes.

Coterminous with these commentaries, the movement to craft a Jewish law code developed primarily among Sefardic Jewry. Starting with the *Rif*[2] (and continuing through, and finally culminating with, *Rambam's*[3] *Mishne Torah*[4]), the first attempt to craft a "code of Jewish law" was undertaken. *Rif*, by deleting all the sections of the Talmud he thought to be non-normative, and *Rambam*, by building on this structure and actively writing a code of Jewish law based on, but distinct from, the Talmud, sought to change the basic structure of Halakha into an ordered, hierarchical system in which every question has one, and only one, correct answer. Had this approach alone taken hold, Jewish law would have developed into a law code similar, at some level, to many other legal systems.

---

2   Rabbi Yitzchak Al-Fasi (1013–1103) of Morocco was best known for his legal code *Sefer Ha-halakhot*, considered the first fundamental work in codified halakhic literature.

3   Moses ben-Maimon; Maimonides (1135–1204) was born in Spain and died either in Egypt or Tiberias. Maimonides was a preeminent philosopher, jurist, and physician and is acknowledged as one of the foremost arbiters of rabbinic law in all of Jewish history.

4   Literally "Repetition of the Torah," subtitled *Sefer Yad ha-Hazaka*, "Book of the Strong Hand." Compiled between 1170 and 1180, *Mishne Torah* consists of fourteen books, subdivided into sections, chapters, and paragraphs. It is the only medieval-era work that details *all* of Jewish observance, including those laws that are only applicable when the Holy Temple is in existence.

Despite *Rambam*'s influence, many of the great men who followed, such as *Rosh*,[5] *Ritva*,[6] *Ramban*,[7] *Rashba*,[8] and *Meiri*,[9] forsook *Rambam*'s approach and adopted the model of the *Baalei HaTosafot*, reverting back to writing Talmudic novella or commentaries. They also frequently concluded that more than one approach was viable and, as a result, steadfastly refused to write definitive conclusions to Talmudic matters. One who wished to determine what "Jewish law" was on a given topic in the 1300s would have encountered the problem that there was not one definitive legal book to consult to answer that question. Rather, there was a compendium of opinions which he would have to consider.

The son of *Rosh*, Rabbi Yaakov ben Asher,[10] recognized this lacuna and sought to fill it by writing another code of law. Unlike the *Mishne Torah*, which was much broader in that it attempted to restate all of Jewish law, Rabbi Yaakov covered only those areas of Halakha that were in practice in his time; it was written to be a

---

5   Rabbi Asher ben Jehiel (Ashkenazi) was born in Germany (in either 1250 or 1259) and died in Spain (in 1327). His abstract of Talmudic law focuses only on the legal (non-aggadic) portions of the text and specifies the final, practical Halakha, leaving out the intermediate discussions and entirely omitting areas of law that are limited to the Land of Israel.

6   Rabbi Yom Tov ben Avraham Asevilli (1250–1330) of Spain is known for his clarity of thought and his commentary on the Talmud, which is extremely concise and remains one of the most frequently referenced Talmudic works today.

7   Rabbi Moses ben Naḥman Girondi (also known as Nahmanides) was born in Gerona, Spain, in 1194 and died in Israel in 1270. A leading medieval philosopher, physician, Kabbalist, and commentator, his commentary on the Talmud, *Hiddushei HaRamban*, often provides a different perspective on a variety of issues addressed by the *Baalei Tosafot*.

8   Rabbi Shlomo ben Aderet (1235–1310) of Spain was the author of thousands of Responsa, various halakhic works, and the *Hiddushei HaRashba* commentary on the Talmud.

9   Rabbi Menachem Meiri (1249–1310) of Barcelona authored his commentary, the *Beit HaBehirah*, which is arranged in a manner similar to the Talmud, presenting first the Mishna and then the discussions and issues that arise from it. He focuses on the final upshot of the discussion and presents the differing views of that upshot and conclusion.

10 Rabbi Yaakov ben Asher, the third son of *Rosh*, was born in Germany in 1270 and died in Spain in 1340.

practical and convenient halakhic guide for people living outside of Israel in a time when there was no Temple. His four-volume work, the *Tur*, divided all of Jewish law into "four pillars" (*Arba Turim*) or areas; namely, daily life (including the laws of Shabbat and Yom Tov), family law, commercial law, and ritual law. Another major difference between the *Tur* and the *Mishne Torah* was that the *Tur* was not a definitive legal code in the same way the *Mishne Torah* was. While the *Rambam* approached legal questions with the assumption that there was only one right answer, Rabbi Yaakov wrote a compendium in which every legal question possessed a number of reasonable answers. As such, while the book is extremely useful, given the alternatives, the reader of the *Tur* is left with little reward but the time it would have taken to look up all the various answers and opinions for himself. Rabbi Yosef Karo's classic commentary on the *Tur*, the *Bet Yosef*, is an expansion of the *Tur*'s methodology. It adds the views of many of the *Rishonim* and connects their views to the Talmudic discussion, but it does not systematically provide a mandate as to what the normative law should be.

To rectify this situation,[11] Rabbi Karo undertook the responsibility of writing yet another legal code, the *Shulhan Arukh*, which was meant to follow the structure of the *Tur* and the methodology of *Rambam,* providing one—and only one—answer to questions of Jewish law in the areas that the *Tur* covered.[12] In fact, the *Shulhan Arukh* derives most of its rules from *Rambam*'s code, though it does frequently deviate from *Rambam*'s rulings, especially when a

---

11   To see a demonstration that Rabbi Karo understood the difficulty of knowing the normative Halakha from reading the *Bet Yosef*, and that he desired that the *Shulhan Arukh* would rectify the problem, see his introduction to the *Shulhan Arukh*, a relevant section of which is found immediately below.

12   There are instances in the *Shulhan Arukh* where Rabbi Karo will give a ruling and will then give another opinion using the phrase, "There are those who say," or something to that effect. When this occurs, Rabbi Karo is not seeking to avoid giving a definitive normative position. Rather, due to the historical difficulties that were discussed above, a truly definitive decision has not been concluded. Therefore, Rabbi Karo tries to account for verifiable alternatives even while indicating the position he deems normative.

unanimous consensus from other authorities rejects the *Rambam*'s view. Calling it the *Shulhan Arukh*, or "Set Table,"[13] to suggest that everything was prepared for its user, he describes his decision to write the book as follows:

> I saw in my heart that it would be good to put the numerous statements [in the *Bet Yosef*] in a condensed form and in a precise language so that the Torah of Hashem will be continuous and fluent in the mouth of every Jew ... so that any practical ruling about which he may have a question will be clear to him when this magnificent book which covers everything is fluent in his mouth. ... Moreover, young students will study it continuously so that they memorize it. Its clear language regarding the practical Halakha will be set on their young lips, so that when they get older they will not deviate from it. Also, scholars will take care of it as if it was light from the Heavens easing them from their troubles, and their souls will be recreated when studying this book which contains all the sweet *halakhot*, decided without controversy.[14]

According to Rabbi Karo, those who would read the *Shulhan Arukh* would be able to discern the laws of daily living and would not need to consult other opinions. Yet, consistent with the historical development of Jewish Law, immediately after the publication of the *Shulhan Arukh*, other *poskim* (decisors) began to write their comments on it, both to explain it and to contradict it. The codification, however, succeeded in that the underlying assumption for its commentators was that it was in fact a "set table" and needed only a few minor adornments or adjustments.

The first to comment and append decisions to the *Shulhan Arukh* so as to provide alternative positions which were considered normative was Rabbi Moses Isserles.[15] Rabbi Isserles, in addition, wrote a work similar to the *Bet Yosef* in that it provides additional information to the *Tur* without systematically providing the

---

13 For a brief note on the titles of books in the Jewish legal tradition, see Appendix D.

14 Rabbi Karo, Introduction to the *Shulhan Arukh*.

15 Rabbi Moses Isserles, also known as *Rema* or Moshe Isserlis, was born in Krakow, Poland, and lived from 1520 to 1572.

normative Halakha, as well as a legal work called *Torat Hatat*. In his glosses on Rabbi Karo's code, the *Shulhan Arukh*, Rabbi Isserles incorporated Ashkenazic Jewry's practices into the predominantly Sefardic-oriented work. These glosses, however, revert back to the practice of accepting juridical ambiguity. *Rema* is inclined to cite more than one opinion as normative, both in theory and in practice, and frequently cites conflicting views without a clear manner of resolving contradiction.

Other commentaries to the *Shulhan Arukh* developed, and conflicts between them added to the uncertainty of how to determine the normative law. The most significant early commentaries that are associated with the *Shulhan Arukh* include the *Taz*,[16] *Bet Shmuel*,[17] *Shakh*,[18] *Sema*,[19] and *Magen Avraham*.[20] In particular, the *Taz* and the *Magen Avraham* wrote detailed commentaries that incorporate a variety of positions found neither in the *Shulhan Arukh* nor in *Rema*'s glosses. These include citations from the Talmud, *Rishonim*, and the *Zohar*[21] and other works of Jewish mysticism, and a detailed account of the sundry customs practiced in Central and Eastern Europe. The *Shulhan Arukh*, along with its codes, was transformed over a relatively short period of time from a set table to a crowded one, in which the right answer was no longer clear.

By 1830, three detailed additions to the section of the *Shulhan Arukh* called *Orah Hayyim* were added, namely the writings of the

---

16 Rabbi David ha-Levi Segal of Poland (1586–1667) authored the *Taz*.

17 Rabbi Shmuel ben Uri Shraga Faivish of Poland, who lived during the second half of the seventeenth century, wrote the *Bet Shmuel*.

18 Rabbi Shabbatai ben Meir ha-Kohen was born in Lithuania in 1621, died in Moravia in 1662, and wrote the *Shakh*.

19 Rabbi Joshua ben Alexander HaCohen Falk of Poland (1555–1614) authored the *Sema*.

20 Rabbi Avraham Avli ben Chaim HaLevi of Poland (1633–1683) wrote the *Magen Avraham*.

21 Lit. "Splendor"; the foundational work in Kabbalistic literature. The Zohar first appeared in Spain in the thirteenth century, and was published by a Jewish writer named Moses de Leon. De Leon ascribed the work to Rabbi Shimon bar Yochai, a second-century Tanna, who hid in a cave for thirteen years studying the Torah to escape Roman persecution and, according to legend, was inspired by the Prophet Elijah to write the Zohar.

Gra,[22] the *Graz*,[23] and Rabbi Akiva Eiger.[24] The methodological gap between the three works is wide. The *Gra* focuses on Talmudic texts, including the Jerusalem Talmud. The *Graz*, otherwise known as the *Shulhan Arukh HaRav*, was written by the first Lubavitcher Rebbe and is a classic synthesis of prior codes (albeit with a Hassidic slant). Rabbi Akiva Eiger brought the sharp insights and the methodology of the *Tosafot* back into the legal discussion. On complex and nuanced questions, they rarely agree. The *Pri Megadim*,[25] who wrote the *Mishbetzot Zahav* and *Eshel Avraham* as super-commentaries on the *Taz* and *Magen Avraham*, respectively, was yet another prominent figure who reanalyzed and elaborated on many areas of daily living.

By the mid-1800s, two additional short but important self-standing legal codes had become popular—the *Hayye Adam*[26] and the *Kitzur Shulhan Arukh*[27]—which attempted to resolve all disputes and provide a single view for easy comprehension by laypeople. While both of these books were written by eminent Jewish scholars, they have totally different styles and approaches to codification. The *Kitzur Shulhan Arukh* is both simple to use and practically strict, whereas the *Hayye Adam*, who was a disciple of the *Gra*, is deeply analytical in his approach.

This approximately 250-year period of crowding the table also saw the rejuvenation and development of responsa literature, which was a separate genre from the commentaries. The responsa, which were questions and answers on matters of Halakha collected into volumes, formed an alternative to the primarily European model of discerning normative law through commentaries. (The primarily Sefardi model was to write restatements.) While the genre had been dormant for many years in acquiescence to the genre of writing

---

22 Rabbi Elijah ben Shlomo Zalman Kramer, known as the Vilna Gaon, was born in 1720, died in 1797, and lived in Vilna, Lithuania.
23 Rabbi Shneur Zalman of Liadi (1745-1813), the first Lubavitcher Rebbe.
24 Rabbi Akiva Eiger was born in Hungary in 1761 and died in Posen in 1837.
25 Rabbi Joseph ben Meir Teomim (1727–1792) lived in Lemberg, Ukraine.
26 Rabbi Avraham ben Yechial Michel of Danzig (1748–1820) lived in Poland.
27 Rabbi Solomon ben Joseph Ganzfried (1804–1886) lived in Hungary.

commentaries, by the 1700s responsa literature was the primary vehicle for some rabbinic authorities.[28] Both the *Noda b'Yehuda*[29] and the *Hatam Sofer*,[30] as well as many major Eastern European *poskim*, chose to write responsa, adding a whole new set of literature to the melting pot of Jewish law.

By the year 1880, Jewish law in Eastern Europe was anything but clear. There were more than a dozen significant codes, commentaries, and other texts illuminating a myriad of topics, from minor customs and practices to major matters of Torah law. It was difficult for a legal scholar, let alone a layperson, to discern what should be the normative halakhic practice, even on simple matters. Needless to say, it was much harder to know where to turn when deciding complicated issues.

Painting with a broad brush, one can say that until the late 1800s works of Halakha generally fell into one of four distinct categories. The first category comprises works such as the *Arba Turim* and the *Bet Yosef*, collections of halakhic opinions with the occasional conclusive decision.[31] The second category, exemplified by the *Shulhan Arukh* and the *Mishne Torah*, consists of works which clearly delineate the laws without commentary or explanation. The intention of these works is to provide an easy guidebook for proper action. Some, like the *Mishne Torah*, were meant to stand independent of any other work; others, such as the *Shulhan Arukh*, are meant for younger students and for quick review, yet presuppose that their audiences will look elsewhere for greater in-depth analysis.[32] The third category, in which the *Rema*'s glosses on the *Shulhan Arukh*

---

28 Rabbinic authorities had always written responsa to answer halakhic questions. The difference is that at this time writing responsa went from being a practical method of discerning Halakha for individuals to being the primary genre that rabbis used to demonstrate what should be the normative Halakha in general.

29 Rabbi Yechezkel ben Yehuda Landau (1713–1793) lived in Poland.

30 Rabbi Moshe Schreiber (1762-1839) lived in Germany, Austria, and Bratislavia.

31 For Rabbi Yaakov ben Asher, the final decision is that of his father Rabbi Asher ben Yehiel; for Rabbi Karo, the decision is determined by the majority opinion cited.

32 Whether such is the actual case or not is irrelevant to the author's intention (referring to the *Mishne Torah* standing independent of any other work).

and the *Raavad*'s[33] glosses on the *Mishne Torah* are included, contains primarily editorial-like super-commentaries, which add or correct information.[34] The fourth category contains works, such as the *Yam Shel Shlomo*,[35] which attempt to collect all relevant information on a topic, from the Talmud to contemporary times, in order to evaluate the subject properly and determine the correct decision. Of course, these categories are not always so distinct that a work can only fit into one of them. For example, works like those of the *Magen Avraham*, *Taz*, and *Shakh* use a hybrid method, and thus can fit into more than one category.

Into this arena at the end of the 1800s entered two halakhic giants. The first, Rabbi Yehiel Epstein,[36] was the author of the *Arukh HaShulhan* and the *Arukh HaShulhan HeAtid*, a nearly twenty-volume code of Jewish law. Rabbi Epstein's work is recognized by all to be remarkable—it is novel and innovative, grounded in the Talmud and classical post-Talmudic codes, and well written. It follows a simple organizational structure, in which each topic starts with a summary of the passages in the Bible, Talmud, and the codes that are relevant to the topic. Legal decisions almost always revolve around two points of reference—what is the best explanation of the Talmudic precedents and what is the best defense of the Lithuanian practice. When the two results coincide, the decision is obvious. When they do not, he struggles to find a balanced approach that best protects both goals. Like the *Gra*, Rabbi Epstein was comfortable with the full gamut of Talmudic literature, and like *Rambam*, he wrote on—and had a unified understanding of—all of Jewish law. Indeed, in testimony to his awesome breadth, he and *Rambam* are the only two writers in the last two thousand years who undertook to provide a comprehensive code of Jewish law, one which would

---

33   Rabbi Avraham ben David (1125–1198) lived in Provence, France.

34   In the *Rema*'s case, additions are meant to include the local practices of Ashkenaz, which are omitted in the *Shulhan Arukh*. In the *Raavad*'s case, additions are meant to correct what are seen as errors.

35   Solomon Luria, also known as *Maharshal* (1510-1573) lived in Lithuania.

36   Rabbi Yehiel Epstein (1829-1908) served as a rabbi in Lithuania.

encompass both contemporary halakhic issues and those that will arise in the Messianic Age. On the methodological level, however, the *Arukh HaShulhan* is a simple work. It has only two principles, Talmudic correctness and contemporary practice. Other opinions are rejected simply as "wrong."[37]

The second giant, and the methodological opposite to Rabbi Epstein, is Rabbi Israel Meir Kagan of Radin,[38] the author of the *Mishna Berura*. At the foundational level, the *Mishna Berura* assumes that virtually all disputes of Jewish law and Talmudic understanding are irresolvable, in the sense that Rabbi Epstein considers them exactly to be resolvable. "Correct" practice is therefore difficult to discern, and the defense of custom is not the sole alternative justification when common practice differs from what should be Jewish law based on one's understanding of the sources. Moreover, according to Rabbi Kagan, even the *Shulhan Arukh* alone,

---

37 Of course, this is somewhat of a simplification of the *Arukh HaShulhan*'s methodology but this assessment is more or less correct. The *Arukh HaShulhan* has many unique features—foremost being the unique process it uses to determine Talmudic correctness—but the only factor that can offset Talmudic correctness is the custom (*minhag*) of the community of its author. Of course, the greatness of the *Arukh HaShulhan* is its unique methodological process for determining Talmudic correctness. We see six factors regularly used. First, it is fiercely independent in its intellectual thought process, and defers to the judgment of no other halakhic authority, including the *Gra*. The *Arukh HaShulhan* is not afraid to make novel insights, or even craft new rules based on the judgment of its author. Second, it is much more comfortable acknowledging the changing social and technological reality than the books of its author's peers were. Third, the *Arukh HaShulhan* uses the Jerusalem Talmud as a significant factor in its halakhic decisions, frequently citing novel passages and understandings of the Jerusalem Talmud and deriving new halakhic rules from them. Fourth, the *Arukh HaShulhan* tends to assign the most prominent role as a posek to the *Rambam*, which is almost unheard of for an Ashkenazi *posek*. Fifth, the *Arukh HaShulhan* seems to believe that Kabbala and Halakha never conflict, and seeks to resolve such tensions through reinterpretation, rather than resolution. Finally, and most importantly, the *Arukh HaShulhan* simply decides which halakhic position is correct, and advises that one follow that position, rather than recommend strategies to avoid resolving disputes. As one who reads this work will see, the *Mishnah Berura* rejects each of these approaches.

38 Rabbi Israel Meir Kagan (1838-1933) lived in a section of Poland that is currently part of Belarus.

the supposed "set table of easily understood rulings for daily practice," and even without the multitude of commentaries and asso-
ciate codes, is not really as clear-cut as Rabbi Karo asserted. As the
primary reason for writing his commentary, the *Mishna Berura*
writes:

> The *Shulhan Arukh*, without with learning the *Tur* along with it, is an
> obscure book, since when the *Bet Yosef* ordered the *Shulhan Arukh*
> his intention was that one would first learn the essential laws and
> their sources from the *Tur* and the *Bet Yosef*, in order to understand
> the ruling, each one according to its reasoning. Since the *Tur* and the
> *Bet Yosef* bring numerous differing opinions for each law, he thus
> decided to write the *Shulhan Arukh* to make known the ruling in prac-
> tice for each law. It was not his intention, however, that we would
> learn it alone, since the law is not able to sit well with a person unless
> he understands the reasoning behind it.[39]

The *Mishna Berura* is thus Rabbi Kagan's attempt to elucidate for the
layperson, and not only for the legal scholar, both *what* should be
the normative halakhic practice and *why* it should be so, for complicated halakhic matters and for simple daily life alike.

By reframing Rabbi Karo's "Set Table" as an ambiguous work
that cannot be studied on its own, the *Mishna Berura* establishes
two essential premises upon which his methodology rests. The first
is that many times the *Shulhan Arukh* will write one ruling in terms
of an *ab initio* perspective and another in terms of an *ex post facto*
perspective, or he will not clarify if something is a Torah obligation
or a rabbinic decree, and if one would read the book without the
Tur and the *Bet Yosef*, he would not be able to comprehend clearly
what to do since the *Shulhan Arukh* does not contain the underlying reasons for its rulings. The second premise is that since most
people do not read the *Shulhan Arukh* along with the *Tur* and the
Bet Yosef, the *Mishna Berura*'s commentary, along with his explanations and interpretations, is essential to understand the

---

39 Introduction to the *Mishna Berura*.

coherence of the *Shulhan Arukh*. By creating a scenario where he can justify that his commentary is necessary to understanding the *Shulhan Arukh*, the *Mishna Berura* is essentially able to recreate the *Shulhan Arukh* in accord with his own halakhic methodology and views. It is that exact methodology that this book seeks to understand.

III

Introduction to Rabbi Israel Meir Kagan and the *Mishna Berura*

Little is known about the early life and influences of the *Hafetz Hayyim*, Rabbi Yisrael Meir Kagan, and how he came to be commonly viewed as both a leader of the Jewish community in Eastern Europe and the most significant halakhic authority of the first half of the twentieth century.[1] These accolades are above and beyond his otherwise well-known reputation as a pious and righteous man about whom legendary stories are told—he seems to have lived the life of a truly ethical and upright human being. From the vast and varied literature that he penned, however, one can catch a glimpse of who he was and how he perceived the world around him, and his perception would lead him to become one of the greatest sages of late nineteenth- and early twentieth-century Ashkenazic Jewry.

---

1   Rabbi Kagan was born in Zhetl, Belarus, on February 6, 1838 and died in Radun, Poland, on September 15, 1933. We are not writing a biography of Rabbi Israel Meir Kagan, although such is sorely needed. Nor are we writing a survey of his general intellectual approach. Rather, this work is an analysis of the methodology of the book *Mishna Berura*. It is neither a social nor an intellectual biography of Rabbi Kagan. Nor is this a study of specific questions in Jewish law. Rather, it is an examination of the methodological approach used to produce the *Mishna Berura*. The goal is to understand how the book addresses and analyzes questions of Jewish law and the practical approach that is taken to deal with legal ambiguity.

Of the many tomes he wrote, the *Mishna Berura*[2] is, without a doubt, Rabbi Kagan's greatest contribution to the canon of Orthodox Jewish law and the most complex; it is a singular work that synthesizes Jewish traditions, laws, and mores into a practical halakhic guide to daily religious life. What is also clear is that for all of his traditionalism, Rabbi Kagan was an iconoclast, and the *Mishna Berura* broke from many of the traditional approaches for deciding halakhic directives, such as the *Shulhan Arukh's* "Majority Rule" and the *Gra's* "Rule of Correctness," and even from other normative Orthodox approaches like Rabbenu Tam's[3] dependence on local Jewish custom (*Minhag Yisrael*). Instead, he favored studying, engaging, and asserting decisions in a nuanced, almost natural approach to how ethical people should live their daily lives in a manner consistent with Jewish law. The specific answers as to how moral people should interact with their world while governed by Jewish law were often to be understood not in simple definitions of "right and wrong," but rather, in terms of the question: "How could one please his Creator and be his most authentic self, in any given situation?" As the terms and turns of life shift like the vagaries of a kaleidoscope, Rabbi Kagan's responses to these realities are equally nimble, subtle, and variegated, yet remain at once clear and defined. His perspective is not about observations of strictness versus leniency as much as it is about evaluating a spectrum of options; the same question could get a different answer depending on the situation. Through his singularly humane prism and holistic analysis of individual cases, he guides the common Jew toward an observant and meaningful life.

It is that very unique approach to comprehending and disseminating Jewish law that makes the *Mishna Berura* such a groundbreaking work. It seems to be an editorial, since it is written as a commentary, but it also shares a similarity to those works in the first

---

2   *Mishnah Berura* was written as a six-volume work, published intermittently from 1884 to 1907. See Mordecai Schreiber, Alvin Schiff, and Leon Klenicki, eds., *The Shengold Jewish Encyclopedia*, 3rd ed. (Rockville: Shengold Books, 2003), 117.

3   Rabbi Jacob ben Meir (1100–c. 1171), grandson of Rashi, was a renowned French Tosafist and the foremost halakhic authority of his generation.

category mentioned above, since it cites sources encyclopedically. At times, it even analyzes information in a manner similar to that of the *Yam Shel Shlomo*, probing the depths of halakhic development. Yet, despite its resemblance to these other forms, its overall halakhic methodology is wholly unique compared to that of both its predecessors and its successors. On the pages of what is known as a whole as the *Mishna Berura*, Rabbi Kagan includes, in addition to his main commentary (which is called *Mishna Berura*), two other commentaries, entitled *Biur Halakha* (on the outer edge of the page) and *Sha'ar HaTziyun* (on the bottom of the page). Though other legal scholars have written multiple works on a single topic, this layout of having different commentaries by one author on a single page is unique, not only because they reference each other but also because they are meant to be read concurrently. In our analysis, we will at times cite the *Biur Halakha* and the *Sha'ar HaTziyun*, but we will not be analyzing the methodologies of the two works on their own. Rather, references from these works will be used to support our analysis of the *Mishna Berura*.[4]

As major world events and subsequent transitions in Jewish history[5] swirled around the enclave of Eastern European Jewry, the

---

4   The reason why we treat the two works as support to the *Mishna Berura* is that, in truth, the *Biur Halakha* and the *Sha'ar HaTziyun* are not wholly independent from the main commentary. Rather, the *Biur Halakha* explains and elaborates on the rulings found in the *Mishna Berura*, and gives detailed analyses of the sources used in the *Mishna Berura* to justify the rulings found therein. As such, the *Biur Halakha* is more similar to a collection of long, academic footnotes than it is another commentary or even a super-commentary. The *Sha'ar HaTziyun* is an even simpler work, since it typically just provides the bibliographic information that is lacking in the *Mishna Berura*, and only occasionally provides a qualification or limitation to the *Mishna Berura*'s rulings. There are, however, a few cases where the *Sha'ar HaTziyun* contradicts the *Mishna Berura*, such as with respect to whether a *Kohen* who is acting as *Hazan* can also recite the *Birkat Kohanim* (*Sha'ar HaTziyun* 128:64), yet such cases are exceedingly rare. Nevertheless, they await scholarly explanation. The *Mishna Berura* also contains a number of "Star Footnotes," which qualify the main text. We hope to explain these "Star Footnotes" in a future publication.

5   The transitions in Eastern Europe from 1860 to 1910 were profound and paradigm-shifting, including the rise of the Reform Movement, the Mussar Movement, and Conservative Judaism, among others.

Mishna Berura served a role as a law book trying to preserve the strength of faith in an often volatile world, a daunting task. Yet, as time has shown, the *Mishna Berura* does manage to live up to the task. Indeed, much of the work deals with the inherent conflicts of a Jewish person's attempt to maintain his traditions and integrity in a chaotic and unyielding society. The consummate juggler, the *Hafetz Hayyim* (as Rabbi Kagan is known, in a reference to another of his works) often addresses the reality of complex situations and steadfastly refuses to limit his halakhic tools only to a few principles; he balances numerous central propositions while resolving uncertainty, all at the same time. For him, the best outcome is the one that is most consistent with the *totality* of the picture—which is what makes the methodology of the *Mishna Berura* so hard to grasp and the work so incredibly sophisticated.[6] Rabbi Kagan also manages to do all this while keeping the work extremely simple and easy to use, so that the reader who simply wants to know the answer to a question can find it without difficulty.

Today, the *Mishna Berura* has gained widespread recognition and is considered authoritative by essentially all of contemporary Orthodox Jewry, a measure of greatness that few works of Halakha have attained. For scholar and layman alike, it exerts widespread normative influence on the daily life of an observant Jew. Of course, it is not the case that every single one of the *Mishna Berura*'s decisions are universally followed, since rulings in *Orah Hayyim*, which cover the ritual aspects of daily life, have continued to maintain diversity as a result of local customary practice or Hassidic affiliations. Nonetheless, the *Mishna Berura* is nevertheless a primary source for those who are looking for what constitutes normative practice within Orthodox Judaism as a whole. As Aharon Feldman, editor of the English translation of the *Mishna Berura*, writes in its introduction:

6　The *Gra*, too, was creative in his approach to defining Jewish law, though his thoughts, inspiration, and analysis tend to center around one central question: right or wrong?

The Mishnah Berurah has undergone countless printings. It is studied and restudied by all rabbis, students, and scholars; it can be found—and is consulted—in the home of every learned Jew. The statement, "The Mishnah Berurah says..." is enough to settle nearly any halachic question.[7]

Similarly, Israeli Supreme Court Justice Eliyakim Rubenstein calls the *Mishna Berura* "the standard commentary on the *Shulhan Arukh* for all of Torah Jewry."[8] Given the *Mishna Berura*'s widespread acceptance as a halakhic authority, it is remarkable how little his halakhic methodology has been critically examined. However, Benjamin Brown, the great scholar of Jewish law and practice, has given an alternative account of the *Mishna Berura*'s methodology. Because the *Mishna Berura* is such a widespread authority in matters of Jewish law, and because there is such a lacuna in the systematic study of its methodology, we have undergone an examination of the methodology of this incredibly successful work.

---

7   Israel Meir, Aharon Feldman, and Aviel Orenstein, *Mishnah Berurah: The Classic Commentary to Shulchan Aruch Orach Chayim, Comprising the Laws of Daily Jewish Conduct* (Spring Valley: Feldheim, 1989), xii.

8   Eliyakim Rubenstein, "Halakha and Mussar for Everyone: On the Life and Works of the Hafetz Hayyim," in *Berakhah le-Avraham Asufat Ma'amarim li-Khevod ha-Rav Prof. Avraham ha-Leyi Shtainberg mi-Peri 'Itam shel Yediday u-Mokiray bi-Melot lo Shishim Shanah; be-Tosefet Ketavim shel Avot ha-Mishpahah*, ed. Yitshak Ilan Shtainberg and Avraham Steinberg (Yerushalayim: Y. Shtainberg, 2008), 462.

IV

Mishna Berura's **Philosophy of Jewish Law**

When attempting to describe an interpretive halakhic methodology in terms of contemporary theories of legal interpretation, it is important to recognize that Jewish law contains certain presumptions that render several theories immediately inapplicable. One example of an approach that must be discarded due to the fact that Jewish law is grounded on incompatible premises is that of intentionalism. The theory of intentionalism is that judges should attempt to ascertain the meaning of a particular provision by determining how its author understood it at the time it was established. Without discussing the various nuances of the different proponents of this theory, in general what is normative is the subjective intent of the author. Critics of intentionalism claim that even if the author had a specific intent, it cannot be identified. While those who defend the theory argue that inherent in the idea of legislative authority are the notions that the author both intends, and has the expertise to articulate, certain legal norms, most recognize that the ability to identify and acknowledge the applicability of that intention is inversely proportional to the amount of time that has lapsed since the law's enactment. As one proponent of intentionalism remarks, "[T]he more ancient a law is the more suspicious one has to be of the relevance of the legislators' intentions."[1]

---

1   Andrei Marmor, *Interpretation and Legal Theory* (Oxford: Clarendon Press, 1992), 182.

Jewish law further complicates the matter, since, except with respect to particular rabbinic enactments, all legal works are themselves interpretative commentaries on legislation that is believed to have begun with Moses at Sinai. Therefore, jurists who try to interpret a legal work such as the *Shulhan Arukh* must recognize that Rabbi Karo did not have the authority to enact legislation himself. Rather, they rely on the belief that he simply had the competence to correctly understand the intent of previous legislation and to accurately reveal it. Moreover, the theological assertion that knowledge of God can only occur within the framework of *via negativa*[2] makes the assumption of access to the intention of the author of Jewish law impossible.

Intentionalism stands in contradistinction with the theory of originalism, which seeks to base normativity on the understanding of the *recipients* of the law at the time that it was enacted. Originalism fares no better in its connection to Jewish law, since the basis for halakhic works to be written down in the first place is the admission that there had been a significant deterioration in the accurate transmission of the Oral law.

Though scripturalism is a popular way to classify orthodox religious adherence from a sociological perspective, textualism, as an interpretative method, is another approach that is, in fact, incongruous with Jewish law. In the most general terms, the belief that a primary text has a meaning of its own, without its authorized and lawful explanation, contradicts the belief in the necessity and the primacy of the Oral Torah. With respect to older versions of textualism, those who have written legal corpora, with the exception of *Rambam*, have admitted in their introductions that their work is not a complete elucidation of the law and can only be used properly if it is approached in conjunction with a greater understanding of the complexity of Jewish law. Even if the particular legal code can give general instructions, understanding the plain meaning of the law, as

---

2   Negative theology is the idea that since God is not a universe or an object in a universe, one can really speak of Him only in terms of what He is not, as opposed to what He is.

penned by the author of the code, for every situation demands a higher level of competency than can be expected of the average reader. With respect to newer versions of textualism (paralleling the intentionalism/originalism distinction), which claims that the reasonable reader is seeking the meaning of the legal text as understood by its readers when first enacted, the history of debate over this issue includes those polemics against both the Karaites and the Sadducees, which put them firmly outside of the rabbinic camp of Judaism.[3]

If one were, however, to attempt to classify the interpretive methodology of the *Mishna Berura*, one could find similarities between the *Mishna Berura*'s approach and that of "purposive interpretation." The theory of purposive interpretation is premised on the idea that law is a means to shape society. Therefore, rules should be understood in light of the purposes they are intended to implement. It is not enough to understand either statutes or customary law through the standard of ordinary or plain usage alone.[4] As Professor Lon Fuller explained in his famous exchange with H.L.A. Hart:

> A statute or a rule of common law has, either explicitly, or by virtue of its relation with other rules, something that may be called a structural integrity. This is what we have in mind when we speak of "the intent of the statute," though we know it is men who have intentions and not words on paper. Within the limits of that structure, fidelity to law not only permits but demands a creative role from the judge, but beyond that structure it does not permit him to go.[5]

---

3   The Sadducees and later the Karaites are sects of Judaism that reject the Oral Law in favor of a religious life based entirely on the Written Torah. As Josephus writes of the Sadducees in his Antiquities, "The Pharisees [Rabbinic Jews] have delivered to the people a great many observances by succession from their father, which are not written in the law of Moses, and for that reason it is that the Sadducees reject them and say that we are to esteem those observances to be obligatory which are in the written word, but are not to observe what are derived from the tradition of our forefathers" (*Antiquities* 13.10.6).

4   Julian B. McDonnell, "Purposive Interpretation of the Uniform Commercial Code: Some Implications for Jurisprudence," *University of Pennsylvania Law Review* 126, No. 4 (April 1978): 797-8.

5   Lon L. Fuller, "Positivism and Fidelity to Law: A Reply to Professor Hart," *Harvard Law Review* 71, No. 4 (February 1958): 670.

According to this view, jurists must first seek to find the *purpose* of the law and not the subjective intention of the legislator, nor the objective intent of the ruling as it arises from the language of the text. Purpose combines both subjective and objective components in searching for the expected goal of a piece of legislation and in examining whether the language of the ruling accurately conveys that goal, given the context of the greater legal framework and the legal community in which it is embedded. Interpretation thus becomes a balancing of different presumptions when they conflict, which allows for greater flexibility than negotiating between conflicting interpretative rules. As a result, the methodology of purposive interpretation allows a jurist to reinterpret rulings that he finds contradictory or incoherent, given the priorities of the legal system, and still claim that he is accurately understanding both the law's meaning and its author's intention, via the medium of expounding its purpose.

The *Mishna Berura* interprets the *Shulhan Arukh* in a manner that seeks to resolve potential contradiction between particular rulings of Rabbi Karo, as well as between the positions of the *Shulhan Arukh* and other legal authorities. As we will see, its jurisprudential priorities reveal its overall desire to create a coherent presentation of the Halakha. Whether by negotiating between positions or by interpreting the language of rulings in a way that justifies what its author believed should be the law, given the greater halakhic discussion (and the greater halakhic purpose or goal), the *Mishna Berura*'s halakhic methodology revolves around more than just the two axes of the *Arukh HaShulhan*. On the contrary, the *Mishna Berura* is a complex, nuanced attempt to transform the laws of daily conduct into a comprehensive, consistent, and unified system which accords to Rabbi Kagan's own perspective.

V

Mishna Berura's Jurisprudence

Given the volatile world in which the *Mishna Berura* was composed, it is obvious that much of Rabbi Kagan's work must address the inherent conflict of the modern Jew's attempt to maintain his tradition in an oftentimes chaotic and unyielding society. Its success in doing so is one of the reasons why the *Mishna Berura* is still the practical halakhic guide to which most observant Jews refer today.

The *Mishna Berura* has two major jurisprudential objectives, and both are responses to the legal and social environment in which its author lived and wrote. Doctrinally, the *Mishna Berura* saw each legal dispute as irresolvable; therefore, any halakhic resolution would have to take into account all the various opinions on a matter, or at least as many as possible. As a matter of social policy, the *Mishna Berura* sought to balance the opposing forces of tradition and modernity. Given these two objectives, the *Mishna Berura* sought to provide definitive halakhic guidance to every question of Jewish law. The manner in which the *Mishna Berura* approached a halakhic dispute was to first ask four central questions:

1. What is the common halakhic practice of the community in a given situation? Does more than one *minhag* (custom) exist?
2. What is the spectrum of answers provided by the *poskim* to the question at hand?
3. What are the minimum halakhic requirements that one should try to fulfill?

4. How can one maximize observance in order to enhance his relationship with God?

Since the *Mishna Berura* could not draw a single, unequivocal ruling because of its doctrinal commitment not to resolve disputes, it also developed second-order guidelines of decision-making which would allow it to determine what to do in a given situation. The following are the *Mishna Berura*'s second-order guidelines or halakhic principles:

1. When a ruling no longer seems to fit the current reality, the *Mishna Berura* provides alternative explanations for the ruling, changes its language, or adapts practices so that they fit with the ruling's spirit.
2. When the codes record both lenient and strict positions, the *Mishna Berura* advises when one should be strict and when one may be lenient.
3. When the codes record multiple normative views that do not exclude the validity of the other or others, the *Mishna Berura* accepts the validity of different practices in different locations, and suggests manners of fulfillment that incorporate the different views.
4. When the codes record two mutually exclusive opinions, the *Mishna Berura* suggests ways to avoid transgression according to either view.
5. When the early codes are lenient and the later commentators are strict, the *Mishna Berura* inclines toward the strict position.
6. When the major codes adopt a lenient position, yet other codes are stricter, the *Mishna Berura* suggests qualifying one's intention to act so as to avoid transgression according to strict position.
7. When people have adopted an unsupported custom, the *Mishna Berura* disapproves of it, yet attempts to justify it for those who will nevertheless continue to follow it.
8. When the codes are easily misunderstood, the *Mishna Berura* clarifies misunderstood rulings and defends widespread practices.

9. When the codes and Kabbala conflict, the *Mishna Berura* minimizes the tension between the two positions.
10. When the codes are in tension and the *Gra* has a strong view, the *Mishna Berura* relies on the position of the *Gra*.

The *Mishna Berura* may use more than one of these guidelines or principles at a time, and will balance them, along with the four central questions it asks, in order to give the proper ruling given its jurisprudential objectives.

Clearly, the author of the *Mishna Berura* was successful in the seemingly impossible endeavor of incorporating so many variables into one cohesive structure.[1] As a result, the book is the hallmark of legal harmony—consensus synthesizing disparate (and often conflicting) sources—and all Ashkenazim accept the work today. Even more significantly, it is precisely *because* the *Mishna Berura* recognizes the complexity of life and gives a spectrum of reasonable answers to difficult halakhic questions that it has stood the test of time and is authoritative more than a century after its publication. It is a rare occasion when a book is both so timely and so timeless.

The approach of the *Mishna Berura* has never been well understood; certainly it has never been ably replicated by any other *posek*. It is unique, and as such it is impossible to understand and systematically decipher without specific keys to guide its student through the process of its legal deliberation. Consequently, this study is meant for the serious student who desires to understand the mechanics of the *Mishna Berura* and, in particular, how the *Mishna Berura* finds consensus among the disparate halakhic opinions and conflicting sources and customs.

Below is a more in-depth analysis of the ten halakhic principles that the *Mishna Berura* uses to answer its four central questions. They are, in no particular order:

---

1   Other rabbinic authorities may have also endeavored to incorporate many variables into one cohesive structure, yet we believe that none have done it so effectively.

1. **When a ruling no longer seems to fit the current reality, the *Mishna Berura* provides alternative explanations for the ruling, changes its language, or adapts practices so that they fit with the ruling's spirit.**

In order to uphold the consistency of the *Shulhan Arukh*, the *Mishna Berura* provides alternative explanations for particular rulings in order for them to maintain their relevancy. The *Mishna Berura* also provides alternative explanations to rulings in order to maintain the legitimacy of a lenient practice which previously rested on faulty reasoning.

At times, the *Mishna Berura* justifies changing the language of a ruling so that it will support what its author believed should be the law. When the language of a ruling or to whom it is attributed differs from what it believes should be the ruling or the attribution, the *Mishna Berura* assumes that the difference is due to a scribal error.

The *Mishna Berura* considers social changes in order to adapt practices so that they concur with the principle of the law given new circumstances. However, the *Mishna Berura* does not always broaden the scope of acceptability when a general trend of laxity in observance develops; there are times when it takes a hard line in order to uphold what its author thought to be the correct practice.

We provide 21 examples of this phenomenon in the *Mishna Berura* from many different areas of Halakha. For an in-depth analysis of how the *Mishna Berura* uses this principle, please see the following examples:

- Example 29: A father purchasing phylacteries for his child in order to teach him how to don them.[2]
- Example 36: A mourner who desires to recite the *Shema* and to pray.

---

2   The number associated with the example relates to its position in the two hundred and fifty illustrative examples.

- Example 76: Bending one's head while praying.
- Example 95: Selling a sanctified object to buy another object of similar sanctity.
- Example 155: Praying *Maariv* Saturday night from *Plag HaMinha* and making *Havdala* immediately afterwards.
- Example 160: The measure of a *kazayit*.
- Example 168: Lending a tool to a Gentile on Shabbat.
- Example 169: Doing activity on Erev Pesach from noon onwards.
- Example 221: Calling a blind person or one who is unable to read from the Torah for an *Aliyah*.
- Example 222: Returning a pot into the oven on Shabbat.
- Example 232: When Kohanim may return to the congregation after *Birkat Kohanim*.
- Example 233: Reciting *Birkat Kohanim* when unable to properly pronounce the Hebrew letters.
- Example 234: The ability for one person to exempt another through his blessing over foods.
- Example 235: Saying the blessings over food eaten after the meal but before reciting *Birkat HaMazon*.
- Example 236: A *Hazan* who is a *Kohen* saying *Birkat Kohanim*.
- Example 237: Renting or lending one's animal to a Gentile.
- Example 238: Reducing one's business activity from *Rosh Hodesh Av* until the fast.
- Example 239: Squeezing fruits on Shabbat.
- Example 240: Kneading dough to make *matzah*.
- Example 241: Listening to a doctor who tells a person to eat on Yom Kippur.
- Example 242: Bringing one's children to hear the *Megilla*.

2. **When the codes record both lenient and strict positions, the *Mishna Berura* advises when one should be strict and when one may be lenient.**

In situations where there are numerous halakhic opinions, and there is no clear decision as to which position is established as the definitive ruling, the *Mishna Berura* creates a hierarchical standard for adherence which takes into account the contingencies inherent in daily life. In this way, it is able to grant validity to different degrees of fulfillment under varying conditions so that people have the ability to perform correctly despite non-ideal circumstances.

When Rabbi Karo records two positions regarding a particular Halakha, the *Mishna Berura* designates the more stringent position as what should be done *ab initio* and consents to the legitimacy of the lenient position *ex post facto*. One of the factors that influences the *Mishna Berura*'s hierarchical synthesis is the situation in which a person may find himself when following one of the alternatives or another. When the *Shulhan Arukh* records an opinion to which many other *poskim* are strongly opposed, the *Mishna Berura* advocates following the more stringent position *ab initio* but consents to the legitimacy of the lenient position when the circumstances of the situation do not allow for ideal performance. The *Mishna Berura* also uses this technique when there is debate is among the *Aharonim*. The *Mishna Berura* defines a time of difficulty as a situation where there is no other alternative. The *Mishna Berura* will give validity to a lenient position when a person is presented with what it refers to as "situation of great loss." Besides taking into account the circumstances of a particular situation, in determining whether to accept a lenient opinion as valid, the *Mishna Berura* also considers the nature of the obligation or prohibition. In particular, the *Mishna Berura* is more prone to accept a lenient opinion when the dispute is over a rabbinic ruling.

We provide 64 examples of this phenomenon in the *Mishna Berura* from many different areas of Halakha. For an in-depth analysis of how the *Mishna Berura* uses this principle, please see the following examples:

- Example 5: Immersing a new dish in a *mikveh* on Shabbat.
- Example 16: Relighting a torch left over from the first day of Yom Tov, that had gone out on the second day of Yom Tov.

- Example 34: Searching for *hametz*.
- Example 37: Drying one's hands after washing *mayim aharonim*.
- Example 38: Assembling a detachable bed on Shabbat.
- Example 39: Finding *hametz* within one's possession on Passover.
- Example 40: Insulating food on Erev Shabbat with something that adds heat.
- Example 41: If a monkey washes a person's hands before his meal.
- Example 42: Having the intention that one's washing of his hands permits him to eat.
- Example 43: Sealing the opening of a hot oven that contains food for Shabbat.
- Example 44: Baking bread on Yom Tov.
- Example 45: Eating legumes on Passover.
- Example 46: Praying *Maariv* for Shabbat on a cloudy day.
- Example 47: Nullifying *hametz* through a representative.
- Example 48: Marrying on the eve of a holiday and having a celebratory meal on the holiday.
- Example 49: Making a tent on Shabbat or on Yom Tov.
- Example 50: If a Gentile ties *tzitzit* on a garment while a Jew is standing over him.
- Example 51: Having sexual relations in the room where one's phylacteries are lying.
- Example 52: Reciting the *Shema* at dawn.
- Example 53: If a doubt arises as to whether something was prepared on the first day of Yom Tov or the day before.
- Example 54: Buying something in exchange for their *hametz* on the day before Passover after the sixth hour of the day.
- Example 55: Mixture of *hametz* on Passover.
- Example 56: Selling something to a Gentile and having him pick it up close to dark before Shabbat.
- Example 57: Praying in a synagogue with the community.
- Example 58: Rabbinic decrees are permitted during *ben-ha'shma-shot* (the time between sunset and nightfall).
- Example 59: A doubt as to whether something is considered *nolad* on a Yom Tov which is preceded by a weekday.

- Example 60: Sitting a hen on her eggs to hatch chicks on *Hol HaMoed*.
- Example 61: If a Hanukah candle becomes mixed with other candles.
- Example 62: Going to guard one's fruit on Shabbat.
- Example 63: If a fire breaks out on Shabbat.
- Example 64: Making an *Eruv Tehumin*.
- Example 65: Reciting the *Shema* if one has a doubt that there is urine in the litter.
- Example 66: If a Gentile bakes bread in a Jew's oven on Shabbat.
- Example 70: A person with a stomach illness donning phylacteries.
- Example 71: One who is watching a corpse is exempt from all other commandments.
- Example 72: Pregnant and nursing women fasting.
- Example 73: Washing one's hands and reciting the blessing *al netilat yadaim*.
- Example 75: Saying *Tahanun*.
- Example 77: Praying silently.
- Example 86: If a community collects money for a certain purpose.
- Example 90: Saying the *Birkat HaMazon* silently.
- Example 91: If, due to sickness or conditions out of his control, a person recites the *Shema* without moving his lips.
- Example 95: Selling a sanctified object to buy another object of similar sanctity.
- Example 97: How much of the hand one must wash when washing before eating bread.
- Example 98: Doing something in a regular manner on *Hol HaMoed*.
- Example 113: Extinguishing a candle for a sick person on Shabbat.
- Example 116: Receiving *hametz* from a Gentile as payment on Passover.
- Example 124: Speaking before hearing *HaMotzi*.
- Example 142: An *androgynous* person or a *tumtum* making a *zimun*.
- Example 143: Bringing a second wine to the table at a meal.

- Example 148: Eating *matzah* in remembrance of the Passover offering.
- Example 149: Renting one's house for Passover.
- Example 151: Saying *Vidui* at *Minha* before Yom Kippur.
- Example 159: How much wine a person must drink for the four cups on Passover.
- Example 160: The measure of a *kazayit*.
- Example 161: If a person rents a house and does not know if it has been checked for *hametz*.
- Example 172: *Okhel Nefesh* on a holiday.
- Example 180: Placing food upon a stove before Shabbat.
- Example 185: Shaving on the day before Yom Tov.
- Example 199: How much one needs to wash for *mayim aharonim*.
- Example 214: *Hashma'at kol* on Shabbat.
- Example 215: *Kiddush* on Shabbat day with a different alcoholic drink.
- Example 234: The ability for one person to exempt another through his blessing over foods.
- Example 243: Designating a bag to always be used for one's phylacteries.

3. **When the codes record multiple normative views that do not contradict each other, the *Mishna Berura* accepts the validity of different practices in different locations, and suggests manners of fulfillment that incorporate the different views.**

When two different ways to fulfill an obligation have become widespread, established practices, and both claim equal validity in terms of their efficacy, the *Mishna Berura* acknowledges both practices as legitimate. If a practice endorsed by the *Shulhan Arukh* is not commonly observed in a particular location, the *Mishna Berura* recommends that one not protest against the lack of adherence. The *Mishna Berura* does not perceive its acceptance of multiple ways of halakhic fulfillment as innovative. Rather, it considers it only as an expansion and development of an already-accepted norm.

When the *poskim* give a number of possible alternatives that do not contradict each other, the *Mishna Berura* at times recommends that a person act in accord with more than one position. Although the *Mishna Berura*'s attempt to incorporate as many opinions as viable may result in advocating a change of practice, it does not recommend a change if the law itself is debated. In such cases, it will accept and further support the current custom in practice. The strength of an established custom may even supersede other halakhic methodological principles due to its social influence. The *Mishna Berura* will maintain an established custom while, at the same time, forbidding its introduction into a different community. The *Mishna Berura* also uses the existence of a custom to measure the validity of a written norm. When a legal dispute exists and there is no established custom in a particular area, the *Mishna Berura* considers the existence of a custom in the same way as the various textual opinions.

We provide 34 examples of this phenomenon in the *Mishna Berura* from many different areas of Halakha. For an in-depth analysis of how the *Mishna Berura* uses this principle, please see the following examples:

- Example 15: *Hametz*-based adhesive.
- Example 20: *Kohanim* turning toward the congregation to say the *Birkat Kohanim*.
- Example 28: Making a hole for the *Tzitzit*.
- Example 29: A father purchasing phylacteries for his child in order to teach him how to don them.
- Example 30: When to say *Kiddush Levana*.
- Example 68: If one interrupts his recitation of *Hallel*.
- Example 69: If a groom, his best men, and all the members of the wedding party are exempt from sitting in a *Sukkah* for the seven days after the wedding.
- Example 86: If a community collects money for a certain purpose.
- Example 87: If alleyways are considered public domains.

- Example 92: Touching one's foreleg or thigh in the middle of a meal.
- Example 94: Carrying on Yom Tov.
- Example 96: The blessing over *Hallel*.
- Example 101: Giving a Gentile a letter to send before Shabbat.
- Example 102: Giving a Gentile money on Friday to buy something.
- Example 103: Setting sail before Shabbat.
- Example 104: Giving food to a person who does not know how to make a blessing over it.
- Example 108: Making a tent on Shabbat with books.
- Example 130: Hiring a *Hazan* to pray on Shabbat.
- Example 135: The blessings over wearing phylacteries.
- Example 145: If a Gentile deposits his *hametz* with a Jew on Passover.
- Example 146: If a Jew gives his *hametz* to a Gentile on the day before Passover.
- Example 147: Preparing tables and drawers for Passover.
- Example 149: Renting one's house for Passover.
- Example 184: Washing for less than the volume of an olive (*kazayit*) of bread.
- Example 186: The person called up to the Torah reading along with the *Hazan*.
- Example 187: The status of a protruding roof when the walls cannot be seen.
- Example 201: Examining one's clothing on Friday close to dark.
- Example 204: Status of a partition that was erected on Shabbat.
- Example 211: How a left-handed person dons his phylactery.
- Example 217: The blessing if one uses horseradish for *marror*.
- Example 225: Washing one's hands, if eating something that is dipped in wine, honey, oil, dew, blood, or water, and is not dried.
- Example 235: Saying the blessings over food eaten after the meal but before reciting *Birkat HaMazon*.
- Example 244: Eating and drinking in the synagogue.
- Example 248: Eating, drinking, and sleeping in a *Sukkah*.

4. When the codes record two mutually exclusive opinions, the *Mishna Berura* suggests ways to avoid transgression according to either view.

When there is a potential contradiction in trying to synthesize different opinions, the *Mishna Berura* uses the technique of introducing a concrete variable into the situation in order to create the synthesis. To avoid transgression, the *Mishna Berura* suggests simply leaving the environment where the conflict between obligation and prohibition exists.

The *Mishna Berura* may demand that a person do something in addition to the requirement set forth by the *Shulhan Arukh* in order to avoid public confusion, which may result in potentially negative consequences. The *Mishna Berura* also suggests that a person take an additional measure to avoid the misconception that one is acting erroneously. The *Mishna Berura* also introduces alternative practices when necessary to avoid potential transgression.

We provide 41 examples of this phenomenon in the *Mishna Berura* from many different areas of Halakha. For an in-depth analysis of how the *Mishna Berura* uses this principle, please see the following examples:

- Example 4: Which garments need *tzitzit*.
- Example 18: "Amen" after "*Ga'al Israel.*"
- Example 74: Where to put on Tallit and Tefillin (Phylacteries).
- Example 82: Calling a *Kohen* for an *Aliyah* after a *Kohen*.
- Example 84: Reciting the *Birkat HaMazon* for others.
- Example 85: Leaving a meal before saying the *Birkat HaMazon*.
- Example 106: Picking up one's son who is holding a stone on Shabbat.
- Example 108: Making a tent on Shabbat with books.
- Example 110: If a person is alone on the road as Shabbat begins.
- Example 120: If the bread for the *Eruv* became moldy and is inedible.

- Example 127: Until when a person can pray in the morning.
- Example 128: Wearing phylacteries on *Hol HaMoed*.
- Example 129: Wearing phylacteries of *Rashi* and of *Rabbenu Tam*.
- Example 131: Eating stolen *matzah* on Passover.
- Example 132: When the Yom Kippur fast begins.
- Example 133: If sleep is considered an interruption in learning Torah.
- Example 134: Accepting Shabbat by candle-lighting.
- Example 137: Eating fruit with a meal.
- Example 138: Forgetting to say *Birkat HaMazon*.
- Example 139: Saying the *Birkat Kohanim* in an impure place.
- Example 140: Incorrect performance of a component of *Birkat Kohanim*.
- Example 141: Who can recite the *Birkat Kohanim*.
- Example 144: If two wines are brought to the table simultaneously.
- Example 146: If a Jew gives his *hametz* to a Gentile on the day before Passover.
- Example 149: Renting one's house for Passover.
- Example 153: When no one can read the Torah properly with the correct accentuation.
- Example 154: If a person delays praying *Minha* until the community has already accepted Shabbat.
- Example 155: Praying *Maariv* Saturday night from *Plag HaMinha* and making *Havdala* immediately afterwards.
- Example 156: Immersing uncooked food into hot water on Shabbat.
- Example 157: Pouring liquid from one cup that contains both liquid and sediment to another on Shabbat.
- Example 158: The status of a protruding roof.
- Example 159: How much wine a person must drink for the four cups on Passover.
- Example 160: The measure of a *kazayit*.
- Example 181: The third meal when Shabbat falls on the fourteenth of *Nissan*.

- Example 183: Saying the *Kedusha* within "*Yotzer*" when praying alone.
- Example 187: The status of a protruding roof when the walls cannot be seen.
- Example 194: A *Kohen* who killed someone saying *Birkat Kohanim*.
- Example 201: Examining one's clothing on Friday close to dark.
- Example 210: If while a *Kohen* is reciting the *Shema* he is called to the Torah.
- Example 227: Saying "amen" after "*Ga'al Israel*."
- Example 232: When Kohanim may return to the congregation after *Birkat Kohanim*.

5. When the early codes are lenient and the later commentators are strict, the *Mishna Berura* inclines toward the strict position.

When the *Shulhan Arukh* rules leniently on a particular matter, but other *poskim* rule stringently, the *Mishna Berura* attempts to incorporate the more stringent position into the ruling of the *Shulhan Arukh*. If incorporation of the more stringent position would result in a potential transgression or contradiction according to the plain understanding of the ruling of the *Shulhan Arukh*, the *Mishna Berura* will incorporate only those aspects of the more stringent position which can be included without conflict. The justification for only partially incorporating a decision against the claim that such an approach leads to arbitrariness and inconsistency is that the approach takes into account the various levels of obligation that the different aspects of a particular performance may entail.

When the *Mishna Berura* is faced with two compelling and contradictory positions on one issue, the first being the ruling of the *Shulhan Arukh* and the second an alternative view which is more stringent, the objective of the *Mishna Berura* is to incorporate the more stringent view in a manner that does not negate the ruling of the *Shulhan Arukh* nor make the new compromise position incoherent. When the *Shulhan Arukh* or the *Rema* rules leniently, yet a person thinks that he may be stringent upon himself, if the self-imposed stringency does not take into consideration that the ruling exempts him from doing something as a way to avoid an unforeseen transgression, the *Mishna Berura* explicitly prohibits him from acting stringently.

We provide 122 examples of this phenomenon in the *Mishna Berura* from many different areas of Halakha. For an in-depth analysis of how the *Mishna Berura* uses this principle, please see the following examples:

- Example 1: If a Jew ties *tzitzit* on a garment without the proper intention.
- Example 3: Learning books of wisdom on Shabbat or Yom Tov.
- Example 5: Immersing a new dish in a *mikveh* on Shabbat.
- Example 7: Making an *Eruv* that contains a public domain.
- Example 8: Fast days due to tragedy.
- Example 9: Walking outside on Shabbat wearing gloves.
- Example 10: When the day before Passover falls on Shabbat, what one does with his remaining bread.
- Example 11: Prohibitions on fast days.
- Example 12: Squeezing grapes into a pot on Shabbat.
- Example 13: Buying meat on Yom Tov.
- Example 14: Putting salt in a *kli rishon* that is no longer on the fire.
- Example 15: *Hametz*-based adhesive.
- Example 16: Relighting a torch left over from the first day of Yom Tov, that had gone out on the second day of Yom Tov.
- Example 17: *Rosh Hodesh* meals.
- Example 21: Saying the passage "The Incense Mixture."
- Example 22: Clothes washed in wheat-water and paper that has a *hametz*-based adhesive on Passover.
- Example 23: Folding an article of clothing on Shabbat.
- Example 24: Using a prayer book when Rosh Hashanah falls on Saturday night.

- Example 25: Making the blessing over spices for *Havdala* if Yom Kippur fell on Shabbat.
- Example 26: Writing salutary letters on *Hol HaMoed*.
- Example 27: Asking one's servant to walk with him and light a candle on Shabbat.
- Example 31: Squeezing unripe grapes into food on Shabbat.
- Example 36: A mourner who desires to recite the *Shema* and to pray.
- Example 37: Drying one's hands after washing *mayim aharonim*.
- Example 38: Assembling a detachable bed on Shabbat.
- Example 39: Finding *hametz* within one's possession on Passover.
- Example 41: If a monkey washes a person's hands before his meal.
- Example 43: Sealing the opening of a hot oven that contains food for Shabbat.
- Example 46: Praying *Maariv* for Shabbat on a cloudy day.
- Example 47: Nullifying *hametz* through a representative.
- Example 49: Making a tent on Shabbat or on Yom Tov.
- Example 52: Reciting the *Shema* at dawn.
- Example 53: If a doubt arises as to whether something was prepared on the first day of Yom Tov or the day before.
- Example 54: Buying something in exchange for their *hametz* on the day before Passover after the sixth hour of the day.
- Example 56: Selling something to a Gentile and having him pick it up close to dark before Shabbat.
- Example 59: A doubt as to whether something is considered *nolad* on a Yom Tov which is preceded by a weekday.
- Example 60: Sitting a hen on her eggs to hatch chicks on *Hol HaMoed*.
- Example 65: Reciting the *Shema* if one has a doubt that there is urine in the litter.
- Example 67: If a person takes a cup of beer or water and makes the blessing for wine.
- Example 68: If one interrupts his recitation of *Hallel*.

- Example 69: If a groom, his best men, and all the members of the wedding party are exempt from sitting in a *Sukkah* for the seven days after the wedding.
- Example 76: Bending one's head while praying.
- Example 77: Praying silently.
- Example 83: Carrying on Yom Tov for unnecessary purposes or for a Gentile.
- Example 85: Leaving a meal before saying the *Birkat HaMazon*.
- Example 88: Whether a hole in a wall bordering a *Karmelit* is considered a *Karmelit*.
- Example 93: How much *matzah* one must eat at the Seder.
- Example 94: Carrying on Yom Tov.
- Example 97: How much of the hand one must wash when washing before eating bread.
- Example 99: Making partitions of a *Sukkah* from linen sheets.
- Example 100: Entering through one door of a synagogue and exiting through another to take a short cut.
- Example 101: Giving a Gentile a letter to send before Shabbat.
- Example 102: Giving a Gentile money on Friday to buy something.
- Example 106: Picking up one's son who is holding a stone on Shabbat.
- Example 107: Moving a tool on Shabbat that has on it both prohibited and permitted objects.
- Example 109: Watering vegetables on Shabbat.
- Example 110: If a person is alone on the road as Shabbat begins.
- Example 117: If one forgot to say a blessing before taking a drink.
- Example 119: Definition of a private domain.
- Example 120: If the bread for the *Eruv* became moldy and is inedible.
- Example 123: If one has a doubt as to whether he mentioned "*Ya'ale ve'Yavo*."
- Example 124: Speaking before hearing *HaMotzi*.
- Example 125: Telling a Gentile to light a candle for the Shabbat meal.
- Example 126: Chewing cinnamon sticks during a fast.

- Example 136: Saying the wrong blessing.
- Example 144: If two wines are brought to the table simultaneously.
- Example 148: Eating *matzah* in remembrance of the Passover offering.
- Example 149: Renting one's house for Passover.
- Example 150: Eating meat or drinking wine on the tenth of *Av*.
- Example 151: Saying *Vidui* at *Minha* before Yom Kippur.
- Example 152: If a person makes a mistake while publicly reading from the Torah.
- Example 153: When no one can read the Torah properly with the correct accentuation.
- Example 154: If a person delays praying *Minha* until the community has already accepted Shabbat.
- Example 155: Praying *Maariv* Saturday night from *Plag HaMinha* and making *Havdala* immediately afterwards.
- Example 156: Immersing uncooked food into hot water on Shabbat.
- Example 159: How much wine a person must drink for the four cups on Passover.
- Example 160: The measure of a *kazayit*.
- Example 162: Lighting Hanukah candles before sunset.
- Example 163: The status of a wall when its gaps make up as much of the wall as the material of the wall itself.
- Example 164: Women doing work on *Rosh Hodesh*.
- Example 165: If one finds *hametz* in his house on *Hol Hamoed*.
- Example 166: Eating the night before fasts which begin at sunrise.
- Example 167: Definition of a *Karmelit*.
- Example 168: Lending a tool to a Gentile on Shabbat.
- Example 169: Doing activity on Erev Pesach from noon onwards.
- Example 171: Entering the synagogue through one door to exit through another.
- Example 173: When a roof is both part of a private domain and next to a public domain.
- Example 176: When to say the blessing *"Elokai Neshama."*

- Example 228: Playing with a ball on Shabbat and Yom Tov.
- Example 229: If a Gentile lights a candle for a Jew on Shabbat.
- Example 230: Going barefoot on *Tisha b'Av*.
- Example 231: Placing the *Bima* in the middle of the synagogue.
- Example 236: A *Hazan* who is a *Kohen* saying *Birkat Kohanim*.
- Example 238: Reducing one's business activity from *Rosh Hodesh Av* until the fast.
- Example 239: Squeezing fruits on Shabbat.
- Example 240: Kneading dough to make *matzah*.
- Example 241: Listening to a doctor who tells a person to eat on Yom Kippur.
- Example 242: Bringing one's children to hear the *Megilla*.
- Example 245: Eating fish on Shabbat.
- Example 246: What to do with clay pots used for *hametz* on Passover.
- Example 249: Eating *Hadash*.
- Example 250: Having a Gentile make a bonfire on Shabbat in cold lands.

6. **When the major codes adopt a lenient position, yet other codes are stricter, the *Mishna Berura* suggests qualifying one's intention to act so as to avoid transgression according to strict position.**

The difficulty of combining opposing positions in a manner that removes doubt in fulfillment often occurs when the *Mishna Berura* seeks to promote leniency. In following a stringent opinion, one would automatically fulfill the opinions with more lenient requirements as well. On the other hand, when a person follows a more lenient opinion, he excludes those opinions with a higher bar for fulfillment. There are times, however, when following a more lenient position may not only preclude fulfillment according to the higher standard, but may also entail potential transgression according to the more stringent standard. In order to maneuver between maximizing the range of fulfillment in accepting a more lenient position while, at the same time, avoiding possible transgressions, the *Mishna Berura* recommends qualifying one's intention when performing the particular action. Similarly, the *Mishna Berura* recommends that a person qualify his intentions when there is no other way to join completely opposing conditions. Although the *Mishna Berura* uses the technique of suggesting that one qualify his intention or make a stipulation about his intention in order to aggregate various opinions, it still recognizes that this is not an optimal method of finding compromise. When a person's intention clearly contrasts the presumed intention behind a particular action, the *Mishna Berura* has difficulty accepting that his personal intention effectively influences the meaning of the action.

We provide 70 examples of this phenomenon in the *Mishna Berura* from many different areas of Halakha. For an in-depth analysis of how the *Mishna Berura* uses this principle, please see the following examples:

- Example 1: If a Jew ties *tzitzit* on a garment without the proper intention.
- Example 2: Working on Friday from *Minha* onward.
- Example 3: Learning books of wisdom on Shabbat or Yom Tov.
- Example 4: Which garments need *tzitzit*.
- Example 6: If the community prays the evening prayer (*Maariv*) while it is still daytime.
- Example 7: Making an *Eruv* that contains a public domain.
- Example 8: Fast days due to tragedy.
- Example 9: Walking outside on Shabbat wearing gloves.
- Example 10: When the day before Passover falls on Shabbat, what one does with his remaining bread.
- Example 11: Prohibitions on fast days.
- Example 12: Squeezing grapes into a pot on Shabbat.
- Example 13: Buying meat on Yom Tov.
- Example 14: Putting salt in a *kli rishon* that is no longer on the fire.

- Example 17: *Rosh Hodesh* meals.
- Example 19: Washing one's hands with soap on Shabbat.
- Example 23: Folding an article of clothing on Shabbat.
- Example 24: Using a prayer book when Rosh Hashanah falls on Saturday night.
- Example 25: Making the blessing over spices for *Havdala* if Yom Kippur fell on Shabbat.
- Example 26: Writing salutary letters on *Hol HaMoed*.
- Example 30: When to say *Kiddush Levana*.
- Example 31: Squeezing unripe grapes into food on Shabbat.
- Example 32: Cutting vegetables finely on Shabbat.
- Example 33: Learning on the day before *Tisha b'Av*.
- Example 34: Searching for *hametz*.
- Example 35: Repeating the phrase "Hashem, your God, is true."
- Example 40: Insulating food on Erev Shabbat with something that adds heat.
- Example 66: If a Gentile bakes bread in a Jew's oven on Shabbat.
- Example 82: Calling a *Kohen* for an *Aliyah* after a *Kohen*.
- Example 84: Reciting the *Birkat HaMazon* for others.
- Example 93: How much *matzah* one must eat at the Seder.
- Example 103: Setting sail before Shabbat.
- Example 105: Discussion during a meal.
- Example 111: If a person rents a house for Passover with the presumption that it has been checked for *hametz* and it is found not to have been checked.
- Example 112: Washing dishes on Shabbat.
- Example 114: Reducing happiness during the month of *Av*.
- Example 115: "Seeking one's needs" on Shabbat.
- Example 118: Spooning out food from a cooking utensil or pot on Shabbat.
- Example 121: Standing during Torah reading.
- Example 156: Immersing uncooked food into hot water on Shabbat.
- Example 157: Pouring liquid from one cup that contains both liquid and sediment to another on Shabbat.

- Example 165: If one finds *hametz* in his house on *Hol Hamoed*.
- Example 166: Eating the night before fasts which begin at sunrise.
- Example 167: Definition of a *Karmelit*.
- Example 170: Trapping flies on Shabbat.
- Example 182: The status of a doubtful *Eruv*.
- Example 194: A *Kohen* who killed someone saying *Birkat Kohanim*.
- Example 198: Materials to use as walls of a *Sukkah*.
- Example 202: Reading a letter delivered on Shabbat.
- Example 203: If a person intentionally cooks food on Shabbat.
- Example 209: If a person offers a Gentile a job and he works on Shabbat.
- Example 210: If while a *Kohen* is reciting the *Shema* he is called to the Torah.
- Example 213: The conclusion of the blessing "*She'hakol.*"
- Example 214: *Hashma'at kol* on Shabbat.
- Example 215: *Kiddush* on Shabbat day with a different alcoholic drink.
- Example 216: When a synagogue's custom is to give the first *Aliyah* on Shabbat Bereshit to a donor, yet a particular *Kohen* does not want to set aside his honor.
- Example 218: Using *noten taam lifgam* to permit mixtures on Passover.
- Example 219: Whether a first-born may partake in a *Seudat Mitzvah* during the Fast of the First Born.
- Example 220: Reciting a blessing over lighting candles for Yom Kippur.
- Example 221: Calling a blind person or one who is unable to read from the Torah for an *Aliyah*.
- Example 222: Returning a pot into the oven on Shabbat.
- Example 223: Building a *Sukkah* in a public domain.
- Example 224: Giving one's clothes to a Gentile to wash, or one's leather to a Gentile to tan, on Friday close to dark.
- Example 233: Reciting *Birkat Kohanim* when unable to properly pronounce the Hebrew letters.

- Example 234: The ability for one person to exempt another through his blessing over foods.
- Example 236: A *Hazan* who is a *Kohen* saying *Birkat Kohanim*.
- Example 238: Reducing one's business activity from *Rosh Hodesh Av* until the fast.
- Example 240: Kneading dough to make *matzah*.
- Example 246: What to do with clay pots used for *hametz* on Passover.
- Example 247: Kashering utensils through *Hagala*.
- Example 249: Eating *Hadash*.

7. **When people have adopted an unsupported custom, the *Mishna Berura* disapproves of it, yet attempts to justify it for those who will nevertheless continue to follow it.**

The *Mishna Berura* will not endorse a custom that has developed if the custom contradicts, or cannot be incorporated into, its greater halakhic methodology. This is the case even if the custom is practiced by those considered to be scrupulous in fulfilling the commandments. Nevertheless, even if a custom is erroneous, the *Mishna Berura* often first searches for means to legitimate it and will only disallow it when it clearly has no support. One should not infer that this demonstrates that the *Mishna Berura* considers the legitimacy of custom to be subordinate to written texts; rather, it shows that it recognizes that not all customs are similar and that some practices develop outside of the four cubits of the Halakha. The *Mishna Berura* also takes into account the reason for the development of a particular erroneous custom in determining how adamantly to oppose it.

Even when the *Mishna Berura* cannot find a way to accept as legitimate a practice which has developed contrary to the Halakha, in order to incorporate those who have such a practice into the realm of halakhic acceptability, it may still try to find some justification for their actions. In its attempt to justify a common practice, the *Mishna Berura* at times dissects a general practice into a number of possible variations in order to validate at least some of the permutations rather than be forced to reject the entire gamut. The *Mishna Berura* attempts to justify many practices even if it does not support them. When the *Mishna Berura* cannot validate a customary practice at all, it attempts to give the practice's adherents some other form of support.

We provide 13 examples of this phenomenon in the *Mishna Berura* from many different areas of Halakha. For an in-depth analysis of how the *Mishna Berura* uses this principle, please see the following examples:

- Example 122: Two *Hatanim* or two *Ba'alei Brit* in the synagogue on Monday or Thursday.
- Example 188: Reading the *Haggadah* after *Minha* on *Shabbat HaGadol*.
- Example 189: Spreading out grasses on *Shavuot* both in the synagogue and at home.
- Example 190: What to wear on the Shabbat preceding *Tisha b'Av*.
- Example 226: Washing one's hands in the morning.
- Example 227: Saying "amen" after "*Ga'al Israel*."
- Example 228: Playing with a ball on Shabbat and Yom Tov.
- Example 229: If a Gentile lights a candle for a Jew on Shabbat.
- Example 230: Going barefoot on *Tisha b'Av*.
- Example 231: Placing the *Bima* in the middle of the synagogue.
- Example 246: What to do with clay pots used for *hametz* on Passover.
- Example 249: Eating *Hadash*.
- Example 250: Having a Gentile make a bonfire on Shabbat in cold lands.

8. **When the codes are easily misunderstood, the *Mishna Berura* clarifies misunderstood rulings, and defends widespread practices.**

When the language of a ruling in the *Shulhan Arukh* is ambiguous and may lead a person to draw an erroneous inference, the

Mishna Berura clarifies its scope in order to save the reader from making what it believes to be false assumptions. When the language of a ruling in the *Shulhan Arukh* is ambiguous and a lenient practice has developed which can be interpreted as being in line with the wording of the *Shulhan Arukh*, the *Mishna Berura* attempts to clarify the language in order to legitimate the lenient practice.

When a prevalent custom contradicts the *Shulhan Arukh*, the *Mishna Berura* still may defend its acceptability as an *ab initio* manner of fulfillment. One way in which it supports such a custom is through applying or elevating legal principles not previously attributed to the custom in order to bolster its legitimacy. The legal principle used to support a custom may sometimes simply be a reprioritization of conflicting values. When there is a common practice that explicitly contradicts the ruling of the *poskim*, and where the *Mishna Berura* cannot add other principles to tilt the scales definitively in the custom's favor, it will explain the rationale behind the custom and leave the final ruling open-ended.

We provide 98 examples of this phenomenon in the *Mishna Berura* from many different areas of Halakha. For an in-depth analysis of how the *Mishna Berura* uses this principle, please see the following examples:

- Example 2: Working on Friday from *Minha* onward.
- Example 10: When the day before Passover falls on Shabbat, what one does with his remaining bread.
- Example 11: Prohibitions on fast days.
- Example 14: Putting salt in a *kli rishon* that is no longer on the fire.
- Example 18: "Amen" after "*Ga'al Israel.*"
- Example 21: Saying the passage "The Incense Mixture."
- Example 36: A mourner who desires to recite the *Shema* and to pray.
- Example 52: Reciting the *Shema* at dawn.
- Example 55: Mixture of *hametz* on Passover.
- Example 60: Sitting a hen on her eggs to hatch chicks on *Hol HaMoed*.

- Example 61: If a Hanukah candle becomes mixed with other candles.
- Example 62: Going to guard one's fruit on Shabbat.
- Example 67: If a person takes a cup of beer or water and makes the blessing for wine.
- Example 72: Pregnant and nursing women fasting.
- Example 82: Calling a *Kohen* for an *Aliyah* after a *Kohen*.
- Example 83: Carrying on Yom Tov for unnecessary purposes or for a Gentile.
- Example 84: Reciting the *Birkat HaMazon* for others.
- Example 85: Leaving a meal before saying the *Birkat HaMazon*.
- Example 86: If a community collects money for a certain purpose.
- Example 87: If alleyways are considered public domains.
- Example 88: If a hole in a wall bordering a *Karmelit* is considered a *Karmelit*.
- Example 89: Preparing something for Shabbat in order to honor it.
- Example 90: Saying the *Birkat HaMazon* silently.
- Example 91: If, due to sickness or conditions out of his control, a person recites the *Shema* without moving his lips.
- Example 92: Touching one's foreleg or thigh in the middle of a meal.
- Example 93: How much *matzah* one must eat at the Seder.
- Example 94: Carrying on Yom Tov.
- Example 95: Selling a sanctified object to buy another object of similar sanctity.
- Example 96: The blessing over *Hallel*.
- Example 97: How much of the hand one must wash when washing before eating bread.
- Example 98: Doing something in a regular manner on *Hol HaMoed*.
- Example 99: Making partitions of a *Sukkah* from linen sheets.
- Example 100: Entering through one door of a synagogue and exiting through another to take a short cut.
- Example 101: Giving a Gentile a letter to send before Shabbat.
- Example 102: Giving a Gentile money on Friday to buy something.
- Example 103: Setting sail before Shabbat.

- Example 104: Giving food to a person who does not know how to make a blessing over it.
- Example 105: Discussion during a meal.
- Example 106: Picking up one's son who is holding a stone on Shabbat.
- Example 107: Moving a tool on Shabbat that has on it both prohibited and permitted objects.
- Example 108: Making a tent on Shabbat with books.
- Example 109: Watering vegetables on Shabbat.
- Example 110: If a person is alone on the road as Shabbat begins.
- Example 111: If a person rents a house for Passover with the presumption that it has been checked for *hametz* and it is found not to have been checked.
- Example 112: Washing dishes on Shabbat.
- Example 113: Extinguishing a candle for a sick person on Shabbat.
- Example 114: Reducing happiness during the month of *Av*.
- Example 115: "Seeking one's needs" on Shabbat.
- Example 116: Receiving *hametz* from a Gentile as payment on Passover.
- Example 117: If one forgot to say a blessing before taking a drink.
- Example 124: Speaking before hearing *HaMotzi*.
- Example 126: Chewing cinnamon sticks during a fast.
- Example 128: Wearing phylacteries on *Hol HaMoed*.
- Example 129: Wearing phylacteries of *Rashi* and of *Rabbenu Tam*.
- Example 130: Hiring a *Hazan* to pray on Shabbat.
- Example 135: The blessings over wearing phylacteries.
- Example 142: An *androgynous* person or a *tumtum* making a *zimun*.
- Example 149: Renting one's house for Passover.
- Example 150: Eating meat or drinking wine on the tenth of *Av*.
- Example 161: If a person rents a house and does not know if it has been checked for *hametz*.
- Example 162: Lighting Hanukah candles before sunset.
- Example 163: The status of a wall when its gaps make up as much of the wall as the material of the wall itself.

- Example 164: Women doing work on *Rosh Hodesh*.
- Example 168: Lending a tool to a Gentile on Shabbat.
- Example 170: Trapping flies on Shabbat.
- Example 171: Entering the synagogue through one door to exit through another.
- Example 172: *Okhel Nefesh* on a holiday.
- Example 173: When a roof is both part of a private domain and next to a public domain.
- Example 174: What to do regarding eating bread when a person is traveling and cannot reach water.
- Example 175: Establishing time to learn Torah.
- Example 180: Placing food upon a stove before Shabbat.
- Example 194: A *Kohen* who killed someone saying *Birkat Kohanim*.
- Example 195: Interruptions between *Kaddish* after *Pesukei d'Zimra* and *Barkhu*.
- Example 197: Lighting Hanukah candles.
- Example 199: How much one needs to wash for *mayim aharonim*.
- Example 200: Going out Friday close to dark with a needle or a pen in one's hand.
- Example 201: Examining one's clothing on Friday close to dark.
- Example 202: Reading a letter delivered on Shabbat.
- Example 203: If a person intentionally cooks food on Shabbat.
- Example 204: Status of a partition that was erected on Shabbat.
- Example 207: Status of holes that are in the walls facing a private domain.
- Example 208: Carrying within four cubits in a public domain on Shabbat.
- Example 209: If a person offers a Gentile a job and he works on Shabbat.
- Example 211: How a left-handed person dons his phylactery.
- Example 217: The blessing if one uses horseradish for *marror*.
- Example 223: Building a *Sukkah* in a public domain.
- Example 224: Giving one's clothes to a Gentile to wash, or one's leather to a Gentile to tan, on Friday close to dark.
- Example 227: Saying "amen" after *"Ga'al Israel."*

- Example 234: The ability for one person to exempt another through his blessing over foods.
- Example 242: Bringing one's children to hear the *Megilla*.
- Example 243: Designating a bag to always be used for one's phylacteries.
- Example 244: Eating and drinking in the synagogue.
- Example 245: Eating fish on Shabbat.
- Example 246: What to do with clay pots used for *hametz* on Passover.
- Example 247: Kashering utensils through *Hagala*.
- Example 248: Eating, drinking, and sleeping in a *Sukkah*.
- Example 249: Eating *Hadash*.
- Example 250: Having a Gentile make a bonfire on Shabbat in cold lands.

9. **When the codes and Kabbala conflict, the *Mishna Berura* minimizes the tension between the two positions.**

The *Mishna Berura* seeks to minimize the inherent tensions between Kabbala and Talmud, even if such interpretations may seem somewhat forced. However, when faced with no alternative, the rulings of the Talmud and *poskim* take precedence over the Kabbalistic literature, and avoiding potential transgression overrides a Kabbalistic instruction. In order to negotiate between conflicting positions in the Talmud and writings of the *poskim* and the Kabbalistic literature, the *Mishna Berura* applies the technique of suggesting that one follows different positions depending on the circumstances. The *Mishna Berura* also reinterprets Kabbalistic texts in order to mitigate opposition. When there is a suggestion among the Kabbalistic sources which does not conflict with the Talmud or *poskim*, the *Mishna Berura* often recommends that one act in accordance with it. The *Mishna Berura*'s method of responding to the challenges that arise in trying to incorporate the Kabbala literature and the Talmud and *poskim* into one coherent halakhic system is, in truth, not innovative. When it spells out its approach explicitly, it attributes it to the *Knesset HaGedola*.

We provide 10 examples of this phenomenon in the *Mishna Berura* from many different areas of Halakha. For an in-depth analysis of how the *Mishna Berura* uses this principle, please see the following examples:

- Example 73: Washing one's hands and reciting the blessing *al netilat yadaim*.
- Example 74: Where to put on Tallit and Tefillin.
- Example 75: Saying *Tahanun*.
- Example 76: Bending one's head while praying.
- Example 77: Praying silently.
- Example 78: How to perform *Hagba*.
- Example 79: Staying awake throughout the night of the holiday of *Shavuot* to study Torah.
- Example 80: Investigating one's actions during the Ten Days of Repentance.
- Example 81: Obligation to form a *zimun*.
- Example 186: The person called up to the Torah reading along with the *Hazan*.

10. When the codes are in tension and the *Gra* has a strong view, the *Mishna Berura* relies on the position of the *Gra*.[3]

Many times when the *Mishna Berura* confronts a disagreement in which it cannot find a compromise that can successfully include opposing positions, it grounds its ultimate suggestion on the opinion of the *Gra*. The *Mishna Berura* also relies on the *Gra* to

---

3 What is amazing about this principle is that the *Mishna Berura* wishes to incorporate the positions of the *Gra*, despite the fact that the *Gra*'s "True vs. False" approach is diametrically opposed to the *Mishna Berura*'s inclusive and holistic priorities, in which alternative views are rarely fully wrong.

    Today it is a common, almost unconscious, automatism in yeshiva circles to defer to the *Gra*'s halakhic rulings; however, despite his great influence on the manner of Talmud study and in contrast to his majestic reputation, before the *Mishna Berura*, the *Gra*'s rulings were generally not influential in shaping halakhic practice, even in Vilna. The uniqueness of the *Mishna Berura*'s deep reliance on the *Gra* is unmistakable when juxtaposed with the *Gra*'s status in the *Arukh HaShulhan* as just one of a number of commentators.

give further support to the ruling of the *Shulhan Arukh* when there are others who rule contrarily. On one occasion, the *Mishna Berura* cites the *Gra* to support its opposition to a custom endorsed by the *Rema*. There are times when the *Mishna Berura* defers to the *Gra* despite the fact that its general methodology would have it rule to the contrary. If the *Mishna Berura* does not suggest following the *Gra*'s opinion in practice, it may still defer to his position intellectually.

The *Mishna Berura* also utilizes the *Gra*'s writings as a means to reinterpret or explain the *Shulhan Arukh* when its author thinks that either Rabbi Karo or the *Rema* contradicts himself. The *Mishna Berura* also utilizes the *Gra*'s writings as a means to reinterpret or explain a *Rishon* when it looks like the *Rishon* contradicts himself. The *Mishna Berura* relies on the *Gra* to give an alternate justification for a position whose initial justification has been rejected. The *Mishna Berura* also reinterprets the *Shulhan Arukh*'s or the *Rema*'s rulings so that they accord with the *Gra*'s position. The *Mishna Berura*, at times, writes that the simple reading of a ruling is misleading and should mean something different i.e., as the *Gra* understands it, or will simply rewrite a ruling to conform to the *Gra*'s understanding. The *Mishna Berura*'s deference to the *Gra* is so substantial that it even reinterprets the *Gra's* writings in order to make certain that the *Gra* remains a consistent foundation upon which to rely.

We provide 46 examples of this phenomenon in the *Mishna Berura* from many different areas of Halakha. For an in-depth analysis of how the *Mishna Berura* uses this principle, please see the following examples:

- Example 19: Washing one's hands with soap on Shabbat.
- Example 30: When to say *Kiddush Levana*.
- Example 40: Insulating food on Erev Shabbat with something that adds heat.

- Example 119: Definition of a private domain.
- Example 135: The blessings over wearing phylacteries.
- Example 158: The status of a protruding roof.
- Example 162: Lighting Hanukah candles before sunset.
- Example 167: Definition of a *Karmelit*.
- Example 176: When to say the blessing "*Elokai Neshama*."
- Example 177: If a community skips the public recital of the Torah portion on Shabbat.
- Example 178: Saying *Kiddush Levana* after Yom Kippur.
- Example 179: If a person forgets and leaves a pot of food that is already fully cooked on the stove on Shabbat.
- Example 180: Placing food upon a stove before Shabbat.
- Example 181: The third meal when Shabbat falls on the fourteenth of *Nissan*.
- Example 182: The status of a doubtful *Eruv*.
- Example 183: Saying the *Kedusha* within "*Yotzer*" when praying alone.
- Example 184: Washing for less than the volume of an olive (*kazayit*) of bread.
- Example 185: Shaving on the day before Yom Tov.
- Example 186: The person called up to the Torah reading along with the *Hazan*.
- Example 187: The status of a protruding roof when the walls cannot be seen.
- Example 188: Reading the *Haggadah* after *Minha* on *Shabbat HaGadol*.
- Example 189: Spreading out grasses on *Shavuot* both in the synagogue and at home.
- Example 190: What to wear on the Shabbat preceding *Tisha b'Av*.
- Example 191: If the three people called to read from the Torah read less than nine verses cumulatively.
- Example 192: Grinding salt on Shabbat.
- Example 193: If a Gentile is going of his own accord to a place where a Jew happens to have a letter to send.

- Example 194: A *Kohen* who killed someone saying *Birkat Kohanim*.
- Example 195: Interruptions between *Kaddish* after *Pesukei d'Zimra* and *Barkhu*.
- Example 196: Leaving the synagogue and talking while the Torah scroll is open.
- Example 197: Lighting Hanukah candles.
- Example 198: Materials to use as walls of a *Sukkah*.
- Example 199: How much one needs to wash for *mayim aharonim*.
- Example 200: Going out Friday close to dark with a needle or a pen in one's hand.
- Example 201: Examining one's clothing on Friday close to dark.
- Example 202: Reading a letter delivered on Shabbat.
- Example 203: If a person intentionally cooks food on Shabbat.
- Example 204: Status of a partition that was erected on Shabbat.
- Example 205: Renting or lending one's animal to a Gentile in order for him to perform prohibited activity on Shabbat.
- Example 206: Wiping up with a sponge on Shabbat.
- Example 207: Status of holes that are in the walls facing a private domain.
- Example 208: Carrying within four cubits in a public domain on Shabbat.
- Example 209: If a person offers a Gentile a job and he works on Shabbat.
- Example 212: How to lean when saying *Tahanun*.
- Example 213: The conclusion of the blessing "*She'hakol*."
- Example 220: Reciting a blessing over lighting candles for Yom Kippur.
- Example 248: Eating, drinking, and sleeping in a *Sukkah*.

VI

The *Mishna Berura's* Technique of Legal Interpretation

The *Mishna Berura*'s methodology of negotiating between the ten halakhic principles is, in truth, only one manifestation of its overall desire to create a coherent presentation of the Halakha. A second demonstration of this desire is the manner in which it presents its analysis. By innovatively interpreting both the rulings of the *Shulhan Arukh* and the canon upon which it is based, the *Mishna Berura* seeks to resolve apparent contradictions, modify and adapt rulings, and, in general, transform the laws of daily conduct into a comprehensive, consistent, and unified system which accords to its own perspective.

In a situation in which a ruling in the *Shulhan Arukh* is ambiguous, the *Mishna Berura* will provide an interpretation that mitigates disagreement among the various interpretative positions in order to achieve the greatest level of juridical consolidation. The *Mishna Berura* also seeks to clarify ambiguity in situations wherein Rabbi Karo gives a general ruling, yet his language raises doubt as to its universality. The *Mishna Berura* also reinterprets a law that seems to contradict the general methodology of the legislator. By claiming that two seemingly opposing rulings do not contradict, but in fact deal with different situations, the *Mishna Berura* is able to achieve coherence even when it must maintain seeming inconsistency. When a ruling seems to contradict an accepted halakhic principle, the *Mishna Berura* will interpret the law to apply to a different context so that it does not conflict with the principle. In order to defend an accepted halakhic principle, the *Mishna Berura* reinterprets the language of legal positions if their plain meaning would present a challenge. This is not limited to Rabbi Karo's wording; the *Mishna Berura* even reinterprets the language of *Aharonim*. The *Mishna Berura* provides alternative explanations for the source of particular *Halakhot* in order to remove contradictions in the perceived derivation of a law. The *Mishna Berura* provides alternative explanations for a Halakha when it seems to contradict the general reasoning behind the legal issue. The *Mishna Berura* not only interprets the *Shulhan Arukh* in a manner that makes Rabbi Karo's opinion consistent with the general halakhic tradition, it reinterprets *Rishonim* to accord with it as well. The *Mishna Berura* reinterprets rulings that, on their face, contradict common practice in order to demonstrate that the law and the people's way of life have not, in fact, diverged. When the halakhic tradition contains two distinct yet valid forms of one practice, the *Mishna Berura* attempts to find a practical application which justifies the distinction.

The author of the *Mishna Berura* also uses his commentary as a way to interpret various positions so that they will accord with what he thinks should be the law. The *Mishna Berura* provides an alternative rationale behind the particular position to which it subscribes in order to justify ruling in its favor. There are times when the *Mishna Berura* explains the justification for a certain opinion in order to reject it.

When confronted with a ruling by Rabbi Karo which it believes inaccurately portrays the normative Halakha, the *Mishna Berura* qualifies or limits its application. On the other hand, when confronted with a ruling by the *Rema* which it believes inaccurately portrays the normative Halakha, the *Mishna Berura* considers this a sole or minority opinion. Therefore, rather than having to approach it as a description of the normative practice in Ashkenaz, he can ignore it completely.

We provide 45 examples of the *Mishna Berura*'s interpretative strategy from many different areas of Halakha. We have categorized the examples into three main strategies that the *Mishna Berura* uses. For an in-depth analysis of how the *Mishna Berura* uses this principle, please see the following examples:

Interprets in a Manner that Seeks to Resolve Potential Contradiction

- Example 82: Calling a *Kohen* for an *Aliyah* after a *Kohen*.
- Example 83: Carrying on Yom Tov for an unnecessary purpose or for a Gentile.
- Example 84: Reciting the *Birkat HaMazon* for others.
- Example 85: Leaving a meal before saying the *Birkat HaMazon*.
- Example 86: If a community collects money for a certain purpose.
- Example 87: If alleyways are considered public domains.
- Example 88: If a hole in a wall bordering a *Karmelit* is considered a *Karmelit*.
- Example 89: Preparing something for Shabbat in order to honor it.
- Example 90: Saying the *Birkat HaMazon* silently.
- Example 91: If, due to sickness or conditions out of his control, a person recites the *Shema* without moving his lips.
- Example 92: Touching one's foreleg or thigh in the middle of a meal.
- Example 93: How much *matzah* one must eat at the Seder.
- Example 94: Carrying on Yom Tov.
- Example 95: Selling a sanctified object to buy another object of similar sanctity.
- Example 96: The blessing over *Hallel*.

Interprets in a Manner that Justifies His Own Opinion

- Example 97: How much of the hand one must wash when washing before eating bread.
- Example 98: Doing something in a regular manner on *Hol HaMoed*.
- Example 99: Making partitions of a *Sukkah* from linen sheets.

- Example 100: Entering through one door of a synagogue and exiting through another to take a shortcut.

Difference in Interpreting Rabbi Karo Versus the *Rema*

- Example 101: Giving a Gentile a letter to send before Shabbat.
- Example 102: Giving a Gentile money on Friday to buy something.
- Example 103: Setting sail before Shabbat.
- Example 104: Giving food to a person who does not know how to make a blessing over it.
- Example 105: Discussion during a meal.
- Example 106: Picking up one's son who is holding a stone on Shabbat.
- Example 107: Moving a tool on Shabbat that has on it both prohibited and permitted objects.
- Example 108: Making a tent on Shabbat with books.
- Example 109: Watering vegetables on Shabbat.
- Example 110: If a person is alone on the road as Shabbat begins.
- Example 111: If a person rents a house for Passover with the presumption that it has been checked for *hametz* and it is found not to have been checked.
- Example 112: Washing dishes on Shabbat.
- Example 113: Extinguishing a candle for a sick person on Shabbat.
- Example 114: Reducing happiness during the month of *Av*.
- Example 115: "Seeking one's needs" on Shabbat.
- Example 116: Receiving *hametz* from a Gentile as payment on Passover.

VII

The *Mishna Berura*'s Use of Key Terms

With a cursory look, it may seem that the *Mishna Berura* uses particular terms simply as rabbinic expressions without any methodology behind their usage. However, upon examination, it becomes clear that its use of different terms has jurisprudential importance, as they signify its opinion regarding the legal merit of particular positions vis-à-vis their alternatives. For example, the *Mishna Berura* reveals a different attitude toward given positions when it uses the term *Yireh Shamayim* (One who fears Heaven), *Ba'al Nefesh* (A Spiritual Person), *Tavo Alav Berakha* (Will come to blessing), *HaMedakdakim* (The Scrupulous), or *Machmir al Atzmo* (Stringent upon Oneself).

Yireh Shamayim: When the *Mishna Berura* writes that one who fears Heaven should be careful to act stringently even though a prevalent practice is more lenient, it means that the lenient practice is here considered legitimate. The *Mishna Berura*'s advice to people who fear Heaven that they should be more stringent is based upon a desire for a person to act in accordance with as many opinions as possible. When other *poskim* use the term "one who fears Heaven," the *Mishna Berura* interprets their use of the term in the same way as its own use.

For an in-depth analysis of how the *Mishna Berura* uses this term, please see the following examples:

- Example 1: If a Jew ties *tzitzit* on a garment without the proper intention.
- Example 2: Working on Friday from *Minha* onward.
- Example 3: Learning books of wisdom on Shabbat or Yom Tov.
- Example 4: Which garments need *tzitzit*.
- Example 5: Immersing a new dish in a *mikveh* on Shabbat.
- Example 6: If the community prays the evening prayer (*Maariv*) while it is still daytime.

Ba'al Nefesh: When a prevalent practice is more lenient than what the *Mishna Berura* believes is the essential ruling, yet it foresees that the practice cannot be changed, the *Mishna Berura* writes that a *Ba'al Nefesh* will act stringently. The *Mishna Berura* also uses the term *Ba'al Nefesh* to describe those who follow the simple ruling of the *Shulhan Arukh*, even when it itself gives a more lenient interpretation of the ruling. The *Mishna Berura* uses the term *Ba'al Nefesh* when confronted with a Halakha which is lenient only as the result of capitulation to ensure community adherence.

For an in-depth analysis of how the *Mishna Berura* uses this term, please see the following examples:

- Example 7: Making an *Eruv* that contains a public domain.
- Example 8: Fast days due to tragedy.
- Example 9: Walking outside on Shabbat wearing gloves.
- Example 10: When the day before Passover falls on Shabbat, what one does with his remaining bread.
- Example 11: Prohibitions on fast days.

Tavo Alav Berakha: If the Halakha follows the majority opinion, yet there is an individual or marginal opinion among the *Rishonim* that is more stringent, the *Mishna Berura* writes that anyone who accepts the more stringent opinion upon himself will come to blessing. The *Mishna Berura*'s use of the expression reflects its use among previous *poskim*. If the number of *poskim* who suggest that one be stringent increases to the point where it no longer seems to be a marginal position, the *Mishna Berura* will aggregate the earlier marginal opinions to give it normative authority.

For an in-depth analysis of how the *Mishna Berura* uses this term, please see the following examples:

- Example 12: Squeezing grapes into a pot on Shabbat.
- Example 13: Buying meat on Yom Tov.
- Example 14: Putting salt in a *kli rishon* that is no longer on the fire.
- Example 15: *Hametz*-based adhesive.
- Example 16: Relighting a torch left over from the first day of Yom Tov, that had gone out on the second day of Yom Tov.

HaMedakdakim: The *Mishna Berura* uses the expression "the scrupulous" to refer to those people who attempt to act in accord with all opinions, yet it does not necessarily imply that the *Mishna Berura* considers their actions to be correct.

For an in-depth analysis of how the *Mishna Berura* uses this term, please see the following examples:

- Example 17: Rosh Hodesh meals.
- Example 18: "Amen" after "Ga'al Israel."
- Example 19: Washing one's hands with soap on Shabbat.
- Example 20: Kohanim turning toward the congregation to say the Birkat Kohanim.
- Example 21: Saying the passage "The Incense Mixture."
- Example 22: Clothes washed in wheat-water and paper that has a hametz-based adhesive on Passover.

Machmir al Atzmo: When the lenient practice is clearly accepted as the Halakha, yet a more stringent practice has strong support among the *poskim,* the *Mishna Berura* will not impose the stringent opinion upon the community. Rather, it will recommend the stringent practice only to those individuals who are able to uphold it. If a particular lenient practice is halakhically acceptable yet may lead to erroneous analogy to other areas of Halakha, the *Mishna Berura* will recommend leniency only to individuals and not to the community as a whole.

For an in-depth analysis of how the *Mishna Berura* uses this term, please see the following examples:

- Example 23: Folding an article of clothing on Shabbat.
- Example 24: Using a prayer book when Rosh Hashanah falls on Saturday night.
- Example 25: Making the blessing over spices for Havdala if Yom Kippur fell on Shabbat.
- Example 26: Writing salutary letters on Hol HaMoed.
- Example 27: Asking one's servant to walk with him and light a candle on Shabbat.

VIII

Examples of the *Mishna* *Berura*'s Methodology

As the above points show, the *Mishna Berura* juggles a number of variables to define proper halakhic practice in any given case, as opposed to the traditional models of creating a legal guide. How the *Mishna Berura* approaches a final decision on any given matter of Jewish law becomes an exercise in what we at first might suspect to be judicial caprice, since there are so many variables at play; as its students, it is hard at first to imagine that it could possibly have a systematic approach.

We hope, however, that in providing a number of in-depth examples below we will demonstrate that the *Mishna Berura*'s wondrous achievement is so much more astounding with the added realization that it did, in fact, have a systematic approach, one that negotiated between these ten principles and did so with such skill that it has become the coherent unified code of Halakha that its author intended it to be.

Our choice of examples is meant to highlight two specific points in addition to the complex nature of the *Mishna Berura*'s methodology. The first point is with respect to its involved nature. Many *poskim* utilize and negotiate between a number of principles, yet they find coherence among them by compartmentalizing their use. For example, both Rabbi Moshe Feinstein and Rav Ovadia Yosef have the principles of being strict and being lenient, and they are each strict or lenient in different areas of Halakha—however, they do not use both principles in the same area of law.[1] Contrary to these two *poskim*, the *Mishna Berura* uses both principles in the same areas of law, and will even use both principles when ruling on a single issue!

The second point is with respect to the status of customs. The reason we deem it important to provide examples that relate to customs is that we have found that the *Mishna Berura*'s approach to the legitimacy of customs in their own right is different than what is popularly assumed. In his seminal article "Rupture and Reconstruction: The Transformation of Contemporary Orthodoxy," which masterfully portrays the shift in Orthodoxy from a mimetic tradition into one which is controlled by textual justification, Dr. Haym Soloveitchik compared the methodology of the *Mishna Berura* to the *Arukh HaShulhan* as it pertains to the legitimacy of customs per se as follows:

> The difference between [the author of the *Mishna Berura*'s] posture and that of his predecessor, the author of the *Arukh ha-Shulhan*, is that he surveys the entire literature and then shows that the practice is plausibly justifiable in terms of that literature. His interpretations, while not necessarily persuasive, always stay within the bounds of the reasonable. And the legal coordinates upon which the *Mishnah Berurah* [sic] plots the issue are the written literature and the written literature alone. With sufficient erudition and inclination, received practice can almost invariably be charted on these axes, but it is no longer inherently valid. It can stand on its own no more.[2]

While Dr. Soloveitchik correctly contends that customs are no longer inherently valid for the *Mishna Berura*, many have incorrectly inferred that the *Mishna Berura* does not consider customs to have any validity vis-à-vis the written literature. It is our contention that this view is incorrect, even including those situations in

---

1   It is beyond this work to explore the jurisprudence of these two modern *poskim*, but suffice it to say that anyone who is familiar with their works would agree with this assertion.

2   This article was initially published in *Tradition* 28, No. 4 (Summer 1994): 64-131, and is posted at http://www.lookstein.org/links/orthodoxy.htm.

which the *Mishna Berura* examines the legitimacy of a custom which either does not have textual support or conflicts with the normative written Halakha. The manner in which the *Mishna Berura* explains a custom's existence and at times accepts its continuation demonstrates that it does believe that customs have halakhic weight, if not inherent validity. In other words, though the *Mishna Berura* utilizes custom as a source for legitimating a practice, it does not allow custom to stand alone. Rather, consistent with its overall methodology, which attempts to promote maximum compliance when possible and accept the broadest range for acceptance when not, an existing custom is only one component, albeit an important one, in the *Mishna Berura's* general approach. In order to exemplify this point more clearly, after some of the examples we will also provide the ruling of the *Arukh HaShulhan* as a point of comparison. However, because this is not an examination of the similarities and differences between the two jurists, we will only provide the ruling of the *Arukh HaShulhan* when the comparison will highlight the unique approach of the *Mishna Berura* and not just present their agreement or disagreement in the substantive rulings.

We have also included an additional 250 examples in a separate section. These additional examples are meant to serve as a reference guide to support the general claims that we have made above. One need not read every (or any) example to understand what we have described as the *Mishna Berura's* jurisprudential methodology. However, if one would like to engage in further research on the *Mishna Berura* or to have concrete examples to fully evidence our claims and would therefore need to accumulate a large number of examples, we have done the work already.

The examples we have chosen show the *Mishna Berura's* use of more than one principle per issue and tend to be of interest to the contemporary reader. They are divided into four categories, namely, (a) adding a new dimension to resolve a disagreement, (b) including all Jews, (c) regarding Jewish-Gentile relations, and (d) regarding the existence of erroneous customs.

(A) Adding a New Dimension to Resolve a Disagreement

Example 1—The *Androgynous* Person and the *Tumtum:* Intersex and Jewish Law

In the following example, the *Mishna Berura* utilizes the following halakhic principles:

2. When the codes record both lenient and strict positions, the *Mishna Berura* advises when one should be strict and when one may be lenient.
4. When the codes record two mutually exclusive opinions, the *Mishna Berura* suggests ways to avoid transgression according to either view.
8. When the codes are easily misunderstood, the *Mishna Berura* clarifies misunderstood rulings and defends widespread practices.

Under Jewish law, at certain prescribed times males that are patrilineal descendants from Aaron, the biblical High Priest, who are as a group called *Kohanim*, or "Priests," are ritually required to bless the nation. The process is called *Birkat Kohanim* (the "Priestly Blessings"). On the *Rema*'s ruling that someone who is not a *Kohen* should not recite the *Birkat Kohanim*,[3] the *Mishna Berura* writes that an "*androgynous* person" or a "*tumtum*" should not recite the blessings. Rather, these people should leave the synagogue before the *Hazan* (cantor) recites "*Retzei,*" the prayer directly preceding the blessings, during which the *Kohanim* are supposed to walk to the front of the synagogue in preparation.[4]

Before discussing the ruling of the *Mishna Berura*, we will first provide a bit of background information to give it context. An *androgynous* person is someone who has both male and female genitalia. A *tumtum* is a person with no visible genitalia. There is a disagreement among the *poskim* as to whether an *androgynous* person should be considered as of neither gender, but rather as a

---

3   *Shulhan Arukh, Orah Hayyim* 128:1.
4   *Biur Halakha* 128: s.v. *v'ein l'zar.*

category unto itself, or whether such a person should be considered someone whose gender is in doubt. If the *androgynous* person is a wholly different gender, someone of that gender should not recite the *Birkat Kohanim*, since that is a task for a male *Kohen*. If there is a possibility that the *androgynous* person may be male, then there would be an obligation to recite the *Birkat Kohanim* since, as we noted above, in the context of *matzah* on Passover, the Halakha inclines toward obligation rather than exemption in the case of doubt regarding a Torah obligation.[5] Furthermore, there is a disagreement among the *Aharonim* as to whether there is a prohibition for someone who is not a *Kohen* to recite the *Birkat Kohanim* or not. Therefore, since there may be a possible obligation and potentially no prohibition, it would seem that an *androgynous* person should, in fact, recite the *Birkat Kohanim* if such a person is classified as potentially a male.

With respect to a *tumtum*, on the other hand, all consider such a person to be a case of doubtful gender: the person is definitely either a male or a female. Therefore, the obligation, or prohibition, for a *tumtum* to recite the *Birkat Kohanim* rests solely on the disagreement among the *Aharonim* over whether or not there is a prohibition for someone who is not a *Kohen* to recite the *Birkat Kohanim*. Despite the categorical distinction between the two, the *Mishna Berura* nevertheless advises indiscriminately that both the *androgynous* person and the *tumtum* should preemptively leave the synagogue.

The assiduousness of the *Mishna Berura*'s recommendation becomes clear in light of a different ruling in the *Shulhan Arukh*. Just a few paragraphs later, the *Shulhan Arukh* states that if a regular *Kohen*, for whatever reason, does not move when the *Hazan* recites "*Retzei*," he is no longer allowed to go up to recite the *Birkat Kohanim*;[6] however, even if a *Kohen* did not move, he is not in violation of a prohibition—he can simply rely on the rabbinic precept of "*shev v'al taaseh*" (literally: "sit and do not act"). By doing nothing, the *Kohen* in question is doing nothing *wrong*; he is just passively

---

5   See *supra* text accompanying note 11.
6   *Shulhan Arukh, Orah Hayyim* 128:8.

not performing a positive commandment.[7] Nevertheless, the *Mishna Berura* recommends that this *Kohen* too should actively leave the synagogue.

The *Mishna Berura*'s reasons not to rely on this principle of "*shev v'al taaseh*" in the case of a regular *Kohen* are twofold. First, *ab initio* a person should not rely on this rabbinic principle if he can help it[8] (the case in the *Shulhan Arukh* is clearly referring to a male *Kohen* who did not move or was unable to move for some other reason during *Retzei* and now wants to know what to do, which is different from someone like an *androgynous* person or *tumtum*, who initially did not know what to do). Additionally, the *Mishna Berura* thinks that the *Kohen* should leave because otherwise people who do not know the reason why he did not "move his feet" and see him standing in the congregation when all of the other *Kohanim* are getting ready to recite the blessings may erroneously think that the reason this particular *Kohen* is not up there is because he has a blemish that makes him unfit to recite the Blessings,[9] casting aspersions and creating a scenario which he would like to avoid. Getting back to our original case, since an *androgynous* person or a *tumtum* need not worry about the second reason, as their condition *does* in fact render them unfit, the *Mishna Berura*'s suggestion that they leave the synagogue rests solely on its discomfort in relying on a valid rabbinic principle in a situation when it is not essential to do so. Its decision here is therefore based on its fourth halakhic principle.

---

7   The reason we say that the person is doing nothing wrong, even though one is generally forbidden to not perform a command through a *shev v'al taaseh*, is that the prohibition applies when no conflicting prohibition exists. If a person is confronted with even a rabbinic prohibition that conflicts with the positive command, then the *shev v'al taaseh* may be applied. In this case, the conflicting prohibition would be based on the statement of Rabbi Yehoshua ben Levi, "Any *Kohen* who does not ascend [the platform] in the Service blessing may not ascend later, as it is said: 'And Aaron lifted up his hands toward the people, and blessed them, and he came down from offering the sin-offering and the burnt-offering and the peace-offering (Leviticus 9:22).' As in this passage [the benediction occurred] during the Service, so here [in the Synagogue] it must be [during the prayers relating to] the Service (BT *Sotah* 38b)."

8   *Sha'ar HaTziyun* 128:14.

9   *Mishna Berura* 128:9.

On a related note, the *Shulhan Arukh* rules that an *androgynous* person should only make a *zimun* (a ritual invitation by a member of a group of three or more men, or three or more women, who have eaten together to the others when they wish to recite the *Birkat HaMazon* [Grace After Meals] as a unit) for other *androgynous* people, and not for either men or women.[10] A *tumtum* should not make a *zimun* at all.[11] In his commentary on the *Shulhan Arukh*'s rulings, the *Mishna Berura* first explains the reason as being that *androgynous* people make up their own category,[12] but also includes the second reason, which expresses a doubt that they may actually be of the opposite gender than the other participants.[13] Though the two opinions are contradictory on their face, the *Mishna Berura* records both of them. Based on the opinion that they are of doubtful gender, *androgynous* people cannot join with men, for fear that they may be women, nor can they join with women, for fear that they may be men.

In the *Sha'ar HaTziyun*, Rabbi Kagan's footnotes to the *Mishna Berura*, he writes that when three *androgynous* people eat together, but not to satiety, one may make a *zimun* with them. This is permissible because the obligation to make a *zimun* when people eat, but not to satiety, is of a rabbinic and not a biblical level. As noted, when dealing with a rabbinic law, the traditional halakhic principle is to be lenient in cases of doubt. The doubt as to what to consider *androgynous* people can therefore be dealt with leniently in this case, and we can assume that they are of the same gender as the new participant. If, however, they have eaten to satiety, ideally one should not join in a *zimun* with them, since the obligation upon men to make a *zimun* is not the same as for women, and the varying levels of obligation (which in our case are in doubt) preclude them from joining together. Nevertheless, *ex post facto* it may be permissible.[14] In contradistinction, the *Mishna Berura* writes that even if

---

10 *Shulhan Arukh, Orah Hayyim* 199:8.
11 *Shulhan Arukh, Orah Hayyim* 199:9.
12 *Mishna Berura* 199:20.
13 *Mishna Berura* 199:21.
14 *Sha'ar HaTziyun* 199:11.

three *tumtumim* eat together, they cannot make a *zimun*, since there is a doubt as to each individual's gender. The same distinctions are made with respect to blowing the *Shofar* for others on Rosh Hashanah[15] and for reading the *Megilla* for others on Purim.[16] Moreover, the *Mishna Berura* explains that an *androgynous* person may not be circumcised on Shabbat since there is a doubt if the person is in fact male, and one does not suspend the laws of Shabbat (biblical in nature) due to doubtful fulfillment.[17] In his explanation of the *Shulhan Arukh* and in his decisions, the *Mishna Berura* utilizes the second halakhic principle in showing in which situations *androgynous* people may partake in rituals *ab initio*, *ex post facto*, or not at all.

For comparison, the *Arukh HaShulhan* writes with respect to people in these categories that an *androgynous* person may make a *zimun* for other *androgynous* people, but cannot make a *zimun* for men or for women. Rather than detailing all of the various positions and situations, he writes simply that the reason for this is that *androgynous* people are the same as each other: they are a category unto themselves. A *tumtum*, on the other hand, may be either a man or a woman; therefore, such a person cannot join even with other *tumtumim*.[18]

Example 2—Tefillin (Phylacteries) of *Rabbenu Tam* and Tefillin on *Hol HaMoed*

In the following example, the *Mishna Berura* utilizes the following halakhic principles:

4. When the codes record two mutually exclusive opinions, the *Mishna Berura* suggests ways to avoid transgression according to either view.

---

15 *Mishna Berura* 589:5-6.
16 *Mishna Berura* 689:9-12.
17 *Mishna Berura* 331:18.
18 *Arukh HaShulhan, Orah Hayyim, Hilkhot Birkat HaMazon*, 199:3; *Hilkhot Megilla* 689:6; *Rosh Hashanah* 589:7.

8. When the codes are easily misunderstood, the *Mishna Berura* clarifies misunderstood rulings, and defends widespread practices.
9. When the codes and Kabbala conflict, the *Mishna Berura* minimizes the tension between the two positions.

The *Shulhan Arukh* provides the following description for the order of the Torah sections which are placed in the box of the phylacteries:

> The order of the sections of the Torah which are placed in the phylacteries according to *Rashi* and *Rambam* are as follows: "*Kadesh*" (Exodus 13:1-10) on the outer left, "*VeHaya Ki YaViacha*" (Exodus 13:11-16) on the inner left, "*Shema*" (Devarim 6:4-9) on the inner right, and "*VeHaya Im Shamoa*" (Deuteronomy 11:13-21) on the outer right. According to *Rabbenu Tam*, the order is "*Kadesh*" (Exodus 13:1-10) on the outer left, "*VeHaya Ki YaViacha*" (Exodus 13:11-16) on the inner left, "*VeHaya Im Shamoa*" (Deuteronomy 11:13-21) on the inner right, and "*Shema*" (Devarim 6:4-9) on the outer right. The universal custom is according to *Rashi* and *Rambam*. Those who fear Heaven will fulfill their obligation through donning both, and they will make two pairs of phylacteries, and while donning them both they will have the intention that the one which is halakhically acceptable will be the one through which they fulfill their obligation and the other one will be as regular straps.... . If they cannot don both at the same time, they will don the set that is according to *Rashi* first and the set that is according to *Rabbenu Tam* second without a blessing.[19]

The opinion of *Rashi* and that of *Rabbenu Tam* are mutually exclusive; moreover, because the dominant halakhic position is that *Rashi*'s opinion is correct, problems arise when wearing *Rabbenu Tam*'s phylacteries if one does not have a certain intention while doing so. If a person dons the phylacteries of both *Rashi* and of *Rabbenu Tam*, he cannot have the intention that both of them fulfill the commandment. Counter-intuitively, the reason is not because one will transgress the prohibition of "*bal tosif*" (adding on to the six hundred thirteen Torah commandments); rather, if a person dons the phylacteries of *Rabbenu Tam* for the sake of fulfilling a commandment, he may find himself transgressing "*bal tigra*" (the

---

19 *Shulhan Arukh, Orah Hayyim* 34:1-2.

prohibition of *subtracting* from the six hundred thirteen commandments in such a way that it is perceived as though one is denying the perfection of the prescribed performance). In the *Biur Halakha*, the *Mishna Berura* explains that *Rambam*'s position is that if one takes away from what is in the Written Torah, or from what is accepted in the Oral Torah, he transgresses the prohibition of "*bal tigra*." Since the *poskim* have accepted that the correct order of the sections in the phylacteries is according to *Rashi*, the phylacteries of *Rabbenu Tam* contain two invalid sections, since they are not in the proper order. Thus, wearing the phylacteries of *Rabbenu Tam* is like wearing phylacteries with only two sections, instead of the required four. To don the phylacteries of *Rabbenu Tam* after those of *Rashi* does not ameliorate the problem, since there are opinions claiming that, according to the Torah, a person is obligated to wear phylacteries throughout the entire day. Therefore, when he dons the phylacteries of *Rabbenu Tam*, he cannot say that he has already fulfilled his obligation and is now just performing a supererogatory act. The difficulty in how to consider the meaning of wearing both the phylacteries of *Rashi* and those of *Rabbenu Tam* is exacerbated by the statement in the *Shulhan Arukh* which states that those who fear Heaven wear both sets of phylacteries, yet when doing so, they have the intention that one of them fulfills the obligation whereas the second is considered as mere straps with no halakhic significance.[20]

The *Mishna Berura* explains the statement in the *Shulhan Arukh* to mean that those who fear Heaven do not have the intention that both phylacteries have the status of being proper, according to the Torah; rather, they seek only to act according to all opinions. Nevertheless, they avoid both potential nonfulfillment and possible transgression, since their intention stipulates that one set is *definitely* invalid, thereby avoiding adding to the commandment by wearing two valid, yet different sets, and that each set be judged on its own, thereby also allowing the phylacteries of *Rashi* to be

---

20 *Shulhan Arukh, Orah Hayyim* 34:2.

deemed fully valid within the conditional stipulation.[21] When a person does not don both sets at the same time, the *Mishna Berura* advises that it is essential that one explicitly have in mind, while donning the phylacteries of *Rabbenu Tam*, that he does so only due to a doubt and not to fulfill a commandment. Acting due to doubt is not so definitive as to be considered *"bal tigra."*[22] When donning the phylacteries of *Rashi*, on the other hand, a person does recite the blessing, since according to the main ruling, it is only with them that a person actually fulfills his obligation.[23] In his explanation of the *Shulhan Arukh* and in his decision, the *Mishna Berura* utilizes the fourth halakhic principle, in finding a way to avoid potential transgression as a result of conflicting priorities, and explanation, in describing how the various positions developed.

After going through the opinions of the various Rishonim up to the opinion of the *Shulhan Arukh*, the *Arukh HaShulhan* writes:

> It should not seem wondrous in your eyes that since the phylacteries of *Rashi* are invalid according to *Rabbenu Tam* and those of *Rabbenu Tam* are invalid according to *Rashi* that it is possible that the great ones of the world and the pious of the generations and all of Israel at various periods did not fulfill the commandment of donning phylacteries and made blessings that were in vain [by wearing both sets of phylacteries], Heaven forefend. Yet so, even in our book of laws it is not appropriate to write of things that are said in a whisper, and the hidden things are for Hashem our God, and in particular because of our many sins we do not have any idea in this matter. Nevertheless, in order so that it should not be a wonder in your eyes, I will explain a little according to our understanding.[24]

He then goes on to give an account of how the opinion of wearing the phylacteries of *Rabbenu Tam* developed.

The *Mishna Berura* is faced with a similar harmonizing challenge with respect to the ruling in the *Shulhan Arukh* that it is prohibited to wear phylacteries on *Hol HaMoed* (the intermediate

---

21 *Mishna Berura* 34:8.
22 *Biur Halakha* 34: s.v. *yaniah shel Rabbenu Tam.*
23 *Mishna Berura* 34:13.
24 *Hilkhot Tefillin* 34:6.

days of the festivals of Sukkot and Passover) because, like Shabbat and Yom Tov (the festivals and holidays themselves), *Hol HaMoed* itself is considered a "sign" of the relationship between Man and God, and one must not have two different signs displayed together.[25] The difficulty is that the *Rema*, on the other hand, rules that a person *is* required to don his phylacteries, since he is of the opinion that *Hol HaMoed* is not considered a sign. Since there is nothing that would prohibit donning phylacteries during those days, one is required to do so.[26] (The reason one must not have two signs together is that it shows contempt for each one. It is also considered a transgression of "*bal tosif*," the prohibition of adding to the commandments given in the Torah in such a way that it is perceived as though one is denying the perfection of the prescribed performance, as if one were saying, "This alone is not good enough.")

With respect to the *Shulhan Arukh*'s reasons for prohibiting the donning of phylacteries during *Hol HaMoed*, the *Mishna Berura* writes that the prohibition of displaying two signs and of "*bal tosif*" applies only to times when a person would don phylacteries for the sake of performing a commandment. If he dons them without such intention, it would neither show contempt for any sign nor would it be a transgression of "*bal tosif*." Also, if a person wears them publicly, it would entail only a rabbinic offense.[27] Therefore, during *Hol HaMoed*, a person should don his phylacteries without saying a blessing and have in mind the following intention: if he is obligated to don phylacteries, then his donning is for the sake of fulfilling a commandment; if not, then it is not.[28]

The *Mishna Berura*'s explanation of the *Shulhan Arukh*'s reasoning gives him the tools to deal with a blatant contradiction and create a compromise in the following way. He first mentions that the *Aharonim* agree with the *Taz* that a blessing on donning

---

25 *Shulhan Arukh, Orah Hayyim* 31:2.
26 Ibid.
27 *Mishna Berura* 31:5.
28 *Mishna Berura* 31:8.

phylacteries during *Hol HaMoed* should not be said. The reason not to say the blessing is that its requirement in the first place is in doubt, since there is a doubt as to whether or not one must don phylacteries at all on these days; and also, even if there is a requirement to don them, missing blessings do not actually impact upon fulfillment of a commandment. Thus, one need not make the blessing. Having removed this otherwise necessary verbal indication that donning phylacteries is certainly required, i.e., the saying of a blessing, which implies that this, the donning of phylacteries, is a required act, *today*, the *Mishna Berura* advises that a person have a particular intention while donning his phylacteries which would allow him to fulfill the potential obligation without running into a possible transgression if donning them *were* really prohibited. It suggests that before a person dons his phylacteries, he should think to himself that if he is obligated to do so, then his donning is for the sake of fulfilling a commandment, and if not, it is not. This stipulation removes the possible transgression of *"bal tosif,"* since one acts without definitiveness, yet it provides enough intention to be considered efficacious if necessary, even, as we said, without a blessing.[29]

Moreover, the *Mishna Berura* cites the *Pri Megadim* that one does not don the phylacteries of Rabbenu Tam on *Hol HaMoed*.[30] The *Pri Megadim* explains that the reason is that the Zohar is very strong in its language of punishment for those who wear phylacteries on *Hol HaMoed*, and the phylacteries of *Rashi* are enough. Also, there is a *sfeik-sfeika* (a case of double-doubt, in which case the rule is to be lenient) that maybe the Halakha is that one is exempt on *Hol HaMoed* from phylacteries, and maybe the Halakha is according to *Rashi*.[31] In his explanation of the *Shulhan Arukh* and in his decisions, the *Mishna Berura* utilizes the fourth halakhic

---

29 Ibid.
30 *Mishna Berura* 31:8. It is noteworthy that while he cites the *Pri Megadim*'s ruling, he does not provide the *Pri Megadim*'s reasons.
31 *Mishbetzos Zahav* 31:2.

principle, in finding a way to avoid potential transgression as a result of conflicting priorities; the eighth halakhic principle, in describing how the various positions developed; and mysticism and Talmud, in discouraging one from donning the phylacteries of *Rabbenu Tam*.

In his discussion of wearing the phylacteries on *Hol HaMoed*, after going through the differing opinions of the *Rishonim*, the *Arukh HaShulhan* writes, "The *Bet Yosef* rules that one should not don phylacteries, but *Rema* writes that there are those who do don them, but make the blessing in a whisper. No Sefardi dons and all Ashkenazim don, but today they don without a blessing, and so it seems proper to act accordingly. And many great *Aharonim* have already written at length regarding this, one saying one thing, and another saying another. Thus, each should continue according to his *minhag*, and now many, even among the Ashkenazim, do not don, and we will not continue at length on this. However, in any case, in one beit midrash people should not be doing different things because of *lo titgedidu* (the rabbinic prohibition to fragment Jewish society through the adoption of various and differing rituals and customs)."[32]

Example 3—Praying the Morning Prayer (*Shaharit*) Late

In the following example the *Mishna Berura* utilizes the following halakhic principles:

2. When the codes record both lenient and strict positions, the *Mishna Berura* advises when one should be strict and when one may be lenient.
4. When the codes record two mutually exclusive opinions, the *Mishna Berura* suggests ways to avoid transgression according to either view.

---

32 *Arukh HaShulhan, Orah Hayyim, Hilkhot Tefillin* 31:4.

The *Shulhan Arukh* rules that a person may pray in the morning until the end of the fourth hour.[33] If one makes a mistake, or purposefully delays, and prays after the fourth hour until midday, even though he does not receive reward for praying on time, he nevertheless receives reward for praying. The *Rema* writes that after noon has passed, it is prohibited to pray the morning prayer.[34] There are opinions which hold that if one purposefully delays his prayer until after the fourth hour, he is no longer allowed to pray at all. Also, there are opinions which allow one to pray the morning prayer until a half-hour past noon.

The *Mishna Berura* is left with the difficulty of reconciling the *Shulhan Arukh*'s ruling that one may pray after the fourth hour with the opinions that prohibit a person from praying after that time. To follow the ruling of the *Shulhan Arukh* means that not only is the person acting according to a lenient opinion, but he may also be potentially *transgressing* the law according to the more stringent opinion. Furthermore, if the *Mishna Berura* were to accept the opinion that allows a person to pray the morning prayer until half past noon, he would be condoning a potential transgression according to those opinions that prohibit it. The *Mishna Berura* is left with the difficulty of maximizing the range of fulfillment in accepting a more lenient position while, at the same time, avoiding possible transgression according to more stringent opinions.

The *Mishna Berura* accepts the ruling that if one prays after the fourth hour he still receives a reward for praying, albeit not for praying on time. Nevertheless, he recommends that one intend that his prayer be a "*nedava*" (a voluntary offering), since there are opinions which hold that if one purposefully delays his prayer until after the fourth hour, he is no longer allowed to pray at all. To unequivocally intend one's prayer to be a "*nedava*," however, precludes the ability to pray the morning prayer if he is allowed to

---

33　According to Jewish law, the hours of the day are calculated by dividing the total daylight hours into twelve proportional hours. Each proportional hour is considered to be an "hour" according to Jewish law.

34　*Shulhan Arukh, Orah Hayyim* 89:1.

do so. Therefore, the *Mishna Berura* advises to stipulate that one's prayer should only be considered a *"nedava"* if, according to the law, it is prohibited to pray the morning prayer after the fourth hour.[35] Similarly, the *Mishna Berura* writes that if one has not yet prayed the morning prayer due to error or compulsion, and noon passes, even though there are some opinions that allow one to pray until a half hour past noon, he should wait until after half past noon, pray *Minha* (the afternoon prayer), and then pray a make-up prayer in place of the morning prayer. *Ex post facto*, however, even if a person prays before half past noon, he fulfills his obligation and need not pray a make-up morning prayer.[36] In presenting his most lenient position, the *Mishna Berura* refers us to the comment of Rabbi Akiva Eiger on the matter, which states that after noon passes, one may pray but only if he says the following stipulation: "If the time for the *Minha* prayer has come, let this be for the sake of the *Minha* prayer. If it has not yet arrived, let this be for the sake of the morning prayer." Furthermore, Rabbi Akiva Eiger recommends that after half past noon, one should pray again with the stipulation that if the first prayer counted as the morning prayer, then this one should be counted for the *Minha* prayer; if the last prayer counted for the *Minha* prayer, then this one should be considered a make-up for the missed morning prayer.[37]

Because, at first glance, his most lenient position seems to conflict with the other positions regarding when a person can pray, one may think that he allows the person to pray without making a stipulation *ex post facto* in order to keep him within the halakhic fold. Such an assumption presumes that his methodology of synthesizing positions only relates to *ab initio* situations. *Ex post facto*, however, a person can rely on any position that legitimizes his performance. This assumption is corrected by his reference to Rabbi Akiva Eiger. Why the *Mishna Berura* only refers us to Rabbi Akiva Eiger's comment and does not state it explicitly, either in the

---

35 *Mishna Berura* 89:6.
36 *Mishna Berura* 89:7.
37 *Hiddushei Rabbi Akiva Eiger* 89: s.v. *mathil ahar hatzot.*

Biur Halakha or *Sha'ar HaTziyun*, is an open question. Yet the reference to it in the main commentary supports the fact that the *Mishna Berura* attempts to find agreement among the various positions regardless of whether it is *ab initio* or *ex post facto*.

For comparison, the *Arukh HaShulhan* rules that if a person purposely misses the morning prayer, he may not make it up. If he errs or was unable to pray due to circumstances out of his control, then he should pray *Minha* twice. He also interprets the *Rema* to be referring to a situation in which a person transgresses and purposely misses the morning prayer.[38] The *Arukh HaShulhan* does not suggest making a stipulation beforehand, indicating that he makes a definitive judgment as to which position is normative and which should be disregarded.

(B) Including all Jews
Example 4—Calling One who is Blind or who Cannot Read to the Torah

In the following example the *Mishna Berura* utilizes the following halakhic principles:

1. When a ruling no longer seems to fit the current reality, the *Mishna Berura* provides alternative explanations for the ruling, changes its language, or adapts practices so that they fit with the ruling's spirit.
6. When the major codes adopt a lenient position, yet other codes are stricter, the *Mishna Berura* suggests qualifying one's intention to act so as to avoid transgression according to the strict position.

The *Shulhan Arukh* rules that neither a blind person nor one who is unable to read from the Torah may be called for an *Aliyah*, which is the public reading from the Torah during synagogue services. If a

---

38 *Arukh HaShulhan, Orah Hayyim, Hilkhot Tefilla*, 89:14.

person who is unable to read from the Torah wants to be called, one must protest. However, if the person is a *Kohen* or a Levi, and there is no one else who can replace him, if he can recite the reading along with the *Hazan* word for word, he may be called to the Torah.[39] The *Rema*, on the other hand, rules that today we can call blind people, as well as those unable to read, to the Torah for an *Aliyah*.[40]

The *Mishna Berura* writes that Rabbi Karo's leniency for giving an *Aliyah* to a *Kohen* or a Levi who is unable to read the Torah himself is because he is still able to read the Torah along with the *Hazan*. Nevertheless, Rabbi Karo only permits this person to be called as a last resort; if there are other people who can be called to the Torah, one should not call a person unable to read.[41]

However, the *Mishna Berura* legitimizes the contemporary custom of calling up a blind person and one unable to read, even when there are others who can be called in their place, by emphasizing the idea that reciting with the *Hazan* is like reading the text oneself.[42] Moreover, the *Mishna Berura* supports the common practice of not checking to see if people can actually read with the *Hazan* through emphasizing the notion that listening is equivalent to reading, and by saying that there is a general presumption that people are able to repeat the words.[43]

Although the *Mishna Berura* remarks that this position is in accord with various *Aharonim*, its acceptance of this lenient custom is not solely based on textual analysis. Rather, it seeks to justify the common practice that has developed. This is evident from the fact that the *Mishna Berura* does not allow this leniency *ab initio* for *Parshat Para* or *Parshat Zakhor*, since some contend that *Parshat Para* is a Torah obligation and *Parshat Zakhor* is unanimously considered so.[44] Its disapproval of this custom when it comes to *Parshat Para* and *Parshat Zakhor* reveals that it recognizes that the

---

39 *Shulhan Arukh, Orah Hayyim* 135:4; 139:2-3.
40 *Shulhan Arukh, Orah Hayyim* 139:3.
41 *Mishna Berura* 139:4.
42 *Mishna Berura* 139:12-13.
43 *Mishna Berura* 135:15.
44 *Sha'ar HaTziyun* 139:6.

prevalent custom is not in accord with the ideals of Halakha, but also shows a willingness to acquiesce to contemporary practice when it contradicts the codes.

The *Arukh HaShulhan* similarly writes, after explaining the reasoning behind Rabbi Karo's ruling, that the great *poskim* of the world have already written that one who cannot read from the Torah, even after the *Hazan*, may still be called for an Aliyah since listening to the *Hazan* recite the words is equivalent to reciting them oneself.[45]

Example 5—Reciting *Birkat HaMazon* for Those Who Cannot

In the following example the *Mishna Berura* utilizes the following halakhic principles:

4. When the codes record two mutually exclusive opinions, the *Mishna Berura* suggests ways to avoid transgression according to either view.
6. When the major codes adopt a lenient position, yet other codes are stricter, the *Mishna Berura* suggests qualifying one's intention to act so as to avoid transgression according to the strict position.
8. When the codes are easily misunderstood, the *Mishna Berura* clarifies misunderstood rulings and defends widespread practices.

The *Shulhan Arukh* rules that with respect to a person reciting the *Birkat HaMazon* for others, there is one who says that a *ba'al ha'bayit* (head of the household) must say the *Birkat HaMazon* aloud in order to include his wife and children in his blessing, so that they may also fulfill their obligation through his recitation.[46] The *Magen Avraham* asks why Rabbi Karo wrote this ruling in the form of "there is one

---

45 *Arukh HaShulhan, Orah Hayyim, Hilkhot Tefilla* 139:3.
46 *Shulhan Arukh, Orah Hayyim* 185:3.

who says," since it is an obvious statement.[47] The *Taz* writes that even though the Halakha is not established in accordance with this opinion, for women who do not understand Hebrew and cannot say the blessing on their own one may rely on it even *ab initio* since it is better than not saying a blessing at all.[48]

In the *Biur Halakha*, the *Mishna Berura* proposes to answer the *Magen Avraham*'s question with the explanation of the *Birkei Yosef* and the *Nahar Shalom*. Rabbi Karo is citing *Rashi*, who holds that a person may include another in his blessing even if the other person does not understand the language. Rabbi Karo uses the phrase, "there is one who says" because he actually agrees with the other *poskim* who are stringent, and does not allow one who cannot understand the language to be included.

The *Mishna Berura* justifies its reasoning based on Rabbi Karo's ruling regarding a *Zimun*, which states, "Two that eat together, even though regarding recital of *HaMotzi* one may include another through his recital, for the recital of *Birkat HaMazon* it is a *mitzvah* to separate and have each recite it for himself. This applies when both know how to recite the *Birkat HaMazon*, but if one knows how and the other does not, the one who knows may include the other person as long as he understands Hebrew but does not know the blessing ... if he does not understand [Hebrew] he cannot be included through listening."[49] In this Halakha, however, Rabbi Karo nevertheless cites *Rashi*'s opinion with respect to a man reciting the *Birkat HaMazon* for his family because it is better to rely on *Rashi*'s opinion, that it is better they all fulfill their obligation through him than that those who cannot understand Hebrew be unable to bless at all. The *Mishna Berura* concludes by referring to the *Taz* as further support for his interpretation.[50]

The *Mishna Berura* also notes that the custom has become to permit women to fulfill their obligation to recite the *Birkat HaMazon* by listening to it, even if they do not understand the language.

---

47 *Magen Avraham* 185:2.
48 *Taz* 193:2.
49 *Shulhan Arukh, Orah Hayyim* 193:1.
50 *Biur Halakha* 185: s.v. *yesh mi she'omer*.

However, in order to be as comprehensive as possible, he advises that they should recite the blessing for themselves, even if they do not understand Hebrew. At the very least, they should repeat word for word after the one reciting the blessing, if possible, so that they may act in accord with all the *poskim*. To maintain the legitimacy of the lenient position *de jure* even if opposing it in practice, the *Mishna Berura* provides a second reason for his advice, namely that it is difficult to maintain concentration when passively listening.[51]

Picking up on the fact that Rabbi Karo prohibits three people to separate to recite the *Birkat HaMazon* individually, the *Mishna Berura* comments that inability to include one who does not understand only applies when there are two people eating a meal together. If three people eat together, the *Mishna Berura* notes that there is a disagreement among the *poskim* as to whether one can include others who do not understand. Although it does not definitively side with a particular position, it notes that many *Aharonim* follow the interpretation of the *Birkat Avraham*, which interprets Rabbi Karo's ruling to mean that the one reciting can include others, and mentions that only the *Bach* and the *Levush* disagree.[52] By including this analysis, the *Mishna Berura* in effect restricts the realm of disagreement between *Rashi* and the majority opinion, thereby reducing the ramifications of inconsistency that Rabbi Karo's rulings entail.

Example 6—Giving Food to One who Doesn't Know the Blessing

In the following example the *Mishna Berura* utilizes the following halakhic principles:

3. When the codes record more than one normative view that does not exclude the validity of the other, the *Mishna Berura* accepts the validity of different practices in different locations, and suggests manners of fulfillment that incorporate the different views.

---

51 *Mishna Berura* 193:5.
52 *Biur Halakha* 193: s.v. *eino yotzei b'shmia*.

8. When the codes are easily misunderstood, the *Mishna Berura* clarifies misunderstood rulings and defends widespread practices.

The *Shulhan Arukh* rules that one may only give food to a person who knows how to make a blessing over it.[53] The *Rema*, however, writes that there are those who are lenient to give to a poor person for the sake of charity.

With respect to the situation of whether one should give food for the sake of charity to a poor person who does not know how to recite a blessing, there is a conflict over differing commandments. In giving food to someone who will not say a blessing, one would be transgressing the prohibition of putting a stumbling block before the blind. On the other hand, giving food to a poor person fulfills the commandment to give charity. Therefore, the *Mishna Berura* must negotiate between the two conflicting commandments in a way that does not invalidate the ruling of the *Shulhan Arukh*.

To do this, the *Mishna Berura* makes a distinction between a person who does not know how to recite the blessing because of his own malice and one who cannot recite the blessing due to forces out of his control. The former should not be given food, yet the latter is still eligible to receive the charity.[54] By distinguishing between people who do not recite blessings out of contempt and those who do not recite blessings out of ignorance, the *Mishna Berura* finds a way to qualify the ruling of the *Shulhan Arukh* without invalidating it. It also finds a way to negotiate between conflicting priorities. Its interpretation is consistent with the wording of the ruling of the *Shulhan Arukh*. Also, because not reciting from ignorance is less of a transgression for the poor person, the transgression of putting a stumbling block before him is also diminished. Therefore, the commandment to give charity trumps it. On the other hand, the obligation to give charity to a wicked person is smaller than the transgression of putting a stumbling block before him. Therefore, one should not give him charity.

---

53 *Shulhan Arukh, Orah Hayyim* 169:2.
54 *Mishna Berura* 169:11.

(C) Jewish-Gentile Relations
Example 7—Carrying for a Gentile on Yom Tov

In the following example, the *Mishna Berura* utilizes the following halakhic principles:

5. When the early codes are lenient and the later commentators are strict, the *Mishna Berura* inclines toward the strict position.
8. When the codes are easily misunderstood, the *Mishna Berura* clarifies misunderstood rulings and defends widespread practices.

The *Shulhan Arukh* rules that the legal principle that allows one to carry on Yom Tov for the sake of eating also allows one to carry for unnecessary purposes, and he gives as examples of things that are unnecessary to carry a child, a lulav, a Sefer Torah, or other utensils. He adds, however, that it is forbidden to carry stones and the like.[55] He also rules that it is prohibited for a Jew to carry anything for the sake of a Gentile on Yom Tov.[56] The *Rema* appends to "other utensils," that they must be needed somewhat, or that the person fears they may be stolen or lost.

The difficulty regarding this ruling is as follows: if one would interpret the Halakha regarding the prohibition to carry for unnecessary purposes in light of the Halakha that prohibits a person to carry for a Gentile, one could assume that the *Rema*'s contribution is meant to explain Rabbi Karo's ruling, since carrying for a Gentile would be carrying without personal need. Yet if such is the case, one must then explain why Rabbi Karo specifically mentions the prohibition to carry stones and the like.

Recognizing the ambiguity of Rabbi Karo's rulings and their relation to the *Rema*'s comment, the *Mishna Berura*, in the *Biur Halakha*, first proposes that Rabbi Karo rules according to *Rashi*'s opinion, which is also that of the *Rif* and the *Rambam*. He therefore mentions

---

55 *Shulhan Arukh, Orah Hayyim* 518:1.
56 *Shulhan Arukh, Orah Hayyim* 518:2.

utensils without any clarification because he does not differentiate between whether they have a need or not. Only objects like stones are outside of the sphere of permissibility due to their being *muktze*. In general, however, one has permission even *ab initio* to carry a utensil not needed for the day. According to this interpretation, one is required to say that the *Rema*'s comment is his own opinion and not a clarification of Rabbi Karo's. Though his language seems to show the contrary, the *Mishna Berura* writes that many times the *Rema* interjects with his own opinion without adding the expression, "there are those who say."

The *Mishna Berura* admits that this explanation is difficult to reconcile with Rabbi Karo's ruling regarding the prohibition to carry for a Gentile. Therefore, it notes that it seems to be more consistent to say that Rabbi Karo also forbids, albeit rabbinically, carrying utensils that are not needed. The *Rema*'s comment is therefore seen as an explanation of Rabbi Karo's ruling. The *Mishna Berura* justifies this perspective with the fact that the *Rema* notes in the *Darkhei Moshe* that Rabbi Karo's conclusion in the *Bet Yosef* is, in fact, that one should be stringent. Moreover, the *Rema*'s omission of the phrase, "there are those who say," is now more coherent. Rabbi Karo's mention of stones, under this interpretation, is meant to provide examples of those things which have no need at all. Despite the fact that the *Mishna Berura* seeks to reconcile Rabbi Karo's language in the two rulings with the *Rema*'s comment, it recognizes that the second explanation—which interprets Rabbi Karo as forbidding, albeit rabbinically, a person to carry completely unnecessary objects—is difficult. For even though this statement accords with *Rashi*, the *Rif*, and the *Rambam*, almost all of the other *poskim* disagree and say that carrying such objects would be a Torah transgression. Therefore, he admits that this ruling still requires further investigation.[57]

In his main commentary, the *Mishna Berura* interprets the *Rema*'s comment as an explanation of Rabbi Karo's ruling, and explains the

____

57 *Biur Halakha* 518: s.v. *mitokh she'hutra hotza'ah*.

mentioning of stones as an example of something completely unnecessary.[58] It does, however, note that as a practical matter, many *poskim* disagree with the ruling in the *Shulhan Arukh*, even as qualified by the *Rema*, and contend that one does not have permission to carry anything except if needed, and that preventing loss is not considered necessary. It continues to say that it is correct to be stringent like this opinion.[59]

In the *Sha'ar HaTziyun*, the *Mishna Berura* writes that based upon the Halakha that prohibits carrying something unnecessary, if it is interpreted in a manner which allows one to carry without any need at all, the prohibition to carry for a Gentile cannot be a valid law. Its validity, however, can be rectified based on the contention that Rabbi Karo rabbinically forbids a person to carry without any need. He gives further support to the law's validity by claiming that based upon the opinion of some *poskim*, doing a prohibited action for a Gentile is worse than doing it for no purpose at all. The *Mishna Berura* thus reclaims the Halakha as valid law.[60]

Example 8—Giving Mail to a Gentile before Shabbat

In the following example the *Mishna Berura* utilizes the following halakhic principles:

3. When the codes record more than one normative view that does not exclude the validity of the other or others, the *Mishna Berura* accepts the validity of different practices in different locations, and suggests manners of fulfillment that incorporate the different views.

5. When the early codes are lenient and the later commentators are strict, the *Mishna Berura* inclines toward the strict position.

---

58 *Mishna Berura* 518:5. In his comment appended to "stones," the *Mishna Berura* explains that Rabbi Karo means stones that have not been previously designated for any use (MB 518:7).

59 *Mishna Berura* 518:6.

60 *Sha'ar HaTziyun* 518:22.

8. When the codes are easily misunderstood, the *Mishna Berura* clarifies misunderstood rulings, and defends widespread practices.

The *Shulhan Arukh* rules that if a Gentile is going of his own accord to another place, which happens to be where a Jew needs to send a letter, it is permissible without restriction for the Jew to give his letter to the Gentile before Shabbat starts.[61] The *Magen Avraham*, the *Elya Rabba*, and other *Aharonim* rule that it is permissible for the Jew to give his letter to the Gentile only if there is enough time before Shabbat for the Gentile to deliver it. This position is also held by the *Maharam*. The *Gra*, however, agrees with Rabbi Karo's position.

The *Shulhan Arukh* clearly states that it is permissible without any restrictions to give the Gentile the letter, and the *Mishna Berura*, in the *Sha'ar HaTziyun*, acknowledges that it is problematic to interpret the ruling of the *Shulhan Arukh* as implying the restriction that there must be enough time before Shabbat for the Gentile to deliver it. However, the *Mishna Berura* also admits that it would be difficult to ignore the more stringent ruling, especially given the *poskim* who affirm this position.[62]

Therefore, the *Mishna Berura* interprets Rabbi Karo's mention of having no restriction to apply specifically to the requirement to set a fee for the Gentile's services. In a situation in which a Gentile is going on his own accord, even if it is to a locale that does not have an established postal system, one need not determine a fixed fee since the Gentile is traveling on his own accord and not for the sake of delivering the letter. Also, with respect to there being enough time before Shabbat to deliver the letter, the *Mishna Berura* qualifies Rabbi Karo's ruling as well. The Jew may only give his letter to the Gentile if there is enough time for him to reach his destination before Shabbat. Otherwise, he may not give him the letter. Even

____

61 *Shulhan Arukh, Orah Hayyim* 247:5.
62 *Sha'ar HaTziyun* 247:17.

though the Gentile travels on his own accord, he nevertheless carries the letter on behalf of the Jew.[63]

The objective of the *Mishna Berura* is to maintain the ruling of the *Shulhan Arukh*, yet to qualify it in such a way that it is possible to incorporate coherently the more stringent position. It does so by interpreting the phrase "without restriction" to apply specifically to a particular situation i.e., fixing a fee, whether or not there exists an established postal system. By directing Rabbi Karo's leniency only to that particular issue, the *Mishna Berura* is able to insert the restriction of having enough time before Shabbat as an implied requirement.

Example 9—Having a Gentile Buy Things for a Jew

In the following example the *Mishna Berura* utilizes the following halakhic principles:

3. When the codes record multiple normative views that do not exclude the validity of others, the *Mishna Berura* accepts the validity of different practices in different locations, and suggests manners of fulfillment that incorporate the different views.
5. When the early codes are lenient and the later commentators are strict, the *Mishna Berura* inclines toward the strict position.
8. When the codes are easily misunderstood, the *Mishna Berura* clarifies misunderstood rulings and defends widespread practices.

The *Shulhan Arukh* rules that it is permitted for a Jew to give a Gentile money on Friday to buy something for him as long as he does not tell him to buy it on Shabbat.[64] The *Magen Avraham*, the *Elya Rabba*, and other *Aharonim* rule that they must determine a fixed price for the Gentile's services beforehand.

---

63 *Mishna Berura* 247:17.
64 *Shulhan Arukh, Orah Hayyim* 307:4.

The issue with which the *Mishna Berura* is confronted is as follows: the *Shulhan Arukh* only gives one restriction, not to tell the Gentile to buy the thing on Shabbat. How can the *Mishna Berura* incorporate the more stringent position without invalidating the ruling of the *Shulhan Arukh*?

The *Mishna Berura* interprets Rabbi Karo's ruling to imply that the two parties will obviously have determined a price for the Gentile's services.[65] He justifies his interpretation by referring to the ruling of the *Shulhan Arukh* which states that it is permissible for a Jew to hire a Gentile to buy something, as long as he designates a fixed wage and he tells him explicitly not to buy it on Shabbat.[66] The *Mishna Berura* makes an interpretative comparison, stating that just as when a Jew hires a Gentile to buy something for him he must establish a fixed wage, so when a Jew gives a Gentile money to buy him something he must establish a fixed wage. In effect, the *Mishna Berura* makes both laws equivalent, and no longer makes it possible for the Gentile to do the Jew a favor.

(D) The Existence of Erroneous Customs
Example 10—*Eruv* and **Public Domains**

In the following example the *Mishna Berura* utilizes the following halakhic principles:

5. When the early codes are lenient and the later commentators are strict, the *Mishna Berura* inclines toward the strict position.
6. When the major codes adopt a lenient position, yet other codes are stricter, the *Mishna Berura* suggests qualifying one's intention to act so as to avoid transgression according to strict position.

An *Eruv* is a ritual enclosure around a community which allows Jews to carry objects on Shabbat when they would otherwise be

---

65 *Mishna Berura* 307:14.
66 *Shulhan Arukh, Orah Hayyim* 245:5.

forbidden to do so. It is meant to symbolize a wall around the community in order to turn it into one unified domain for the purpose of carrying on Shabbat. The *Shulhan Arukh* rules that one cannot make an *Eruv* that contains a public domain, unless the openings in the walls contain doors that actually close at night. He admits, however, that some say if they are not closed at night, the *Eruv* may still be valid on the condition that they are at least *able* to be closed at night.[67]

To define what constitutes a public domain, Rabbi Karo, in the *Shulhan Arukh*, writes that a public domain is defined as streets and markets that are sixteen cubits wide and which are not roofed or walled. If the area was enwalled yet its gates were not closed at night, it would still be considered a public domain. He adds that there are those who say that any place that does not contain six hundred thousand people in it every day is not considered a public domain.[68]

With respect to how to define a public domain, the *Mishna Berura* writes that its author has searched through all of the *Rishonim* who require six hundred thousand people, but could not find the stipulation that the people must be present every day. Rather, they mean that there is a possibility that they would be found there in general.[69] In the *Biur Halakha* (Rabbi Kagan's gloss on the *Mishna Berura*), it is noted that if the presence of six hundred thousand people was actually a necessary stipulation, the Talmud would not have omitted mentioning it.[70] However, despite the lack of textual justification, the prevalent custom had, in fact, become to build a *Tzurat HaPetah* (the form of a doorway opening, with two doorposts and an overhead lintel, which, in Jewish law, is enough of a structure to maintain the continuity required of a wall—that is, unless it cuts across a public domain) across the open areas when constructing an *Eruv* which includes streets that are very wide and

---

67 *Shulhan Arukh, Orah Hayyim* 364:2.
68 *Shulhan Arukh, Orah Hayyim* 345:7.
69 *Mishna Berura* 345:24.
70 *Biur Halakha* 252: s.v. *she'ein shishim ribo.*

open from one end of the city to the other, i.e., streets that might otherwise be public domains. The justification to use a *Tzurat HaPetah* is grounded on the opinion that a public domain requires six hundred thousand people. Based on that requirement, the streets would not be public domains; therefore, a *Tzurat HaPetah* would be effective in constructing an *Eruv*.

The *Mishna Berura* writes that even though many *Rishonim* disagree with this opinion, one cannot protest against those who act leniently and use a *Tzurat HaPetah* to make an *Eruv*; nevertheless, a *Ba'al Nefesh* (a conscientious person) should be stringent upon himself.[71] By stating that one cannot protest against those who follow the lenient custom, he demonstrates that he does not believe that the lenient position is the essential normative opinion. However, because some *poskim* have found it to have legal worth, and in order to spread the net of halakhic legitimacy as widely as possible so as to maintain a unified system of Halakha such that the existence of different opinions does not result in the Torah becoming two Torahs,[72] the *Mishna Berura* condones it. A *Ba'al Nefesh*, on the other hand, should follow what it thinks is the proper halakhic position. As will be shown in greater detail elsewhere in the examples section of the book, when a prevalent practice is more lenient than what the *Mishna Berura* believes is the essential ruling, yet it foresees that the practice cannot be changed, the *Mishna Berura* writes that a *Ba'al Nefesh* should, and will, act stringently. In his explanation of the *Shulhan Arukh* and in his decision, the *Mishna Berura* utilizes the halakhic principles of being strict, since it advises a *Ba'al Nefesh* to act according to the stringent position; and also of being lenient, in its condoning of the lenient practice.

Like the *Mishna Berura*, the *Arukh HaShulhan* does not accept the established custom to use a *Tzurat HaPetah* per se. On the contrary, its author follows the opinion that the Halakha does not consider population when defining a public domain, which would mean that

---

71 *Mishna Berura* 345:23; 364:8.
72 See BT *Sanhedrin* 88b.

it thinks using a *Tzurat HaPetah* would be ineffective for the streets in question. However, it also accepts the more lenient opinion, out of a desire to incorporate those who follow it into the realm of observance. After explaining how the requirement of six hundred thousand people actually being present is not found in any of the *Rishonim*, he writes:

> But in any case what will result in continuing [to deride this position] at length after the *Eruvin* that have spread throughout the majority of cities in Israel for many hundreds of years are based only on this leniency, and it is as if the *Bat Kol* (Heavenly voice) went forth and said that the Halakha is according to this opinion, and if we come and restrain it not only will they not listen but it seems as if they have gone crazy.[73]

Of course, the *Arukh HaShulhan* does not rely solely on the assumption that "the Heavenly Voice went forth and said that the Halakha is according to this opinion"; rather, after making this statement, it also goes back and attempts to support the leniency via textual analysis. This textual analysis, however, serves only a justificatory purpose; it is predicated on the legitimacy of the established custom, reflecting its basic methodology of making the Talmudic texts consistent with the common practice.

Example 11—Saying "Amen" After "*Ga'al Israel*"

In the following example the *Mishna Berura* utilizes the following halakhic principles:

4. When the codes record two mutually exclusive opinions, the *Mishna Berura* suggests ways to avoid transgression according to either view.
7. When people have adopted an unsupported custom, the *Mishna Berura* disapproves of it, yet attempts to justify it for those who will nevertheless continue to follow it.

---

73 *Arukh HaShulhan, Orah Hayyim* 345:18.

8. When the codes are easily misunderstood, the *Mishna Berura* clarifies misunderstood rulings and defends widespread practices.

The *Shulhan Arukh* rules that a person should not say "amen" after "*Ga'al Israel*," the concluding words of the blessing after the recital of the *Shema* which is said immediately before the recital of the *Amida*, since it would be an interruption between "*Geula*" and "*Tefilla*."[74] The *Rema*, on the other hand, notes that some say that one should answer "amen" after the *Hazan* recites the blessing, and that such is the custom.[75] He writes, however, that there are those who are of the opinion that the necessity of juxtaposing "*Geula*" and "*Tefilla*" only applies to weekdays and holidays; on Shabbat, on the other hand, it is not required. He concludes by saying that it is good to be stringent and not interrupt if it is not necessary to do so.[76]

The *Rema*'s advice to be strict may seem like he is deferring to the opinion of Rabbi Karo; however, when one takes his suggestion in light of what he writes in his *Darkhei Moshe*, it becomes clear that he does not retract his position that saying "amen" is permissible. In the *Darkhei Moshe*, the *Rema*'s concern is that since Shabbat does not require "*Tefilla*" to immediately follow "*Geula*," one may think it permissible to engage in any type of interruption, even if it has nothing to do with the prayer service. Therefore, he specifically remarks that things not associated with the service would be considered a prohibited interruption. For those necessary interruptions, such as responding for *Kaddish* or *Kedusha*, on the other hand, the Rema writes that one may rely on the *Or Zarua* and not consider an interjection to be prohibited.[77] The reason that the *Rema* does not consider "amen" to be an interruption is that it is part of the conclusion of the blessing. Rabbi Karo, on the other

---

74　*Shulhan Arukh, Orah Hayyim* 66:7-8; 111:1.
75　*Shulhan Arukh, Orah Hayyim* 66:7.
76　*Shulhan Arukh, Orah Hayyim* 111:1.
77　*Darkhei Moshe, Orah Hayyim* 111.

hand, bases his decision that "amen" is considered an interruption on the *Zohar*.

The *Mishna Berura* interprets the *Rema's* statement—that it is good to be stringent—in a different way than the *Darkhei Moshe* connotes. Where the *Darkhei Moshe's* stringency relates to superfluous interruptions, the *Mishna Berura* attributes it to a doubt regarding whether Shabbat is actually excluded from the prescription or not. According to the *Mishna Berura*, the *Rema's* comment now refers to the fact that Rabbi Karo disagrees with making any distinction between Shabbat and other days, and due to the negative consequences of interrupting, "it is good to be stringent."[78] The *Mishna Berura* does, however, maintain that it is legitimate to be lenient regarding necessary interruptions on Shabbat, since the opinion is a legally valid one.[79]

The *Mishna Berura* also notes that there are those who are scrupulous and try during the week to fulfill their obligation according to all opinions by pausing at *"Tzur Israel"* or *"Shira Hadasha,"* in order to answer "amen" after the *Hazan* finishes the blessing. It disapproves of this strategy, and states that all the *Aharonim* agree that this is not a good practice, since one should not say an additional "amen" within a blessing, nor should one refrain from starting the *Amida* with the congregation. With the intention of correctly fulfilling the obligation according to all opinions, the *Mishna Berura* gives alternative advice. One should intend to finish the blessing at the same time as the *Hazan*, thus negating the obligation to say "amen." Likewise, he could say the introductory verse of the *Amida* slightly before the *Hazan* finishes the blessing, which would also negate the obligation to say "amen," and he would still be considered as starting the *Amida* with the congregation.[80]

---

78 *Mishna Berura* 111:8.
79 *Mishna Berura* 111:9; *Biur Halakha* 111: s.v. *tov l'hahmir*.
80 *Mishna Berura* 66:35.

Example 12—Eating *Hadash*[81]

In the following example the *Mishna Berura* utilizes the following halakhic principles:

5. When the early codes are lenient and the later commentators are strict, the *Mishna Berura* inclines toward the strict position.
6. When the major codes adopt a lenient position, yet other codes are stricter, the *Mishna Berura* suggests qualifying one's intention to act so as to avoid transgression according to the strict position.
7. When people have adopted an unsupported custom, the *Mishna Berura* disapproves of it, yet attempts to justify it for those who will nevertheless continue to follow it.
8. When the codes are easily misunderstood, the *Mishna Berura* clarifies misunderstood rulings, and defends widespread practices.

According to the *Shulhan Arukh*, it is prohibited to eat *Hadash* even today, whether it is bread, parched grain, or roasted grain, until the night of the eighteenth of *Nissan*, and in the land of Israel until the night of the seventeenth of *Nissan*.[82] The *Rema*, on the other hand, rules that all unmarked grain is permitted after Passover by virtue of a *sfeik-sfeika* (a double doubt). The first doubt is with respect to whether the grain was from the previous year or not; the second is that even if you want to say that the grain is from the current year, it may nevertheless still have taken root before the sixteenth of *Nissan*.[83] Despite the *Rema*'s ruling, there are *Aharonim* who write that in Poland, a person can only be lenient with regards to wheat and rye, since most of it is planted in *Heshvan* so *Hadash* does not apply to it. The great majority of barley, oats, and spelt, on

---

81 *Hadash* is a concept within the Jewish dietary laws. It is the biblical requirement not to eat any grain of the new year, or any products made therefrom, prior to the sixteenth day of *Nissan*. The prohibition applies to the five classical grains of Judaism, namely, wheat, barley, oat, spelt, and rye.
82 *Shulhan Arukh, Orah Hayyim* 489:10.
83 *Shulhan Arukh, Yoreh Deah* 293:3.

the other hand, are planted after Passover; therefore, where it is not normal to import it from elsewhere when they plant it earlier, one cannot be lenient.

Even though the prohibition of eating *Hadash* is a biblical commandment, in the *Mishna Berura*'s time the majority of people were not careful at all regarding it. Since it was so difficult to be careful, they relied on those few *Rishonim* that argued that *Hadash* outside the land of Israel is only a rabbinic obligation, and even then it applies only for those lands close to Israel, like Egypt and Babylon. They also relied on the fact that there are some *poskim* who hold that *Hadash* only applies to grain owned by Jews at the time of growing, but not to grain owned by Gentiles.

Due to these circumstances, the *Mishna Berura* writes that we are unable to protest against those who are lenient. Nevertheless, it notes that a *Ba'al Nefesh* will not rely on these leniencies and will be stringent upon himself as much as he can.[84] In the *Biur Halakha*, the *Mishna Berura* repeats that we should not protest against those who are lenient regarding *Hadash*. Yet again it continues, saying that it seems that those who are careful to avoid the suspicion of transgression regarding other prohibitions, but are lenient with respect to *Hadash*, make the exception for *Hadash* because they think that if a person wants to be careful in observing a commandment, he must be careful regarding all the stringencies of a particular matter. Therefore, they rely on the custom to be lenient completely. The *Mishna Berura* writes, however, that it is not correct to be lenient completely in everything when it is easy to fulfill one's obligation properly in at least some respects. It concludes by saying that in certain instances it is quite easy to not rely on leniency, and that people should at least make a distinction between certain and doubtful *Hadash*. He assures those who are willing to be more stringent that they will be able to acquire *Yashan* in the winter as well.[85]

---

84 *Mishna Berura* 489:45.
85 *Biur Halakha* 489: s.v. *af bazman ha'zeh.*

IX

Alternative Views of the *Mishna Berura*'s Methodology

Simcha Fishbane's *The Method and Meaning of the "Mishnah Berurah"*

In his book *The Method and Meaning of the "Mishnah Berurah,"* Simcha Fishbane has provided an alternative view of the halakhic methodology of the *Mishna Berura*. He states that the *Mishna Berura* will seem to rule leniently in order to implicitly convey the message that it is not difficult to remain observant in order to prevent people from joining liberal movements in Judaism, yet in reality it is predominantly strict in its adjudication.[1] He writes as follows:

> In his desire to combat secularism [the author of the *Mishna Berura*] sought to strengthen and regulate the spiritual boundaries of the Orthodox Jew. Therefore in regard to contemporary issues he felt compelled to inculcate stringent behavior. At the same time he could imply to observant readers that Jewish law allows an accommodative attitude and that there was no need to turn to liberal or secular Judaism.[2]

This view, however, adopts two difficult assumptions. First is that the *Mishna Berura* believed that strict rulings would protect those already flirting with secularism from leaving the Orthodox camp. Second is that already-observant readers would not turn to secularism because of the text's accommodative lenient attitude.

---

1   Simcha Fishbane, *The Method and Meaning of the "Mishnah Berurah"* (Hoboken: Ktav Publishing House, 1991), 8.

2   Ibid., 169.

With respect to when the *Mishna Berura* takes an accommodative stance, Fishbane argues that this occurs only as long as the ruling remained within the halakhic boundaries set by the *Aharonim*. In particular, they must be previously formulated by the majority of the *Aharonim*. Also, regarding his contemporaries, Fishbane writes that the *Mishna Berura* would not allow itself to incorporate their opinions and rulings unless it had no alternative, and then it would incorporate them only to rule stringently.[3]

We believe that this view is incorrect, and we will give one example to demonstrate why. (For other examples, one may look to the next section where we bring 250 examples.) According to Fishbane, lenient rulings would be directed to the observant, and stringent rulings would be directed to those "on the fence." Also, the *Mishna Berura*'s lenient ruling will be in accord with a majority position among the *Aharonim*. Contemporary positions will have no influence. However, this schema does not concur with how the *Mishna Berura* reconciles the ruling in the *Shulhan Arukh*, i.e., that from *Rosh Hodesh Av* until the fast people should reduce their business activities,[4] with the fact that due to economic circumstances and social changes, Jews were not reducing their business activities in the *Mishna Berura*'s time.

Regarding this matter, the *Mishna Berura* states that there are some *poskim* who hold that the obligation to refrain is with respect to business activities that give a person happiness, such as buying silver objects or things needed for a wedding, but a person does not need to reduce his regular business activity at all. Others, on the other hand, hold that all business activity must be reduced, and only that which a person needs to do in order to make a living is permitted. The *Mishna Berura* remarks that today we have the custom to be lenient, since we consider everything today as being needed to make a living.[5] This lenient ruling is presented in its main commentary both for the observant Jew and for the fence-sitter.

---

3   Ibid., 169.
4   *Shulhan Arukh, Orah Hayyim* 551:2.
5   *Mishna Berura* 551:11.

In the *Sha'ar HaTziyun*, it is stated that there are communities which have the custom of not conducting any business at all, yet it is also noted that this is a stringency that is not in accord with the law. He indicates that it is possible that the custom was made as a protective measure, and, therefore, if a person wants to conduct business in such a place he must receive permission to do so.[6] By calling the stringent custom contrary to the law, the *Mishna Berura* in fact rules against how Fishbane proposes it would.

Also, with respect to the lenient custom, the *Mishna Berura* writes in the *Sha'ar HaTziyun* that it seems from the *Magen Avraham* that a person should nevertheless refrain from conducting those business activities which make him happy, though the *Taz* and the *Elya Rabba* seem to be lenient even in this type of activity, since a person might not be able to procure what he wants afterwards. The *Mishna Berura* concludes, saying that even if it is true that one might not be able to procure the goods afterwards, it is good to be stringent.[7] The *Mishna Berura*'s recommendation to be stringent is placed in a section of its commentary that observant readers would read more often than fence-sitters. Moreover, according to Fishbane's schema, we should have expected the *Mishna Berura* to be lenient like the *Taz* and the *Elya Rabba*, and not stringent like the *Magen Avraham*, since the lenient opinion has a majority among the *Aharonim* that he brought. Therefore, it seems that his strict recommendation is to the observant and his lenient one is to those who need to be spiritually strengthened.

Benjamin Brown's "Soft Stringency"

Benjamin Brown, the brilliant historian of another great rabbinical authority, the *Chazon Ish*, has also provided an alternative view of the halakhic methodology of the *Mishna Berura*. He claims it is founded upon the principle of "soft stringency" and not the complex

---

6   *Sha'ar HaTziyun* 551:11.
7   *Sha'ar HaTziyun* 551:13.

analysis we put forward in this book. Much as we admire Professor Brown's work, we think this approach is mistaken.[8]

Brown argues that, as opposed to "hard stringency," which demands that everyone follow the more stringent opinion, the principle of "soft stringency" allows the individual to decide for himself whether to adhere to the stringent or to the lenient opinion, both of which are effective. Stringent suggestions are exactly that; they are optional norms whose adherence stems from an extra-halakhic motive and an attempt to democratize Jewish law. Of course, the *Mishna Berura* encourages its readers to adhere to the stringent opinion, yet encouragement falls far short of requirement. Before defending his claim that the *Mishna Berura*'s intention to use the principle of "soft stringency" is to democratize the halakhic process, Brown gives a possible alternative explanation. His alternative answer is that the *Mishna Berura* was deliberately ambiguous in terms of providing normative conclusions out of a sense of deference to its predecessors.[9] It could not render a decision that would be in opposition to the ruling of a *posek* it thought greater than itself.[10] Brown rejects this conjecture based on the fact that the *Mishna Berura* does at times make definitive recommendations, and because the *Mishna Berura* states in its introduction that its purpose is to provide clarity with respect to what to do in practice when differences of opinion exist about a given matter.[11]

We think this approach is incorrect: because the *Mishna Berura*'s multifaceted recommendations are not the result of avoiding decision, but rather are deliberately constructed decisions in themselves, Brown contends that the *Mishna Berura*'s halakhic methodology is not strictly juridical. Rather, it has the underlying premise that within the Halakha, there are preferred behaviors that are not

---

8 See generally Benjamin Brown, "*Soft Stringency in the Mishnah Berurah*: The Jurisprudential, Sociological and Ideological Aspects of Halakhic Formulation," *Contemporary Jewry* 27 (2007): 1-41.

9 Ibid., 7.

10 Ibid.

11 Ibid.

universally obligatory, but rather are ideals toward which individuals should aspire. As Brown describes it, "This is an approach that perceives two levels of halakhic norms: a uniform norm that is equally obligatory for all Jews without exception, and a hierarchical norm that merely is suggested, designed for those who wish to serve God on a higher level."[12] The principal of "soft stringency" informs those who wish to aspire toward the higher level to know how to act and provides an opening for everyone else to follow the legitimate lenient opinion.

In claiming that the *Mishna Berura* deliberately gives ambiguous rulings in order to accommodate various degrees of legitimate religious observance, Brown asserts that the *Mishna Berura*'s methodology demonstrates the notion of "open texture," as understood by H.L.A. Hart.[13] In reference to the *Mishna Berura*, Brown writes, "[Kagan], too, tried to clarify the differences of opinion and display their variety [in the *Mishna Berura*], but in all the many cases where he did not decide between them, he actually was willing to accept the open texture caused by that variety. The final decision between them was not made through an intellectual coping with the text, but through the choice of the layman, which was based on other considerations."[14] While his commentary does demonstrate the notion of open texture, contrary to Brown's assertion, the *Mishna Berura* attempts to adjudicate given the open texture of the *Shulhan Arukh*; it does not deliberately create vagueness in the law in order to give the layman autonomy for self-legislation.

Benjamin Brown explains Hart's notion of open texture to be the ambiguity of a law which thereby requires interpretation. Based upon this understanding, he claims that the *Mishna Berura*'s halakhic methodology presupposes that a ruling need not be categorical. In his discussion of the open texture of a law, however, Hart explicitly defines open texture in terms of uncertainty in matters of

---

12 Ibid., 8.
13 See *supra* note 9.
14 Brown, *supra* note 98, at 10.

fact.[15] Given a particular piece of legislation, written in a manner that provides for a general rule to be followed, a particular situation may arise in which there is uncertainty as to whether the rule applies. The particular case shares some features with the general description given in the rule, yet has other features that distinguish it. The difficulty lies not in understanding what is required by the rule; rather, the ambiguity lies in determining whether the rule applies in this situation.

Because uncertainty is based upon deviation from a general norm, ambiguity in a law must, by definition, lie at the extremes of its authority and not at its foundation. Hart's example to describe the open texture of a given rule is, regarding a rule about vehicles, how far the meaning of vehicle can be stretched: it includes a motor-car, but does it also include an airplane, a bicycle, or roller-skates?[16] To give an example from the Halakha, given the rule that a person must pray in the morning, does the morning include only the first three hours of the day, the first four, or until noon? Just as one citizen cannot choose to include roller-skates within the definition of a vehicle while another includes an airplane, if a Jewish law community is to maintain any social stability, community ties would deteriorate if any layman can determine the meaning of morning for himself. In both cases, the authority of interpretation is vested in the adjudicators. As Hart writes, "The open texture of law means that there are, indeed, areas of conduct where much must be left to be developed by courts of officials striking a balance, in the light of circumstances, between competing interests which vary in weight from case to case."[17] As a text that admits it is interpreting laws, the *Mishna Berura*'s commentary should be seen as an attempt to resolve the tension resulting from the open texture in the *Shulhan Arukh,* as it relates to varying situations which all seem to fall

---

15   *The Concept of Law, supra* note 9, 128.

16   Ibid., 126.

17   Ibid., 135.

under the same Halakha. This would explain why the *Mishna Berura* calls the *Shulhan Arukh* a closed book, and gives as justification for its commentary that the *Shulhan Arukh* writes one ruling in terms of an *ab initio* perspective and another in terms of an *ex post facto* perspective. These perspectives relate not to the desire of different adherents but rather to differing details of a given situation in which observance is necessary.

A few examples follow to demonstrate that when the *Mishna Berura* mentions that a particular act is required *ab initio* and a different act suffices *ex post facto*, it does not imply that the individual may choose how to observe the particular command, but rather refers to the external circumstances in which a person must observe it. The *Shulhan Arukh* rules that one must make an *Eruv Tavshilin* (a mixing of cooked dishes that allows one to cook on a Festival for Shabbat when Shabbat immediately follows it) with bread and a dish of food, but if he only made it with a dish of food, it is effective.[18] The *Mishna Berura* comments that if he remembers before it gets dark that he only made the *Eruv Tavshilin* with a dish of food, he *must* add bread to it and designate the bread as part of the *Eruv*. If the voluntary *ex post facto* observance sufficed, the *Mishna Berura* would have only suggested, and not required, the person to add the bread.[19] It makes this requirement since the circumstances characterized the situation as *ab initio*; therefore, it must follow the *ab initio* requirement. Once it turns dark, the person cannot make an *Eruv*; therefore, this is a situation where *ex post facto* requirements suffice.

As another example, the *Rema* rules that we have the custom to pray *Maariv* (the evening prayer) beginning from *Plag HaMinha* (one and a quarter hours before sunset), and one should not pray *Minha* (the afternoon prayer) after *Plag*. He concludes, however, to say that *ex post facto* or in a time of difficulty, praying *Minha* then would still be effective.[20] The *Mishna Berura* interprets the *Rema* to mean that since it is a time of difficulty, it would be permitted *ab initio* to pray

---

18 *Shulhan Arukh, Orah Hayyim* 527:2.
19 *Mishna Berura* 527:7.
20 *Shulhan Arukh, Orah Hayyim* 233:1.

Minha at that time. To understand the *Mishna Berura*'s comment as Brown has described it, namely that *ab initio* is the ideal form of observance and *ex post facto* is the lenient way of the multitudes, does not make sense. One must understand the *Mishna Berura*'s use of *ab initio* to mean that given the difficult situation in which the person finds himself, what is normally considered an *ex post facto* fulfillment is now the *ab initio* requirement. The facts of the case and not the desire of the self-legislator determine the level of stringency necessary.[21] In other cases in which the *Mishna Berura* distinguishes between degrees of observance, he discusses *ex post facto* fulfillment in a situation where someone performs part of an act erroneously,[22] or if the *ab initio* requirement would have the undesired consequence of great monetary loss, or of limiting one's *Simhat Yom Tov* (holiday joy).[23]

Despite the fact that we have shown that the *Mishna Berura*'s confrontation with open texture relates to questions of fact which raises doubts as to whether a given situation is under the influence of a particular law, its use of terms such as "it is good to be stringent" or "it is correct to be stringent" still seem to confirm its use of the principle of soft stringency and its acceptance of the autonomy of the layman. In the *Sha'ar HaTziyun*, the *Mishna Berura* at times gives an account for its use of these phrases, which may help determine whether they should be interpreted to imply soft stringency. A first example deals with saying the words, "May the expressions of my mouth and the thoughts of my heart find favor before you, God, my Rock and My Redeemer," after the *Amida* prayer. The *Mishna Berura* writes that if a person has reached the point where he would say these words but has not yet said them, and the *Hazan* begins to recite the *Kaddish* prayer after his repetition, the person may answer the *Kaddish*; however, he should be cautious not to put himself in this situation.[24] This type of language would seem to imply soft strin-

---

21 *Mishna Berura* 233:13.
22 *Biur Halakha* 455: s.v. *yesh l'smokh aleihem*.
23 *Biur Halakha* 455: s.v. *mayim shelanu*.
24 *Mishna Berura* 122:1.

gency, since the *Mishna Berura* says that a person may answer, yet encourages him to be strict and ideally not to answer. In the *Sha'ar HaTziyun*, it is explained that the use of this language is because the *Rema* forbids a person to interrupt his prayer to answer the *Kaddish*, yet the *Gra* writes that the *Rema*'s ruling is, in fact, not compulsory. In order to give a suggestion that reduces the ambiguity of having conflicting opinions, the *Mishna Berura* writes that one should be cautious to avoid the situation entirely, thereby avoiding the question of whether this extreme case falls under the authority of a disputed law. However, when the situation is unavoidable, the *Mishna Berura* definitively sides with the *Gra* in opposition to the *Rema*, thereby giving clarity as to what one should do in practice if this extreme case occurs.[25] In other places, the *Mishna Berura* explains its use of the phrase, "it is good," for the same reason.[26] It similarly explains its use of the phrase, "it is correct to be stringent."[27]

---

25 *Sha'ar HaTziyun* 122:5.
26 *Sha'ar HaTziyun* 128:7; 273:16.
27 *Sha'ar HaTziyun* 246:13.

IX

Conclusion

As our examples show (and the 250 other examples in our next section prove), the *Mishna Berura*, rather than just allowing its reader to autonomously choose his own manner of fulfilling a particular obligation, does give fairly concrete instructions. The seeming variability is the consequence of the book's attempt to negotiate between its ten core halakhic principles in a manner that best answers its four central, guiding questions.

Because, as he remarks in his introduction, to study the *Shulhan Arukh* alone will not allow one to come to a proper conclusion (since no rule is able to satisfy every situation unless a person understands its intention and reasoning—its *purpose*), and because the increase of disagreements found in the *Aharonim* has caused great difficulty in determining the proper action, the *Mishna Berura* seeks to provide enough information to allow its reader always to act correctly, accounting for various circumstances and differing opinions. At the same time, it desires to construct a unified, coherent halakhic corpus.

Rabbi Israel Meir Kagan's *Mishna Berura* is one of the two premier works of Jewish law written in the last one hundred fifty years. It undertook to survey and clarify all areas of Jewish ritual law found in one of the four sections of the classical Jewish law code, the *Shulhan Arukh*. Unlike many of his contemporaries, who adopted the basic stance that it was the duty of the decisor or commentator to endorse a particular view as the most analytically correct when matters are in dispute, or to adopt the functionally easiest plausible one, the author takes a unique legal approach. The *Mishna Berura* asserts that to adopt the most comprehensively preferred method is ideal, to adopt an answer that most commentators endorse is proper, and in times of need or urgency, the adoption of any resolution endorsed by a significant group of decisors is acceptable. Its innovative approach, fundamentally invented by this work, can perhaps best be summarized by one of its own sayings:

ואשרי מי שעובד ה' בשמחה

Content is the one who worships God with Happiness.[1]

---

1   *Mishna Berura* 477:5.

Two Hundred Fifty Illustrative Examples from the *Mishna Berura*

Explanatory Introduction to the Two Hundred Fifty Examples

The examples taken from the *Mishna Berura* are organized in two ways. The first way is according to the three general strategies and two techniques for resolution through which the *Mishna Berura* applies its ten halakhic principles, namely (1) by the use of specific terminology, (2) through negotiating juridical priorities, (3) via interpretation, (4) by introducing new elements, and (5) by relying on the position of the *Gra*. There will also be a sixth category (6), namely the role that custom plays within the general methodology of the *Mishna Berura*. The reason for putting examples regarding the role of custom into their own category is that we have found that the *Mishna Berura* approaches customs in a manner that is not easily seen when integrated into the others. In a word, its approach to the legitimacy of customs in their own right is different than what is popularly assumed.

The second way in which they are organized is according to the ten principles themselves. Of course, due to the complexity of the *Mishna Berura*, the two organizational structures will at times overlap, and especially according to the second manner, a particular example will have more than one halakhic principle apply. Nevertheless, by organizing the examples in the following two ways, it is our hope that they will be categorized efficiently both to convey the structure of the *Mishna Berura* and to ease further research.

The order in which the examples are arranged follows the first manner of organization. Each strategy/technique is contained in a section, with subsections which further divide each strategy/technique into its particular components. At the beginning of each subsection, there is a short explanation of the *Mishna Berura*'s approach, which is meant to highlight the primary factors which are taken into account. The outline of the examples according to this arrangement is as follows:

Strategy & Techniques	Examples
Terminology	
Yireh Shamayim (One Who Fears Heaven)	1-6
Ba'al Nefesh (A Spiritual Person)	7-11
Tavo Alav Berakha (Will Come to Blessing)	12-16
HaMedakdakim (The Scrupulous)	17-22
Machmir al Atzmo (Stringent upon Oneself)	23-27
Juridical Strategy	
The Legitimacy of Multiple Ways of Fulfillment	28-36
Synthesizing Conflicting Views Into One Unifying Hierarchy	37-67
Combining Different Aspects of Conflicting Views Into One Performance	68-72
Relationship Between Kabbala and Talmud	73-81
Interpretative Strategy	
Interprets in a Manner that Seeks to Resolve Potential Contradiction	82-96
Interprets in a Manner that Justifies his Own Opinion	97-100
Difference in Interpreting Rabbi Karo Versus the *Rema*	101-126
The Accretive Technique	
In Addition to Juridical Strategy	
Qualified Intention	127-136
Introducing Another Variable	137-144
Doubling One's Efforts	145-151
Requiring Something Additional for Public Benefit	152-155
Giving an Alternative to Avoid Transgression	156-160

Strategy & Techniques	Examples
In Addition to Interpretative Strategy	
Clarifies in Order to Add	161-167
Provide Alternative Explanation so that the Halakha Remains Relevant	168-170
Typographical Errors and *Girsa* Changes	171-175
Reliance on the *Gra*	
In Addition to Juridical Strategy	
Gra as the Deciding Factor	176-193
In Addition to Interpretative Strategy	
Gra as Basis for Interpretation	194-209
The Role of Custom	
Custom When the Law is Debated	210-220
Custom Contrary to the Written Halakha	221-225
An Erroneous Custom Does Not Uproot Halakha	226-231
Contemporary Changes	232-242
Limmud Zekhut	243-250

Each example is also numbered in order to identify which examples correspond to any one of the ten halakhic principles. The directory which identifies the halakhic principles which the *Mishna Berura* applies for each example is below.

Halakhic Principles	Examples
(1) When a ruling no longer seems to fit the current reality, the *Mishna Berura* provides alternative explanations for the ruling, changes its language, or adapts practices so that they fit with the ruling's spirit.	29, 36, 76, 95, 155, 160, 168-169, 221-222, 232-242
(2) When the codes record both lenient and strict positions, the *Mishna Berura* advises when one should be strict and when one may be lenient.	5, 16, 34, 37-66, 70-73, 75, 77, 86, 90-91, 95, 97-98, 113, 116, 124, 127, 142-143, 148-149, 151, 159, 160-161, 172, 180, 185, 199, 214-215, 234, 243

(3) When the codes record multiple normative views that do not contradict each
other, the *Mishna Berura* accepts the
validity of different practices in different
locations, and suggests manners of fulfillment that incorporate the different views.

15, 20, 28-30, 68-69, 86-87, 92,
94, 96, 101-104, 108, 130, 135,
145-147, 149, 184, 186-187, 201,
204, 211, 217, 225, 235, 244, 248

(4) When the codes record two mutually
exclusive opinions, the *Mishna Berura*
suggests ways to avoid transgression
according to either view.

4, 18, 74, 82, 84-85, 106, 108,
110, 120, 127-129, 131-134,
137-141, 144, 146, 149, 153-160,
181, 183, 187, 194, 201, 210, 227,
232

(5) When the early codes are lenient and the
later commentators are strict, the *Mishna
Berura* inclines toward the strict position.

1, 3, 5, 7-17, 21-27, 31, 36-39, 41,
43, 46, 47, 49, 52-54, 56, 59-60,
65, 67-69, 76-77, 83, 85, 88,
93-94, 97, 99-102, 106-107,
109-110, 117, 119-120, 123-126,
136, 144, 148-156, 159-160,
162-169, 171, 173, 176, 179, 182,
191-193, 195-196, 198, 200,
204-206, 210, 214-216, 218-220,
225, 228-231, 236, 238-242,
245-246, 249-250

(6) When the major codes adopt a lenient
position, yet other codes are stricter, the
Mishna Berura suggests qualifying one's
intention to act so as to avoid transgression according to the strict position.

1-4, 6-14, 17, 19, 23-26, 30-35, 40,
66, 82, 84, 93, 103, 105, 111-112,
114-115, 118, 121, 156-157, 165-167,
170, 182, 194, 198, 202-203,
209-210, 213-216, 218-224,
233-234, 236, 238, 240, 246-247,
249

(7) When people have adopted an unsupported custom, the *Mishna Berura* disapproves of it, yet attempts to justify it for
those who will nevertheless continue to
follow it.

122, 188-190, 226-231, 246,
249-250

Halakhic Principles	**Examples**
(8) When the codes are easily misunderstood, the *Mishna Berura* clarifies misunderstood rulings, and defends widespread practices.	2, 10-11, 14, 18, 21, 36, 52, 55, 60-62, 67, 72, 82-117, 124, 126, 128-130, 135, 142, 149-150, 161-164, 168, 170-175, 180, 194-195, 197, 199-204, 207-209, 211, 217, 223-224, 227, 234, 237, 242-250
(9) When the codes and Kabbala conflict, the *Mishna Berura* minimizes the tension between the two positions.	73-81, 186
(10) When the codes are in tension and the *Gra* has a strong view, the *Mishna Berura* relies on the position of the *Gra*.	19, 30, 40, 119, 135, 158, 162, 167, 176-209, 212-213, 220, 248

Each example begins with a Halakha and its challenges, whether they are the existence of alternative positions, seeming contradictions with other areas of law, or ambiguity in the law's language or application, among other matters. It will then proceed to give the *Mishna Berura*'s position and an explanation for how the *Mishna Berura* arrives at its conclusion. Some examples also contain further discussion to clarify certain points that are relevant and/or necessary to understand and appreciate the *Mishna Berura*'s methodology.

Yireh Shamayim (One Who Fears Heaven)

When the *Mishna Berura* writes that one who fears Heaven should be careful to act stringently even though a prevalent practice is more lenient, its intention is to indicate that the lenient practice is legitimate. Its advice for the one who fears Heaven to be more stringent is based upon a desire for a person to act in accordance with as many of the major opinions that it deems authoritative as possible. When other *poskim* use the term "one who fears Heaven," the *Mishna Berura* interprets their use of the term in the same way as its own use.

1.

Shulhan Arukh — If a Jew ties *tzitzit* on a garment without the proper intention, and he does not have another garment that contains *tzitzit*, he may rely on the *Rambam*'s opinion that the garment is kosher to wear, yet he should not recite a blessing on wearing it.[1]

Discussion — Rabbi Karo believes that *ab initio* a Jew should tie *tzitzit* on a garment with the proper intention. If a Jew ties *tzitzit* on a garment without the proper intention, he may only wear it if he has no other alternative. This does not mean, however, that the garment is unequivocally kosher, since he writes that the person should not recite a blessing on wearing it. Rather, the garment has the status of being doubtfully kosher, based upon the doubt as to whether one can rely on the *Rambam*'s ruling or not. If the person does have another garment whose *tzitzit* were tied with the proper intention, he may not wear the garment with the *tzitzit* tied without the proper intention.

Alternative Positions — At the time of the writing of the *Mishna Berura*, the common practice was that people were no longer careful to have the proper intention when tying their *tzitzit*.[2]

Issue — The *Mishna Berura* is faced with a common practice that is more lenient than the ruling in the *Shulhan Arukh*. Because he does not want to dismiss the many Jews who act leniently, he must find a way to explain the lenient practice in order to legitimate it. Since the vast majority of people tie *tzitzit* without the proper intention, it is likely that none of the garments that an individual owns would be kosher. Therefore, the individual would be able to rely on the *Rambam*'s position, as indicated by the *Shulhan Arukh*. By legitimating the lenient practice, the *Mishna Berura* would still in fact be providing a judgment that is in accordance with the ruling of the *Shulhan Arukh*.

The *Mishna Berura*'s Position — In the *Biur Halakha*, the *Mishna Berura* discusses at length the various opinions regarding the

---

1   *Shulhan Arukh, Orah Hayyim* 14:2.
2   *Biur Halakha* 14; s.v. *lo yevarekh alav*, at the end.

necessity of having the proper intention when tying *tzitzit* to garments in order to justify the custom that has arisen where people are not careful in having the proper intention. It nevertheless concludes by saying that one who fears Heaven should be stringent upon himself to be careful and say explicitly while tying his *tzitzit* that he is acting with the proper intention.[3]

Halakhic Principles — 5, 6

2.

Shulhan Arukh — One who does work on Friday from *Minha* onwards will not see a blessing from it. There are those who interpret *Minha* to be *Minha Gedola* and there are those who interpret it to mean *Minha Kettana*.[4]

Discussion — The original purpose for this ruling was to make sure that people would come in from the fields early enough to have time to prepare for Shabbat. Today, there is not the same need for everyone to stop working in order to prepare; therefore, the custom has lost its influence.

Alternative Positions — At the time of the writing of the *Mishna Berura*, people would normally continue to work until the onset of Shabbat.

Issue — The *Mishna Berura* does not want to exclude those who work until the onset of Shabbat, yet still are able to get ready in time, from being within the realm of halakhic acceptability. On the other

---

3   *Biur Halakha* 14; s.v. *lo yevarekh alav*. Interestingly, in his main commentary (*Mishna Berura* 14:8), Kagan advises all of his readers to act this way *ab initio* and does not limit his suggestion only to those who fear Heaven, yet in the *Sha'ar HaTziyun,* he refers his readers to the *Biur Halakha*. The difference in perspective between the three commentaries demonstrates one of the objectives behind having different commentaries. The main commentary is meant to be an interpretation and explanation of the *Shulhan Arukh* proper, as well as making it more contemporary by including various later commentaries. The *Biur Halakha* expands upon the main commentary by considering the broader discussion as found among the *Rishonim*, as well as including contemporary practice and custom. The *Sha'ar HaTziyun* is meant to provide justificatory sources for the main commentary and to give a final practical word when needed.

4   *Shulhan Arukh, Orah Hayyim* 251:1.

hand, the historical reason for a ruling's origin is irrelevant in terms of the legal process of nullifying the law. Therefore, the *Mishna Berura* must find a way to maintain the law while allowing for leniency based on current practice.

The *Mishna Berura*'s Position — In the *Biur Halakha*, the *Mishna Berura* writes that the reason why we do not have this custom today is because there is not the same need for everyone to stop working in order to prepare; therefore, the custom has lost its influence. Nevertheless, those who fear Heaven should refrain from working in the fields from *Minha Kettana* onwards, if this would not entail financial loss, and many are also stringent to refrain even from performing work around the house.[5]

Discussion — The *Mishna Berura* changes the ruling in the *Shulhan Arukh* to the status of a custom in order to remove the difficulty of finding a legal means of abrogation. Because the original reason for the custom no longer applies, the custom is no longer applicable. Nevertheless, the *Mishna Berura* does not completely annul its status as law so as not to remove the normativity of the *Shulhan Arukh*'s ruling *de jure*; rather, it relegates its application to those who fear Heaven.

Halakhic Principles — 6, 8

3.

Shulhan Arukh — On Shabbat or on Yom Tov it is prohibited to learn anything except for words of Torah (*Divrei Torah*). Even books of wisdom are forbidden. There is an opinion that allows a person to read from books of wisdom.[6]

Discussion — Originally, people would gather in the afternoons in the synagogues on Shabbat and Yom Tov to listen to public rabbinic lectures. At that time, people were not allowed to learn Scriptures privately on Shabbat and Yom Tov in order to encourage attendance at the lectures. When the custom of giving public lectures on Shabbat

---

5   *Biur Halakha* 251: s.v. *v'yesh mefarshim minha kettana.*
6   *Shulhan Arukh, Orah Hayyim* 307:17.

and Yom Tov ended, the prohibition to read Scriptures privately was also annulled.

Alternative Positions — The majority of the *poskim* understood the repeal to apply only to holy books in order to encourage Torah learning despite the lack of public lectures. People would still be prohibited from reading books containing works of general wisdom, so as not to take away from the opportunity of Torah learning. The *Rashba*, however, held that it was permissible to read books of general wisdom. At the time of the writing of the *Mishna Berura*, common practice was to allow the reading of general books of wisdom on Shabbat and Yom Tov, in accordance with the opinion of the *Rashba*.

Issue — The *Mishna Berura* does not want to exclude those who follow the more lenient opinion, especially since Rabbi Karo mentions it. Moreover, the fact that Rabbi Karo mentions the lenient opinion means that, though he does not agree with it, it may still be considered within the realm of halakhic acceptability.

The *Mishna Berura*'s Position — The *Mishna Berura* writes that today the custom is to be lenient, but it cites the *Elya Rabbah*, who writes that those who fear Heaven will see fit to be stringent, since the *Rambam* and the *Ran* prohibit it.[7]

Halakhic Principles — 5, 6

4.

Shulhan Arukh — Only a garment made from either linen or lamb's wool is required by the Torah to have *tzitzit*; all other materials require *tzitzit* by rabbinical decree.

Rema — Garments made of any type of material require *tzitzit* by the Torah.[8]

Discussion — It seems as if the *Rema*'s opinion is more stringent, since he incorporates more materials into the Torah obligation, which means that if a person does not put *tzitzit* on such a garment he breaks a Torah command, whereas according to Rabbi Karo he

---

7   *Mishna Berura* 307:65.

8   *Shulhan Arukh, Orah Hayyim* 9:1.

would only transgress a rabbinic command. In truth, however, the *Rema* is actually more lenient than Rabbi Karo. Since people would put *tzitzit* on all four-cornered garments regardless, stringency and leniency should not be seen from the perspective of obligation, but rather from that of fulfillment. According to the *Rema*, a person can fulfill a Torah obligation with a garment made of any material; according to Rabbi Karo, he can only fulfill a Torah command with a garment of linen or lamb's wool.

Alternative Positions — The majority of *Aharonim* rule in accordance with the *Rema*.

Issue — If the *Mishna Berura* were to rule in accord with the *Rema*, it would be agreeing with common practice, yet ignoring its methodological principle of including as many halakhic positions as possible. If it were to rule in accord with Rabbi Karo, it would subsume the opinion of the *Rema*, since it is more lenient, yet would ignore the methodological principle of including as many people within the realm of halakhic acceptability as possible.

The *Mishna Berura*'s Position — The *Mishna Berura* writes that the majority of the *Aharonim* rule as the *Rema*, and thus believe that a garment made of any material requires *tzitzit* by the Torah;[9] however, it writes that one who fears Heaven will be stringent upon himself to defer to Rabbi Karo's opinion and wear a *tallit* made of wool in order to act in accordance with all opinions.[10]

Halakhic Principles — 4, 6

5.

Shulhan Arukh — On Shabbat it is permitted to immerse a new dish that needs to be immersed in a *mikveh*, yet there are those who prohibit immersion on Shabbat. Those who fear Heaven will act in accord with everyone by giving the dish to a Gentile as a gift and then asking him to borrow it. The dish will then not need to be immersed before the Jew uses it.[11]

---

9 *Mishna Berura* 9:4.
10 *Mishna Berura* 9:5.
11 *Shulhan Arukh, Orah Hayyim* 323:7.

Discussion — Immersing a new dish into a *mikveh* (a ritual pool) will "fix" it so that it can be used. Because the "fixing" is not material, there is a disagreement as to whether one may do it on Shabbat, when there is a prohibition to fix vessels.

The *Mishna Berura*'s Position — The *Mishna Berura* explains that when Rabbi Karo makes this suggestion for those who fear Heaven, it implies that he believes the lenient opinion to be the essential ruling and not an *ex post facto* permissibility. With respect to its own position, the *Mishna Berura* rules with the *Rema* that the immersion is prohibited. However, if a person transgresses and immerses the vessel, it is possible that he may still use it since there are those, namely Rabbi Karo, who allow immersion *ab initio*. The *Mishna Berura* is thus interpreting Rabbi Karo's use of the term "those who fear Heaven" as legitimating the lenient practice as opposed to simply accepting it as a minority opinion.[12]

Halakhic Principles — 2, 5

6.

Shulhan Arukh — If the community prays the evening prayer (*Maariv*) while it is still daytime, one should recite the *Shema* and its blessings with the community and pray with them, and when the obligation to recite the *Shema* arises he should repeat the *Shema* without its blessings.[13]

Alternative Position — In the *Bet Yosef*, Rabbi Karo expresses the opinion that it is sufficient to repeat only the first two paragraphs, since the person has fulfilled his obligation of recounting the Exodus when he recited the *Shema* with the community. The *Magen Avraham* also writes that it is enough to recite only the first two paragraphs. That volume comments, however, that the custom has become to consider one's obligation to be fulfilled by the recital with the community even if it is a bit early, but prefers that a person should be stringent on himself and recite the whole *Shema* on his bed, or at least the first two paragraphs, with the intention to fulfill his

---

12   *Mishna Berura* 323:33.
13   *Shulhan Arukh, Orah Hayyim* 235:1.

obligation. The *Sha'agat Aryeh*, on the other hand, writes that those who fear Heaven will be careful to repeat all three paragraphs.

The *Mishna Berura*'s Position — The *Mishna Berura* writes that according to the law the person need only recite the first two paragraphs of the *Shema*. He does not need to recite the third paragraph since the obligation to remember the Exodus from Egypt was fulfilled with the earlier recital. The *Mishna Berura* does, however, cite the *Sha'agat Aryeh*, who writes that those who fear Heaven will be careful to repeat all three paragraphs.[14]

Discussion — The *Mishna Berura* writes that according to the law a person need only recite the first two paragraphs, even though Rabbi Karo writes that one must repeat the *Shema* without making any distinction between paragraphs. It does this to clarify the ruling in the *Shulhan Arukh* based on what is written in the Bet Yosef, and to account for those who agree to it, such as the *Magen Avraham*. Moreover, some opinions specifically advise a person to repeat all three paragraphs. If it were interested in simply encompassing as many opinions as possible into its ruling, the *Mishna Berura* could have ruled that one must repeat all three paragraphs. By saying that only those who fear heaven should repeat three paragraphs, the *Mishna Berura* is legitimating the more lenient practice while still advocating that one follow the more stringent one. Furthermore, by attributing the ruling to the *Sha'agat Aryeh*, it is assuming that the *Sha'agat Aryeh* is using the category of "one who fears Heaven" in the same way it is.

Halakhic Principles — 6

Ba'al Nefesh (A Spiritual Person)

When a prevalent practice is more lenient than what the *Mishna Berura* believes is the essential ruling, yet it foresees that the practice cannot be changed, the *Mishna Berura* writes that a *Ba'al Nefesh* will act stringently. This is different from the term *Yireh Shamayim*, since in this case it does not legitimate the lenient

---

14 *Mishna Berura* 235:11.

ruling but rather accepts it due to extenuating circumstances. A *Ba'al Nefesh* seeks to avoid what would be a transgression if not for the overarching acceptance of the practice; one who is *Yireh Shamayim* seeks to fulfill his obligation according to a higher standard without denigrating the more lenient one. The *Mishna Berura* also uses the term *Ba'al Nefesh* to describe those who follow the simple ruling of the *Shulhan Arukh*, even when it itself gives a more lenient interpretation of the ruling. The *Mishna Berura* uses the term *Ba'al Nefesh* when confronted with a Halakha which is lenient only as the result of capitulation to ensure community adherence.

7.

Shulhan Arukh — One cannot make an *Eruv* that contains a public domain except if the openings in the walls contain doors that actually close at night. Some say that if they are not closed at night, the *Eruv* may still be valid on the condition that they are able to be closed at night.[15]

Discussion — An *Eruv* is a ritual enclosure around a community, which allows Jews to carry objects on Shabbat when it would otherwise be forbidden to do so. It is meant to symbolize a wall around the community in order to turn it into one unified domain for the purpose of carrying on Shabbat. To define what constitutes a public domain, Rabbi Karo, in the *Shulhan Arukh*, writes that a public domain is defined as streets and markets that are sixteen cubits wide which are not roofed or walled. If the area is enwalled yet its gates are not closed at night, it would still be considered a public domain. He adds that there are those who say that any place that does not contain six hundred thousand people in it every day is not considered a public domain.[16]

Alternative Positions — With respect to how to define a public domain, the *Mishna Berura* writes that it has searched through all of the *Rishonim* who require six hundred thousand people but could

---

15 *Shulhan Arukh, Orah Hayyim* 364:2.
16 *Shulhan Arukh, Orah Hayyim* 345:7.

not find the stipulation that the people must be present every day. Rather, they mean that there is a possibility that they would be found there in general.[17] In the *Biur Halakha*, it is noted that if the presence of six hundred thousand people was an actual necessary stipulation, the Talmud would not have neglected to mention it.[18] Despite the lack of textual justification, the prevalent custom has become to use a *Tzurat HaPetah* when constructing an *Eruv* which includes streets that are very wide and open from one end of the city to the other, meaning that they are public domains. The justification to use a *Tzurat HaPetah* is grounded on the opinion that a public domain requires six hundred thousand people. Based on that requirement, the streets would not be public domains; therefore, a *Tzurat HaPetah* would be effective in constructing an *Eruv*.

The *Mishna Berura*'s Position — The *Mishna Berura* writes that even though many *Rishonim* disagree with this opinion, one cannot protest against those who act leniently and use a *Tzurat HaPetah* to make an *Eruv*; nevertheless, a *Ba'al Nefesh* should be stringent upon himself.[19]

Discussion — By stating that one cannot protest against those who follow the lenient custom, the *Mishna Berura* demonstrates that it does not believe this is a correct opinion. However, because some *poskim* have found it to have legal worth, and in order to spread the net of halakhic legitimacy as widely as possible so as to maintain a unified system of Halakha, the *Mishna Berura* condones it. A *Ba'al Nefesh*, on the other hand, should follow what the *Mishna Berura* thinks is the proper halakhic position.

Halakhic Principles — 5, 6

8.

Shulhan Arukh — Rabbi Karo enumerates days in which tragedies occurred in Jewish history, and on which it is appropriate to fast. He also remarks that even though some of the days fall on *Rosh Hodesh*

---

17 *Mishna Berura* 345:24.
18 *Biur Halakha* 252: s.v. *she'ein shishim ribo.*
19 *Mishna Berura* 345:23; 364:8.

(the New Month), there is an opinion which states that a person should still fast on those days.[20]

Alternative Positions — The *Mishna Berura* refers to the *Bet Yosef*, in which Rabbi Karo mentions that there are a number of *Rishonim* who disagree and warn not to fast on those days that fall on *Rosh Hodesh*. On the other hand, those who justify fasting even though it is *Rosh Hodesh* draw support from the fact that these days of fasting were decreed since the times of the Talmud.

The *Mishna Berura*'s Position — The *Mishna Berura* concludes by saying that a *Ba'al Nefesh* should be stringent upon himself to fast if he is able to do so.[21]

Halakhic Principles — 5, 6

9.

Shulhan Arukh — It is permitted to walk outside on Shabbat wearing gloves, yet there is an opinion that is stringent to require them to be sewed or tied to one's coat, and it is proper to defer to this opinion.[22]

Discussion — Gloves may not be considered to be like an ordinary garment; therefore, wearing gloves may be considered carrying them and not actually wearing them. There is a concern that someone may take his gloves off and forget and walk four *amot* in the public domain while holding them.[23]

The *Mishna Berura*'s Position — The *Mishna Berura* comments that today the custom is to be lenient, yet proposes that the leniency stems from the fact that according to many *poskim*, there is no such thing as a Torah-level public domain. (This *Mishna Berura* does in fact believe that there could be a Torah-level public domain today.) It continues, however, that though it seems from the *Aharonim* that

---

20 *Shulhan Arukh, Orah Hayyim* 580:1.
21 *Mishna Berura* 580:1.
22 *Shulhan Arukh, Orah Hayyim* 301:37.
23 *Mishna Berura* 301:138.

one should not protest against those who use this leniency, nevertheless it is appropriate for a *Ba'al Nefesh* to be stringent.[24]
Halakhic Principles — 5, 6

10.

Shulhan Arukh — When the day before Passover falls on Shabbat, after a person finishes his morning meal, he may give his remaining bread to a Gentile on the condition that he does not take it into a public domain.[25]

The *Mishna Berura*'s Position — The *Mishna Berura* explains that Rabbi Karo does not mean that he should make an explicit stipulation with the Gentile not to take the bread outside, but rather that he should not make an explicit stipulation for him to take it outside. If the person just gives the Gentile his bread without saying anything, it is acceptable. Nevertheless, the *Mishna Berura* concludes to say that it is appropriate for a *Ba'al Nefesh* to make the exact stipulation which it has just disregarded.[26]

Discussion — While this example may seem to contradict the general claim that the *Mishna Berura* uses the term *Ba'al Nefesh* in relation to what it thinks is the essential ruling, in this example, a *Ba'al Nefesh* does exactly what the *Shulhan Arukh* states and does not follow the *Mishna Berura*'s more lenient interpretation of it. By writing that a *Ba'al Nefesh* should make the stipulation, the *Mishna Berura* expresses the desire to avoid a potential transgression by taking a lenient interpretation, even if it is a justifiable one.
Halakhic Principles — 5, 6, 8

11.

Shulhan Arukh — On all rabbinic fasts except for *Tisha b'Av*, it is permitted to wash and anoint oneself, wear shoes, and have marital relations. Also, one need not stop eating the previous night.[27]

---

24 *Mishna Berura* 301:141.
25 *Shulhan Arukh, Orah Hayyim* 444:4.
26 *Mishna Berura* 444:17.
27 *Shulhan Arukh, Orah Hayyim* 550:2.

Discussion — The *Mishna Berura* explains that when the Jewish community agreed to observe these fasts, they did not make them as strict as *Tisha b'Av* because the majority of the community would not be able to uphold them.

The *Mishna Berura*'s Position — Given that the reason for leniency is the ability for community-wide adherence, the *Mishna Berura* advises that a *Ba'al Nefesh* should be as stringent on all of the fasts as he is on *Tisha b'Av*.[28] In the *Sha'ar HaTziyun*, this opinion is justified with the statement that today we find many decrees made upon the Jews by the Gentiles, and because of them the obligations of the other fasts would now be the same as that of *Tisha b'Av* according to the *Ramban*[29] and the *Gra*. He also cites the *Elya Rabba*, who writes in the name of the *Shlah* that a *Ba'al Nefesh* will stop eating the night before the other fasts.[30]

Discussion — In this example, the *Shulhan Arukh* rules leniently, yet the *Mishna Berura*, by advising a *Ba'al Nefesh* be stringent, disagrees with Rabbi Karo as to the essential ruling. By doing so, it demonstrates that the decision to rule leniently in order to secure community adherence is a compromise position, similar to an *ex post facto* validity. Also, by advising that a *Ba'al Nefesh* be stringent and not demanding that everyone be stringent, and by attributing the ruling to the *Elya Rabba* and the *Shlah*, it is assuming that the *Elya Rabba* and the *Shlah* are using the category of "*Ba'al Nefesh*" in the same way as it is.

Halakhic Principles — 5, 6, 8

Tavo Alav Berakha (Will Come To Blessing)

If the Halakha follows the majority opinion, but there is an individual or marginal opinion among the *Rishonim* that is more stringent, the *Mishna Berura* writes that anyone who accepts the more stringent opinion upon himself will come to blessing. If, over time, the number of *poskim* who suggest that one be stringent increases to

---

28 *Mishna Berura* 550:6.
29 See his *Torat Ha-Adam, Sha'ar Ha'Evel, Inyan Aveilot Yeshana*.
30 *Sha'ar HaTziyun* 550:9.

the point that, at the writing of the *Mishna Berura*, it no longer seems to be a marginal position, the *Mishna Berura* will include the previously marginal opinion as one of the major factors it considers when deciding how to rule. The *Mishna Berura*'s use of the expression that one who acts stringently will come to blessing reflects its use among previous *poskim*.

12.

Shulhan Arukh — On Shabbat, one is permitted to squeeze grapes into a pot that contains food in order to enhance the food. On the other hand, it is forbidden to squeeze grapes into an empty pot.[31]

Alternative Position — *Rabbenu Hananel* prohibits a person to squeeze grapes even onto food.

The *Mishna Berura*'s Position — The *Mishna Berura* writes that although the majority of *poskim* disagree with *Rabbenu Hananel*, one who is stringent will come to blessing. He attributes the ruling and the expression to the *Rosh*, implying that he uses the expression in the same way as he does.[32]

Halakhic Principles — 5, 6

13.

Shulhan Arukh — One may not buy meat on Yom Tov by setting a price, yet he may acquire it without setting a price.[33]

Alternative Position — Although it is explicit from the *Tosefta* that a person may be counted as having a share in an animal without setting a price, the *Rashba* rules stringently, and does not allow a person to acquire meat in this manner on Yom Tov.

The *Mishna Berura*'s Position — After analyzing the reasoning of the *Rashba*, the *Mishna Berura* concludes by citing the *Pri Hadash*,

---

31 *Shulhan Arukh, Orah Hayyim* 320:4.
32 *Mishna Berura* 320:17.
33 *Shulhan Arukh, Orah Hayyim* 500:1.

who writes that although the essential ruling is not in accord with the *Rashba*'s view, he who is stringent will come to blessing.[34]
Halakhic Principles — 5, 6

14.

Shulhan Arukh — On Shabbat, one may put salt in a *kli rishon* that is no longer on the fire and whose contents are completely cooked yet is still *yad soledet bo*. There is a single opinion, however, that prohibits putting salted meat into this pot.

Rema — There are those who prohibit a person to put salt even into a *kli sheni* as long as it is *yad soledet bo*, and he who is stringent will come to blessing.[35]

Discussion — A *kli rishon* (first vessel) is a vessel that was heated directly on a flame or other source of heat. Even when removed from the source of heat, this vessel maintains its status as a *kli rishon*, and possesses the capacity to cook any type of food placed within it. This capacity remains until the pot and its contents cool below the temperature of *yad soledet bo* (the degree of heat "from which the hand recoils").

The *Mishna Berura*'s Position — The *Mishna Berura* explains the *Rema*'s use of the expression to mean that because the majority of the *poskim* rule leniently but there exists a minority who are stringent, the *Rema* writes that he who is stringent will come to blessing. This interpretation reflects the *Mishna Berura*'s own understanding of the term.[36]
Halakhic Principles — 5, 6, 8

---

34 *Biur Halakha* 500: s.v. *b'pisuk damim*. Because it refers its readers to the *Biur Halakha* in *Mishna Berura* 500:3, one can assume that the *Mishna Berura* agrees with the *Pri Hadash* and does not just mention it as another opinion.
35 *Shulhan Arukh, Orah Hayyim* 318:9.
36 *Mishna Berura* 318:71.

15.

Rema — One may use a *hametz*-based adhesive to stick paper onto his windows within thirty days before Passover, yet some are stringent if the adhesive can be seen from the outside.[37]

Alternative Positions — In the *Sha'ar HaTziyun*, the *Mishna Berura* cites the *Terumat HaDeshen*, who writes that one who is stringent and uses plaster will come to blessing.[38] In the *Biur Halakha*, the *Mishna Berura* writes that it seems that the *Aharonim* rule *ab initio* according to the stringent opinion, yet mentions that the *Pri Hadash* and the *Taz* rule leniently.[39]

The *Mishna Berura*'s Position — Because it perceives a common tendency toward stringency among the later *poskim*, the *Mishna Berura* writes that a person must make the *hametz*-based adhesive very runny and place it in between the cracks so that it cannot spread out at all and will therefore not be visible.[40] He is not stringent to the point of not permitting its use at all, since its use is common practice, but he attempts to incorporate the suspicions of those who incline toward stringency.

Discussion — Because the stringent position is no longer a marginal opinion but has gained broader legal acceptance, the *Mishna Berura* feels the need to incorporate it into the halakhic system in a more integrative manner. However, since it is still a minority opinion and the accepted lenient opinion is halakhically legitimate, it cannot simply discard the lenient opinion for the more stringent one. Therefore, in accord with its methodological principles, the *Mishna Berura* finds a compromise situation which allows *hametz*-based adhesives, yet in a manner that is consistent with the more stringent position.

Halakhic Principles — 3, 5

---

37 *Shulhan Arukh, Orah Hayyim* 442:3.
38 *Sha'ar HaTziyun* 442:32.
39 *Biur Halakha* 442: s.v. *v'yesh mahmirin im nireh mi'bahutz.*
40 *Mishna Berura* 442:17.

16.

Rema — If a torch left over from the first day of Yom Tov has gone out, it may be relit even on the second day of Rosh Hashanah. Similarly, if it was left over from Shabbat, it may be relit on the Yom Tov that follows Shabbat.[41]

Alternative Positions — In the *Sha'ar HaTziyun*, the *Mishna Berura* cites the *Taz*, the *Elya Rabba*, and the *Pri Hadash*, who write that he who is stringent and does not relight it will come to blessing.[42]

The *Mishna Berura*'s Position — Due to the increase in the number of *poskim* that commend stringency, in his main commentary the *Mishna Berura* writes that *ab initio* it is good and correct to act in accord with all opinions and prepare a new wick, or at least light the old wick in an abnormal manner.[43]

Discussion — Though its immediate predecessors only commend acting stringently in accord with the minority opinion, once the opinion gains strength, the *Mishna Berura* makes it obligatory *ab initio*.

Halakhic Principles — 2, 5

HaMedakdakim (The Scrupulous)

The *Mishna Berura* uses the expression "the scrupulous" to refer to those people who attempt to act in accord with all opinions, but does not necessarily imply that the *Mishna Berura* considers their actions to be correct.

17.

Shulhan Arukh — It is a *mitzvah* to increase the amount of food at one's *Rosh Hodesh* meal.[44]

The *Mishna Berura*'s Position — Recognizing that Rabbi Karo says that it is a *mitzvah* and not an obligation, the *Mishna Berura* writes that even though there is no essential obligation to say the grace after

---

41 *Shulhan Arukh, Orah Hayyim* 501:7.
42 *Sha'ar HaTziyun* 501:43.
43 *Mishna Berura* 501:34.
44 *Shulhan Arukh, Orah Hayyim* 419:1.

meals (*Birkat HaMazon*) on *Rosh Hodesh*, to have a meal is praise-worthy.[45] Once a person decides to have a meal, in terms of what the meal consists, the *Mishna Berura* adds that those who are scrupulous have the custom of making an extra dish above what they normally have for the specific purpose of honoring *Rosh Hodesh*.[46] It does not, however, commend or suggest imitating the practice.

Halakhic Principles — 5, 6

18.

Shulhan Arukh — One should not say "amen" after "*ga'al Israel* (who redeemed Israel)," the concluding words of the blessing after the recital of the Shema which is said immediately before the recital of the *Amida*, since it would be an interruption between "*geula*" and "*tefilla*" (the blessing for redemption and prayer).[47]

Rema — Some say to answer "amen" after the *Hazan* recites the blessing, and that such is the custom.[48] The *Rema* also writes that there are those who are of the opinion that the requirement to juxtapose "*geula*" and "*tefilla*" only applies to weekdays and holidays; Shabbat, on the other hand, does not require it. Yet, he concludes, it is good to be stringent and not interrupt, if it is not necessary to do so.[49]

Discussion — The advice of the *Rema* to be strict may seem like he is agreeing with the opinion of Rabbi Karo; however, when one reads his comment in the context of what he writes in his *Darkhei Moshe*, it becomes obvious that he does not waver from considering saying "amen" to be permissible. In the *Darkhei Moshe*, the *Rema's* concern is that since Shabbat does not require "*tefilla*" to immediately follow "*geula*," one may think it permissible to engage in any type of interruption, even those that have nothing to do with the prayer service. Therefore, he specifically remarks that things not associated with the service would be considered a prohibited interruption, in agreement with what Rabbi Karo writes in the

---

45 *Mishna Berura* 419:1.
46 *Mishna Berura* 419:2.
47 *Shulhan Arukh, Orah Hayyim* 66:7-8; 111:1.
48 *Shulhan Arukh, Orah Hayyim* 66:7.
49 *Shulhan Arukh, Orah Hayyim* 111:1.

Bet Yosef; but for those necessary interruptions, such as responding for *Kaddish* (an Aramaic recitation of God's glory) or *Kedusha* (the proclamation of God's exaltedness that is based on that which the angels are recorded to say), one may rely on the *Or Zarua* and not consider them prohibited.[50] The reason that the *Rema* does not consider "amen" to be an interruption is that it is the conclusion of the order of blessings; Rabbi Karo, on the other hand, bases his decision on the *Zohar*.

The *Mishna Berura*'s Position — The *Mishna Berura* interprets the *Rema*'s statement that it is good to be stringent in a different way than the *Darkhei Moshe*'s. Where the *Darkhei Moshe*'s stringency relates to superfluous interruptions, the *Mishna Berura* attributes it to a doubt in interpreting the justification for Shabbat's excusal from the prescription. Placing the *Rema*'s statement within his comment that Shabbat is not a time of distress, it notes that Rabbi Karo disagrees with making any distinction between Shabbat and other days, and due to the negative consequences of interrupting, "it is good to be stringent."[51] It does, however, maintain the legitimacy of leniency when it is necessary on Shabbat, since the opinion is a legally valid one.[52]

The *Mishna Berura*'s Position II — The *Mishna Berura* notes that there are those who are scrupulous and try during the week to fulfill their obligation according to all opinions by pausing at *"tzur Israel"* or *"shira hadasha,"* which are words in the blessing after the recital of the Shema which is said immediately before the recital of the Amida that precede *"ga'al Israel,"* in order to answer "amen" after the *Hazan*'s blessing. It disapproves of this strategy, writing that all the *Aharonim* agree that this is not a good practice since one should not say an additional "amen" within the blessing nor should he refrain from starting the *Amida* with the congregation. With the intention of correctly fulfilling the obligation according to all opinions, the *Mishna Berura* gives alternative advice. One should intend to finish the

---

50 *Darkhei Moshe, Orah Hayyim* 111.
51 *Mishna Berura* 111:8.
52 *Mishna Berura* 111:9; *Biur Halakha* 111: s.v. *tov l'hahmir*.

blessing at the same time as the *Hazan*, thus negating the obligation to say "amen." Likewise, he could say the introductory verse of the *Amida* slightly before the *Hazan* finishes the blessing, which would also negate the obligation to say "amen" and would still be considered as starting the *Amida* with the congregation.[53]
Halakhic Principles — 4, 8

19.

Rema — On Shabbat it is prohibited to wash one's hands with soap that is made from prohibited fat (*Helev*), which liquefies in one's hands, since it would be *Nolad*.[54]

Discussion — Objects that come into existence on Shabbat are considered *muktze* and may not be handled on Shabbat under a restriction called *Nolad*.

Alternative Positions — In the *Biur Halakha*, the *Mishna Berura* writes that according to the *Gra*, as well as other great *poskim*, this is prohibited even during the week, since smearing is equivalent to drinking and it is prohibited to consume *Helev*. Therefore, in any case it should be prohibited at least rabbinically. *Rabbenu Tam*, on the other hand, permits it completely.

The *Mishna Berura*'s Position — The *Mishna Berura* writes that though the universal custom is to wash one's hands with soap made from *Helev*, certain scrupulous people are careful to refrain from this. It adds that if an alternative is readily available it is certainly correct to be stringent.[55]
Halakhic Principles — 6, 10

20.

Shulhan Arukh — As the *Kohanim* turn towards the congregation to say the *Birkat Kohanim* (*dukhan*), they should recite the blessing over *Birkat Kohanim*.[56]

---

53 *Mishna Berura* 66:35.
54 *Shulhan Arukh, Orah Hayyim* 326:10.
55 *Biur Halakha* 326: s.v. *b'sha'ar helev*.
56 *Shulhan Arukh, Orah Hayyim* 128:11.

Alternative Positions — The *Mishna Berura* mentions that some *Rishonim* rule that the *Kohanim* should recite the blessing before they turn to face the congregation.

The *Mishna Berura*'s Position — The *Mishna Berura* notes that those who are scrupulous will try to fulfill their obligation according to both opinions by beginning the blessing while their backs are still toward the people and begin to turn toward them while in the middle of the recitation.[57]

Halakhic Principles — 3

21.

Rema — Some say the passage, "The Incense Mixture," in the evening and in the morning after prayer, yet there are those who write that one should be careful to recite "The Incense Mixture" from a written text and not by heart, since it is said in place of performing the Incense Offering, and we suspect that he may skip a spice which would make him liable to the death penalty. Therefore, we have the custom to only recite "The Incense Mixture" on Shabbat.[58]

Alternative Position — Although it is an established custom, the *Mishna Berura* remarks that Rabbi Karo challenges this premise, since reciting the passage and actually offering the incense are not exactly equivalent and because the death penalty is not imposed for an accidental offence.

The *Mishna Berura*'s Position — The *Mishna Berura* notes Rabbi Karo's challenge of the custom so as to affirm the passage's recital, and also notes that one would be guilty of the death penalty only if he transgresses intentionally; therefore, it writes that because of these reasons those who are scrupulous have the custom to recite it every day.[59]

Halakhic Principles — 5, 8

22.

Shulhan Arukh — Clothes washed in wheat-water, and paper that has a *hametz*-based adhesive, etc., are permissible to have in one's

---

57 *Mishna Berura* 128:40.
58 *Shulhan Arukh, Orah Hayyim* 132:2.
59 *Mishna Berura* 132:17.

possession on Passover since the *hametz* out of which the cleansing liquid or adhesive is composed is no longer considered *hametz*.[60]

The *Mishna Berura*'s Position — Though far afield from the *Shulhan Arukh*'s actual leniency, *Mishna Berura* notes that those who are scrupulous have the custom not to wash their clothes in wheat-water for the thirty days before Passover.[61] In the *Sha'ar HaTziyun*, it is stated that the source of this custom is a stringent opinion of the Geonim regarding this matter.[62]

Halakhic Principles — 5

Machmir al Atzmo (Stringent upon Oneself)

When the lenient practice is clearly accepted as the Halakha, yet a more stringent practice has strong support among the *poskim*, the *Mishna Berura* will not impose the stringent opinion upon the community. Rather, he will recommend it only to those individuals who are able to uphold it. If a particular lenient practice is halakhically acceptable, yet may lead to erroneous analogy to other areas of Halakha, the *Mishna Berura* will recommend leniency only to individuals and not to the community as a whole.

23.

Shulhan Arukh — A person may fold an article of clothing on Shabbat to wear that day, yet only on the conditions that only one person folds it, it is new and has not yet been washed, it is white, and he does not have another article of clothing to wear instead. If any one of these conditions is not met, it is prohibited. There is one opinion that permits a person to fold the first fold in an irregular manner, and the Halakha seems to be in accord with this opinion.[63]

Discussion — The reason one is forbidden to fold clothes is because it is as if one is repairing them. Either folding into their creases 'repairs' them by accenting the folds, or folding irons out the creases.

---

60 *Shulhan Arukh, Orah Hayyim* 442:3.
61 *Mishna Berura* 442:16.
62 *Sha'ar HaTziyun* 442:30.
63 *Shulhan Arukh, Orah Hayyim* 302:3.

The *Mishna Berura*'s Position — The *Mishna Berura* writes that the *Aharonim*, in general, rule according to the latter opinion; nevertheless, for the one who wants to be stringent upon himself and not fold at all, it is certainly preferable.[64] In the *Sha'ar HaTziyun*, the author limits his preferred stringency to that of the first opinion, and does not advise a more stringent approach, such as prohibiting one to fold under any circumstance.[65]
Halakhic Principles — 5, 6

24.

The *Mishna Berura* writes that when Rosh Hashanah falls on Saturday night, it is the custom to pray from a prayer book (*Siddur*) even though the community has not recited the blessing "*boreh me'oreh ha'esh* (the blessing over creation of fire)." It justifies the practice by citing the *Sha'are Teshuva*, who reasons that people are not really benefitting from the light completely, since they know the prayer partially by rote.
Discussion — Using the light to see the prayer book would constitute benefitting from the light. One should not benefit from something without first making a blessing over the benefit.
The *Mishna Berura*'s Position — The *Mishna Berura* writes that he who is stringent should be stringent upon himself only, and should not teach others to be stringent.[66]
Discussion — In this case, the *Mishna Berura* uses the expression that "one should be stringent upon himself only" because the lenient action does not lead to a transgression even in the eyes of those who are stringent. Nor is the more stringent opinion actually better. Therefore, the *Mishna Berura* need not legitimate or condone the lenient position, since it holds it to be the essential law.
Halakhic Principles — 5, 6

---

64 *Mishna Berura* 302:19.
65 *Sha'ar HaTziyun* 302:21.
66 *Mishna Berura* 599:1.

25.

Shulhan Arukh — At the conclusion of Yom Kippur one should make *Havdala* on a cup of wine, but he should not recite a blessing over spices even if Yom Kippur fell on Shabbat.[67]

Discussion — The *Mishna Berura* explains that the reason for Rabbi Karo's ruling is that we smell spices at the conclusion of Shabbat during *Havdala* in order to appease our souls after the *Neshama Yetera* (the extra soul one is traditionally believed to receive on Shabbat) has left. On Yom Kippur, one does not receive a *Neshama Yetera*; therefore, smelling the spices is not needed.

Alternative Position — The *Mishna Berura* notes that many of the *Aharonim* disagree with Rabbi Karo's ruling and hold that when Yom Kippur falls on Shabbat, one still recites a blessing on smelling spices, and it is not a superfluous blessing since one nevertheless derives benefit from it.

The *Mishna Berura*'s Position — The *Mishna Berura* writes that one should not teach the opinion of the *Aharonim* to the community, nor should he protest against a place that has the custom not to recite a blessing on spices. Rather, when the person is at home and makes *Havdala* he may then recite the blessing on the spices.[68] To add further support in favor of reciting the blessing for smelling spices, it mentions in the *Sha'ar HaTziyun* that according to a number of *Aharonim*, the *Neshama Yetera* does come when Yom Kippur falls on Shabbat.[69]

Halakhic Principles — 5, 6

26.

Rema — We have the custom to be stringent and prohibit writing salutary letters on *Hol HaMoed* even in our own script, which is like "*Rashi* script" and does not entail professional work.[70]

67　*Shulhan Arukh, Orah Hayyim* 624:3.
68　*Mishna Berura* 624:5.
69　*Sha'ar HaTziyun* 624:6.
70　*Shulhan Arukh, Orah Hayyim* 545:5.

Alternative Position — The *Mishna Berura* writes that according to many *Aharonim*, in our lands we have the custom to be lenient with respect to scripts that do not require a professional to write them. In the *Biur Halakha*, the *Mishna Berura* cites the *Mor U'Ketzia* who considers writing in "*Rashi* script" to be a professional practice when done by a scribe, and therefore rules that one should not write in a nice script even in the vernacular since any script can be that of a professional or an amateur regardless of language.

The *Mishna Berura*'s Position — The *Mishna Berura* writes that those who are lenient have support to justify their actions. Those who are stringent should be stringent upon themselves only.[71] In the *Biur Halakha*, however, it is written that even though the world has the custom to be lenient and we should not protest against it, it is nevertheless good to defer to the *Mor U'Ketzia*'s words when there is not a great need to write.[72]

Halakhic Principles — 5, 6

27.

Shulhan Arukh — On Shabbat a person cannot ask his servant to walk with him and light a candle, even if the servant would need the candle, since the act is essentially for the Jew.

Rema — It is permitted to say to a Gentile who is already holding a lit candle to walk with him, since the Gentile is not doing anything but generally carrying something which a Jew cannot carry.[73]

The *Mishna Berura*'s Position — The *Mishna Berura* limits the *Rema*'s permission only to *Bnei-Torah*, and justifies its qualification on the assumption that people may get confused as to what is permitted and what is not, and thus come to think that certain quasi-analogous yet forbidden acts are permitted.[74]

Halakhic Principles — 5

---

71   *Mishna Berura* 545:35.
72   *Biur Halakha* 545: s.v. *afilu bi'khtiva.*
73   *Shulhan Arukh, Orah Hayyim* 276:3.
74   *Mishna Berura* 276:29.

The Legitimacy of Multiple Ways of Fulfillment

When two different ways to fulfill an obligation have become widespread, established practices, and both claim equal validity in terms of their efficacy, the *Mishna Berura* acknowledges both practices as legitimate. If a practice endorsed by the *Shulhan Arukh* is not commonly observed in a particular location, the *Mishna Berura* recommends that one not protest against the lack of adherence. The *Mishna Berura* does not perceive its acceptance of multiple ways of halakhic fulfillment as innovative. Rather, it considers them only as an expansion and development of an already-accepted norm.

28.

Shulhan Arukh — One must make a hole for the *tzitzit* relative to the length of the *tallit*. It must not be above three finger-breadths; for otherwise, its location would not be called a corner. It cannot be below the measurement from the joint of the thumb until the nail since it says "on the corner." If it was below the full measurement made from the joint of the thumb, it is below the corner (and invalid). **Alternative Positions** — The *Mishna Berura* records a position mentioned in the *Bet Yosef* regarding the practice of making two holes in one's garment through which one ties *tzitzit*. Regarding this practice, Rabbi Karo states that one need not worry about this position, and he who is stringent upon himself to act according to it acts surprisingly, since it makes him look haughty. The *Mishna Berura* cites the *Bach* who writes that one should make two holes to tie *tzitzit* to a *tallit-kattan*, and since it is not visible he does not look haughty.

As described in *Shulhan Arukh*   Alternative Position

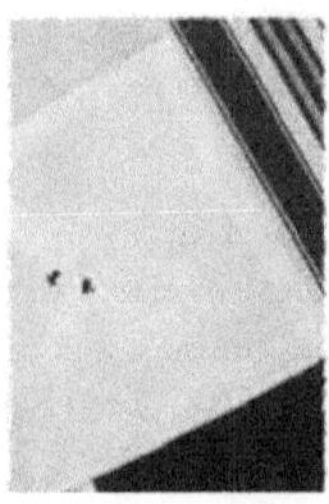

The *Mishna Berura*'s Position — The *Mishna Berura* writes that the custom has spread through Poland to follow the position cited by the *Bach*, but in Hungary and in Ashkenaz it is not the custom, and every river has its own course, i.e., every place has its own practices.[75]
Halakhic Principles — 3

29.

Shulhan Arukh — A father is obligated to purchase phylacteries for his child in order to teach him how to don them if his son knows how to keep them pure.

Rema — There are those who say that the child to whom Rabbi Karo refers is one who is at least thirteen years and one day old, and such is the custom and should not be changed.[76]

Alternative Position — The *Mishna Berura* writes that the current custom is to have the child don phylacteries two or three months beforehand in order to teach him.[77]

The *Mishna Berura*'s Position — In the *Biur Halakha*, the *Mishna Berura* justifies this custom, though it directly contradicts the *Rema*'s counsel, by referring to the *Bach* and the *Pri Megadim*, which state that a twelve-year-old who learns and understands Talmud may don phylacteries. It concludes by saying that if the child can fulfill the requirements set forth by Rabbi Karo and can keep his phylacteries pure, one may certainly rely on this opinion.[78]
Halakhic Principles — 1, 3

30.

Shulhan Arukh — One should not say *Kiddush Levana* until seven days after the new moon.[79]

Alternative Position — The *Mishna Berura* writes that the majority of *Aharonim* disagree and hold that one should recite *Kiddush Levana* after three days and should not delay the opportunity to do a *mitzvah*.

---

75 *Mishna Berura* 11:39.
76 *Shulhan Arukh, Orah Hayyim* 37:3.
77 *Mishna Berura* 37:12.
78 *Biur Halakha* 37: s.v. *v'khen nahagu.*
79 *Shulhan Arukh, Orah Hayyim* 426:4.

The *Mishna Berura*'s Position — To reconcile this contradiction, the *Mishna Berura* first writes that if the third day of the month is a weekday, it is correct to wait until *Motzei Shabbat* (after Shabbat), since both Rabbi Karo and the *Rema*[80] agree that this would be the correct procedure. However, because many *Aharonim*, the *Gra* among them, require a person to say *Kiddush Levana* on the third day even when it is during the middle of the week, the *Mishna Berura* concludes that he who has this practice certainly has support upon which to rely, especially during the winter and rainy seasons during which alacrity to recite it would be praiseworthy.[81]

Halakhic Principles — 3, 6, 10

31.

Shulhan Arukh — There is an opinion which permits squeezing unripe grapes into food on Shabbat, but *Rabbenu Tam* prohibits it.[82]

Alternative Position — If the unripe grapes can be eaten, albeit with some difficulty, the *Olat Shabbat* and the *Taz* rule leniently. The *Magen Avraham*, on the other hand, is stringent.

Discussion — Squeezing grapes in order to have their juice as a liquid would constitute the prohibition of *Mefarek* (separating) on Shabbat. The opinion that allows one to squeeze the juice out onto food reasons that the person does not intend to have the juice as a liquid and that he intends to eat it immediately. The opinion that prohibits it holds that squeezing the juice onto food would still constitute separating the juice, which is food, from the unripe grapes, which is inedible, and thus constitute the prohibition of *Borer* (sorting) on Shabbat. The one who prohibits it does not allow for the leniency of immediate consumption, since for unripe grapes, this would be the regular way to sort the juice from the inedible parts.

The *Mishna Berura*'s Position — The *Mishna Berura* writes that even though it is correct to defer to the stringent opinion, one should

---

80 See his comment on *Shulhan Arukh, Orah Hayyim* 426:2.
81 *Mishna Berura* 426:20.
82 *Shulhan Arukh, Orah Hayyim* 320:5.

not protest against a person who relies on the words of the *Olat Shabbat* and the *Taz*.[83]
Halakhic Principles — 5, 6

32.

Rema — The prohibition to cut vegetables finely on Shabbat only applies when one cuts the vegetables for later consumption. If he cuts them immediately prior to eating them, it is permitted to cut them finely, just as sorting is permitted prior to eating.[84]

Alternative Positions — Rabbi Karo writes in the *Bet Yosef* that even if one intends to eat the vegetables immediately, he should still be careful to cut slightly larger pieces. Many *Aharonim* advocate to act in accordance with this suggestion.

The *Mishna Berura*'s Position — The *Mishna Berura* writes that one should not protest against a person who cuts onions or radishes finely since they have justification upon which to rely, as long as it is done immediately before the meal.[85]
Halakhic Principles — 6

33.

Rema — We have the custom not to learn on the day before *Tisha b'Av* from noon onwards except for those topics that relate to *Tisha b'Av*.[86]

Alternative Positions — The *Mishna Berura* notes that many *Aharonim* follow the custom mentioned by the *Rema*, yet some voice strong opinions against it. The *Rashal* writes that he himself learns and permits others to do so as well. The *Gra* and the *Hayye Adam* write that the custom is only a stringency, and the *Ma'amar Mordekhai* writes at length that this custom will cause many to decrease their Torah learning in general.

---

83 *Mishna Berura* 320:20.
84 *Shulhan Arukh, Orah Hayyim* 321:12.
85 *Mishna Berura* 321:45.
86 *Shulhan Arukh, Orah Hayyim* 553:2.

The *Mishna Berura*'s Position — The *Mishna Berura* writes that one should not protest against a person who wants to be lenient and learn in the afternoon before *Tisha b'Av*.[87]

Halakhic Principles — 6

34.

Shulhan Arukh — Before one begins to search for *hametz*, he should recite the blessing, "That we have been sanctified with His commandments and have been commanded to destroy *hametz*."

Rema — If the person began to search for *hametz* before he recited the blessing, he may still recite it at any time before he completes the search.[88]

Alternative Position — There are *Aharonim* who hold that if the person did not recite the blessing beforehand, he may only recite it during the search itself. If he decides to recite the blessing the next day at the time of burning of the *hametz*, he may only do so if he omits from the blessing God's name and mention of His kingship.

The *Mishna Berura*'s Position — The *Mishna Berura* writes that if a person did not recite the blessing before he completed his search, he may recite the blessing (without God's name and mention of His kingship) the following day when he burns the *hametz* and one should not protest against it, since he has halakhic support on which to rely.[89] In the *Sha'ar HaTziyun*, the *Mishna Berura* justifies his opinion by saying that there are many *Aharonim* who hold this position.[90]

Halakhic Principles — 2, 6

35.

Shulhan Arukh — When the *Hazan* finishes reciting the *Shema* and says to himself, "Hashem, your God, is true," he should repeat the phrase aloud so the community hears it.[91]

---

87 *Mishna Berura* 553:8.
88 *Shulhan Arukh, Orah Hayyim* 432:1.
89 *Mishna Berura* 432:4.
90 *Sha'ar HaTziyun* 432:4.
91 *Shulhan Arukh, Orah Hayyim* 61:3.

The *Mishna Berura*'s Position — The *Mishna Berura* writes that in a place where such is not the custom, one should not protest.[92]

Note — Older texts of the *Mishna Berura* (as well as the text in the Bar Ilan University Responsa Project) have "one should protest." However, in the *Sha'ar HaTziyun*,[93] the *Mishna Berura* says that its ruling is based on the *Magen Avraham*,[94] which states that one should not protest.

Halakhic Principles — 6

36.

Shulhan Arukh — One whose relative has died [and is not yet buried] is obligated to mourn. Even if the deceased is not before him, he is exempt from reciting the *Shema* and from prayer. Even if he wants to be stringent upon himself to recite them, he may not. If, however, there is someone who can take care of everything for him regarding the burial, and the mourner wants to be stringent upon himself to recite the *Shema* and prayer, one should not protest against it.[95]

Discussion — Regarding Rabbi Karo's first statement, that the mourner may not be stringent upon himself, the *Mishna Berura* gives two explanations. The first explanation is that Rabbi Karo means that when the person does not have anyone to help him, he may not be stringent upon himself to recite the *Shema* and prayer. The implication of this explanation is that when the mourner does have someone to take care of everything for him, one should not protest since it is permissible. The *Mishna Berura*'s second explanation is that Rabbi Karo means that the person should never be stringent upon himself due to his obligation to honor the deceased. Therefore, when he writes that one should not protest if the mourner has someone who can take care of the burial necessities, he means that one should not protest even though he essentially forbids it, since

---

92 *Mishna Berura* 61:9.
93 *Sha'ar HaTziyun* 61:3.
94 *Magen Avraham* 61:1.
95 *Shulhan Arukh, Orah Hayyim* 71:1.

those who have the practice do this have some halakhic support. The *Mishna Berura* states that the second interpretation is, in fact, Rabbi Karo's main intention.[96]

Ambiguity — The *Mishna Berura* supports its contention that the latter interpretation is the essential one by referring to what Rabbi Karo writes in *Shulhan Arukh, Yoreh Deah* 341:1. However, in the ruling in *Yoreh Deah*, Rabbi Karo writes that the mourner is exempt from all the *mitzvot* mentioned in the Torah even if he does not need to take care of any burial needs, such as when he has another who can do those tasks for him. He then adds that there are those who say that if he wants to be stringent upon himself he is not allowed to do so.[97] Rabbi Karo's use of the expression "there are those who say" implies that he does not consider it to be the essential ruling and would consider it more halakhically acceptable to impose stringency upon oneself to recite the *Shema* and to pray. The *Mishna Berura* notes that this interpretation is, in fact, what was originally the common practice, yet the practice later changed to prohibit a person to be stringent upon himself.[98]

The *Mishna Berura*'s Position — The *Mishna Berura* states that the second interpretation, which essentially forbids a person to say the *Shema* and to pray out of respect for the deceased, is the main interpretation, rather than the first interpretation, which places the ability to say the *Shema* and to pray within the bounds of the normative Halakha.

Discussion — The change in the current custom supports the difference in the *Mishna Berura*'s use of the expression that one should not protest from what seems to be Rabbi Karo's. Where Rabbi Karo's statement that one should not protest may very well mean that the practice is within the bounds of normative Halakha, the *Mishna Berura* uses the expression to mean that despite the fact that the practice is not in accord with what it considers to be the essential

---

96 *Mishna Berura* 71:5.
97 *Shulhan Arukh, Yoreh Deah* 341:1.
98 *Mishna Berura* 71:6.

ruling, it should nevertheless be overlooked for the purpose of maintaining communal unity.

Halakhic Principles — 1, 5, 8

Synthesizing Conflicting Views into One Unifying Hierarchy

In situations in which there are numerous halakhic opinions, and there is no clear decision as to which position is established as the essential Halakha, the *Mishna Berura* creates a hierarchical standard for adherence which takes into account the contingencies inherent in daily life. In this way, it is able to grant validity to different degrees of fulfillment under varying circumstances so that people have the ability to perform correctly despite non-ideal conditions.

When Rabbi Karo records two positions regarding a particular Halakha, the *Mishna Berura* designates the more stringent position as what should be done *ab initio* and consents to the legitimacy of the lenient position *ex post facto*. One of the factors that influences the *Mishna Berura*'s hierarchical synthesis is the situation in which a person may find himself given which position is normative. When the *Shulhan Arukh* records an opinion to which many other *poskim* are strongly opposed, the *Mishna Berura* advocates following the more stringent position *ab initio* but consents to the legitimacy of the lenient position when the circumstances of the situation do not allow for ideal performance. The *Mishna Berura* also uses this technique when there is debate among the *Aharonim*. The *Mishna Berura* defines a time of difficulty as a situation in which there is no other alternative. The *Mishna Berura* will give validity to a lenient opinion when a person is presented with what he refers to as a "situation of great loss." Besides taking into account the circumstances of a particular situation, in determining whether to accept a lenient opinion as valid, the *Mishna Berura* also considers the nature of the obligation or prohibition. In particular, the *Mishna Berura* is more prone to accept a lenient opinion when the dispute is over a rabbinic ruling.

37.

Shulhan Arukh — There are those who do not require a person to dry his hands after washing *mayim aharonim,* but according to the *Rambam* he should dry his hands and then recite *Birkat HaMazon.*[99]

Discussion — The *Shulhan Arukh* seems to rule that one need not dry his hands after washing *mayim aharonim* since that is the opinion of the majority and only the *Rambam* disagrees.

The *Mishna Berura*'s Position — The *Mishna Berura* writes that although it seems that Rabbi Karo rules leniently on this matter, nevertheless *ab initio* it is good to dry one's hands in order to act in accord with all opinions.[100]

Discussion — The *Mishna Berura* does not directly contradict the lenient ruling of the *Shulhan Arukh.* However, because the *Rambam*'s ruling was mentioned, the *Mishna Berura* can confidently suggest adhering to his position as good advice in order to conform to all opinions.

Halakhic Principles — 2, 5

38.

Shulhan Arukh — It is forbidden to assemble, or reassemble, a detachable bed on Shabbat. If one tightens its joints he is liable to bring a *Hatat* offering. On the other hand, a detachable bed, which is (normally) loosely constructed, is permitted *ab initio* to re-assemble (as long as he does not tighten the joints). Also, it is permitted to assemble and separate on Shabbat the pieces of a cup made of different parts; however, there is an opinion that says that a cup has the same ruling as a bed.[101]

Discussion — A *Hatat* offering is a sin offering which is brought when someone commits a Torah transgression. There is a difference between a detachable bed that is tightly constructed (like the products bought at IKEA) and a detachable bed that is loosely

---

99 *Shulhan Arukh, Orah Hayyim* 181:8.
100 *Mishna Berura* 181:19.
101 *Shulhan Arukh, Orah Hayyim* 313:6.

constructed (which can be taken apart and reconstructed quite easily). The former is prohibited to put together by Torah law; the latter is permitted, as long as the person does not tighten the joints. With respect to the disagreement over whether a person can assemble a cup made of prefabricated parts, some *Rishonim* hold that since it never reaches an objective level of "firm assembly" (equivalent to hammering with nails) it is permissible to assemble it. Others hold that since the cup can be assembled tightly (in a relative sense) it is rabbinically prohibited to put the pieces together.

The *Mishna Berura*'s Position — With respect to assembling the cup, even though Rabbi Karo cites the lenient position first and in a manner that indicates that such is the law in practice, the *Mishna Berura* writes that *ab initio* one should defer to the stringent opinion and not attach the cup even loosely. Nevertheless, it accepts the validity of the lenient opinion *ex post facto* only on the condition that a person needs to use the cup on Shabbat.[102]

Discussion — Like the example above, the *Mishna Berura* does not oppose the permissibility of assembling the cup. Rather, he limits it to certain situations and to the *ex post facto*. *Ab initio*, the *Mishna Berura* defers to the more stringent opinion, in order to cover as many positions as possible in its ruling.

Halakhic Principles — 2, 5

39.

Shulhan Arukh — With respect to finding *hametz* within one's possession on Passover, there is one who says that the second day of Yom Tov is considered like *Hol HaMoed*,[103] which means that he may remove it and burn it immediately.

Alternative Positions — The *Shayarei Kenesset HaGedola* writes that many *poskim* disagree with this, and equate the second day of Yom Tov with the first day in all respects.

---

102 *Mishna Berura* 313:46.
103 *Shulhan Arukh, Orah Hayyim* 446:2.

The *Mishna Berura*'s Position — The *Mishna Berura* cites the *Aharonim* who conclude that the Halakha in practice is that if the person had already nullified his *hametz* through a verbal declaration of disownment, the second day is like the first, and he cannot burn it. Rather, he must cover it and wait until *Hol HaMoed*, when it would be permitted to burn it. If he did not nullify his *hametz*, or it leavened on Passover, everyone agrees that he transgresses "*bal yira'eh*" and "*bal yimatze* (possessing *hametz* on Passover)"; therefore, he may rely on the opinion which allows him to move the *hametz* and throw it into the sea or toilet, especially since many *Rishonim* already permitted one to do this on the first day of Yom Tov as well.[104]

Discussion — Though in the latter situation the *Mishna Berura* equates the second day with the first, it still does not allow a person to burn the *hametz*. Rather, he only allows the person to rid himself of the *hametz* in a way that would not constitute a transgression of the prohibitions of Yom Tov.

Halakhic Principles — 2, 5

40.

Shulhan Arukh — One may not insulate food on Erev Shabbat with something that adds heat. If he did, the food is prohibited even *ex post facto*. The prohibition *ex post facto* refers to food that was originally cold or food that would be improved by heating, but if it retains its original temperature it is permitted to eat the food.

Rema — There are those who say that if he forgot and accidently insulated the food in a substance that adds heat, the food would be permitted.[105]

Alternative Positions — According to the *Magen Avraham*, the *Taz*, and the *Gra*, Rabbi Karo holds that the food is prohibited until after Shabbat, even when insulated accidently.

The *Mishna Berura*'s Position — The *Mishna Berura* writes that in a situation of necessity, one can rely on the opinion cited by the *Rema*, since many *Aharonim* side with it, especially if the food is

---

104 *Mishna Berura* 446:8.
105 *Shulhan Arukh, Orah Hayyim* 257:1.

fully cooked.[106] The *Sha'ar HaTziyun* gives supports to this decision by saying that because it is a matter of rabbinic decree, we can rely on the lenient opinion.[107] In the *Biur Halakha*, the *Mishna Berura* writes that the *Gra* dismisses the opinion cited by the *Rema*, but qualifies the *Gra*'s opinion to mean that he dismisses it only as the essential ruling. The *Mishna Berura* admits that it is difficult to rule stringently *ex post facto* since the *Rema*, himself, relies on the lenient opinion *ex post facto* in a similar situation.[108]

Discussion — The *Mishna Berura*'s ruling reflects its desire to incorporate both positions in a manner that legitimates the largest realm of acceptability of halakhic practice. The ruling of the *Shulhan Arukh* is deemed the essential ruling, and the *Rema* is accepted when necessary. The *Gra*'s ruling is interpreted to allow for the *Rema*'s position, even though its simple understanding would be that it rejects the *Rema* outright.

Halakhic Principles — 2, 6, 10

41.

Shulhan Arukh — If a monkey washes a person's hands before his meal, some disregard it as proper washing and some permit it, and the ruling seems to be according to the latter.

Rema — Nevertheless, it is proper to be stringent.[109]

The *Mishna Berura*'s Position — The *Mishna Berura* writes that *ex post facto* it is effective. He cites the *Elya Rabba*, however, who writes that even *ex post facto* a person should rewash his hands, albeit without a blessing, if he has enough water to do so.[110]

Discussion — Though the *Mishna Berura* orders the two rulings in terms of *ab initio* and *ex post facto*, he also suggests an alternative practice which avoids relying on the *Rema*'s leniency when possible. The alternative practice, to wash without a blessing, is a compromise

---

106 *Mishna Berura* 257:10.
107 *Sha'ar HaTziyun* 257:9.
108 *Biur Halakha* 257; s.v. *yesh omrim d'im shakhah ve'hitmin*.
109 *Shulhan Arukh, Orah Hayyim* 159:12.
110 *Mishna Berura* 159:74.

which implies that the original washing has doubtful efficacy. The efficacy is doubtful because the *Elya Rabba* writes that if the person has extra water, the person must rewash his hands. Only when he does not have extra water can he rely on the leniency.
Halakhic Principles — 2, 5

42.

Shulhan Arukh — *Ab initio* one should have the intention that his washing permits him to eat.[111]

Alternative Position — The *Magen Avraham* writes that the washing is ineffectual even *ex post facto* if one does not have the proper intention at all. The *Gra*, on the other hand, does not require any intention for the washing to be effective.

The *Mishna Berura*'s Position — The *Mishna Berura* writes that *ex post facto* one may certainly rely on the lenient opinion if one does not have any more water to wash his hands.[112] In the *Biur Halakha*, the *Mishna Berura* writes that if one does have more water, it seems as if the *Rema* would require a person to rewash his hands, without a blessing; however, it suggests that in this situation one should make his hands impure to force the obligation to rewash his hands, and therefore be able to say the requisite blessing.[113]
Halakhic Principles — 2

43.

Rema — It is only permitted to seal the opening of a hot oven that contains food for Shabbat during the day before, when all of the dishes are fully cooked. In the evening, when it is close to the time of insulating the food, if there is a doubt whether the dishes are fully cooked, it is forbidden to seal the oven's opening since it will cause the food to cook.[114]

---

111 *Shulhan Arukh, Orah Hayyim* 159:13.
112 *Mishna Berura* 159:75.
113 *Biur Halakha* 159: s.v. *u'l'khathila yekhaven.*
114 *Shulhan Arukh, Orah Hayyim* 259:7.

The *Mishna Berura's* Position — The *Mishna Berura* explains that if a person did seal the oven the food would be forbidden even *ex post facto* when the food has not yet been cooked to the level of *ma'akhal ben-Derosai* (1/3-1/2 cooked). If it has reached the level of *ma'akhal ben-Derosai*, the food would not be prohibited *ex post facto*.[115] The *Sha'ar HaTziyun* explains the distinction. Although there is an opinion which holds that even after the level of *ma'akhal ben-Derosai*, further cooking would be a violation of Shabbat (*Bishul*), which means that it should be prohibited if the person sealed the oven, nevertheless, the *Mishna Berura* writes that it cannot negate the *Rema*'s ruling *ex post facto* when there are others who hold it as the essential ruling.[116] *Ab initio*, however, the *Mishna Berura* remarks that the *Rema* himself mentions that the food must be fully cooked.[117]

Halakhic Principles — 2, 5

44.

Shulhan Arukh — It is permitted on Yom Tov to fill one's oven with bread to bake even if he only needs one loaf. This specifically applies only to the types of ovens in Talmudic times, which were small, and in which the bread would stick to the walls, since filling the oven with bread would improve baking. In our ovens [those of the time of the writing of the *Shulhan Arukh*, which are similar to contemporary ovens in terms of size and the amount of heat produced], one can only bake what he needs.[118]

Alternative Positions — The *Mishna Berura* notes that there are *poskim* who assert that one may put additional loaves of bread into our ovens [those of the time of the writing of the *Mishna Berura* which are similar to contemporary ovens in terms of of size and the amount of heat produced] to bake, but only if at least one loaf is needed for the day. If a person connives to justify baking for a

---

115 *Mishna Berura* 259:25.
116 *Sha'ar HaTziyun* 259:24.
117 *Sha'ar HaTziyun* 259:25
118 *Shulhan Arukh, Orah Hayyim* 507:6.

weekday, it is prohibited.[119] The *Sha'ar HaTziyun* explains that those who permit adding loaves in our ovens reason that when there is not a lot of bread in the oven, it may get too hot and burn the bread; therefore, adding loaves serves the same purpose of improving baking as in Talmudic ovens.[120]

The *Mishna Berura*'s Position — The *Mishna Berura* writes that in a time of difficulty, such as when one has not made an *Eruv Tavshilin* and needs bread for Shabbat, one may rely on the lenient opinion to bake a lot of bread before the morning meal, still on the condition that he needs in any case at least one loaf. To cook a number of loaves only to eat a little in a manner that seems to be conniving to legitimate cooking for Shabbat is prohibited.[121]

Discussion — An *Eruv Tavshilin* (mixing of [cooked] dishes) is when one prepares a cooked food prior to a holiday that will be followed by Shabbat. Normally, cooking is allowed on holidays, but only for consumption on that day, and not for consumption after the holiday. Technically, if such a holiday occurs on Friday, cooking is allowed for the Sabbath, but the rabbis forbade this in order to prevent confusion during other years (when the holiday does not immediately precede the Sabbath) unless the ritual of *Eruv Tavshilin* is performed, which would remind the people of the reasons for the exception.[122]

Halakhic Principles — 2

45.

Rema — There are those who prohibit eating legumes on Passover and such is the custom in Ashkenaz and it should not be changed.[123]

The *Mishna Berura*'s Position — The *Mishna Berura* writes that at a time of difficulty when a person does not have anything to eat, it is permitted to cook anything except the five species of grains.

---

119 *Mishna Berura* 507:35.
120 *Sha'ar HaTziyun* 507:49.
121 *Mishna Berura* 507:35.
122 BT *Pesahim* 46b.
123 *Shulhan Arukh, Orah Hayyim* 453:1.

Also, it is obvious that such is also the case for someone who is sick, even if he is not dangerously so.[124] The *Sha'ar HaTziyun* writes that it is known that sages throughout the generations have permitted people to cook legumes on Passover many times in years of drought.[125]

Halakhic Principles — 2

46.

Shulhan Arukh — If, on a cloudy day, the community errs and thinks that it is dark and lights candles and prays *Maariv* for Shabbat, and afterwards the clouds disperse and the sun shines, they may return to performing those activities normally prohibited on Shabbat since their acceptance was in error.[126]

Alternative Position — The *Mishna Berura* writes that the *Aharonim* cite many of the great *poskim* to contend that erroneously accepting Shabbat via prayer is still an effective acceptance. The only practical difference is that in such a situation the few who did not accept Shabbat with the community need not be obligated to follow the majority in accepting Shabbat.

The *Mishna Berura*'s Position — The *Mishna Berura* concludes by saying that one should not be lenient against these *poskim*; however, in a time of difficulty one may rely on the opinion in the *Shulhan Arukh*.[127]

Halakhic Principles — 2, 5

47.

Shulhan Arukh — One is able nullify his *hametz* through a representative.[128]

Discussion — With respect to using a representative, the *Mishna Berura* explains Rabbi Karo's ruling by saying that even though it is

---

124 *Mishna Berura* 453:7.
125 *Sha'ar HaTziyun* 453:6.
126 *Shulhan Arukh, Orah Hayyim* 263:14.
127 *Mishna Berura* 263:56.
128 *Shulhan Arukh, Orah Hayyim* 434:4.

usually the case that a person can only nullify his property himself and not through the use of an agent, since the transgression of having *hametz* on Passover is actually having it in one's possession, revealing one's intention (by telling the representative) that one does not desire to have the *hametz* allows use of a representative.

The *Mishna Berura*'s Position — The *Mishna Berura* notes, however, that there are those who are stringent in this matter; therefore, it advises that a person can only be lenient in times of difficulty.[129]

Halakhic Principles — 2, 5

48.

Shulhan Arukh — Anyone is permitted to marry on the eve of a holiday and have a celebratory meal on the holiday.[130]

Alternative Positions — The *Mishna Berura* notes that the *Aharonim* write that one should be careful *ab initio* to have the wedding in the morning so that the couple may celebrate and so that the first meal may take place on the day before the holiday. However, if for any reason it must be delayed or it is a time of difficulty, the *Elya Rabba* permits one to marry even close to dark. The *Magen Avraham*, on the other hand, writes that the current custom is to not have weddings at all on the eve of a holiday.

The *Mishna Berura*'s Position — The *Mishna Berura* writes that if there is a great need to marry, one should not be stringent.[131]

Halakhic Principles — 2

49.

Shulhan Arukh — It is forbidden to make a tent on Shabbat or on Yom Tov, even if it is only temporary. This prohibition refers to the roof; partitions, on the other hand, are allowed to be erected when they do not serve the purpose of permitting a *Sukkah* or permitting one to carry.

---

129 *Mishna Berura* 434:15.
130 *Shulhan Arukh, Orah Hayyim* 546:3.
131 *Mishna Berura* 546:9.

Rema — A partition erected for privacy is also permitted. It is likewise permitted to erect a partition to protect against the sun or the cold, or in front of candles so as to prevent the wind from extinguishing them. It is forbidden, however, to erect a partition in front of a candle or in front of *Sefarim* (religious books) in order to be able to have relations or to relieve oneself, except if he extends an already in-place partition of at least a *tefach*.[132]

Alternative Positions — With respect to making a partition in front of a candle or in front of *Sefarim*, the *Magen Avraham* writes that the prohibition applies only when they can be seen above the partition. If the partition would totally hide the candle or the *Sefarim*, it would in essence function as a covering and not as a partition. Therefore, it would be permitted to erect it. The *Mishna Berura* notes that there are *Aharonim* who disagree with the *Magen Avraham*'s distinction and contend that it is always forbidden to erect a partition for the purpose of having relations or to relieve oneself.

The *Mishna Berura*'s Position — The *Mishna Berura* writes that at a time of difficulty one may rely on the *Magen Avraham*'s position.[133] In the *Biur Halakha*, the *Mishna Berura* gives an example of a time of difficulty. It refers to the *Nishmat Adam*, which states that in a case where a person's inclination may overpower him, he is permitted to rely on the *Magen Avraham* to make a temporary partition. In such a situation, he even permits the light to be seen above the partition. When such is not the case, however, Heaven forfend that he acts leniently in this.[134]

Halakhic Principles — 2, 5

50.

Shulhan Arukh — If a Gentile ties *tzitzit* on a garment while a Jew is standing over him and says that he should do it with the proper

---

132 *Shulhan Arukh, Orah Hayyim* 315:1.
133 *Mishna Berura* 315:10.
134 *Biura Halakha* 315: s.v. *im lo.*

intention, according to the *Rambam* it is *pasul* (unfit) but according to the *Rosh* it is kosher.[135]

The *Mishna Berura*'s Position — The *Mishna Berura* writes that only at a time of difficulty, such as when one cannot find a Jew who will tie them with the proper intention, can one rely on the opinion of the *Rosh*.[136]

Halakhic Principles — 2

51.

Shulhan Arukh — It is prohibited to have sexual relations in the room where one's phylacteries are lying until the phylacteries are placed within two coverings, neither of which is the designated covering which normally holds the phylacteries.

Rema — If the inner covering is not its designated covering yet the outer one is, it is still permitted.[137]

The *Mishna Berura*'s Position — The *Mishna Berura* adds that the same discussion applies to a *Humash* (Pentateuch) or a *Siddur* (prayer book), whether handwritten or printed, and that the book's cover does not count as one of the coverings. However, he cites the *Havvat Ya'ir*, who writes that one may be lenient regarding counting the cover of a book as a cover in a time of difficulty when he does not have something else with which to cover it.[138]

Halakhic Principles — 2

52.

Shulhan Arukh — If a person recites the *Shema* at dawn, even if he is not compelled to do so, he still fulfills his obligation *ex post facto*.[139]

Discussion — By stating that it is legitimate only *ex post facto*, the *Shulhan Arukh* recognizes that the performance is not ideal.

---

135 *Shulhan Arukh, Orah Hayyim* 11:2.
136 *Mishna Berura* 11:11.
137 *Shulhan Arukh, Orah Hayyim* 40:2.
138 *Mishna Berura* 40:4.
139 *Shulhan Arukh, Orah Hayyim* 58:4.

The *Mishna Berura*'s Position — The *Mishna Berura* writes that this is the case only if he does this *ad hoc*; if, on the other hand, he does this regularly, he will not have fulfilled his obligation even *ex post facto* and will have to repeat it later. However, if this is at a time of difficulty, even if he does it regularly it is efficacious, for what else can he do?[140]

Discussion — The reason for the *Mishna Berura*'s initial rejection of *ex post facto* legitimacy is that by regularly reciting the *Shema* at dawn, the person is in essence relying on the ruling *ab initio*. However, external factors change the circumstances to allow the recital *ex post facto* even when the external factors are constant.

Halakhic Principles — 2, 5, 8

53.

Shulhan Arukh — With respect to something in which a doubt arises as to whether it was prepared on the first day of Yom Tov or the day before, it would be permitted to enjoy it on the second day of Yom Tov due to the fact that there is a *sfeik-sfeika*.[141]

Discussion — A *sfeik-sfeika* is when there exists a two-faceted doubt in the status of an object. In a situation where a *sfeik-sfeika* exists, one usually rules leniently. The *Mishna Berura* explains the *sfeik-sfeika* to be that there is a doubt as to when the item was prepared and there is an additional doubt as to whether the second day of Yom Tov is actually a holiday.

Alternative Positions — The *Mishna Berura* first writes that in such a case we need not be stringent and consider the object to be a *davar she'yesh lo matirin* (an item which is currently forbidden, but will eventually become permitted), which would require the person to wait until after the two days of Yom Tov are finished. The *Mishna Berura* notes, however, that there are those who disagree and do not consider the second day of Yom Tov to be a doubtful holiday, since the Sages decreed it to be a full holiday based on an established custom. Therefore, in this case there would be only one doubt,

---

140 *Mishna Berura* 58:19.
141 *Shulhan Arukh, Orah Hayyim* 497:4.

namely when the object was prepared. As such, the object should be prohibited until after the two days of Yom Tov are finished because it is considered to be a *davar she'yesh lo matirin*.[142]

The *Mishna Berura*'s Position — The *Mishna Berura* concludes that one should be stringent except in a situation of great loss.[143]

Halakhic Principles — 2, 5

54.

Shulhan Arukh — On the day before Passover after the sixth hour of the day, if a person buys something in exchange for their *hametz*, the thing bought is permissible, since *hametz* does not forbid what is exchanged for it.[144]

Alternative Positions — The *Mishna Berura* writes that Rabbi Karo's ruling is not a unanimous opinion; many great *poskim* hold that, though others may derive benefit from it, the Sages penalized the one who made the exchange since it entails a transgression.

The *Mishna Berura*'s Position — The *Mishna Berura* suggests that one should be stringent in accordance with these *poskim* unless there would be a great loss.[145] In the *Biur Halakha*, the *Mishna Berura* cautions that the entire discussion above deals only with a situation where the person has already received the object of exchange. If he did not yet receive it, he should not, since accepting the object entails a transgression. Even if the Gentile had already acquired the *hametz* and all that is left is for the Gentile to give the Jew the object of exchange, *ab initio* the Jew may not receive it.[146]

Halakhic Principles — 2, 5

55.

Shulhan Arukh — *Hametz* on Passover is forbidden even when it is only part of a mixture, whether the mixture is of the same type of

---

142 See *Sha'ar HaTziyun* 497:17-19.
143 *Mishna Berura* 497:11.
144 *Shulhan Arukh, Orah Hayyim* 443:3.
145 *Mishna Berura* 443:16.
146 *Biur Halakha* 443: s.v. *eino tofes*.

food or of different types. Normally forbidden food can be nullified depending on the proportions of the mixture. On Passover, however, *hametz* is forbidden in any amount and for any benefit.

Rema — The entire mixture must be burnt, and it is not enough to redeem the value of the *hametz* and sell the mixture.[147]

Discussion — The *Mishna Berura* writes that the *Rema* means to exclude the ruling of those *poskim* that hold that it is sufficient to throw the monetary value of the *hametz* into the sea and then sell or give the forbidden mixture to a Gentile. The *Mishna Berura* notes, however, that the *Aharonim* write that in a situation of very great loss, one need not burn the entire mixture. Rather he may sell it to a Gentile for less than the value of the *hametz*; since he does not receive money for it, he is thus not benefitting from the prohibited substance.[148] This position is, in fact, consistent with Rabbi Karo's ruling regarding the situation where one finds wheat in his cooked chicken on Passover, yet the *Rema* obligates him to burn everything in this case as well.[149]

The *Mishna Berura*'s Position — In the *Sha'ar HaTziyun*, the *Mishna Berura* writes that one may accept this leniency in the case of a very great loss, at least according to the *Hok Yaakov*, who says that he who relies on this will not lose out, though he remarks that from the other *Aharonim* this position does not seem to be correct.[150]

Halakhic Principles — 2, 8

56.

Shulhan Arukh — It is permitted for a Jew to sell something to a Gentile and have him pick it up from his house close to dark before Shabbat, as long as he leaves the house before Shabbat starts.

Rema — There are those who permit the Gentile to remove the object on Shabbat if, on the day before, the Jew designated a place from

---

147 *Shulhan Arukh, Orah Hayyim* 447:1.
148 *Mishna Berura* 447:3.
149 *Shulhan Arukh, Orah Hayyim* 467:10.
150 *Sha'ar HaTziyun* 447:1.

which the Gentile can remove the object, yet one should be stringent.[151]

The *Mishna Berura*'s Position — The *Mishna Berura* notes that the *Aharonim* agree that the essential ruling is that one should be stringent; therefore, he concludes that one may not follow the lenient opinion unless it will cause loss or there is a great need.[152]

Halakhic Principles — 2, 5

57.

Shulhan Arukh — A person should endeavor to pray in the synagogue with the community. If, however, he is unable to go to the synagogue due to an external compulsion, he should intend to pray at the same time as the community.[153]

The *Mishna Berura*'s Position — The *Mishna Berura* writes regarding what it means to be unable to pray with the community due to financial reasons as follows: if it will cause him financial loss, he may pray alone; if, on the other hand, it will only cause him to forgo profit, he is not exempt from praying with the community, since there is a difference between losing what one has and not getting what one thinks he can.[154] In the *Sha'ar HaTziyun*, the *Mishna Berura* gives for one meaning of "a great need" a time when there is the desire to remove bodily pain or discomfort.[155] Though this definition comes from another context, it sheds light onto what the *Mishna Berura* thinks the parameters may be for something to constitute being a "great need" or a reason to allow leniency.

Halakhic Principles — 2

58.

Rashal — Regarding a matter of potential great loss or of great need, rabbinic decrees are permitted during *ben-ha'shmashot* (the time

---

151 *Shulhan Arukh, Orah Hayyim* 252:1.
152 *Mishna Berura* 252:11.
153 *Shulhan Arukh, Orah Hayyim* 90:9.
154 *Mishna Berura* 90:29.
155 *Sha'ar HaTziyun* 307:24.

between sunset and nightfall) on Shabbat, particularly the decree prohibiting telling a Gentile to do something for a Jew.[156]

The *Mishna Berura*'s Position — In the *Sha'ar HaTziyun*, the *Mishna Berura* adds that many *Aharonim* cite the *Rashal* as the law.[157]

Halakhic Principles — 2

59.

Shulhan Arukh — If there is a doubt as to whether something is considered *nolad* on a Yom Tov which is preceded by a weekday, it is prohibited.[158]

Alternative Positions — The *Mishna Berura* comments that if the object is mixed with other things, there are *poskim* who hold that it cannot be nullified in the mixture since it is a *davar she'yesh lo matirin*. On the other hand, there are *Aharonim* who disagree and hold that since it is only a rabbinic prohibition, one can be lenient and consider the object nullified even if in a mixture of one in two.

The *Mishna Berura*'s Position — The *Mishna Berura* suggests that in a situation of loss one may rely on the lenient opinion.[159] In the *Sha'ar HaTziyun*, the *Mishna Berura* writes that this would not be the case if it were a Yom Tov which was after a Shabbat, since there would be a doubt with respect to a Torah prohibition; therefore, one cannot be lenient regarding a mixture.[160]

Halakhic Principles — 2, 5

60.

Shulhan Arukh — One cannot sit a hen on her eggs to hatch chicks on *Hol HaMoed*, yet if he placed the hen on her chicks before *Hol HaMoed* and she escaped, she may be returned to her chicks within three days of her escape.[161]

---

156 *Mishna Berura* 261:16.
157 *Sha'ar HaTziyun* 342:5.
158 *Shulhan Arukh, Orah Hayyim* 513:2.
159 *Mishna Berura* 513:5.
160 *Sha'ar HaTziyun* 513:8.
161 *Shulhan Arukh, Orah Hayyim* 536:4.

Discussion — The *Mishna Berura* writes that from the general wording of Rabbi Karo, one can infer that in the case where three days had not passed since the hen sat on the eggs, and the eggs did not completely ruin and could still be sold at a lower price, it would still be permitted to return the hen, since there would be in any case a small loss if she were not returned. However, according to the *Rosh* and the *Tur*, one can only be lenient if the prohibition to do work on *Hol HaMoed* is a rabbinic decree. If one considers the prohibition to be a Torah law, one cannot be lenient in returning the hen unless she had already sat on the eggs for three days, whereby they would no longer be fit to eat since they would have begun to germinate. Then it would be a matter of loss if the hen was not returned.

The *Mishna Berura*'s Position — Since many of the *Rishonim* consider the prohibition of work on *Hol HaMoed* to be a Torah law, the *Mishna Berura* writes that one cannot be lenient except when there is a potential loss of many eggs. The case would then fit the description of what the rabbis permitted on *Hol HaMoed* despite the fact that work in general is prohibited by Torah law.[162]

Halakhic Principles — 2, 5, 8

61.

Rema — If a Hanukah candle becomes mixed with other candles, it is prohibited to use any candle of the mixture, since the candles are counted objects.[163]

Discussion — Hanukah candles cannot be used for any other purpose. Also, mixtures of objects which are usually counted individually are not considered to be classical mixtures. Each item retains its individual status; therefore, a prohibited object cannot be nullified.

Alternative Position — The *Rashal* rules that the Hanukah candle would be nullified in a mixture of one in two.[164] In the *Sha'ar*

---

162 *Mishna Berura* 536:10.
163 *Shulhan Arukh, Orah Hayyim* 673:1.
164 *Mishna Berura* 673:22.

HaTziyun, the *Mishna Berura* writes that the *Magen Avraham* cites the *Rashal* but does not make a decision regarding whom to follow. **The *Mishna Berura*'s Position** — From the *Magen Avraham*'s omission of a verdict, the *Mishna Berura* infers that in a situation of great loss it is possible to be lenient, since it regards a rabbinic decree.[165]

Halakhic Principles — 2, 8

62.

Shulhan Arukh — If one goes to guard his fruit on Shabbat, he is permitted to traverse through water, but he may not return by traversing through water.[166]

Discussion — The *Mishna Berura* explains that guarding one's money is a small *mitzvah*; therefore, it is permitted. On the other hand, the rabbis did not permit his return since it would not consist of a *mitzvah*.[167]

The *Mishna Berura*'s Position — In the *Sha'ar HaTziyun*, the *Mishna Berura* cites the *Tosafot Yeshanim*, who wrote that due to a potential loss of money, the Sages did not prohibit traversing through water as a protective decree to prevent a person from potentially wringing out his garments.[168]

Halakhic Principles — 2, 8

63.

Shulhan Arukh — If a fire breaks out on Shabbat, a Jew may say in front of a Gentile that anyone who extinguishes the fire will not lose out; he may even call a Gentile to come, even though it is certain that he will extinguish the fire.[169]

The *Mishna Berura*'s Position — The *Mishna Berura* writes that the Jew may not tell the Gentile directly to extinguish the fire.[170]

---

165 *Sha'ar HaTziyun* 673:25.
166 *Shulhan Arukh, Orah Hayyim* 301:6.
167 *Mishna Berura* 301:14.
168 *Sha'ar HaTziyun* 301:14.
169 *Shulhan Arukh, Orah Hayyim* 334:26.
170 *Mishna Berura* 334:68.

The *Sha'ar HaTziyun* explains that even according to the opinion that a *melakha she'eina tzrikha l'gufa* (prohibited work that is not done for the purpose of the work's main intention) is a rabbinic prohibition, and it is established that rabbinic prohibitions are permitted via a Gentile's performance in a situation of great loss, in this situation there are other reasons to be stringent.[171]

Halakhic Principles — 2

64.

Shulhan Arukh — One should not make an *Eruv Tehumin* except if one needs it to perform a *mitzvah*.[172]

Discussion — An *Eruv Tehumin* (mixed borders) enables a Jew to travel farther than is normally allowed on Shabbat or on a holiday.

Alternative Position — The *Mishna Berura* notes that there is a disagreement among the *poskim* as to whether there is a difference between making an *Eruv* with bread or through acquiring a place by sitting there when Shabbat begins. Some hold that one can make a *Eruv* through sitting in a place at the onset of Shabbat even for a permitted matter and not only for the purpose of later performing a *mitzvah*, and some hold that one can only make an *Eruv* for the purpose of later performing a *mitzvah*, regardless of how it is made.

The *Mishna Berura*'s Position — The *Mishna Berura* writes that in a situation of need one can be lenient in accordance with the first opinion.[173] In the *Sha'ar HaTziyun*, however, it restricts its leniency to the situation of great need, and also justifies the leniency by explaining that it is a case of a rabbinic decree.[174]

Halakhic Principles — 2

65.

Shulhan Arukh — If one has a doubt that there is urine in the litter, one is still permitted to recite the *Shema*, since the Torah

---

171 *Sha'ar HaTziyun* 334:57.
172 *Shulhan Arukh, Orah Hayyim* 415:1.
173 *Mishna Berura* 415:1.
174 *Sha'ar HaTziyun* 415:3.

only prohibits a person to recite the *Shema* in front of a stream of urine; after it has formed a puddle it is only prohibited by rabbinic decree.[175]

The *Mishna Berura*'s Position — The *Mishna Berura* adds that if one knows that there is urine yet is in doubt if a *revi'it* (a liquid measure equal to about 3oz) of water has been poured on it, the *Hayye Adam* writes that since there is a presumption of its presence, one must be stringent even in the case of a rabbinic prohibition. Nevertheless, in a time of difficulty, such as when one would lose the chance to recite the *Shema* or prayer, one can rely on the *poskim* even in this case and be lenient since it is a matter of rabbinic decree. However, regarding a situation in which one knows that there was feces in the house but has a doubt as to whether it was removed, it seems that it would be prohibited to recite the *Shema* or to pray until one clarifies the situation, since it is a matter of Torah law.[176]

Halakhic Principles — 2, 5

66.

Shulhan Arukh — If a Gentile bakes bread in a Jew's oven on Shabbat against the Jew's will, and gives him some bread as payment for this use, the Jew is prohibited to benefit from it.[177]

The *Mishna Berura*'s Position — The *Mishna Berura* cites the *Bach*, who writes that if the Gentile uses the oven on other days as well, even if it is not against the Jew's will, the Jew may receive payment for the use of the oven on Shabbat.[178] The reason is that even though he transgressed in allowing the Gentile to use the oven on Shabbat, *ex post facto* the rabbis did not prohibit one to benefit from the

---

175 *Shulhan Arukh, Orah Hayyim* 76:7.
176 *Mishna Berura* 76:25.
177 *Shulhan Arukh, Orah Hayyim* 245:6.
178 The point that the Gentile uses the oven on other days as well is necessary to allow the Jew to rely on the leniency of *havla'ah*, whereby it is permitted to receive a single lump sum as compensation for use that was both during the week and on Shabbat. *Havla'ah* means that the payment for use on Shabbat is mixed in with the payment for use on a weekday.

payment since the prohibition was only due to *Ma'arit Ayin* (giving the appearance that something impermissible is permitted).[179]
Halakhic Principles — 2, 6

67.

Shulhan Arukh — If a person takes a cup of beer or water and makes the blessing for wine, yet *tokh k'dei dibbur* (a break of less time than it takes to say *"shalom alecha rebbi"*) he remembers his mistake and says the end of the proper blessing, he has fulfilled his obligation.[180]

The *Mishna Berura*'s Position — The *Mishna Berura* writes that with respect to being lenient *tokh k'dei dibbur*, this only applies to blessings that are rabbinically decreed. If one makes a similar mistake regarding blessings which one is obligated to say by Torah law, such as *Birkat HaMazon*, he must go back and recite the blessing properly.[181]
Halakhic Principles — 5, 8

Combining Different Aspects of Conflicting Views into One Performance

When the *Shulhan Arukh* rules leniently on a particular matter, yet other *poskim* rule stringently, the *Mishna Berura* will attempt to incorporate the more stringent position into the ruling of the *Shulhan Arukh*. If incorporation of the more stringent position would result in a potential transgression or contradiction according to the plain understanding of the ruling of the *Shulhan Arukh*, the *Mishna Berura* will incorporate only those aspects of the more stringent position which can be included without conflict. The justification for only partially incorporating a decision against the claim that such an approach leads to arbitrariness and inconsistency is that the approach takes into account the idea that each ruling may be dealing with

---

179 *Mishna Berura* 245:23.
180 *Shulhan Arukh, Orah Hayyim* 209:2.
181 *Mishna Berura* 209:6.

numerous actions or situations, all with varying levels of obligation. Therefore, the *Mishna Berura* can incorporate certain aspects of a ruling and not others, while still being able to provide a coherent position.

When the *Mishna Berura* is faced with two compelling and contradictory positions on one issue, the first being the ruling of the *Shulhan Arukh* and the second being a more stringent alternative view, the objective of the *Mishna Berura* is to incorporate the more stringent view in a manner that does not negate the ruling of the *Shulhan Arukh* nor make the new, compromise position incoherent. When the *Shulhan Arukh* or the *Rema* rules leniently, yet a person thinks that he may be stringent upon himself, if the self-imposed stringency does not take into consideration that the *Shulhan Arukh*'s or *Rema*'s ruling is meant to avoid an unforeseen transgression (i.e., to avoid a *humra ha'mevia liydei kula*), the *Mishna Berura* explicitly prohibits him from acting stringently.

68.

Shulhan Arukh — If one interrupts his recitation of *Hallel*, even for the amount of time it would take to complete it, he need not start again from the beginning.[182]

Stringent Alternative Ruling — The *Mishna Berura* cites the *Levush* and the *Bach*, who rule stringently and demand that the person return to the beginning.

Discussion — If one were to interrupt his saying the *Shema* for the amount of time that it would take to complete it, even if the interruption was due to forces out of his control, he would have to return to the beginning. Nevertheless, because the recitation of *Hallel* is only rabbinically mandated, Rabbi Karo, in the *Shulhan Arukh*, rules that one need not return to the beginning. Rather, he can continue where he left off. According to the position which asserts that one must return to the beginning, the part of *Hallel* that has already been said is considered as naught. Therefore, before he

---

182 *Shulhan Arukh, Orah Hayyim* 422:5.

begins over again, he should also repeat the blessing related to saying *Hallel*. According to Rabbi Karo, however, repeating the blessing would entail the transgression of saying God's name in vain through a superfluous blessing.

Issue — How can the *Mishna Berura* incorporate the position which demands repeating the *Hallel* without nullifying the ruling of the *Shulhan Arukh* or leading one to transgression according to the *Shulhan Arukh*?

The *Mishna Berura*'s Position — It is good to return to the beginning, yet one should not repeat the blessing.[183]

Discussion — The objective of the *Mishna Berura* is to incorporate the more stringent position into the ruling of the *Shulhan Arukh*. By saying that it is good to return to the beginning, it is not saying that it is required. Therefore, it does not contradict the *Shulhan Arukh*. Also, the recitation of the introductory blessing does not affect the efficacy of fulfilling one's obligation to recite the *Hallel*. Therefore, by recommending that one not repeat the blessing, it avoids leading a person to infer that it disagrees with the *Shulhan Arukh*, while, at the same time, does not deny the benefit of following the more stringent opinion. Due to the level of obligation related to the recitation of the introductory blessing, the *Mishna Berura* is able to incorporate only part of the stringent position without causing incoherence or contradiction within the suggested performance.

Halakhic Principles — 3, 5

69.

Shulhan Arukh — A groom, his best men, and all the members of the wedding party are exempt from sitting in a *Sukkah* for the seven days after the wedding.[184]

Stringent Alternative Ruling — The *Mishna Berura* cites the *Rosh* and others who rule stringently and obligate them to sit in a *Sukkah*.

---

183 *Mishna Berura* 422:25.
184 *Shulhan Arukh, Orah Hayyim* 640:6.

Discussion — The *Shulhan Arukh* relies on the concept that if one is engaged in a commandment, he is exempt from fulfilling other potential commandments. Because there is a commandment to rejoice with a groom, the groom, his best men, and all the members of the wedding party would be exempt from sitting in a *Sukkah*. Those *poskim* who rule stringently argue that the concept does not apply in this case, since it is possible to perform both commandments simultaneously. Rejoicing can occur inside a *Sukkah*. If the commandment to sit in a *Sukkah* still applies, they would also recite the blessing related to sitting in a *Sukkah*.

Issue — How can the *Mishna Berura* incorporate the stringent position without nullifying the ruling of the *Shulhan Arukh*, since advising the groom to sit in the *Sukkah* and say the blessing would presume that he has an obligation?

The *Mishna Berura*'s Position — It is appropriate that the groom be stringent upon himself to sit in a *Sukkah*, yet he should not recite the blessing for sitting in it. The same applies to the best men when they are with the groom; when they are not with him they are obligated to sit in a *Sukkah* and recite the blessing.[185]

Discussion — The objective of the *Mishna Berura* is to incorporate the more stringent position into the ruling of the *Shulhan Arukh*. Because the recitation of the introductory blessing does not affect the efficacy of fulfilling one's obligation to sit in the *Sukkah*, by not requiring the groom to say the blessing, even while advising that it is appropriate for him to be stringent upon himself, the *Mishna Berura* does not openly contradict the ruling of the *Shulhan Arukh*. Also, the *Mishna Berura*'s suggestion fits within the wording of the *Shulhan Arukh*, since one may still perform a commandment from which he is temporarily exempt. Due to the level of obligation related to the recitation of the introductory blessing, the *Mishna Berura* is able to incorporate only part of the stringent position without causing incoherence or contradiction within the suggested performance.

Halakhic Principles — 3, 5

---

185 *Mishna Berura* 640:33.

70.

Shulhan Arukh — A person with a stomach illness is exempt from donning phylacteries.

Rema — He is exempt even if he is not in pain, yet for other illnesses his pain must cause him mental disturbance to exempt him.[186]

Discussion — The *Shulhan Arukh* exempts a person with a stomach illness from donning phylacteries for fear that he may soil himself or break wind while wearing them, which one is prohibited to do. A person, however, may think that he is healthier than he actually is and insist on donning phylacteries, since the *Shulhan Arukh* only exempts him and does not prohibit him from wearing them.

Issue — How can the *Mishna Berura* reinforce the concern which underlies the ruling of the *Shulhan Arukh* without seeming to contradict it?

The *Mishna Berura*'s Position — One who has a stomach illness, even if he can still go to the markets, is nevertheless still exempt; and he may not be stringent upon himself, except during the time of reciting the *Shema* and during prayer, if he knows that he can keep from soiling himself.[187] For one with a different illness, on the other hand, if he wants to be stringent, he may be so.[188]

Discussion — The *Mishna Berura* does not outright prohibit a person from donning phylacteries since that would contradict the *Shulhan Arukh*; rather, he prohibits a person from being stringent upon himself to not accept the exemption. Though it may seem to be a matter of semantics, the *Mishna Berura* maintains the priority of adhering to the language of the *Shulhan Arukh*. Though the *Mishna Berura* uses similar wording (*assur lo l'hahmir al atzmo*) to the *Magen Avraham* (*assur l'hahmir al atzmo*), our interpretation of it is different in light of the *Mishna Berura*'s later comment on the ruling of the *Rema*. In its comment regarding the *Rema*'s exemption when suffering from other types of illness, the *Mishna Berura* writes that if a person wants to be stringent on himself, he is

---

186 *Shulhan Arukh, Orah Hayyim* 38:1.
187 *Mishna Berura* 38:4.
188 *Mishna Berura* 38:5.

permitted. The *Magen Avraham* makes no such comment. Also, due to the similarity of statements in the *Mishna Berura*, it is reasonable to interpret them in light of each other. Moreover, in both cases the emphasis is on the exemption itself and not on the legitimacy of the action. Also, there is a difference between the *Mishna Berura* writing *assur l'hahmir al atzmo* and *assur l'hahmir*.[189] The latter means that the seemingly more stringent action is prohibited; the former phrase means that the person is prohibited to be stringent and act when exempt.

Halakhic Principles — 2

71.

Shulhan Arukh — One who is watching a corpse, even if it is not that of a deceased relative, is exempt from all other commandments.[190]

Discussion — Though the *Shulhan Arukh* exempts a person watching a corpse from all other commandments, the person may think that he can watch the corpse and still recite the *Shema* or pray without a problem arising. This assumption is supported by the position of the *Be'er Heitiv*, who comments that if a person can perform both commands he is not only permitted but obligated to perform them both.[191] However, the *Shulhan Arukh* rejects that position based upon the principle that one who is engaged in a commandment is exempt from others, and because of the gravity of the respect due to watching a corpse.

Issue — How can the *Mishna Berura* reinforce the concern which underlies the ruling of the *Shulhan Arukh* without seeming to contradict it?

The *Mishna Berura*'s Position — One is not allowed to be stringent upon himself and perform other commandments, since a person engaged in the performance of one command is exempt from performing others.[192]

---

189 *Mishna Berura* 63:5.
190 *Shulhan Arukh, Orah Hayyim* 71:3.
191 *Be'er Heitiv* 71:7.
192 *Mishna Berura* 71:12.

Discussion — The *Mishna Berura* does not outright prohibit a person from performing other commandments, since that would contradict the *Shulhan Arukh*; rather, he prohibits a person from being stringent upon himself to not accept the exemption. Though it may seem to be a matter of semantics, the *Mishna Berura* maintains the priority of adhering to the language of the *Shulhan Arukh*.

Halakhic Principles — 2

72.

Rema — Pregnant and nursing women who would be in great pain should not fast during any of the minor fasts besides *Tisha b'Av*. Even if they would not be in pain, they are not actually obligated to fast, yet they have the custom to be stringent upon themselves to do so.[193]

Discussion — The *Rema*'s ruling is ambiguous when it comes to people who are sick yet not dangerously ill, as well as pregnant and nursing women who are weak yet would not be in great pain if they fasted. These people may assume that they must be stringent upon themselves and fast, even though it may be detrimental to their health to do so. Moreover, putting one's health at risk is a transgression of Jewish law.

The *Mishna Berura*'s Position — A person who is sick, even if not dangerously ill, certainly must not fast and is forbidden to be stringent upon himself to do so.[194] The *Mishna Berura* also qualifies the *Rema*'s statement by saying that it seems that pregnant and nursing women should not be stringent if they are weak.[195]

Discussion — The *Mishna Berura* expands and clarifies the *Rema*'s statement to include those people who may incorrectly infer that they should fast and thereby transgress Jewish law by endangering their health.[196]

Halakhic Principles — 2, 8

---

193 *Shulhan Arukh, Orah Hayyim* 550:1.

194 *Mishna Berura* 550:4.

195 *Mishna Berura* 550:5.

196 In the *Sha'ar HaTziyun* 550:2, the *Mishna Berura* notes that in the beginning of a pregnancy, the fetus is still vulnerable and any suffering may endanger it as well as the mother; therefore, the one who is lenient will be rewarded without a doubt.

Relationship between Kabbala[197] and Talmud

The rulings of the Talmud and *poskim* take precedence over the Kabbalistic literature, and avoiding potential transgression overrides a Kabbalistic instruction. In order to negotiate between conflicting positions in the Talmud and *poskim* and the Kabbalistic literature, the *Mishna Berura* applies the technique of suggesting that one follows different positions depending on the circumstances. The *Mishna Berura* also reinterprets Kabbalistic texts in order to mitigate opposition. When there is a suggestion among the Kabbalistic sources which does not conflict with the Talmud or *poskim*, the *Mishna Berura* often recommends that one act in accordance with it. The *Mishna Berura*'s method to respond to the challenges that arise in trying to incorporate the Kabbala literature and the Talmud and *poskim* into one coherent halakhic system is, in truth, not innovative. When it spells out its approach explicitly, it attributes the approach to the *Knesset HaGedola*.

Explicit Guideline — When the Kabbala literature disagrees with the Talmud and *poskim*, the law is according to the Talmud and *poskim*. However, if the masters of the Kabbala literature are stringent, one may be stringent as well. If the matter regards something that is not mentioned in the Talmud and *poskim*, yet is mentioned in Kabbala, we cannot force it upon the people to become a practice. A directive from Kabbala literature which is not refuted by the Talmud and halakhic decisors may become law. Also, where the *poskim* disagree, the Kabbala literature decides the matter.[198]

---

197 Kabbala is the school of thought concerned with Jewish mysticism. It seeks to explain the nature of the universe and the human being, knowledge of which allows one to attain spiritual realization. While kabbalistic teachings are meant to give inner meaning of both the Bible and traditional rabbinic literature, as well as to explain the significance of Jewish practices, it is not considered as part of the halakhic corpus.

198 The *Mishna Berura*'s method to respond to the challenges that arise in trying to incorporate the Kabbala literature and the Talmud and *poskim* into one coherent halakhic system is, in truth, not innovative. When he spells out his approach explicitly, he attributes it to the *Knesset HaGedola*. See *Mishna Berura* 25:42.

73.

Shulhan Arukh — In the morning, a person should wash his hands and recite the blessing *al netilat yadaim*.[199]

Alternative Positions — The *Mishna Berura* cites the *Shlah*, a sixteenth century Kabbalist, who cautions that as soon as one awakens he must wash his hands while still lying down, and must not walk four cubits without washing his hands. The *Mishna Berura* continues by referring to the *Zohar*, the primary work within the Kabbala literature, which endorses this practice with a threat of great punishment if one does not wash his hands immediately, since the person continues to keep a spirit of impurity (*ruah ha'tumah*) on his hands.

The *Mishna Berura*'s Position — Despite the grave language of the Kabbalistic texts, the *Mishna Berura* writes, "Nevertheless, Heaven forfend that one should transgress any prohibition out of fear of not having his hands washed," such as withholding oneself from going to the bathroom or in taking another person's water without permission."[200] In the *Sha'ar HaTziyun*, he writes that it is obvious and thus needs no textual justification that one should not look to account for the warnings in the Kabbalistic literature if doing so may possibly lead to committing a sin.[201] He also writes that if one awakens and does not have enough water to wash his hands properly, he should not abstain from learning Torah. Rather, he should clean his hands in any way he can, make the requisite blessings, and study, as ruled by the Talmud and *poskim*.[202]

Halakhic Principles — 2, 9

74.

Shulhan Arukh — One who is careful about wearing a *tallit-kattan*[203] should put it on in the morning, don his phylacteries at home, and

---

199 *Shulhan Arukh, Orah Hayyim* 4:1.
200 *Mishna Berura* 1:2.
201 *Sha'ar HaTziyun* 1:3.
202 *Mishna Berura* 1:2.
203 The *tallit-katan* (small *tallit*) is a fringed undergarment worn by Jewish males that has special twined and knotted fringes known as *tzitzit* attached to its four corners.

then should walk to the synagogue, where he should enwrap himself in his *tallit-gadol*.[204]

Rema — The universal custom is to enwrap oneself in his *tallit-gadol*, then don phylacteries, and then walk to the synagogue.[205]

Discussion — The *Mishna Berura* remarks that the source of both Rabbi Karo's and the *Rema*'s ruling is the *Zohar*, and refers its readers to the source, saying that it is a substantial matter.

The *Mishna Berura*'s Position — Despite the Kabbalistic source of the ruling, the *Mishna Berura* nevertheless qualifies the directive in order to prevent potential transgression. It writes that if a person knows that he will walk through dirty streets or through an area populated by Gentiles, and cannot cover his phylacteries during the walk, he should instead don them in the courtyard of the synagogue.[206] Moreover, the same also applies to enwrapping oneself in his *tallit-gadol*.[207]

Discussion — The reason for the *Mishna Berura*'s qualification is a statement in the Talmud that one may not wear phylacteries in baths or in a privy, i.e., places of filth.[208] Therefore, the potential of passing filth when walking through dirty streets overrides the *Zohar*'s injunction. Also, the *Mishna Berura*'s proviso with respect to an area populated by Gentiles reflects the ruling of the *Rema* regarding going barefoot during *Tisha b'Av*.[209]

Halakhic Principles — 4, 9

75.

Shulhan Arukh — *Tahanun* should be said while sitting.[210]

Alternative Position — *Rivash* permits *Tahanun* to be said while standing.

---

204 The *tallit-gadol* (big *tallit*) is the traditional Jewish prayer shawl.
205 *Shulhan Arukh, Orah Hayyim* 25:2.
206 *Mishna Berura* 25:8.
207 *Mishna Berura* 25:10.
208 BT *Berakhot* 23a.
209 *Shulhan Arukh, Orah Hayyim* 554:17. The ninth of *Av* is a day of mourning for the destruction of the Temple in Jerusalem.
210 *Shulhan Arukh, Orah Hayyim* 131:2.

Discussion — *Tahanun*, meaning "supplication," is a prayer that is recited following the weekday prayer in the morning and in the afternoon.

The *Mishna Berura*'s Position — The *Mishna Berura* remarks that the position of the *Shulhan Arukh* is based on Kabbalistic reasons; therefore, in a time of need one may rely on the *Rivash*, who permits *Tahanun* to be said while standing.[211]

Halakhic Principles — 2, 9

76.

Shulhan Arukh — While praying, a person must bend his head slightly so that his eyes are pointing downward.[212]

Discussion — The *Zohar* states that while praying, a person must cover his head and eyes so as not to look upon the Divine Presence, and that one whose eyes are open will encounter the Angel of Death before his time.[213]

The *Mishna Berura*'s Position — Regarding the comment from the Zohar, the *Mishna Berura* writes that one may keep his eyes open to be able to read from the prayer book. Only those who raise their head and eyes upwards toward the ceiling while praying are chastised.[214] In the *Biur Halakha*, the *Mishna Berura* acknowledges that according to the Talmud, there is no prohibition of keeping one's eyes open as long as they point downwards, contrary to the *Zohar*.

Discussion — In order to mitigate the opposition between its ruling and the *Zohar*, the *Mishna Berura* gives the explanation of the *Hayye Adam*, who writes that the essential prohibition in the *Zohar* is of looking around while praying, but that having one's eyes pointed downwards, albeit open, is permissible. Nevertheless, the *Mishna Berura* concludes that it is proper, *ab initio*, to keep one's eyes closed,

---

211 *Mishna Berura* 131:10.
212 *Shulhan Arukh, Orah Hayyim* 95:2.
213 *Mishna Berura* 91:6.
214 *Mishna Berura* 95:5.

yet changes the reason from not gazing upon the Divine Presence to not looking around while praying.[215]
Halakhic Principles — 1, 5, 9

77.

Shulhan Arukh — One may not pray solely in his heart; he must hear his own whispering.[216]

Alternative Positions — The *Mishna Berura* writes that according to some, a person should take into account the words of the *Zohar*, that even *ab initio* he should not hear anything.[217] In the *Biur Halakha*, it mentions that the *Magen Avraham* and the *Nefesh HaHayyim* rule that one who prays solely in his heart has not fulfilled his obligation, even *ex post facto*.[218] In order to find a bridge between the position of the *Shulhan Arukh* and that of the *Zohar*, it cites the *Gra*, who states that the intention of the *Zohar* is actually like that of the *Shulhan Arukh*.

The *Mishna Berura*'s Position — The *Mishna Berura* concludes by saying that, *ab initio*, it is better for a person to hear himself praying, yet *ex post facto*, if he only moves his lips he has fulfilled his obligation according to everyone.[219]
Halakhic Principles — 2, 5, 9

78.

Shulhan Arukh — When performing *Hagba*, the person should show the writing of the Sefer Torah to the people both to the right and to the left, since it is a *mitzvah* for everyone to see the writing.[220]

Discussion — After the Torah reading, before the Torah is returned to the holy ark (*Aron Kodesh*), the Torah is lifted (*Hagba*) and a prayer is sung. As the Torah is raised, it is customary for people in the congregation to raise their fingers up toward the Torah just as the words "This is the Torah that God gave to Moses" are being recited.

---

215 *Biur Halakha* 95: s.v. *tzarikh.*
216 *Shulhan Arukh, Orah Hayyim* 101:2.
217 *Mishna Berura* 101:5.
218 *Biur Halakha* 101: s.v. *b'libo.*
219 *Mishna Berura* 101:5.
220 *Shulhan Arukh, Orah Hayyim* 134:2.

The *Mishna Berura*'s Position — Basing his interpretation on the writings of the Kabbalists, the *Mishna Berura* writes that it is good to get close enough to the Sefer Torah during *Hagba* so that one is able to read the letters, and that doing so brings a great light to the person.[221]

Halakhic Principles — 9

79.

The *Mishna Berura*'s Position — As a way to encourage the practice of staying awake throughout the night of the holiday of *Shavuot* to study Torah, the *Mishna Berura* cites the *Zohar*, which states that this was a practice of the first *Hasidim*, as well as the *Ari*, who states that whoever does not sleep and studies Torah is assured to have his sleep repaid and no injury come to him.[222]

Halakhic Principles — 9

80.

Rema — During the Ten Days of Repentance,[223] each person should investigate his actions and repent.[224]

The *Mishna Berura*'s Position — The *Mishna Berura* adds that during these days one should act in accordance with the *Zohar*, to repent before going to bed at night and to bemoan his sins and investigate his actions.[225]

Halakhic Principles — 9

81.

Shulhan Arukh — When three people eat together, they are obligated to form a *zimun*. One person should say, "Let us bless He whose [food] we have eaten." The others should respond, "Blessed is He of

---

221 *Mishna Berura* 134:11.

222 *Mishna Berura* 494:1.

223 The Ten Days of Repentance are the first ten days of the Hebrew month of *Tishrei*, beginning with the holiday of *Rosh Hashanah* and ending with the conclusion of *Yom Kippur*.

224 *Shulhan Arukh, Orah Hayyim* 603:1.

225 *Mishna Berura* 603:2.

Whose [food] we have eaten and through Whose goodness we live." The first person should then repeat their words and begin the *Birkat HaMazon*.[226]

Discussion — A *zimun* is a formal invitation to say *Birkat HaMazon* after a meal.

The *Mishna Berura*'s Position — The *Mishna Berura* writes that the *Zohar* warns that we should say before reciting the *zimun*, "Give us a cup and let us bless," or "Come, let us bless," as a verbal introductory summons to arouse holiness.[227]

Halakhic Principles — 9

Interpret in a Manner that Seeks to Resolve Potential Contradiction

In a situation where a ruling in the *Shulhan Arukh* is ambiguous, the *Mishna Berura* will provide an interpretation that mitigates disagreement among the various interpretative positions in order to achieve the greatest level of juridical consolidation. The *Mishna Berura* also seeks to clarify ambiguity in a situation where Rabbi Karo gives a general ruling, yet his language raises doubt as to its universality. It also reinterprets a law that seems to contradict the general methodology of the legislator. By claiming that two seemingly opposing rulings do not contradict each other but in fact deal with different situations, the *Mishna Berura* is able to achieve coherence even when he must maintain seeming inconsistency. When a ruling seems to contradict an accepted halakhic principle, the *Mishna Berura* will interpret the law to apply to a different context so that it does not conflict with the halakhic principle. In order to defend an accepted halakhic principle, the *Mishna Berura* reinterprets the language of a legal position if the plain meaning would present a challenge. This is not limited to Rabbi Karo's wording; the *Mishna Berura* even reinterprets the language of *Aharonim*. It provides alternative explanations for the source of a

---

226 *Shulhan Arukh, Orah Hayyim* 192:1.
227 *Mishna Berura* 192:2.

particular Halakha in order to remove contradictions in the perceived derivation of a law. The *Mishna Berura* provides alternative explanations for a Halakha itself when it seems to contradict the general reasoning behind the legal issue. It does not only interpret the *Shulhan Arukh* in a manner that makes Rabbi Karo's opinion consistent with the general halakhic tradition, it also reinterprets *Rishonim* to accord with it as well. The *Mishna Berura* re-interprets rulings that, on their faces, contradict common practice, in order to demonstrate that the law and the people's way of life have not in fact diverged. When the halakhic tradition contains two distinct yet valid forms of one practice, the *Mishna Berura* attempts to find a practical application which justifies the distinction.

Note: Because this section is meant to demonstrate a method of interpretation, the examples used are a bit involved and therefore may be difficult for those who do not have a deep background in Jewish law.

82.

Shulhan Arukh — A *Kohen* may be called for an *Aliyah* after a *Kohen* only if an Israel is called in between them and if the *Hazan* states regarding the second, "Even though he is a *Kohen*," when calling him to the Torah. The same applies for a Levi who is called after a Levi.[228]

Rema — Therefore, a *Kohen* or a Levi is permitted to be called to recite the *Maftir*. However, there are those who say that they should not receive one of the five *Aliyot* usually designated for Israelites. Additional *Aliyot* that are included after the primary seven, on the other hand, may be assigned either to a *Kohen* or a Levi. The *Rema* concludes that such is the custom in Ashkenaz, yet one may rely on the first opinion in a time of need.[229]

Discussion — Rabbi Karo's statement about calling the second Levi is ambiguous. It may refer to the order in which *Aliyot* may be

---

228 *Shulhan Arukh, Orah Hayyim* 135:10.
229 *Shulhan Arukh, Orah Hayyim* 135:10.

given, or it may relate only to the necessity for the *Hazan* to declare that he is also a Levi. If it is the former, then a Levi can only follow a *Kohen*. If it is the latter, then the second Levi called need not be preceded by a *Kohen*. The interpretation of Rabbi Karo's statement is further complicated by the *Rema*'s comment. If a Levi may be called for the *Maftir* without any further stipulation, it would imply that he need not be preceded by a *Kohen*. Therefore, it would seem that the latter interpretation is correct and thus the required order for *Aliyot*, in which first a *Kohen* is called and then a Levi, followed by an Israelite, is only for the first three *Aliyot* and need not be repeated. However, because the *Maftir* is a separate *Aliyah*, and since the *Rema* writes that neither a *Kohen* nor a Levi should be called for the first seven, it is not necessary that the latter interpretation is the correct one. It could be that there is a distinction between the primary *Aliyot*, which necessitate following the prescribed order, and additional *Aliyot*. Alternatively, one could simply assume that the *Rema* and Rabbi Karo disagree regarding the customary practice.

The *Mishna Berura*'s Position — The *Mishna Berura* explains Rabbi Karo's opinion to be that a second *Kohen* may be called only after the established order of *Kohen*, Levi, and then Israel is completed, yet a second Levi may be called for an *Aliyah* without the need to restart the decreed order.[230] The *Mishna Berura* still advises that one follow the alternative interpretation of Rabbi Karo, and the second opinion in the *Rema*, in order to be more inclusive of divergent opinions in practice. He writes that it is proper to be cautious and defer to the opinion that requires that the *Aliyot* accord to the decreed order, even for additional *Aliyot* that are included after the primary seven.

Discussion — In the *Sha'ar HaTziyun*, the *Mishna Berura* explains why it chose to interpret Rabbi Karo's statement in the way that it did. It notes that its interpretation is in accord with the explanation of the *Elya Rabba* and the *Pri Megadim*. According to the *Levush*,

---

230 *Mishna Berura* 135:31.

the *Magen Avraham*, and the *Gra*, however, Rabbi Karo does not mean to permit a second *Kohen* or a second Levi to be called for an *Aliyah* unless the decreed order for *Aliyot* is repeated. Nevertheless, the *Mishna Berura* states that it refrained from including this interpretation in its main commentary since it seemingly contradicts Rabbi Karo's statement that a Levi can follow a Levi with only an Israelite in between them. Moreover, the latter interpretation would cause Rabbi Karo and the *Rema* to disagree regarding the permission for a Levi to receive *Maftir* without a *Kohen* preceding him. Interpreting Rabbi Karo's statement to accord with the *Rema* regarding the *Maftir* also explains the *Rema*'s use of the word "therefore" when adding that a *Kohen* or Levi may be called for *Maftir*, and allows one to understand the *Rema*'s reference to "there are those who say" to be an alternative opinion which requires the prescribed order. This explanation allows for the greatest consistency between Rabbi Karo and the *Rema*. Nevertheless, the *Mishna Berura* feels the need to state that the potential difficulties with the *Magen Avraham*'s and the *Gra*'s interpretations are nevertheless answerable, albeit with difficulty, so that it may incorporate their opinions into its explanation, thereby presenting a comprehensive and unified legal analysis.[231]

Although its interpretation of Rabbi Karo provides legal consistency, the *Mishna Berura* still advises one to follow the alternative interpretation of Rabbi Karo, and the second opinion in the *Rema*, in order to be more inclusive of divergent opinions in practice. It states that it is proper to be cautious and defer to the opinion that requires that the *Aliyot* accord to the decreed order, even for additional *Aliyot* that are included after the primary seven. Even though this opinion would require that one not call a *Kohen* or a Levi for *Maftir*, it notes that we can be lenient in that particular matter based upon the fact that the world has already accepted the custom to do so.[232]

Halakhic Principles — 4, 6, 8

---

231 *Sha'ar HaTziyun* 135:31.
232 *Mishna Berura* 135:37.

83.

Shulhan Arukh — The legal principle that allows one to carry on Yom Tov for the sake of eating also allows one to carry for unnecessary purposes, and he gives as examples a child, a Lulav, a Sefer Torah, or other utensils. It is forbidden to carry stones and the like.[233] It is prohibited for a Jew to carry anything for the sake of a Gentile on Yom Tov.[234]

Rema — The *Rema* appends to "other utensils," that they must be needed somewhat or that the person fears they may be stolen or lost.

Alternative Positions — The *Rambam* writes that a person may be punished by lashes for performing on Yom Tov any labor for which he is liable on Shabbat if it is not necessary for the preparation of food, except for the transfer of articles from one domain to another and kindling a fire. Since it is permitted to transfer articles for the sake of preparing food, it is permitted to carry even when it is not necessary for the sake of preparing food. Therefore, it is permitted to transfer an infant, a Torah scroll, a key, or the like from one domain to another. Similarly, it is permitted to kindle a fire, even though it is not for the purpose of preparing food.[235] *Rashi*[236] and the *Rif*[237] rule similarly.

Discussion — If one would interpret the Halakha regarding the prohibition to carry for unnecessary purposes in light of the Halakha that prohibits a person to carry for a Gentile, one could assume that the *Rema*'s contribution is meant to explain Rabbi Karo's ruling, since carrying for a Gentile would be carrying without personal need. Yet if such is the case, one must then explain why Rabbi Karo specifically mentions the prohibition to carry stones and the like.

The *Mishna Berura*'s Position — Recognizing the ambiguity of Rabbi Karo's rulings and their relation to the *Rema*'s comment, the

---

233 *Shulhan Arukh, Orah Hayyim* 518:1.
234 *Shulhan Arukh, Orah Hayyim* 518:2.
235 *Hilkhkot Yom Tov* 1:4.
236 Rashi, BT *Beitsa* 12a.
237 Rif, *Beitsa dapei haRif* 5b.

Mishna Berura, in the *Biur Halakha*, first proposes that Rabbi Karo rules according to *Rashi*'s opinion, which is also that of the *Rif* and the *Rambam*. He therefore mentions utensils without any clarification because he does not differentiate between whether they have a need or not. Only objects like stones are outside of the sphere of permissibility due to their being *muktze*. In general, however, one has permission even *ab initio* to carry a utensil not needed for the day. According to this interpretation, one is required to say that the *Rema*'s comment is his own opinion and not a clarification of Rabbi Karo's. In order to answer any question that his language seems to be to the contrary, the *Mishna Berura* writes that many times the *Rema* interjects with his own opinion, without adding the expression "there are those who say."

The *Mishna Berura* admits that this explanation is difficult to reconcile with Rabbi Karo's ruling regarding the prohibition of carrying for a Gentile. Therefore, he writes that it seems to be more consistent to say that Rabbi Karo also forbids, albeit rabbinically, carrying utensils that are not needed. The *Rema*'s comment is therefore seen as an explanation of Rabbi Karo's ruling. The *Mishna Berura* justifies this perspective with the fact that the *Rema* notes in the *Darkhei Moshe* that Rabbi Karo's conclusion in the *Bet Yosef* is, in fact, that one should be stringent. Moreover, the *Rema*'s omission of the phrase, "there are those who say," is now more coherent. Rabbi Karo's mention of stones, under this interpretation, is meant to provide examples of those things which have no need at all. Despite the fact that the *Mishna Berura* seeks to reconcile Rabbi Karo's language in the two rulings with the *Rema*'s comment, he recognizes that his second explanation—which he interprets as Rabbi Karo forbidding, albeit rabbinically, a person to carry completely unnecessary objects—is difficult. For even though it accords with *Rashi*, the *Rif*, and the *Rambam*, almost all of the other *poskim* disagree and say that carrying such objects would be a Torah transgression. Therefore, he admits that this ruling still requires further investigation.[238]

---

238 *Biur Halakha* 518: s.v. *mitokh she'hutra hotza'ah.*

In his main commentary, the *Mishna Berura* interprets the *Rema*'s comment as an explanation of Rabbi Karo's ruling, and explains the mentioning of stones as an example of something completely unnecessary.[239] He does, however, note that as a practical matter, many *poskim* disagree with the ruling in the *Shulhan Arukh*, even as qualified by the *Rema*, and contend that one does not have permission to carry anything except if he is in great need to do so, and that preventing loss does not count as a great need. He continues to say that it is correct to be stringent like this opinion.[240]

In the *Sha'ar HaTziyun*, the *Mishna Berura* writes that based upon the Halakha which prohibits carrying something unnecessary, the prohibition to carry for a Gentile, if interpreted in a manner which allows one to carry completely without any need, cannot be a valid law. Its validity, however, can be rectified based on the contention that Rabbi Karo rabbinically forbids a person to carry without any need. He gives further support to the law's validity by claiming that based upon the opinion of some *poskim*, doing a prohibited action for a Gentile is worse than doing it for no purpose at all. The *Mishna Berura* thus reclaims the Halakha as valid law.[241]

Halakhic Principles — 5, 8

84.

Shulhan Arukh — With respect to a person reciting the *Birkat HaMazon* for others, there is one who says that a *ba'al ha'bayit* (head of the household) must say the *Birkat HaMazon* aloud in order to include his wife and children in his blessing so that they may also fulfill their obligation through his recitation.[242]

Alternative Positions — The *Magen Avraham* asks why Rabbi Karo wrote this ruling in form of "there is one who says" since it is an

---

239 *Mishna Berura* 518:5. In his comment appended to "stones," the *Mishna Berura* explains that Rabbi Karo means stones that have not been previously designated for any use (MB 518:7).

240 *Mishna Berura* 518:6.

241 *Sha'ar HaTziyun* 518:22.

242 *Shulhan Arukh, Orah Hayyim* 185:3.

obvious statement.[243] The *Taz* writes that even though the Halakha is not established in accordance with this opinion, for women who do not understand Hebrew and cannot say the blessing on their own, one may rely on it even *ab initio* since it is better than not blessing at all.[244]

The *Mishna Berura*'s Position — In the *Biur Halakha*, the *Mishna Berura* proposes to answer the *Magen Avraham*'s question with the explanation of the *Birkei Yosef* and the *Nahar Shalom*. Rabbi Karo is citing *Rashi*, who holds that a person may include another in his blessing even if the other person does not understand the language. Rabbi Karo uses the phrase "there is one who says" because he actually holds the same opinion as the other *poskim* who are stringent, and does not allow one who cannot understand the language to be included.

Discussion — The *Mishna Berura* justifies his reasoning based on Rabbi Karo's ruling regarding a *Zimun*, which states, "Two that eat together, even though regarding recital of *HaMotzi* one may include another through his recital, for the recital of *Birkat HaMazon* it is a *mitzvah* to separate and have each recite it for himself. This applies when both know how to recite the *Birkat HaMazon*, but if one knows how and the other does not, the one who knows may include the other person as long as he understands Hebrew but does not know the blessing ... if he does not understand [Hebrew] he cannot be included through listening."[245] In this Halakha, however, Rabbi Karo nevertheless cites *Rashi*'s opinion with respect to a man reciting the *Birkat HaMazon* for his family because it is better to rely on *Rashi*'s opinion, that they can all fulfill their obligation through him, than for those who cannot understand Hebrew to be unable to bless at all. The *Mishna Berura* concludes by referring to the *Taz* as further support for its interpretation.[246]

---

243 *Magen Avraham* 185:2.
244 *Taz* 193:2.
245 *Shulhan Arukh, Orah Hayyim* 193:1.
246 *Biur Halakha* 185: s.v. *yesh mi she'omer*.

The *Mishna Berura* also notes that the custom has become to permit women to fulfill their obligation to recite the *Birkat HaMazon* by listening to it, even if they do not understand the language. However, in order to be as comprehensive as possible, it advises that they should recite the blessing for themselves, even if they do not understand Hebrew. At the very least, they should repeat word for word after the one reciting the blessing, if possible, so that they may act in accord with all the *poskim*. To maintain the legitimacy of the lenient position *de jure* even if opposing it in practice, the *Mishna Berura* provides a second reason for its advice, namely that it is difficult to maintain concentration when passively listening.[247]

Picking up on the fact that Rabbi Karo prohibits three people to separate to recite the *Birkat HaMazon* individually, the *Mishna Berura* comments that inability to include one who does not understand only applies when there are two people eating a meal together. If three people eat together, the *Mishna Berura* notes that there is a disagreement among the *poskim* as to whether one can include others who do not understand. Although it does not definitively side with a particular position, it writes that many *Aharonim* follow the interpretation of the *Birkat Avraham*, which interprets Rabbi Karo's ruling to mean that the one reciting can include others, and mentions that only the *Bach* and the *Levush* disagree.[248] By including this analysis, the *Mishna Berura* in effect restricts the realm of disagreement between *Rashi* and the majority opinion, thereby reducing the ramifications of inconsistency that Rabbi Karo's rulings entail.

Halakhic Principles — 4, 6, 8

85.

Rema — *Ab initio*, one should not leave a meal without first saying the *Birkat HaMazon*, since we suspect that he may forget to return to his meal.[249]

---

247 *Mishna Berura* 193:5.
248 *Biur Halakha* 193: s.v. *eino yotzei b'shmia.*
249 *Shulhan Arukh, Orah Hayyim* 178:2.

Discussion — In the *Biur Halakha*, the *Mishna Berura* remarks that the necessity to recite *Birkat HaMazon* upon leaving is only according to the opinion that leaving one's place is considered an end to the meal. According to the opinion that leaving is not considered an indication of the end of the meal per se, the *ab initio* requirement to recite *Birkat HaMazon* would cause the person to recite a superfluous blessing. This creates a difficulty not only because this is a case where stringency in one area of law inevitably causes an erroneous leniency in another, but also because the *Rema*'s position contradicts his general adherence to the *Rosh*'s opinion regarding whether leaving the table during a meal indicates its conclusion or not.[250]

The *Mishna Berura*'s Position — The *Mishna Berura* writes that *ab initio* it is certainly correct to not leave the table for any general purpose. Nevertheless, if one does leave he should not say the concluding blessing if he leaves on the condition that he will return immediately and finish his meal, since in this case the blessing may be superfluous. On the other hand, if he assumes that it is possible that he will be away for a long time, it is correct to recite the *Birkat HaMazon* and then leave.[251]

Discussion — To resolve this difficulty, the *Mishna Berura* initially offers that the source of the *Rema*'s ruling is in fact *Tosafot* and the *Rosh*, who do not consider leaving the table to indicate the end of a meal. Nevertheless, they provide, as good advice, that one should say the *Birkat HaMazon* upon leaving, since the person may delay to the point where he may become hungry again, and thus lose the ability to recite the blessing over what he has previously eaten. This explanation, however, still does not address the fact that the person may be reciting a superfluous blessing. Therefore, in order to avoid contradiction within the positions of *Tosafot* and the *Rosh*, the *Mishna Berura* proposes that when they offered the idea as good advice in their Talmudic commentaries, it was meant to apply only within the perspective of Rav Sheshet, who considers leaving

---

250 *Biur Halakha* 178: s.v. *b'bayit ehad.*
251 *Mishna Berura* 178:35.

the table to be diverting one's attention from the meal, and, as such, its completion. According to the opinion that leaving is not considered a diversion of attention, one should not say *Birkat HaMazon* when leaving.

Because the *Mishna Berura* cannot find a way to resolve the *Rema*'s ruling with the *Rosh* as practical Halakha, it then proffers the idea that the *Rema*'s ruling has support from the opinions of the *Kol Bo* and the *Ma'or*, who hold that one may only leave the table during a meal for the purpose of fulfilling a commandment. Leaving in general would indicate the desire to end a meal, or at least it would be a diverting of attention, which would create the obligation to recite *Birkat HaMazon*. The *Mishna Berura* rejects this explanation, however, since neither the *Kol Bo* nor the *Ma'or* say explicitly that one must recite the *Birkat HaMazon* upon leaving.

Unable to find solid support for the *Rema*'s ruling, the *Mishna Berura* concludes that if one thinks he will be away for a long time he should say the *Birkat HaMazon* before leaving, and should not worry that it would be a superfluous blessing, since he can rely on the opinion of Rabbi Karo.[252]

In his main commentary, the *Mishna Berura* explains the *Rema*'s ruling to be consistent with the *Kol Bo* and the *Ma'or* without any qualification, and says that *ab initio* it is certainly correct not to leave the table for any general purpose. Nevertheless, if one does leave, he should not say the concluding blessing if he leaves on the condition that he will return immediately and finish his meal, since in this case the blessing may be superfluous. On the other hand, if he assumes that it is possible that he will be away for a long time, it is correct to recite the *Birkat HaMazon* and then leave.[253] By adding that the one leaving the table should consider whether he will return or not, the *Mishna Berura* subtly removes the difficulty caused by the idea that leaving the table for any reason implies a diversion of attention. It allows the one leaving the table to actually consider his meal to be over if he thinks he will be away for a

---

252 *Biur Halakha* 178: s.v. *be'lo berakha*.
253 *Mishna Berura* 178:35.

long time, thereby also removing the suspicion of reciting a superfluous blessing. The *Mishna Berura*'s addition to the *Rema*'s ruling also makes it consistent in practice with the opinion of the *Rosh* and thus coherent with the *Rema*'s general legal methodology.
Halakhic Principles — 4, 5, 8

86.

Shulhan Arukh — If a community collects money for a certain purpose, and then wants to use the money for something else, the money may only go toward something of increased sanctity. If, however, a building is built for the purpose of being a synagogue, it does not become sanctified until the community prays in it.[254]

Rema — If a community purchases wood and stones, they become sanctified through their purchase. Therefore, if the community wants to use the materials to build something else, it must be of greater sanctity.[255]

Ambiguity — Rabbi Karo's ruling seems contradictory, especially in light of the *Rema*'s comment, since a community can build a synagogue which does not become sanctified before using it, but the wood and stones do become sanctified upon purchase.

The *Mishna Berura*'s Position — The *Mishna Berura* first explains that Rabbi Karo holds that a synagogue is not sanctified until people pray in it, since designation alone is not effective.[256] Because the *Mishna Berura* wants to explain that the *Rema* does not contradict Rabbi Karo's ruling but only expands upon it, it describes the case to be a situation in which either the money was not specifically raised for a particular need but rather for some undefined purpose or one in which everyone brought his own materials to build the synagogue, rather than that the materials were collected by the community leaders.[257] In these two cases specifically, the

---

254 *Shulhan Arukh, Orah Hayyim* 153:8. This is a paraphrase of the Halakha brought in the *Shulhan Arukh* and not a straight translation.
255 *Shulhan Arukh, Orah Hayyim* 153:5.
256 *Mishna Berura* 153:49.
257 *Mishna Berura* 153:18.

synagogue would not become sanctified until the community prays in it. However, if the money or material was given for the specific purpose of building a synagogue, it is prohibited to divert them to be used for a less sanctified purpose.

Although the money cannot be used for a less sanctified purpose, one could nevertheless still infer that according to Rabbi Karo the materials themselves would not be sanctified as long as the synagogue is not built and people have not prayed in it. Therefore, the *Mishna Berura* provides a different reason to explain the prohibition against using the materials for something else. The *Mishna Berura* writes that, in fact, the materials are not sanctified by virtue of their intention to be part of a synagogue; rather, the prohibition to use them for another purpose stems from the requirement to fulfill one's *Neder* (vow) to give the materials for a specific purpose. The *Sha'ar HaTziyun* justifies this explanation by saying that since a synagogue is generally a public necessity, it would mean that the donor of the materials would be making an implied *Neder* even when he does not make one explicitly.[258] In the *Biur Halakha*, the *Mishna Berura* writes that this explanation is meant to buttress the concept that designation is not effective against any challenge that these rulings may raise.[259]

Halakhic Principles — 2, 3, 8

87.

Shulhan Arukh — Some *poskim* consider alleyways that are thirteen and a third cubits wide and have both ends open to a public domain to also be a public domain.[260]

Ambiguity — Elsewhere, Rabbi Karo writes that an alleyway that has both ends open to a public domain is not considered a public domain.[261]

---

258 *Sha'ar HaTziyun* 153:48.
259 *Biur Halakha* 153: s.v. *ein m'shanin.*
260 *Shulhan Arukh, Orah Hayyim* 345:9.
261 *Shulhan Arukh, Orah Hayyim* 364:1.

The *Mishna Berura*'s Position — In order to reconcile this contradiction, the *Mishna Berura* explains that when Rabbi Karo writes that the alleyway is not a public domain, he is either referring to an alleyway that is not thirteen cubits wide or to one in which many people do not enter from the public domain. If, on the other hand, an alleyway is the requisite length or does have many people entering into it, it would be considered a public domain.[262]

Discussion — In the *Biur Halakha*, the *Mishna Berura* writes that Rabbi Karo's statement regarding an alleyway that is thirteen and a third cubits wide and has both ends open to a public domain actually should be included with his immediately preceding statement. Rabbi Karo writes, "Some say that alleyways that are sixteen cubits wide, whose ends taper to less than sixteen cubits, if their length runs along a public domain, should be considered public domain."[263] However, putting the two statements together seems difficult, since they are derived from different sources. The first is based upon the *Rashba* and the second is based on the *Rosh* in the name of the *Ri*. Moreover, the two opinions are contradictory. The first position would declare an alleyway that is less than thirteen cubits wide a public domain, yet the second would limit it specifically to thirteen cubits. To reconcile the contradiction of this combination, the *Mishna Berura* notes that Rabbi Karo often includes dissenting opinions into one ruling.[264]

In his main commentary, the *Mishna Berura* interprets the two rulings as if they explain each other. He writes that Rabbi Karo means that an alleyway that is sixteen cubits wide and tapers at its end is considered by some to be a public domain. Also, even if the alleyway is less than sixteen cubits wide, it will still be considered a public domain if it runs along a public domain. Since Rabbi Karo does not give an exact minimum width for this latter case, even if the alleyway is less than thirteen cubits wide, it would be still be

---

262 *Mishna Berura* 345:27.
263 *Shulhan Arukh, Orah Hayyim* 345:8.
264 *Biur Halakha* 345: s.v. *13 amot u'shlish.*

considered a public domain according to this opinion.[265] His inference that this position would consider an alleyway less than thirteen cubits wide to be a public domain is based on the assumption that it disagrees with the position in the following Halakha. If the alleyway needed to be wider to be considered a public domain, this position would not be adding any practical difference; the width would determine its status regardless of location by virtue of the latter position. Though in this case the *Mishna Berura* does not reconcile opposing positions by claiming that they refer to different situations, it does use opposing positions to interpret the situation to which they refer.

Halakhic Principles — 3, 8

88.

Shulhan Arukh — Cavities in a wall bordering a *Karmelit* are not automatically considered a *Karmelit*; rather, they are judged according to their height and width.[266]

The *Mishna Berura*'s Position — The *Mishna Berura* explains that the holes in question are those which face a *Karmelit*, such as holes in a wall of a house that open to a valley yet do not pass through the wall.[267] If the holes measure four by four *tefahim* and are between three and ten *tefahim* from the ground, they would be considered a *Karmelit*. If they are less than four by four, or if they are higher than ten *tefahim* from the ground, they would be considered a *Makom Patur*.[268] In the *Biur Halakha*, the *Mishna Berura* writes that even though the *Rema* rules that a *Makom Patur* cannot exist in a *Karmelit* since they are of the same category of domain types, one can still make a distinction between a *Makom Patur* that is in the middle of a *Karmelit*, and that of the present case where it is on its edge.[269]

Halakhic Principles — 5, 8

---

265 *Mishna Berura* 345:25.
266 *Shulhan Arukh, Orah Hayyim* 345:17.
267 *Mishna Berura* 345:70.
268 *Mishna Berura* 345:71.
269 *Biur Halakha* 345: s.v. *horei karmelit.*

89.

Shulhan Arukh — Even if a person has a lot of servants, he should still try to prepare something for Shabbat in order to honor it.[270]

Discussion — In the *Sha'ar HaTziyun*, the *Mishna Berura* admits that this ruling conflicts with the principle that when others can perform a *mitzvah*, a person should not interrupt his learning to fulfill it. In this case, preparation could be done by the person's servants, yet Rabbi Karo still insists that the person should make an effort to prepare something for Shabbat.

The *Mishna Berura*'s Position — To resolve this difficulty, the *Mishna Berura* proposes that there is a difference between a *mitzvah* that does not relate to one's self, such as performing an act of *Hesed* for another, and a *mitzvah* that does relate to one's self, such as honoring and enjoying Shabbat. With respect to the former, one need not interrupt his learning, since another could perform the deed, yet for the latter, it is better for the person to perform it himself rather than through a representative. The *Mishna Berura* also gives another justification for Rabbi Karo's prescription, namely that specifically in the case of giving honor to Shabbat we are stringent to require a Torah scholar to interrupt his learning. In other words, the importance of honoring Shabbat overrides the principle that one should continue his learning. In the end, it leaves the issue up for further investigation.[271] In its main commentary, the *Mishna Berura* finds a third resolution, writing that the obligation to honor Shabbat is incumbent upon everyone and that it is better for a *mitzvah* to be done by the person than by his representative, but also adds that this is the rule for all *mitzvot*.[272]

Discussion — By extending the concept to all *mitzvot*, the *Mishna Berura* in effect changes Rabbi Karo's ruling to be a suggestion for ideal action, that it is better to act oneself than through another, yet it is not obligatory nor will it detract from the efficacy of designating a representative. This applies to everyone and not just Torah scholars.

---

270 *Shulhan Arukh, Orah Hayyim* 250:1.
271 *Sha'ar HaTziyun* 250:9.
272 *Mishna Berura* 250:3.

A Torah scholar in the midst of his learning, on the other hand, must find a balance between the benefit of acting personally and that of continuing his learning. That Rabbi Karo does not directly contradict the principle that one should continue his learning, but rather only highlights a competing principle, is justified by his statement that one should try to prepare something rather than by making an actual command to do so.

Halakhic Principles — 8

90.

Shulhan Arukh — When saying the *Birkat HaMazon*, one must hear what he is saying. If he does not hear his words, he can fulfill his obligation as long as his lips were moving.[273]

Alternative Positions — The *Magen Avraham* states that if a person only reflects on the words in his heart, and does not mouth them, if he is sick or it is a time when he is unable to recite it, "*yatza*."

The *Mishna Berura*'s Position — Though the word "*yatza*" usually denotes fulfillment of an obligation, the *Mishna Berura* explains that "*yatza*" in this particular case does not mean that, since reflection does not have the same efficacy as speech. Rather, what the *Magen Avraham* means is that when a person reflects on the words of the *Birkat HaMazon* in a situation where he is unable to actually say them, he will still receive reward for his contemplation. In truth, however, he has not fulfilled his obligation. If he would still have time to recite the *Birkat HaMazon* when the hindrance is removed, he should say it.[274]

Halakhic Principles — 2, 8

91.

Shulhan Arukh — If, due to sickness or conditions out of his control, a person recites the *Shema* in his heart [without moving his lips]—"*yatza*."

---

273 *Shulhan Arukh, Orah Hayyim* 185:2.
274 *Mishna Berura* 185:2.

Rema — A person may act in such a manner even *ab initio* if he is in a place that is not completely clean, or if he is unable to properly clean himself, as long as neither he nor the place is completely sullied.[275]

The *Mishna Berura*'s Position — The *Mishna Berura* changes the meaning of the word "*yatza*" from implying that that he has fulfilled his obligation to mean, rather, that God will establish reward for his contemplation; however, he did not actually fulfill his obligation. In the same fashion as above, he says that if the impediment is removed while there is still time to recite the *Shema* he is obligated to do so.[276]

Discussion — The *Mishna Berura*'s rejection of the simple meaning of "*yatza*" as used in the *Shulhan Arukh* and by the *Magen Avraham* in these two examples is due to the force of the *Rishonim*'s opinions in the *Mishna Berura*'s attempt to find coherence in the Halakha. For him, the concept that thoughts do not have the same efficacy as words cannot be doubted, since the majority of the *Rishonim* hold this opinion. Moreover, it appears that even the *Shulhan Arukh* adheres to the principle in other rulings. Though the *Rambam* and the *Smag* hold that, *ex post facto*, thoughts are like words regarding blessings, even with respect to the *Birkat HaMazon*, which unlike other blessings is a Torah obligation, according to the *Mishna Berura*, one must repeat blessings that he only contemplated. This prescription contradicts the *Mishna Berura*'s principle that one may rely on a lenient opinion *ex post facto* to avoid potential transgression (which in the case of repeating the *Birkat HaMazon* would be the transgression of saying an unnecessary blessing), yet in this case he defends his position by saying, "the one who relies on all the *Rishonim* above will certainly not lose out."[277] The reason for his decision in this case is that systemic halakhic coherence is a greater priority than spreading a wide, inclusive net of halakhic acceptability.

Halakhic Principles — 2, 8

---

275 *Shulhan Arukh, Orah Hayyim* 62:4.
276 *Mishna Berura* 62:7.
277 *Biur Halakha* 62: s.v. *yatza.*

92.

Shulhan Arukh — If a person is in the middle of a meal and remembers that he touched either his foreleg or his thigh, or another area which is not normally exposed, or if he scratches his head, etc., he must rewash his hands and recite the blessing over washing.

Rema — Rabbi Karo's mention of other areas not normally exposed includes places on one's body that are usually sweaty and dirty.[278]

Alternative Positions — The *Rashal* states that he need not recite the blessing even if he has to rewash his hands in the middle of the meal after using the bathroom unless it is a substantial interruption.

The *Mishna Berura*'s Position — The *Mishna Berura* notes that many *Aharonim* share the *Rashal*'s position in practice; therefore, the Halakha is that when one uses the bathroom or touches an unclean part of his body, or if he substantially interrupts the meal, he must repeat the blessing. If, on the other hand, a person only touches a place normally covered, or goes to urinate, even if he cleans his hands, he must rewash but does not say the blessing.[279]

Discussion — In the *Biur Halakha*, the *Mishna Berura* cites the *Pri Megadim*, who writes that the opposing positions are based on a disagreement between *Rashi* and his teachers. *Rashi* requires a person to recite the blessing when he rewashes his hands in the middle of a meal because the requirement to wash one's hands before a meal is modeled after the requirement to do so when eating *Terumah*. *Rashi*'s teachers and the *Rambam*, on the other hand, do not require a person to recite the blessing, since even if the requirement before a meal is based upon the necessity of purifying one's hands in order to eat *Terumah*, touching an unclean part of one's body during a meal is not a parallel situation; therefore, he rewashes his hands without a blessing.

Given the *Pri Megadim*'s understanding of the disagreement, the *Mishna Berura* questions how Rabbi Karo and the *Rema* could

---

278　*Shulhan Arukh, Orah Hayyim* 164:2.
279　*Mishna Berura* 164:13.

follow the position of the *Ramban* and the *Rashba*, who require a person to recite a blessing even after touching covered or sweaty body parts, especially when the *Rambam* and *Rashi*'s teachers hold that touching unclean body parts does not cause one to repeat the blessing.

In order to vindicate Rabbi Karo and the *Rema*, the *Mishna Berura* gives an alternate explanation for the rabbinic decree to wash one's hands. Based upon its understanding of *Rabbenu Hananel*, the Sages, in truth, had two reasons for the decree, namely, to guard oneself from impurity, and so that one's hands are clean and sanctified. Therefore, the disagreement regarding the recital of the blessing in the middle of a meal does not center on the aspect of purity but rather on the aspect of keeping one's hands clean. Based on this second reason, the *Ramban* and the *Rashba* consider touching sweaty body parts to require washing with a blessing as a consequence of the decree.

By providing a different interpretation, the *Mishna Berura* gives both Rabbi Karo and the *Rema* a solid legal foundation. Therefore, even though the *Mishna Berura* usually suggests that a person not recite a blessing when its necessity is in question, in this case he writes that one certainly not protest against those who act in accordance with Rabbi Karo's and the *Rema*'s position. He does provide a compromise position, yet it is only owing to his principle to cover all bases.[280]

Halakhic Principles — 3, 8

93.

Shulhan Arukh — Before starting the *Seder* meal, a person first washes his hands and recites the blessing. He then takes all the *matzot*, namely the two whole *matzot* and the broken one in between, recites "*HaMotzi*" and "*al akhilat matzah*," and then grabs the top whole *matzah* and the broken middle *matzah*, dips them in salt, and eats them both while leaning. He must eat a *kazayit* from both the

____

280 *Biur Halakha* 164: s.v. *la'hazor v'litol yadav.*

whole and the broken *matzah*. If he is unable to eat two *zaytim* at the same time, he may first eat a *kazayit* from the one upon which "*HaMotzi*" was recited and then eat a *kazayit* from the one upon which "*al akhilat matzah*" was recited.[281]

Ambiguity — In the *Biur Halakha*, the *Mishna Berura* writes that Rabbi Karo's ruling seems to be very questionable, since it requires an innovation from the traditional halakhic view, namely that on the first night of Passover a person must now eat two *zaytim* instead of one. The intention behind reciting one blessing on one *matzah* and the other blessing on the other *matzah* is only so that the two *matzot* will not be bundled together. However, the truth of the matter is that the *matzot* are one item, just as the two loaves on Shabbat are one item.

The *Mishna Berura*'s Position — Because the *matzot* are, in truth, one item, the *Mishna Berura* writes that the main ruling is that one may eat from whichever *matzah* one desires. Nevertheless, because each *matzah* has a blessing specifically directed to it, it would be good to take a taste from each one. Certainly, however, one *kazayit* aggregated from both *matzot* is sufficient. The *Mishna Berura* notes that Rabbi Karo would concede that this is the law, since he rules that one should hold both *matzot* together when saying both blessings. Therefore, both blessings are directed toward both of the *matzot*. The *Mishna Berura* does, however, qualify his suggestion with an admission that more investigation is needed.[282]

Discussion — To explain Rabbi Karo's ruling, as stated in the *Shulhan Arukh*, the *Mishna Berura* writes that he mentions a *kazayit* from each *matzah* based on the idea that a person is required to eat a *kazayit* of the *matzah* designated with the blessing "*al akhilat matzah*" and there is a disagreement among the *poskim* as to which *matzah* that would be. Eating a *kazayit* of both *matzot* would, therefore, remove any doubt of fulfillment.[283] In the same vein, eating the two *zaytim*, one from each *matzah*, simultaneously would remove

---

281 *Shulhan Arukh, Orah Hayyim* 475:1.
282 *Biur Halakha* 475: s.v. *kazayit mikol ekhad*.
283 *Mishna Berura* 475:9.

any potential interruption between reciting the blessing over a specific *matzah* and then eating it.[284] The *Mishna Berura* obviously interprets Rabbi Karo's ruling as specifying an *ab initio* scenario suggested so as to remove doubtful fulfillment. *Ex post facto*, he argues that Rabbi Karo would agree with the general halakhic norm that eating one *kazayit* between the two *matzot* is sufficient.[285]

Halakhic Principles — 5, 6, 8

94.

Shulhan Arukh — On Yom Tov, even though it is permitted to carry unnecessarily, one should still not carry large objects as one would during a weekday. Rather, a person must carry the object differently, so that it is clear that he is doing it for the sake of the Yom Tov.[286]

Ambiguity — In the *Biur Halakha*, the *Mishna Berura* notes that Rabbi Karo begins his ruling by citing the words of the *Rambam*, yet ends with those of the *Tur*. The two *Rishonim*, however, are not in complete agreement. The *Tur* requires one to carry large objects differently than he would during the week even if they are for the Yom Tov meal. The language of the *Rambam*, on the other hand, seems to refer to objects that are not for the sake of *Okhel Nefesh* (necessary food preparation), meaning that he would allow a person to carry needed objects in the normal manner.

The *Mishna Berura*'s Position — The *Mishna Berura* writes that it is very difficult to say that the *Rambam* disagrees with all of the other *poskim* regarding the permissibility of carrying a needed object in a normal manner, especially when the Talmud explicitly states that even something needed for the Yom Tov must be carried in a different way. The *Mishna Berura* attempts to resolve this contradiction by saying that perhaps the *Rambam* also prohibits a person to carry an object needed for Yom Tov in a normal way. His statement, as cited by Rabbi Karo, which states, "Even though it is permitted," should be interpreted to mean that even if we are lenient when it comes to

---

284 *Mishna Berura* 475:8.
285 *Mishna Berura* 475:11; *Sha'ar HaTziyun* 475:11.
286 *Shulhan Arukh, Orah Hayyim* 510:8.

carrying for no need at all, nevertheless, when carrying we are stringent in requiring a person to carry an object differently than usual even when it is needed for the Yom Tov. Emphasizing its inclination to maintain as coherent and consistent a halakhic tradition as possible, it notes that this explanation is meant only to defend the opinion of the *Rambam*, since Rabbi Karo's conclusion demonstrates that he is referring to a person who is carrying something for the sake of the Yom Tov.[287]

Halakhic Principles — 3, 5, 8

95.

Shulhan Arukh — There are two opinions regarding whether a person may sell a sanctified object to buy another object that has the same level of sanctity. There are those who prohibit this type of exchange and those who permit it.[288]

Discussion — The disagreement is based on whether the idea that "things should increase in sanctity and not decrease" emphasizes the prescription of increasing in sanctity or the proscription of decreasing in sanctity.

Ambiguity — The *Mishna Berura* writes that the disagreement only concerns *ex post facto* cases; *ab initio* it is forbidden to sell an object to buy another of equal sanctity. There must certainly be an increase in sanctity from the exchange.[289] This stringent position, however, contradicts the practice of selling *sefarim* in order to buy others, which is a violation of the *ab initio* requirement to increase sanctity.

The *Mishna Berura*'s Position — In order to avoid a widespread practice clearly contradicting the Halakha, the *Mishna Berura* cites the *Taz*, who states that today when one buys a *Sefer*, at the time of purchase he has in mind the intention to sell it, whether out of necessity or if he finds a better alternative, albeit with the same level of sanctity. He is considered to have this intention even if he does not make an explicit stipulation of it. He also cites the *Elya*

---

287 *Biur Halakha* 510: s.v. *afilu…d'mukhah.*
288 *Shulhan Arukh, Orah Hayyim* 153:4.
289 *Mishna Berura* 153:11.

Rabbah, who explains the custom's legitimacy based on textual grounds, rather than grounding it on a presumption. Sellers of *sefarim* rely on the opinion cited in the *Shulhan Arukh* that permits an individual to sell his personal Sefer Torah and do what he likes with the money, as long as the Sefer Torah was not donated for public readings. This position is not unanimous, however; there is an opinion that forbids the sale unless the money is used for Talmud Torah or to marry.[290]

Halakhic Principles — 1, 2, 8

96.

Shulhan Arukh — One should recite the blessing "*ligmor ha'hallel.*"[291]

Rema — One should say "*likrot ha'hallel*" instead.[292]

The *Mishna Berura*'s Position — The *Mishna Berura* explains that the reason for the *Rema*'s wording is that if a person accidently skips a word or letter, if he said "*ligmor,*" the blessing said may be in vain. Nevertheless, in the places where the custom is to say "*ligmor,*" one should not abrogate his custom.[293] In the *Sha'ar HaTziyun*, he questions this reasoning, saying that such a distinction seems to be incorrect since if one says "*likrot*" and skips parts of *Hallel* he would not fulfill his obligation, just as is the case if he skips parts when reading the Megilla. Therefore, the blessing would still be said in vain. The *Mishna Berura* proffers that the *Rema* rules according to the opinion that states that we are not scrupulous about reading the *Megilla*, so that if a person reads a word incorrectly he still fulfills his obligation. The same would apply for *Hallel*. Therefore, the one who says "*likrot*" does not have the suspicion of reciting a blessing in vain, whereas the one who says "*ligmor*" may, if he says something incorrectly.[294]

Halakhic Principles — 3, 8

---

290 *Mishna Berura* 153:11.
291 *Shulhan Arukh, Orah Hayyim* 644:1.
292 *Shulhan Arukh, Orah Hayyim* 488:1.
293 *Mishna Berura* 488:3.
294 *Sha'ar HaTziyun* 488:3.

Interprets in a Manner That Justifies his Own Opinion

The *Mishna Berura* uses his commentary as a way to interpret various positions so that they will accord with what he thinks should be the law. The *Mishna Berura* provides an alternative rationale behind the particular position to which he subscribes in order to justify ruling in its favor. There are times when the *Mishna Berura* explains the justification for a certain opinion in order to reject it.

97.

Shulhan Arukh — When washing one's hands before eating bread, a person should have the water cover up to his wrist. Some say up to where the fingers join the palm. However, it is appropriate to act according to the first opinion.[295]

Background — There are two reasons for why the Sages established that a person must wash his hands before eating bread. The first reason is because a person regularly touches things; therefore, during the time when *Kohanim* ate *Terumah* in a state of purity, they would need to wash their hands before eating in order that they would not make their food impure. Since the *Kohanim* would regularly wash their hands, the Sages decreed that everyone should wash their hands before eating bread. Today, when *Kohanim* do not eat *Terumah*, the decree is still not annulled in order for people to be accustomed to washing their hands when the Temple in Jerusalem will be rebuilt and *Kohanim* will be able to eat *Terumah* again. The second reason for why the Sages decreed that a person must wash his hands before eating bread is so that the person's hands are clean and sanctified. They support the decree with the exegesis "Sanctify yourselves (Lev. 11:44)" — this refers to washing of the hands before the meal; "And be holy" — this refers to washing of the hands after the meal (BT Berakhot 53b).

Discussion — From the wording of the *Shulhan Arukh*, it seems clear that the law is according to the second, more lenient, opinion. This

---

295 *Shulhan Arukh, Orah Hayyim* 161:4.

opinion is also the position of many of the *poskim*, such as *Rashi*, *Tosafot*, *Rosh*, and others. The *Rif*, however, holds the more stringent position.

The *Mishna Berura*'s Position — In the *Biur Halakha*, the *Mishna Berura* first advises that a person follow the position of the *Rif*, since it is not much more difficult to follow and it allows him to avoid controversy. However, he then contends that the first opinion is actually the law, and not just an *ab initio* deferring to the stringent opinion, since it adheres more closely to the Talmudic discussion of the matter.[296] In his main commentary, the *Mishna Berura* writes that if a person wants to act according to the lenient opinion one should not protest against him, since all matters of doubt should be ruled leniently; nevertheless, *ab initio* it is appropriate to be stringent according to the first opinion. Moreover, the world has such a practice.[297] If, on the other hand, a person is in a situation of difficulty where he does not have ample water, he may rely on the lenient opinion.[298]

Discussion — The *Mishna Berura* reinterprets the *Shulhan Arukh*'s use of the phrase "It is appropriate" to mean that it is obligatory. However, since it cannot completely annul the ruling of the *Shulhan Arukh*, it writes that one cannot protest against those who interpret the wording of the ruling simply as appropriate, which would imply that the second, more lenient, opinion is completely acceptable.

Halakhic Principles — 2, 5, 8

98.

Shulhan Arukh — One may do something in a regular manner on *Hol HaMoed* that if not done would cause loss.[299]

Alternative Positions — The *Magen Avraham* writes that if the matter is in doubt, one can be lenient and perform the deed. The *Hayye Adam* writes that in such a case it should be done through a

---

296 *Biur Halakha* 161: s.v. *v'raui linhog.*
297 *Mishna Berura* 161:21.
298 *Mishna Berura* 161:22.
299 *Shulhan Arukh, Orah Hayyim* 537:1.

Gentile and not by the Jewish person himself.[300] The *Pri Megadim*, the *Mahatzit HaShekel*, and the *Levushi Serad* all concur that the reason the *Magen Avraham* holds that a doubtful loss should be ruled leniently is because he considers the performance of forbidden activity on *Hol HaMoed* to be only rabbinically prohibited.

The *Mishna Berura*'s Position — Contrary to the above-mentioned opinions that support the position of the *Magen Avraham*, the *Mishna Berura* contends that the issue does not depend on whether the prohibition is of Torah law or rabbinic decree but rather that the essential distinction is between whether failure to act will commonly lead to loss or not. Therefore, according to the *Mishna Berura*, if there is a doubt where loss is probable, we may be lenient even if the prohibition is of Torah law. If the matter does not usually lead to loss, we should be stringent even if the prohibition is rabbinic.[301] Also, if the matter will probably lead to loss, he need not ask a Gentile to perform the work, he may even do it himself, but he should do it privately if possible, as a way to take heed of the opinion of the *Hayye Adam*.[302] In this example, the *Mishna Berura* does not accept the commonly-held interpretation of why there may be leniencies due to doubt on *Hol HaMoed*, but rather proffers its own.

Halakhic Principles — 2, 8

99.

Shulhan Arukh — It is not correct to make all the partitions of a *Sukkah* from linen sheets without poles interspersed even if they are well tied, for at times the knots may loosen without one's knowledge and a person will have a partition that cannot stand up to a regular wind. If one wants to make the partitions out of sheets, it is good to weave them with poles less than three *tefahim* apart.[303]

---

300 *Mishna Berura* 537:1.
301 *Biur Halakha* 537: s.v. *davar ha'aved*.
302 *Mishna Berura* 537:1.
303 *Shulhan Arukh, Orah Hayyim* 630:10.

Alternative Position — The *Taz* writes that one of the required three walls may be made out of linen. Many *Aharonim* infer from the wording of the *Shulhan Arukh* that even one partition should not be made out of linen unless it is interwoven with poles less than three *tefahim* apart. Regarding a fourth wall, on the other hand, everyone agrees it can be made out of linen since one only needs three walls according to the law.[304]

The *Mishna Berura*'s Position — In the *Sha'ar HaTziyun*, the *Mishna Berura* cites the *Nahar Shalom* and the *Elya Rabba* who write that the *Taz*'s leniency is based upon the permissibility to use an animal as one of the walls of a *Sukkah*. They distinguish between permitting the use of an animal and forbidding the use of a linen sheet based on the fact that one will see if the animal runs away, thus making the wall invalid, but he may not see if the knot keeping the sheet tight loosens, which would also make the wall invalid. For this reason, the *Mishna Berura* concludes that we have no justification to rely on the *Taz*'s leniency at all.[305] In this example, the *Mishna Berura* does not accept the *Taz*'s position to incorporate it as acceptable under difficult circumstances or to broaden the scope of what is acceptable. Rather, it rejects it based on the rejection of what it sees as a faulty comparison to the use of an animal.

Halakhic Principles — 5, 8

100.

Shulhan Arukh — If a synagogue has two doors, a person should not enter through one door and exit through the other in order to take a shortcut.[306]

Discussion — In the *Biur Halakha*, the *Mishna Berura* cites the *Rambam*, who explains the reason for the ruling to be that one may only enter a synagogue in order to perform a *mitzvah*. The *Mishna Berura* then cites the *Pri Megadim*, who states that if a person is

---

304 *Mishna Berura* 630:50.
305 *Sha'ar HaTziyun* 630:48.
306 *Shulhan Arukh, Orah Hayyim* 151:5.

making a short cut because he is on the way to perform a *mitzvah*, it is possible that it would be permitted.

The *Mishna Berura*'s Position — The *Mishna Berura* rejects the *Pri Megadim*'s opinion, stating that, from the words of the *Rambam*, there is no justification for this leniency, especially since the *mitzvah* that one hopes to perform could be done without turning the synagogue into a short cut.[307]

Halakhic Principles — 5, 8

Difference in Interpreting Rabbi Karo versus the *Rema*

When confronted with a ruling by Rabbi Karo which he believes inaccurately portrays the normative Halakha, the *Mishna Berura* qualifies or limits its application. On the other hand, when confronted with a ruling by the *Rema* which it perceives as inaccurately portraying the normative Halakha, the *Mishna Berura* considers it as a sole or minority opinion. Rather than having to approach it as a description of the normative practice in Ashkenaz, he can ignore it completely.

101.

Shulhan Arukh — If a Gentile is going of his own accord to another place, which happens to be where a Jew needs to send a letter, it is permissible without restriction for the Jew to give his letter to the Gentile before Shabbat starts.[308]

Alternative Positions — The *Magen Avraham*, the *Elya Rabba*, and other *Aharonim* rule that it is permissible for the Jew to give his letter to the Gentile only if there is enough time before Shabbat for the Gentile to deliver it. This position is also held by the *Maharam*. The *Gra* agrees with Rabbi Karo's position.

Discussion — The *Shulhan Arukh* clearly states that it is permissible without any restrictions to give the Gentile the letter, and the *Mishna Berura*, in the *Sha'ar HaTziyun*, acknowledges that it is

---

307 *Biur Halakha* 151: s.v. *l'katzer darko.*
308 *Shulhan Arukh, Orah Hayyim* 247:5.

problematic to interpret the ruling of the *Shulhan Arukh* as implying the restriction that there must be enough time before Shabbat for the Gentile to deliver it. However, the *Mishna Berura* also admits that it would be difficult to ignore the more stringent ruling, especially given the *poskim* who affirm this position.[309]

The *Mishna Berura*'s Position — The *Mishna Berura* interprets Rabbi Karo's mention of having no restriction to apply specifically to the requirement to set a fee for the Gentile's services. In a situation in which a Gentile is going of his own accord, even if it is to a locale that does not have an established postal system, one need not determine a fixed fee since the Gentile is traveling of his own accord and not for the sake of delivering the letter. With respect to there being enough time before Shabbat to deliver the letter, the *Mishna Berura* does qualify Rabbi Karo's ruling. The Jew may only give his letter to the Gentile if there is enough time for him to reach his destination before Shabbat. Otherwise, he may not give him the letter. Even though the Gentile travels of his own accord, he carries the letter on behalf of the Jew.[310]

Discussion — The objective of the *Mishna Berura* is to maintain the ruling of the *Shulhan Arukh*, yet to qualify it in such a way that it can coherently incorporate the more stringent position. He does this by interpreting the phrase "without restriction" to apply specifically to a particular situation, i.e., whether there must exist an established postal system or not. By directing Rabbi Karo's leniency only to that particular issue, the *Mishna Berura* is able to insert the restriction of having enough time before Shabbat as an implied requirement. This is not to say that the *Mishna Berura* is offering what it thinks is the simple reading of the *Shulhan Arukh*'s reading. On the contrary, as stated above, in the *Sha'ar HaTziyun*, it notes that its interpretation is a stringent one, yet maintains it because it believes that it is difficult to rule leniently.[311]

Halakhic Principles — 3, 5, 8

---

309 *Sha'ar HaTziyun* 247:17.
310 *Mishna Berura* 247:17.
311 *Sha'ar HaTziyun* 247:17.

102.

Shulhan Arukh — It is permitted for a Jew to give a Gentile money on Friday to buy something for him as long as he does not tell him to buy it on Shabbat.[312]

Alternative Positions — The *Magen Avraham*, the *Elya Rabba*, and other *Aharonim* rule that they must determine a fixed price for the Gentile's services beforehand.

Issue — The *Shulhan Arukh* only gives one restriction–to not tell the Gentile to buy the thing on Shabbat. How can the *Mishna Berura* incorporate the more stringent position without invalidating the ruling of the *Shulhan Arukh*?

The *Mishna Berura*'s Position — The *Mishna Berura* interprets Rabbi Karo's ruling to imply that there will obviously be a deter-mined price for the Gentile's services.[313] It justifies this interpreta-tion by referring to the ruling of the *Shulhan Arukh* (*Orah Hayyim* 245:5), which states that it is permissible for a Jew to hire a Gentile to buy something as long as they designate a fixed wage and the Jew explicitly tells the Gentile not to buy it on Shabbat. The *Mishna Berura* makes an interpretative comparison: just as when a Jew hires a Gentile to buy something for him he must establish a fixed wage, so when a Jew gives a Gentile money to buy him something he must establish a fixed wage. In effect, the *Mishna Berura* makes both laws equivalent, and no longer makes it possible for the Gentile to do the Jew a favor.

Halakhic Principles — 3, 5, 8

103.

Shulhan Arukh — It is permitted to set sail, even on Friday, if one is going for the purpose of performing a commandment, yet a Jew doing so should stipulate with the ship's captain that he will not sail [on Shabbat]. If afterward the captain does not stop sailing, it is of no consequence. If he is taking the trip for personal matters and not to

---

312 *Shulhan Arukh, Orah Hayyim* 307:4.
313 *Mishna Berura* 307:14.

fulfill a commandment, then he should not set sail less than three days before Shabbat.[314]

Discussion — This ruling is based on a discussion in the Talmud. Rebbi requires the Jew to make the stipulation with the ship's captain, yet Rabbi Shimon ben Gamliel states that it is unnecessary.[315] Based upon the wording of the *Shulhan Arukh*, it seems as if the Jew must actually make the stipulation, he may not just suggest it to the ship's captain, which means that he rules according to Rebbi. If, after agreeing to the stipulation, the ship's captain does not adhere to the agreement, it is of no consequence since the Jew is not in a position of any control.

Alternative Positions — The *Olat Shabbat* raises the concern of how to rule in a situation where the ship's captain says that he will not stop when the Jew asks for such a stipulation. The majority of the *Aharonim* rule that making a stipulation is only a *"mitzvah b'alma"* (generally good idea) and not an obligation. Therefore, failure to make the stipulation after the Jew suggests stopping on Shabbat does not prevent him from being able to set sail. In effect, the position of the *Aharonim* is a compromise position, which is in accord with Rabbi Shimon ben Gamliel, who states that the stipulation is not necessary, yet defers to Rebbi's requirement when possible.

The *Mishna Berura*'s Position — The *Mishna Berura* cites the position of the *Aharonim*.[316] In the *Sha'ar HaTziyun*, it states that even though one can infer from the *Magen Avraham* that failure to make a stipulation would prevent him from being allowed to set sail, the *Elya Rabba*, the *Shakh*, and the *Graz* hold that one need not be particular about it. Moreover, the *Mishna Berura* gives jurisprudential support for the lenient opinion in citing the *Tur*, who rules according to Rabban Shimon ben Gamliel based on the principle that Rebbi's position is preferred over those of his contemporaries but not over the position of his father. To support

---

314 *Shulhan Arukh, Orah Hayyim* 248:1.
315 BT *Shabbat* 19a.
316 *Mishna Berura* 248:3.

changing the meaning of the *Shulhan Arukh*, the *Mishna Berura* cites Rabbi Karo's ruling in *Hoshen Mishpat* 290:16 where he rules according to Rabban Shimon ben Gamliel and not Rebbi.[317] It concludes to say that more investigation is needed to determine the ruling conclusively.

Discussion — The *Mishna Berura* changes Rabbi Karo's ruling into the position of the Aharonim by interpreting "should stipulate" as "it is a good idea to stipulate" rather than "it is obligatory to stipulate." In this way, its interpretation still fits with the language of the *Shulhan Arukh* yet is able to adhere to the alternative position.

Halakhic Principles — 3, 6, 8

104.

Shulhan Arukh — One may only give food to a person who knows how to make a blessing over it.[318]

Rema — There are those who are lenient to give to a poor person for the sake of charity.

Discussion — With respect to the situation of whether one should give food for the sake of charity to a poor person who does not know how to recite a blessing, there is a conflict over differing commandments. In giving food to someone who will not say a blessing, one would be transgressing the prohibition of putting a stumbling block before the blind. On the other hand, giving food to a poor person fulfills the commandment to give charity.

Issue — How can the *Mishna Berura* negotiate between the two conflicting commandments in a way that does not invalidate the ruling of the *Shulhan Arukh*?

The *Mishna Berura*'s Position — The *Mishna Berura* makes a distinction between a person who does not know how to recite the blessing because in his own malice he did not learn how to do so, and one who cannot recite the blessing due to forces out of his

---

317 *Sha'ar HaTziyun* 248:1.
318 *Shulhan Arukh, Orah Hayyim* 169:2.

control. The former should not be given food, yet the latter is still eligible to receive the charity.[319]

Discussion — By distinguishing between people who do not recite blessings out of contempt and those who do not recite blessings out of ignorance, the *Mishna Berura* finds a way to qualify the ruling of the *Shulhan Arukh* without invalidating it. It also finds a way to negotiate between conflicting priorities. Its interpretation is consistent with the wording of the ruling of the *Shulhan Arukh*. Also, because not reciting from ignorance is less of a transgression for the poor person, the transgression of putting a stumbling block before him is also diminished. Therefore, the commandment to give charity trumps it. On the other hand, the obligation to give charity to a wicked person is smaller than the transgression of putting a stumbling block before him. Therefore, one should not give him charity.

Halakhic Principles — 3, 8

105.

Shulhan Arukh — There should be no discussion during a meal for fear that food may go down the wrong pipe.[320]

Discussion — Though the ruling of the *Shulhan Arukh* is grounded in a legitimate fear, there is also a commandment to speak words of Torah at every meal.

Issue — How can the *Mishna Berura* reconcile the two conflicting priorities in a way that does not invalidate the ruling of the *Shulhan Arukh*?

The *Mishna Berura*'s Position — The *Mishna Berura* explains that Rabbi Karo means that one should not talk specifically while eating. Between dishes it is not only permissible to speak; it is, in fact, a commandment, since one is required to learn Torah at every meal.[321]

Halakhic Principles — 6, 8

---

319 *Mishna Berura* 169:11.
320 *Shulhan Arukh, Orah Hayyim* 170:1.
321 *Mishna Berura* 170:1.

106.

Shulhan Arukh — On Shabbat, if his son is holding a stone, a father may still pick him up as long as the father does not consider the stone to be of any importance,[322] and his son so longs to be with his father that if he does not pick him up his son will be ill.[323]

Discussion — On Shabbat, stones are considered to be *muktze*, which means that a person is forbidden to move them. If the father gave consideration to the stone, then it would be as if he was carrying it through his carrying of his son. This would be the case even if he did not give consideration to the stone, but the child was not attached to the stone either.[324] If he does not give consideration to the stone, but the child is attached to it, then it is obvious that he picks up his child for the sake of the child and not the stone. Therefore, he would be permitted to pick up the child, despite his holding the stone, since the child's health takes precedence over the rabbinic transgression of carrying *muktze*. If, however, the father and son were in a public domain, where carrying something is a Torah prohibition, in addition to the rabbinic transgression of *muktze*, then the concern for the child would not overrule the Torah prohibition of carrying. Because the ruling of the *Shulhan Arukh* does not differentiate between whether this incident happens in a public domain or a private domain, it appears as if the ruling is incorrectly lenient.

Issue — How can the *Mishna Berura* address the implied leniency in a way that does not invalidate the ruling of the *Shulhan Arukh*?

The *Mishna Berura*'s Position — The *Mishna Berura* explains that Rabbi Karo's ruling only applies to the situation in which both the father and his child are in a courtyard, so that the only prohibition at stake is that of moving *muktze*. The *Mishna Berura*

---

322 We interpret the ruling in the *Shulhan Arukh* in this manner since he makes a distinction between a stone and a *dinar* (a type of coin). If the child is holding a *dinar*, the father may not pick him for fear that the *dinar* will drop and the father will pick it up the coin. The *Shulhan Arukh* does not have such a fear when the child is carrying a stone.

323 *Shulhan Arukh, Orah Hayyim* 309:1.

324 *Mishna Berura* 309:3.

justifies this interpretation of Rabbi Karo's ruling by noting that it is consistent with the discussion in the Talmud from which the ruling derives.[325] Though this may not be considered a full reinterpretation of the *Shulhan Arukh*, but rather as a clarification so that the reader does not make any wrong assumptions, the distinction between the two is a matter of approach. The objective difference is between qualification through one's own words (which would constitute changing the simple meaning of the ruling directly) and qualification through placing those words in the intent of another (which would constitute changing the simple meaning of the ruling indirectly). Though it gives sources for its qualifications in the *Sha'ar HaTziyun*, in the *Mishna Berura* this is given as if commentating on the *Shulhan Arukh* and not as providing alternative rulings.

Halakhic Principles — 4, 5, 8

107.

Shulhan Arukh — On Shabbat, if a tool has upon it both prohibited and permitted objects, it is permitted to move it when the permitted thing is more important that the forbidden one. If, on the other hand, the forbidden object is more important, one may not move it.[326]

Discussion — Just as there is a prohibition of carrying *muktze* on Shabbat, there is also a prohibition of carrying a permitted object which has a *muktze* object on top of it, since it would be carried indirectly. This case is similar to the situation of the father and his child who is carrying a stone. In this case, the ruling of the *Shulhan Arukh* is ambiguous when it comes to the situation in which there are two objects, one which a person is permitted to carry and the other which is *muktze*, on top of another permitted object.

The *Mishna Berura*'s Position — The *Mishna Berura* writes that if the *muktze* object and the permitted object are of equal importance,

---

325 *Mishna Berura* 309:1.
326 *Shulhan Arukh, Orah Hayyim* 310:8.

it is forbidden to move the tool. It also explains how to establish importance, namely that consideration of importance is based on the opinion of the person and is not socially determined.[327]

Halakhic Principles — 5, 8

108.

Shulhan Arukh — A person is permitted to place a *Sefer* (book) on one side and a *Sefer* on the other side and place a *Sefer* on top of the other two without fear of the prohibition of making a tent.[328]

Discussion — Rabbi Karo records this ruling in his laws of Shabbat, which is why he mentions that it is unnecessary to worry about making a tent, since making a tent is prohibited on Shabbat. However, regardless of the day which one would do this, one must still beware that he does not use the *Sefarim* (books) in a disrespectful manner. Because the *Shulhan Arukh* does not mention this latter concern, it seems as if one need not worry about it.

Issue — How can the *Mishna Berura* address the implied leniency in a way that does not invalidate the ruling of the *Shulhan Arukh*?

The *Mishna Berura*'s Position — The *Mishna Berura* cites the *Taz*, who writes that a person may only arrange the *Sefarim* in such a manner when he needs to learn from all of them. Otherwise, it is considered as if he is dishonoring the *Sefarim* and this would be prohibited even during the week. He does, however, note that the *Magen Avraham* and the *Hayye Adam* are lenient in the respect that one need not worry about disrespecting the *Sefarim*.[329]

Discussion — The *Mishna Berura* adds the *Taz*'s suggestion as a parenthetical concern, as if Rabbi Karo implies that he is only dealing with the ramifications of such an act in relation to Shabbat without excluding additional consequences. However, because the parenthetical interjection may seem to be forced, and because there are alternative positions which are also lenient regarding the potential disrespect one may cause the *Sefarim*, the *Mishna Berura*

---

327 *Mishna Berura* 310:33.
328 *Shulhan Arukh, Orah Hayyim* 315:7.
329 *Mishna Berura* 315:30.

also records the more lenient interpretation. By recording both positions, the *Mishna Berura* negotiates between the priority of incorporating more stringent positions when possible and the priority of maintaining the coherence of the *Shulhan Arukh*.

Halakhic Principles — 3, 4, 8

109.

Shulhan Arukh — On Shabbat, it is permitted to water vegetables not attached to the ground so that they do not wither.[330]

Discussion — It is a Torah prohibition to water vegetables that are attached to the ground on Shabbat. The reason why it is prohibited is because it is part of the planting and growing process. The general understanding of the permission to water cut vegetables is because they do not continue to grow by virtue of being cut from the ground; however, it is possible for vegetables that are not attached to the ground to continue to grow if left in water for an extended period of time. The wording of the ruling in the *Shulhan Arukh* does not seem to take this possibility into consideration.

Issue — How can the *Mishna Berura* address the implied leniency in a way that does not invalidate the ruling of the *Shulhan Arukh*?

The *Mishna Berura*'s Position — The *Mishna Berura* inserts that the type of vegetables to which the ruling refers are those vegetables that are fit to be consumed that day. Something that is not fit to eat that day, even if not attached to the ground, cannot be watered.[331] The *Mishna Berura* also refers the reader to the *Pri Megadim*'s ruling in *Siman* 336. In this *Siman*, the *Rema* allows one to stand tree branches in water on Shabbat as long as they do not have flowers on them, since the flowers would open in water.[332] The *Pri Megadim* writes that it seems that Rabbi Karo would allow one to stand them in water prepared on the previous day, but not to add water to them, since that would constitute too much exertion

---

330 *Shulhan Arukh, Orah Hayyim* 321:11.
331 *Mishna Berura* 321:37.
332 *Shulhan Arukh, Orah Hayyim* 336:11.

on Shabbat. In the *Sha'ar HaTziyun,* the *Mishna Berura* writes that one may rely on this if he forgot to stand them in water on Friday, since the fact that they do not have flowers would prevent a transgression of a Torah prohibition.[333] He does not, however, extend the leniency to vegetables.

Halakhic Principles — 5, 8

110.

Shulhan Arukh — If a person is alone on the road as Shabbat begins, he may carry his purse by moving less than four cubits at a time.[334] However, the *Shulhan Arukh* rules elsewhere that it is prohibited to carry something less than four cubits at a time, even when it is *ben ha'shmashot* (at the onset of Shabbat) and even in a *Karmelit.*[335]

Discussion — In order to understand the challenges that the *Mishna Berura* faces when confronting this ruling, it is first necessary to provide a brief account of the prohibition to carry on Shabbat. There are four different types of spaces, each of which has a different relation to carrying on Shabbat. In a private domain and in a place where there is an exemption due to the dimensions of the space, a person is permitted to carry. In a *Karmelit,* which is a space that is considered a public domain solely by rabbinic standards, it is rabbinically prohibited to carry. In a public domain proper, it is a Torah prohibition to carry four cubits, yet it is a rabbinic prohibition to carry an object less than four cubits at a time repeatedly for fear that the person will carry four cubits at once. Because carrying less than four cubits at a time repeatedly is a rabbinic prohibition, in the event that a person is in a position which interferes with fulfilling the commandment to enjoy Shabbat or is in potential danger, the rabbinic prohibition may be deferred, under cautious consideration. However, it is also a Torah prohibition to carry something from a public domain to a private domain

---

333 *Sha'ar HaTziyun* 336:48.
334 *Shulhan Arukh, Orah Hayyim* 266:7.
335 *Shulhan Arukh, Orah Hayyim* 359:5.

and a rabbinic prohibition to carry from a *Karmelit* to either a public or private domain. If a person is caught on the road at the onset of Shabbat, he does not only need to worry about carrying while on the road, but he must consider whether he is able to bring anything which he is carrying from the street into his house, which would be a transfer from a public to a private domain. The *Shulhan Arukh* does not explicitly deal with this issue in the ruling which seems to imply that one need not consider it.

Issue — How can the *Mishna Berura* address the implied leniency in a way that does not invalidate the ruling of the *Shulhan Arukh*?

The *Mishna Berura*'s Position — The *Mishna Berura* writes that this leniency only applies when there is no one else around, so that the person has no other alternative than walking less than four cubits at a time or leaving the object where it is. In such a case, because it is a situation of loss and people panic over their money, the sages allowed for leniency.[336] Also, the *Mishna Berura* writes that this is only when one is within a public domain or a *Karmelit*, where the prohibition is to walk four cubits. When traveling from a *Karmelit* to a private domain or to a public domain, or from a public domain to a private domain, where the prohibition is the transfer from one domain to another, a person cannot even move half of a cubit. Walking less than four cubits would not save him from transgression. In order to mitigate the difficulty of the latter situation, the *Mishna Berura* offers that when the person comes close to his house, which is a private domain, he should throw his purse in an abnormal way into the house, which is justified only because of the potential loss involved.[337]

Discussion — The prohibition to transfer an object only applies at its full effect when done in a normal manner. When done abnormally, it would be a rabbinic transgression, which can be deferred in a situation of great need.

Halakhic Principles — 4, 5, 8

---

336 *Mishna Berura* 266:16.
337 *Mishna Berura* 266:17.

111.

Shulhan Arukh — If a person rents a house for Passover with the presumption that it has been checked for *hametz*, and it is found not to have been checked, the renter must search for *hametz* without remuneration. It is not considered an erroneous transaction even in a place where people pay to have their houses searched, since he is doing a *mitzvah* by searching for *hametz*.

Rema — There are those who say that the landlord must pay for the price of checking the house for *hametz* if they made an explicit stipulation that the house had been checked.[338]

Alternative Positions — The *Pri Hadash* writes that Rabbi Karo and the *Rema* are only alluding to a general case in which the question of whether the house was checked did not arise, or the landlord said that it was checked and the renter remained quiet. If the renter made an explicit stipulation that he was renting the house on condition that it had been checked, then both Rabbi Karo and the Rema would agree that it is an erroneous transaction. To explain the language of the *Rema*, which seems to refer to making a specific stipulation, he explains that the *Rema*'s language in the phrase "since he made an explicit stipulation that the house was checked" is not specific; rather, he means to say that the landlord said it was checked and in general the renter assumed that the landlord told the truth and relied on his statement that he was renting a checked house.[339]

Discussion — The *Pri Hadash* assumes that the disagreement between Rabbi Karo and the *Rema* is only over whether a presumption can be considered an explicit stipulation. Rabbi Karo believes that it cannot, while the *Rema* contends that it should be so considered. While this may actually be the case, the *Pri Hadash* must drastically change the meaning of the language which the Rema uses. Moreover, the *Shulhan Arukh* does not explicitly endorse the *Pri Hadash*'s assumption that there is a difference between a presumption and an explicit stipulation.

---

338 *Shulhan Arukh, Orah Hayyim* 437:3.
339 *Biur Halakha* 437: s.v. *v'yesh omrim.*

Issue — How can the *Mishna Berura* address the ambiguity between the language of Rabbi Karo and the *Rema*, and take into consideration the interpretation of the *Pri Hadash*, without adversely affecting the trust one may have that the language of the *Shulhan Arukh* is coherent?

The *Mishna Berura*'s Position — The *Mishna Berura* explains the ruling of Rabbi Karo and the *Rema* according to the simple understanding of their language in his main commentary, and cites the *Pri Hadash* in the *Biur Halakha*. It concludes by relying on a technique used primarily in financial cases. He endorses the view of Rabbi Karo, that the landlord need not repay the renter for the cost of the search, because the landlord can claim that such is the ruling and it is the onus of the renter to provide proof that he deserves compensation.

Halakhic Principles — 6, 8

112.

Shulhan Arukh — On Shabbat, one may wash dishes that are needed for the day, but after the third meal he should not wash any more. Cups, on the other hand, he may wash all day, since one can continue to drink even after finishing the third meal.[340]

Discussion — There is a prohibition to prepare on Shabbat for after Shabbat, and cleaning dishes to be used after Shabbat would fall under that prohibition. Because the third meal occurs so late in the day, it is most likely that any dish used after the meal would be for after Shabbat. Therefore, cleaning it would be prohibited. Since a person would still be able to drink on Shabbat after the third meal, and could take any glass to do so, it would be permitted to wash the used glasses that he has. However, this leniency can provide an opportunity to potentially transgress the prohibition of preparing for after Shabbat by claiming that one may want to drink again when really he has no intention of doing so.

---

340 *Shulhan Arukh, Orah Hayyim* 323:6.

Issue — How can the *Mishna Berura* deal with this room for transgression without annulling the legitimacy of the *Shulhan Arukh*'s ruling?

The *Mishna Berura*'s Position — The *Mishna Berura* explains that Rabbi Karo's ruling speaks only in general terms. The truth of the matter, he proffers, is that whenever a person thinks he may eat or drink again, he may wash utensils. When he thinks he will no longer eat or drink, then he may no longer wash utensils.[341]

Halakhic Principles — 6, 8

113.

Shulhan Arukh — On Shabbat, a person is permitted to extinguish a candle so that one who is dangerously ill may sleep.[342]

Alternative Position — The Mishna in Tractate Shabbat records the position that one who extinguishes a lamp so that a sick person may fall asleep is not liable. In his commentary on the Mishna, the *Rambam* writes that it is permitted only if the sick person is dangerously ill and as long as it is impossible to move it/him to another place and he cannot block the light from it/him. Because the Hebrew language gives a gender to neuter objects, the Rambam's wording is ambiguous. It may mean either that it is impossible to move the candle or that it is impossible to move the person.

Discussion — Besides the ambiguity of the *Rambam's* language, there is also the concern regarding extinguishing a candle itself. If one were to extinguish the candle for its own sake, such as to enhance the wick, it would constitute a Torah transgression. To extinguish the candle for a reason not related to the candle itself is a *melakha she'eina tzarikh l'gufa*, meaning that it is not a Torah transgression only by virtue of the fact that the extinguishing was for the purpose of a different intention. Though it is not a Torah prohibition, it is still prohibited by virtue of rabbinic decree. Also, the consideration of allowing one to perform a *melakha she'eina tzarikh l'gufa* is weightier than it is with other rabbinic decrees, since a

---

341 *Mishna Berura* 323:28-9.
342 *Shulhan Arukh, Orah Hayyim* 278:1.

melakha she'eina tzarikh l'gufa is closer to an actual Torah prohibition (*melakha*) than acts prohibited by other rabbinic safeguards, since all the act is missing to be a Torah transgression is the correct intention.

Issue — How can the *Mishna Berura* deal with the ambiguity of the *Rambam's* language as well as the fact that the Mishna seems to be more lenient than either the *Rambam* or Rabbi Karo regarding the danger of the illness without challenging the ruling of the *Shulhan Arukh*?

The *Mishna Berura*'s Position — The *Mishna Berura* cites the *Rambam*, but changes the wording to communicate that that permission is only granted if it is impossible to bring the sick person to another room or to block the light.[343] In the *Biur Halakha*, it is acknowledged that the words "the sick person" were added to what the *Rambam* wrote. The *Mishna Berura* justifies this insertion by saying that if one reads the *Rambam*'s commentary one would be sure that he meant the sick person and not the candle. He further explains that everyone is stringent not to extinguish the candle when there is another alternative, since even though it is a *melakha she'ein tzarikh l'gufa*, extinguishing the candle comes very close to a Torah prohibition. That is the reason why it is treated more stringently than other rabbinic prohibitions which are overridden even for one who is sick but not dangerously so.[344] The *Mishna Berura* does extend the qualified leniency to a person who is not dangerously ill, if a doctor says that he will become sicker and may become dangerously so if he does not sleep.[345]

Discussion — In order to support the ruling of the *Shulhan Arukh*, the *Mishna Berura* interprets the language of a *Rishon* to comply with Rabbi Karo's understanding. Also, because the Mishna does not explicitly limit the permission to the case in which the sick person is dangerously ill, the *Mishna Berura* is able to find support

---

343 *Mishna Berura* 278:1.
344 *Biur Halakha* 278: s.v. *muter.*
345 *Biur Halakha* 278: s.v. *bishvil she'yishan.*

to broaden the permissibility to help someone who may become dangerously ill but is not so currently.

Halakhic Principles — 2, 8

114.

Shulhan Arukh — When the month of *Av* begins, we reduce our happiness.[346]

Alternative Position — The Magen *Avraham* writes that what Rabbi Karo means is that there should be no happiness at all.[347]

Discussion — In the *Sha'ar HaTziyun*, the *Mishna Berura* explains that the *Magen Avraham*'s ruling is based on *Tosafot*'s comment about a fast instituted due to a lack of rain, where the mention of restricting joy implies its complete elimination. The *Magen Avraham* applies the rationale behind the case of a fast due to lack of rain to the decrease of joy in *Av*. The *Mishna Berura*, however, writes that this view of what it means to decrease happiness is only the opinion of *Tosafot* in the first chapter of Tractate *Megilla*. In Tractate *Yevamot* (43a), *Tosafot* contradicts this ruling and contends that one may buy that which is needed for a wedding, which entails happiness, on *Rosh Hodesh Av* and continue to do so during the month. The *Mishna Berura* further draws an analogy to Rabbi Karo's discussion of "restricting one's business" by which he means reducing it and not eliminating it completely.

The *Mishna Berura*'s Position — The *Mishna Berura* posits that "restricting one's happiness" has the same connotation as "restricting one's business," meaning that one should reduce it but not eliminate it completely.[348]

Halakhic Principles — 6, 8

---

346 *Shulhan Arukh, Orah Hayyim* 551:1.
347 *Magen Avraham* 551:1.
348 *Sha'ar HaTziyun* 551:1.

115.

Shulhan Arukh — "Seeking your needs," such as evaluating one's assets to see what needs to be done the following day, is forbidden on Shabbat.[349]

Alternative Positions — The *Magen Avraham* and other *Aharonim* rule that the prohibition only applies when one is obvious about it. The *Hayye Adam*, on the other hand, rules stringently and forbids a person to evaluate his assets, even in a manner which is not recognizable to anyone. Furthermore, this issue is also a matter of dispute among the *Rishonim*. The *Ramban*, the *Rashba*, and the *Ritva* rule leniently, and allow a person to act *incognito*. Some interpret the *Rambam* and the *Smag* as prohibiting a person to "seek his needs" in any manner, yet the *Mishna Berura* argues that after investigating their words, it is not conclusive that they disagree with those who are lenient.

Discussion — The prohibition of "seeking one's needs" is only rabbinic. When there is a doubt with respect to a rabbinic decree, even when the doubt is in which position to follow, the common stance is to judge according to the lenient opinion. The *Shulhan Arukh*, however, seems to rule stringently, since it does not make a distinction between acting in obvious or discreet ways.

Issue — How can the *Mishna Berura* incorporate the seemingly contrary, lenient opinion, which is the normative opinion among the *Aharonim*, without causing a conflict with the ruling of the *Shulhan Arukh*?

The *Mishna Berura*'s Position — The *Mishna Berura* writes that Rabbi Karo's ruling applies only to those actions that are recognizable as such; if a person acts in a manner whereby it is not obvious that he is "seeking his needs," his evaluating is considered general contemplation and is permitted.[350] In the *Biur Halakha*, it is written that because the dispute among the *Rishonim* can be dismissed based on its understanding of the *Rambam* and the *Smag*, and since

---

349 *Shulhan Arukh, Orah Hayyim* 306:1.
350 *Mishna Berura* 306:1.

the matter is only of rabbinic degree, it decided not to mention the more stringent opinion in its main commentary.[351]

Discussion — By interpreting the history of debate among the *poskim* in a way that makes the more lenient approach an obvious understanding of the issue, the *Mishna Berura* is able to interpret the ruling of the *Shulhan Arukh* as if the leniency was implied.

Halakhic Principles — 6, 8

116.

Shulhan Arukh — If a Jew receives a roll each week from a Gentile as an interest payment, he should say to the Gentile before Passover that for the week of Passover he should give him either wheat or money. Since he made such a stipulation, if after Passover the Gentile gives him a *hametz* roll, he can consider it to be in exchange for the wheat or the money that is owed to him; therefore, it is permitted.[352]

Discussion — Since the Gentile is required to give the Jew a roll each week, there is a concern that the Gentile would designate a roll on Passover for the Jew which would be halakhically considered as if it were now owned by the Jew. The Jew would then inadvertently transgress the prohibition of owning leavened bread on Passover. On the other hand, if the Jew were to make the Gentile give him either wheat or money for the week of Passover, then even if the Gentile designated a roll for him, it would not be considered as if the Jew owned it, since it was not what he wanted.

Alternative Positions — The *Shulhan Arukh* does not qualify the ruling so that it applies only in certain situations; the *Aharonim*, however, rule that this is only an *ab initio* requirement. *Ex post facto*, if the Jew did not make a stipulation, he may still receive the *hametz* roll after Passover even if the Gentile designated it for him on the holiday. The reason for its permissibility is that the roll is not considered to be truly owned by the Jew until it comes into his possession. Before that time, the Jew possesses only a credit for a roll and not the

---

351 *Biur Halakha* 306: s.v. *she'me'ayen nekhasav.*
352 *Shulhan Arukh, Orah Hayyim* 450:2.

roll itself. The designated roll remains in the possession of the Gentile during Passover.[353]

Issue — How can the *Mishna Berura* incorporate the seemingly contrary, lenient opinion, which is the normative opinion among the *Aharonim*, without causing a conflict with the ruling of the *Shulhan Arukh*?

The *Mishna Berura*'s Position — In its main commentary, the *Mishna Berura* cites the position of the *Aharonim*.

Discussion — Though the *Mishna Berura* explains the reasoning behind the ruling of the *Shulhan Arukh* and then cites the position of the *Aharonim*, by maintaining the more stringent position of the *Shulhan Arukh* as obligatory *ab initio*, it maintains its juridical validity despite accepting the more lenient conclusion of the later *poskim*.

Halakhic Principles — 2, 8

117.

Shulhan Arukh — If one forgot to say a blessing before taking a drink, he should swallow the liquid and not recite the introductory blessing.

Rema — There are those who say that one should make the blessing and that it seems that this would be the main opinion.[354] This would entail pushing the liquid one has in one's mouth to a side and saying the blessing.

Alternative Positions — The *Raavad* and the *Rashba* rule that a person should spit out what is in his mouth when he has additional liquid that he can make the blessing on. Other *Rishonim*, however, do not mention this advice.

Issue — In this case, the ruling of the *Shulhan Arukh* and the *Rema* directly contradict each other. Also, neither takes the alternative position of spitting out the liquid.

The *Mishna Berura*'s Position — The *Mishna Berura* explains that when Rabbi Karo writes that one should not make the introductory

---

353 *Mishna Berura* 450:4.
354 *Shulhan Arukh, Orah Hayyim* 172:1.

blessing, he refers to a case in which there is no more liquid left to drink and the person needs the water. If there is more liquid, he should spit out what he has in his mouth so as not to benefit without saying a blessing.[355] In the *Biur Halakha*, however, the *Mishna Berura* qualifies its statement by saying that only *ab initio* is it proper to consider the position of the *Raavad* and the *Rashba* to spit out what is in one's mouth when one has additional liquid. Other *Rishonim*, on the other hand, do not mention this advice; therefore, one need not protest against one who is lenient and swallows the liquid.[356] Regarding the position of the *Rema*, the *Mishna Berura* writes that the majority of the *poskim* rule, contrary to the *Rema*, that a person should not make the introductory blessing on the liquid he has in his mouth.[357]

Discussion — The *Mishna Berura* interprets the ruling of the *Shulhan Arukh* in a way that incorporates the alternative stringent opinion. At the same time, it blatantly rejects the *Rema*'s position. **Halakhic Principles — 5, 8**

118.

Shulhan Arukh — On Shabbat, one may not spoon out food from a cooking utensil or pot that was removed from the fire if the food is not fully cooked, because it is stirring. If it is fully cooked, it is permitted.

Rema — *Ab initio* one should be careful not to spoon out food from a pot under any circumstance.[358]

Discussion — The stirring process, as well as the process of removing food, plays an active role in cooking the food, which is prohibited on Shabbat. The ruling of the *Shulhan Arukh* is more lenient than that of the *Rema* since it allows a person to remove fully cooked food from the pot, yet the *Rema* does note that his position is only to be considered *ab initio*.

---

355 *Mishna Berura* 172:2.
356 *Biur Halakha* 172: s.v. *v'aino mevarekh alehem*.
357 *Mishna Berura* 172:5.
358 *Shulhan Arukh, Orah Hayyim* 318:18.

The *Mishna Berura*'s Position — The *Mishna Berura* writes that the *Aharonim* are not stringent like the *Rema*; in truth the main position is that if the food is fully cooked a person may even stir the pot. If someone wants to be stringent, he may be so with respect to stirring, but to spoon out food, one should not be stringent at all if the food is fully cooked and not on the fire.[359]

Halakhic Principles — 6

119.

Shulhan Arukh — A private domain is a place surrounded by partitions that are ten handbreadths high, and contains an area of at least four handbreadths by four handbreadths.

Rema — Some say the required measure to be considered a private domain is equal to a square of the length of the hypotenuse of four by four.[360]

The *Mishna Berura*'s Position — The *Mishna Berura* explains that according to Rabbi Karo and the majority of the *poskim*, the area of four by four must be measured inside of the partitions; the width of the partitions cannot join to the measure of the area. He does note, however, that there are *Rishonim* who write that the width of the walls is included in the measurement.[361] With respect to the *Rema*'s statement, the *Mishna Berura* writes that the *Levush* does not mention this opinion, and that the *Elya Rabba* writes that the *Levush* was correct to omit it, since it is an individual opinion with which all the *Rishonim* disagree. The *Mishna Berura* concludes, saying that the *Gra* also rejects this opinion, since the measure of a private domain is not analogous to the measure of walking four cubits in a public domain.[362]

Halakhic Principles — 5, 10

---

359 *Mishna Berura* 318:117.
360 *Shulhan Arukh, Orah Hayyim* 345:2.
361 *Mishna Berura* 345:3.
362 *Mishna Berura* 345:6.

120.

Shulhan Arukh — If the bread for the *Eruv* became moldy and is inedible, it is invalid and new bread is required.

Rema — Because of this risk, the custom is to make an *Eruv* from *matzot* which do not become moldy so quickly. Another reason is that the *Eruv* can then also be used on Passover as well as throughout the year. This is preferred to establishing an *Eruv* each Shabbat, since people may forget to set an *Eruv*; however, if they want to set an *Eruv* every Friday and eat it every Shabbat they are permitted to do so.[363]

The *Mishna Berura*'s Position — The *Mishna Berura* writes that according to the *Aharonim* it is better to make an *Eruv* every Friday, since *matzah* can also become ruined over time. The *Mishna Berura* does, however, suggest that the ideal would be for a person to make an *Eruv* each Shabbat and include the entire community, and in this way he will not have to worry if the *Eruv* in the synagogue goes bad. He should, nevertheless, not recite a blessing on making the *Eruv*.[364]

Halakhic Principles — 4, 5

121.

Shulhan Arukh — It is not necessary to stand during Torah reading.

Rema — There are those who are stringent to stand as practiced by the *Maharam*.[365]

The *Mishna Berura*'s Position — The *Mishna Berura* cites the *Pri Hadash* and the *Gra* to say that the main ruling is like Rabbi Karo and that such is our practice. It also cites the *Bach* to say that even the *Maharam* agreed that such is the ruling, but nevertheless thought it is appropriate to give honor by standing.[366]

Halakhic Principles — 6

---

363 *Shulhan Arukh, Orah Hayyim* 368:5.
364 *Mishna Berura* 368:21.
365 *Shulhan Arukh, Orah Hayyim* 146:4.
366 *Mishna Berura* 146:19.

122.

Rema — In the event that there are two *Hatanim* or two *Ba'aleiBrit* in the synagogue on Monday or Thursday, it is permissible to add a fourth *Aliyah* since, for them, the day is equivalent to a holiday.[367]

The *Mishna Berura*'s Position — The *Mishna Berura* writes it is not the custom to add *Aliyot* in these cases.[368]

Halakhic Principles — 7

123.

Rema — If one has a doubt as to whether he mentioned *"Ya'ale ve'Yavo,"* he need not repeat the *Amida*.[369]

Discussion — Since thirty days have not passed since last mentioning *"Ya'ale ve'Yavo,"* the Rema considers that there is not a full presumption that he certainly did not mention it.

The *Mishna Berura*'s Position — The *Mishna Berura* writes that despite the *Rema*'s reasoning, we do not consider his position to be the Halakha, since almost all of the *Aharonim* disagree and hold that if there is a doubt a person must repeat the *Amida*, since in general one does not say *"Ya'ale ve'Yavo."*[370]

Halakhic Principles — 5[371]

124.

Rema — When a group begins a meal and someone speaks about a matter unrelated to the blessing over the bread before the one who recited the blessing over bread for the group has eaten, the person must repeat the blessing over bread. If the one who made the blessing

---

367 *Shulhan Arukh, Orah Hayyim* 135:1.

368 *Mishna Berura* 135:3.

369 *Shulhan Arukh, Orah Hayyim* 422:1.

370 *Mishna Berura* 422:10.

371 This instance of being strict, however, also includes the leniency that the person may be repeating the prayer superfluously. Because of this suspicion, the *Be'er Heitiv* quotes the opinion that it is best for a person to repeat the prayer as a *nedava* (voluntary offering) so as to avoid the transgression of saying an obligatory prayer superfluously. The *Mishna Berura* does not cite this opinion, giving further credence to the notion that it rejects the *Rema*'s opinion when it is in the great minority rather than trying to incorporate it.

has eaten some of the bread, even if the other members of the meal have not, it is not considered to be an interruption between the blessing and eating.[372]

The *Mishna Berura*'s Position — The *Mishna Berura* first interprets the *Rema*'s comment to refer only to an *ex post facto* situation, claiming that even the *Rema* holds that *ab initio* it is forbidden for a person to speak until he has eaten. It then states that this ruling is only the position of the *Rema*. Almost all of the *Aharonim* disagree with him, requiring the person to repeat the blessing for himself if he talks before eating.[373] In the *Biur Halakha*, the *Mishna Berura* explains that the source of the *Rema*'s ruling is the *Rokeah* and the *Or Zarua*, yet argues that the *Rema* misinterprets their words.[374]

Halakhic Principles — 2, 5, 8

125.

Rema — There is an opinion which states that it is permitted to ask a Gentile to light a candle for the Shabbat meal since it would be permitted to tell a Gentile to do something completely prohibited for the sake of a *mitzvah*. Many people are accustomed to be lenient and command a Gentile to light a candle for the needs of a meal, particularly when there is a wedding or a celebratory meal for a *brit milah*, and one should not protest against them. There are also those who are stringent in a situation where the action is not of great need, since many *poskim* disagree with this reasoning.[375]

The *Mishna Berura*'s Position — Rather than claiming that this is a minority opinion upon which one can rely in times of need, or that one should not protest against those who accept the lenient position as the Halakha, the *Mishna Berura* explains the *Rema*'s directive not to protest to be because it is better that the people who follow the position err unintentionally than purposefully.[376]

---

372 *Shulhan Arukh, Orah Hayyim* 167:6.
373 *Mishna Berura* 167:43.
374 *Biur Halakha* 167: s.v. *aval ahar-kakh.*
375 *Shulhan Arukh, Orah Hayyim* 276:2.
376 *Mishna Berura* 276:23.

Discussion — By interpreting the *Rema*'s leniency as a way for those who do not know the correct Halakha to avoid more serious repercussions for transgressing intentionally, the *Mishna Berura* implies that the *Rema*'s leniency is not a legitimate opinion on which one may rely. In its comments on the *Rema*'s ruling, the *Mishna Berura* continually attempts to toe the line between disregarding the lenient position as legitimate and maintaining its acceptability when it can prevent people from sinning.[377]

Halakhic Principles — 5

126.

Rema — During a fast it is permitted to chew cinnamon sticks, other spices, or sweet sticks, and spit them out in order to moisten one's throat, except on Yom Kippur where it is forbidden.[378]

The *Mishna Berura*'s Position — The *Mishna Berura* writes that the *Rema* does not actually consider this to be the Halakha. Rather, he is only quoting the opinion of the *Mordekhai*. The *Mishna Berura* justifies this interpretation by saying that based upon what the *Rema* writes regarding prohibiting tasting on all fasts, he would also prohibit chewing cinnamon.[379]

Discussion — By interpreting the *Rema*'s statement to be a citation of another's opinion, the *Mishna Berura* negates the possibility that the *Rema*'s words are his own ruling on the matter.

Halakhic Principles — 5, 8

Qualified Intention

The difficulty of combining opposing positions in a manner that removes doubt in fulfillment often occurs when the *Mishna Berura* seeks to promote leniency. In following a stringent opinion, one

---

377 For example, see *Mishna Berura* 276:25, which states that even though the majority of *poskim* disagree, one is nevertheless allowed to tell a Gentile to fix an *Eruv* that fell down on Shabbat so as not to put a stumbling block in front of the masses.

378 *Shulhan Arukh, Orah Hayyim* 567:3.

379 *Mishna Berura* 567:13.

would automatically fulfill the opinions with more lenient require-ments as well. On the other hand, when a person follows a more lenient opinion, he excludes those opinions with a higher bar for fulfillment. There are times, however, when following a more lenient position may not only preclude fulfillment according to the higher standard, it may also entail potential transgression according to the more stringent standard. In order to maneuver between maximizing the range of fulfillment in accepting a more lenient position while, at the same time, avoiding possible transgression, the *Mishna Berura* recommends qualifying one's intention when performing the partic-ular action. The *Mishna Berura* recommends that a person qualify his intentions when there is no other way to join completely opposing conditions. Although the *Mishna Berura* uses the technique of suggesting that one qualify his intention or to make a stipulation about his intention in order to aggregate various opinions, it still recognizes that this is not an optimal method of finding compro-mise. When a person's intention clearly contrasts with the presumed intention behind a particular action, the *Mishna Berura* has diffi-culty considering his personal intention as effectively influencing the meaning of the action.

127.

Shulhan Arukh — A person may pray in the morning until the end of the fourth hour.[380] If one makes a mistake, or purposefully delays, and prays after the fourth hour until midday, even though he does not receive a reward for praying on time, he nevertheless receives a reward for praying.

Rema — After noon has passed, it is prohibited to pray the morning prayer.[381]

Alternative Positions — There are opinions which hold that if one purposefully delays his prayer until after the fourth hour, he

---

380 According to Jewish law, the hours of the day are calculated by dividing the total daylight hours into twelve proportional hours. Each proportional hour is considered to be an "hour" according to Jewish law.

381 *Shulhan Arukh, Orah Hayyim* 89:1.

is no longer allowed to pray at all. On the contrary, there are also opinions which allow one to pray the morning prayer until a half hour past noon.

Discussion — The *Mishna Berura* is left with the difficulty of reconciling the *Shulhan Arukh*'s ruling that one may pray after the fourth hour with the opinions that prohibit a person from praying after such time. To follow the ruling of the *Shulhan Arukh* entails not only that the person is acting according to a lenient opinion, but that he may potentially be transgressing the law according to the more stringent opinion which prohibits a person from praying at that time. Furthermore, if the *Mishna Berura* were to accept the opinion that allows a person to pray the morning prayer until half past noon, it would be condoning a potential transgression according to those opinions that prohibit it.

Issue — How can the *Mishna Berura* maximize the range of fulfillment in accepting a more lenient position while, at the same time, avoiding possible transgression according to more stringent opinions?

The *Mishna Berura*'s Position — The *Mishna Berura* accepts the ruling that if one prays after the fourth hour he still receives reward for praying, albeit not for praying on time. Nevertheless, it recommends that one intend that his prayer be a "*nedava*" (a voluntary offering) since there are opinions which hold that if one purposefully delays his prayer after the fourth hour he is no longer allowed to pray at all. To unequivocally intend one's prayer to be a "*nedava*," however, precludes the ability to pray the morning prayer if he is allowed to do so. Therefore, the *Mishna Berura* advises that one stipulate that one's prayer should only be considered a "*nedava*" if according to the law it is prohibited to pray the morning prayer after the fourth hour.[382] Similarly, the *Mishna Berura* writes that if one has not yet prayed the morning prayer due to error or compulsion, and noon passes, even though there are some opinions that allow one to pray until a half hour past noon, he should wait until after half past

---

382 *Mishna Berura* 89:6.

noon, pray *Minha* (the afternoon prayer), and then pray a make-up prayer in place of the morning prayer. *Ex post facto*, however, even if a person prays before half past noon, he fulfills his obligation and need not pray a make-up morning prayer.[383] In presenting his most lenient position, the *Mishna Berura* refers us to the comment of Rabbi Akiva Eiger on the matter, which states that after noon passes, one may pray, but only if he provides this stipulation: if the time for the *Minha* prayer has come, let this be for the sake of the *Minha* prayer. If it has not yet arrived, let this be for the sake of the morning prayer. Furthermore, Rabbi Akiva Eiger recommends that after half past noon, one should pray again with the stipulation that if the first prayer counted as the morning prayer, then this one should be counted for the *Minha* prayer; if the last prayer counted for the *Minha* prayer, then this one should be considered a make-up for the missed morning prayer.[384]

Discussion — Because, at first glance, the *Mishna Berura*'s most lenient position seems to conflict with the other positions regarding when a person can pray, one may think that it allows the person to pray without making a stipulation *ex post facto* in order to keep him within the halakhic fold. Such an assumption presumes that its methodology of synthesizing positions only relates to *ab initio* situations. *Ex post facto*, however, a person can rely on any position that legitimizes his performance. This assumption is corrected by the *Mishna Berura*'s reference to Rabbi Akiva Eiger. Why the *Mishna Berura* only refers us to Rabbi Akiva Eiger's comment and does not state it explicitly, either in the *Biur Halakha* or *Sha'ar HaTziyun*, is an open question. Nonetheless, this reference to it in the main commentary supports the assumption that it attempts to find agreement among the various positions regardless of whether it is *ab initio* or *ex post facto*.

Halakhic Principles — 2, 4

---

383 *Mishna Berura* 89:7.
384 *Hiddushei Rabbi Akiva Eiger* 89: s.v. *mathil ahar hatzot.*

128.

Shulhan Arukh — It is prohibited to wear phylacteries on *Hol HaMoed* because, like Shabbat and Yom Tov, *Hol HaMoed* itself is considered a sign, and one must not have two signs displayed together.[385]

Rema — A person is required to don his phylacteries, since *Hol HaMoed* is not considered a sign which would prohibit donning phylacteries during those days.[386]

Discussion — The reason one must not have two signs together is that it shows contempt for each one. It is also a transgression of "*bal tosif*," which is the prohibition of adding to the six hundred thirteen commandments given in the Torah in such a way that it is perceived as if one is denying the perfection of the prescribed performance.

The *Mishna Berura*'s Position — With respect to the *Shulhan Arukh*'s reasons for prohibiting the donning of phylacteries during *Hol HaMoed*, the *Mishna Berura* writes that the prohibitions of displaying two signs and of "*bal tosif*" only apply to times when a person would don phylacteries for the sake of performing a commandment. If he dons them without such intention, it would neither show contempt nor be a transgression. Also, if a person wears them publicly, it would only entail a rabbinic offense.[387] During *Hol HaMoed*, a person should don his phylacteries without saying a blessing and have in mind the following intention: if he is obligated to don phylacteries, then his donning is for the sake of fulfilling a commandment; and if not, it is not.

Discussion — The *Mishna Berura*'s explanation of the *Shulhan Arukh*'s reasoning gives it the tools with which to deal with a blatant contradiction and create a compromise in the following way. It first mentions that the *Aharonim* agree with the *Taz* that a blessing on donning phylacteries during *Hol HaMoed* should not be said. The reason not to say the blessing is because its

---

385 *Shulhan Arukh, Orah Hayyim* 31:2.
386 Ibid.
387 *Mishna Berura* 31:5.

requirement is first of all in doubt, since there is a doubt as to whether one must don phylacteries at all; also even if there is a requirement to don them, blessings do not restrain fulfillment of a commandment. Once it removes the verbal indication that donning phylacteries is certainly required, as saying a blessing over it would imply, the *Mishna Berura* advises that a person have a particular intention while donning his phylacteries, which would allow him to fulfill the potential obligation without running into a possible transgression if donning them were prohibited. It states that before a person dons his phylacteries, he should think to himself that if he is obligated to do so, then his donning is for the sake of fulfilling a commandment; and if not, it is not. This stipulation removes the possible transgression of *"bal tosif,"* since one acts without definitiveness, yet provides enough intention to be considered efficacious if necessary.[388]

Halakhic Principles — 4, 8

129.

Shulhan Arukh — The order of the sections of the Torah which are placed in the phylacteries according to *Rashi* and *Rambam* are as follows: *"Kadesh"* (Exodus 13:1-10) on the outer left, *"VeHaya Ki YaViacha"* (Exodus 13:11-16) on the inner left, *"Shema"* (Devarim 6:4-9) on the inner right, and *"VeHaya Im Shamoa"* (Deuteronomy 11:13-21) on the outer right. According to *Rabbenu Tam*, the order is *"Kadesh"* (Exodus 13:1-10) on the outer left, *"VeHaya Ki YeViacha"* (Exodus 13:11-16) on the inner left, *"VeHaya Im Shamoa"* (Deuteronomy 11:13-21) on the inner right, and *"Shema"* (Devarim 6:4-9) on the outer right. The universal custom is according to *Rashi* and *Rambam*. Those who fear Heaven will fulfill their obligation through donning both, and they will make two pairs of phylacteries, and while donning them both they will have the intention that the one which is halakhically acceptable will be the one through which they fulfill their obligation and the other one will be as regular

---

388 *Mishna Berura* 31:8.

straps; if they cannot don both at the same time, they will don the set that is according to *Rashi* first and the set that is according to *Rabbenu Tam* second without a blessing.[389]

Discussion — The opinion of *Rashi* and that of *Rabbenu Tam* are mutually exclusive; moreover, because the dominant halakhic position is that *Rashi*'s opinion is correct, problems arise when wearing *Rabbenu Tam*'s phylacteries if one does not have a certain intention while doing so. If a person dons the phylacteries of both *Rashi* and *Rabbenu Tam*, he cannot have the intention that both of them fulfill the commandment. Counter-intuitively, the reason is not because one will transgress the prohibition of *"bal tosif"*; rather, if a person dons the phylacteries of *Rabbenu Tam* for the sake of fulfilling a commandment, he may find himself transgressing *"bal tigra,"* the prohibition of subtracting from the six hundred thirteen commandments in such a way that it is perceived as if one is denying the perfection of the prescribed performance. In the *Biur Halakha*, the *Mishna Berura* explains: It writes that the *Rambam*'s position is that if one takes away from what is in the Written Torah or from what is accepted in the Oral Torah, he transgresses the prohibition of *"bal tigra."* Since the *poskim* have accepted that the correct order of the sections in the phylacteries is according to *Rashi*, the phylacteries of *Rabbenu Tam* contain two invalid sections since they are not in the proper order. Thus, wearing the phylacteries of *Rabbenu Tam* is like wearing phylacteries with only two sections, instead of the required four. To don the phylacteries of *Rabbenu Tam* after that of *Rashi* does not ameliorate the problem, since there are opinions that claim that according to the Torah a person is obligated to wear phylacteries throughout the whole day. Therefore, when he dons the phylacteries of *Rabbenu Tam*, he cannot say that he has already fulfilled his obligation and is now just performing a super-erogatory act. The difficulty in how to consider the meaning of wearing both the phylacteries of *Rashi* and those of *Rabbenu Tam* is exacerbated by the statement in the *Shulhan Arukh* that those

---

389 *Shulhan Arukh, Orah Hayyim* 34:1-2.

who fear Heaven wear both sets of phylacteries, yet when doing so, they have the intention that one of them fulfills the obligation whereas the second is considered as mere straps with no halakhic significance.[390]

The *Mishna Berura*'s Position — The *Mishna Berura* explains the statement in the *Shulhan Arukh* to mean that those who fear Heaven do not have the intention that both phylacteries have the status of being proper according to the Torah; rather, they seek only to act according to all opinions. Nevertheless, they avoid both potential non-fulfillment and possible transgression since their intention stipulates that one set is definitely invalid, thereby they avoid adding to the commandment by wearing two valid yet different sets, and that each set be judged on its own, thereby allowing the phylacteries of *Rashi* to be deemed fully valid within the conditional stipulation.[391] When a person does not don both sets at the same time, the *Mishna Berura* advises that it is essential that one explicitly has in mind while donning the phylacteries of *Rabbenu Tam* that he does so only due to a doubt and not to fulfill a commandment. As we saw above regarding "*bal tosif,*" to act due to doubt is not so definitive as to be considered "*bal tigra.*"[392] When donning the phylacteries of *Rashi*, on the other hand, a person recites the blessing, since according to the main ruling, only with them does a person fulfill his obligation.[393]

Halakhic Principles — 4, 8

130.

Shulhan Arukh — It is prohibited to hire a *Hazan* to pray on Shabbat, yet there is an opinion that permits it.

Rema — If he is hired for an extended period of time, such as a year or a month, it is permitted according to everyone.[394]

---

390 *Shulhan Arukh, Orah Hayyim* 34:2.
391 *Mishna Berura* 34:8.
392 *Biur Halakha* 34: s.v. *yaniah shel Rabbenu Tam.*
393 *Mishna Berura* 34:13.
394 *Shulhan Arukh, Orah Hayyim* 306:5.

Alternative Position — The *Aharonim* write that we have the custom to be lenient and hire a person solely for Shabbat.

Discussion — It is rabbinically forbidden to receive wages for work done on Shabbat, even if that work is permissible to do. Though the primary prohibition applies to receiving wages; it includes giving wages as well. Leniency is given, however, if one receives payment for work done over a period of time such as a month, week, or year even if Shabbat is included.[395]

The *Mishna Berura*'s Position — The *Mishna Berura* explains that the reason for permitting a community to hire a *Hazan* solely for Shabbat is that for the sake of a *mitzvah* the rabbis did not make a decree to prohibit it. He adds, however, that the *Hazan* will not see a sign of blessing from his wages.[396] He also remarks that though the *Aharonim* write that we have the custom to be lenient and hire a person solely for Shabbat, the *Mishna Berura* suggests that for one who is concerned for those who prohibit it, he should not determine the *Hazan*'s wages initially, but that whatever he is given afterwards should be in the form of a gift.[397]

Halakhic Principles — 3, 8

131.

Shulhan Arukh — A person cannot fulfill his obligation to eat *matzah* on Passover with stolen *matzah*. On the other hand, if he stole wheat or flour and made *matzah* from it, he can use it to fulfill his obligation since the wheat or flour were acquired via their change in form (*shinui koneh*).[398]

Discussion — According to the Halakha, a physical change in an object's form creates acquisition. It is known as *Shinui Koneh*. The value of the stolen object must nevertheless be returned.

---

395 *Shulhan Arukh, Orah Hayyim* 306:4.
396 *Mishna Berura* 306:23.
397 *Mishna Berura* 306:24.
398 *Shulhan Arukh, Orah Hayyim* 454:4.

The *Mishna Berura*'s Position — The *Mishna Berura* writes that according to many *poskim*, a person must be careful when he bakes his *matzah* in the same oven along with many other people, since someone can accidentally take another's *matzah*. In such a situation, it is correct that each person say before baking, "Anyone who takes my *matzah*, let it be a gift to him," since if each does not say this there would be a suspicion that people may have stolen *matzah*. It also recommends the same technique at the time a person mills his grain.[399]

Discussion — By making such a stipulation, the *Mishna Berura* finds a way for people to avoid the probable transgression of taking other people's *matzah* and grain. If each person makes such a stipulation, then no one will be liable for inadvertent theft.

Halakhic Principles — 4

132.

Shulhan Arukh — On the day preceding Yom Kippur, if one stops eating while it is still daytime, he may resume eating as long as he did not accept upon himself the Yom Kippur fast.[400]

Alternative Position — The *Mishna Berura* cites those who write that there is a custom that after one stops eating he is forbidden to resume, since they consider stopping to eat as equal to stating verbally that he accepts the fast upon himself.

The *Mishna Berura*'s Position — The *Mishna Berura* recommends that a person say explicitly (or at least have in mind) before reciting *Birkat HaMazon* that he is not accepting the fast.[401]

Halakhic Principles — 4

133.

Shulhan Arukh — If one sleeps a deep sleep during the day, it is considered an interruption [between the morning blessings over learning Torah and his continuing to learn when he awakens]. There

---

399 *Mishna Berura* 454:15.
400 *Shulhan Arukh, Orah Hayyim* 608:3.
401 *Mishna Berura* 608:12.

are those who say that it is not considered an interruption, and such is the custom.[402]

Discussion — Usually, the morning blessings over learning Torah includes the Torah a person learns throughout the entire day, since it is presumed that learning Torah is continually on a person's mind. When a person falls asleep, however, there is a doubt as to whether the presumption can still hold. If it is an interruption, he would have to repeat the blessings. If it is not considered an interruption, he need not repeat the blessings. Because the *Shulhan Arukh* records the first opinion as a matter of fact yet records the second opinion with the expression, "There are those who say," it is possible to assume that the first opinion, which requires a person to repeat the blessings, is the true Halakha, and the practice of not repeating them is only a custom that had developed contrary to what Rabbi Karo believes is correct. The *Mishna Berura* quotes, however, the *Lehem Hamudot*, which states that those who do recite the blessings will have blessing come upon them; moreover, it lists a number of *Rishonim* and *Aharonim* who also rule that one should repeat the blessings. It also notes that the *Pri Megadim* infers that it is possible to rely on the custom that one need not recite the blessing, but notes that nevertheless it seems obvious that one who relies on those *poskim* that mention that one should say the blessing will not lose out.[403]

The *Mishna Berura*'s Position — In order to limit the problem as much as possible while not having to choose sides in the disagreement, the *Mishna Berura* recommends that, if one sleeps during the day, he have the study of Torah in mind while saying the evening blessing, "*ahavat olam*," which is the second of the two blessings said before the recital of the *Shema* in the evening in which one thanks God for the Torah and asks for the wisdom to understand it properly. It says that its recital should also fulfill the obligation of

---

402 *Shulhan Arukh, Orah Hayyim* 47:11.
403 *Mishna Berura* 47:25.

reciting the blessings on the Torah if necessary, just as "*ahava rabbah*" would in the morning.[404]

Halakhic Principles — 4

134.

Shulhan Arukh — According to the *Ba'al Halakhot Gedolot*, lighting Shabbat candles causes the one who lights to accept Shabbat; therefore, upon lighting, all creative activity[405] becomes forbidden. Because of this, a few women have the practice, after reciting the blessing and lighting the candles, of releasing the wick from their hands so as not to extinguish it. There are those who say that if she would make a stipulation before lighting that she does not accept Shabbat upon herself until the *Hazan* says *Barkhu*, it would be an effective stipulation. Others, however, disagree.

Rema — The custom in Ashkenaz[406] is for women who light Shabbat candles to thereby accept Shabbat upon themselves if they did not stipulate otherwise. If a woman makes the stipulation in her heart yet does not say it explicitly, it is still sufficient.[407]

The *Mishna Berura*'s Position — The *Mishna Berura* notes that because men do not have the custom to accept Shabbat by lighting candles, if a man does light he is still permitted to perform creative activity afterwards. Nevertheless, the *Mishna Berura* proposes that it is good for him to make a stipulation to ensure that lighting the

---

404 *Mishna Berura* 47:13.

405 "Creative activity" (*melakha*) is the name for those actions which are prohibited to perform on Shabbat due to the commandment to "Guard the Shabbat." This work has the connotation of being creative due to the use of the same word in Genesis 2:1-3 which describes God's work in creating the world, and the categories of "creative activity" are determined through those categories of work that were done in erecting the Tabernacle (*Mishkan*).

406 Ashkenaz is the medieval Hebrew name for the Jewish communities along the Rhine in Germany from Alsace in the south to the Rhineland in the north. Later, Jews from Western and Central Europe came to be called "Ashkenaz" because the main centers of Jewish learning were located in Germany.

407 *Shulhan Arukh, Orah Hayyim* 263:10.

candles does not imply that he is accepting Shabbat upon himself.[408] Despite this suggestion, however, the *Mishna Berura* writes regarding making stipulations over lighting Shabbat candles in general that one should do so only when necessary, since there are those who disagree and hold that they are not effective.[409]

Discussion — The *Mishna Berura* may give this warning only because Rabbi Karo mentions explicitly that in this case there are those who write that they are not effective. Yet, in any case, his reservation demonstrates that he does not support this technique unconditionally.

Halakhic Principles — 4

135.

Shulhan Arukh — A person should have in mind when donning phylacteries that God commanded him to don the four sections ... and he should don the arm phylactery first and say the blessing "on donning the phylactery," and afterwards don the head phylactery and not say a blessing since there is one blessing for both of them.

Rema — There are those who say to recite on the head phylactery, "on the commandment of phylacteries," even when there is no interruption between the two, and also it has become the custom in Ashkenaz to recite two blessings, but that it is good to always say after the second blessing, *"Barukh Shem Kevod Malkhuto LeOlam Va'ed."*[410]

Discussion — The custom in Ashkenazim to say *"Barukh Shem Kevod Malkhuto LeOlam Va'ed"* after donning the head phylactery develops as a compromise position between the rulings of *Rashi*, the *Rif*, and the *Rambam* on one side and *Rabbenu Tam* and the *Rosh* on the other regarding whether the blessing *"l'haniah tefillin* (to don the phylactery)" applies to the donning of the head

---

408 *Mishna Berura* 263:42.
409 *Mishna Berura* 263:44.
410 *Shulhan Arukh, Orah Hayyim* 25:5.

phylactery or not. According to *Rashi*, the *Rif*, and the *Rambam*, and so rules Rabbi Karo, the blessing applies both to the head and the arm phylacteries. According to the *Rosh*'s explanation of *Rabbenu Tam*, the blessings were established in the following sequence. First, when a person dons the arm phylactery he says "*l'haniah* (to don)," which also applies to the head. Afterward, when he affixes the head phylactery, he also says the blessing "*al mitzvat tefillin* (regarding the commandment of phylacteries)" on the conclusion of the *mitzvah*.

The *Mishna Berura*'s Position — The *Mishna Berura* is quick to explain the *Rema*'s reasoning: that we recite this expression due to the doubt of whether to say the second blessing or not. This statement is not satisfactory, however, since a person cannot justify saying a superfluous blessing by following it with "*Barukh Shem...*" The *Mishna Berura*, therefore, explains that Ashkenazim follow the ruling of *Rabbenu Tam*, which would require a person to say the second blessing, yet the custom of saying "*Barukh Shem*" arose to avoid any criticism about potentially saying a superfluous blessing.[411] In the *Biur Halakha*, the *Mishna Berura* reveals reservations over this compromise and adds that the *Gra* rules according to the *Shulhan Arukh*. It also cites a recommendation by Rabbi Akiva Eiger which is meant to ameliorate the difficulty of covering both opinions, which states that a person should intend at the time of saying "*l'haniah*" that if the Halakha is according to *Rashi*, the blessing "*l'haniah*" should not apply to the head phylactery. The second blessing for the head phylactery would then be necessary.[412] By suggesting the stipulation, the *Mishna Berura* is able to include the two contradictory opinions as equally valid while making sure that doing so does not lead to inadvertent transgression in another area of law. Nevertheless, it cites the *Pri Megadim*, who discourages the use of Rabbi Akiva Eiger's advice, and suggests that the reason for the *Pri Megadim*'s

---

411 *Mishna Berura* 25:21.
412 This would leave a question as to the necessity to say "*Barukh Shem.*"

opposition is that it may cause one to criticize established customs founded on the opinion of many of the *Rishonim*.[413]

Halakhic Principles — 3, 8, 10

136.

Shulhan Arukh — If a person takes a cup of beer or water and begins to recite the blessing with the intention of ending with "*She'hakol*"[414] but errs and says "*Boreh Pri HaGafen*"[415] he need not repeat the blessing, since when he recited God's name and mentions His kingship, he had the correct intention.[416]

The *Mishna Berura*'s Position — The *Mishna Berura* writes that this is the opinion of the *Rambam*, yet almost all *poskim* disagree, and maintain that the fulfillment of obligation does not always follow from the intention of the person performing the act. Therefore, since the person said the wrong blessing, he has not fulfilled his obligation and must say the correct one. It concludes by saying that the *Aharonim* write that this opinion should be taught.[417]

Halakhic Principles — 5

Introducing Another Variable:

When there is a potential contradiction in trying to synthesize different opinions, the *Mishna Berura* uses the technique of introducing a concrete variable into the situation in order to create the synthesis. To avoid transgression, the *Mishna Berura* suggests simply leaving the environment where the conflict between obligation and prohibition exists.

137.

Shulhan Arukh — Since fruit is usually brought during a meal to clean a person's palate, if someone eats fruit without bread along

---

413 *Biur Halakha* 25: s.v. *v' tov.*
414 The most general blessing over food.
415 The blessing said specifically over wine.
416 *Shulhan Arukh, Orah Hayyim* 209:1.
417 *Mishna Berura* 209:1.

with it, he must say a blessing prior to eating it. The fruit is not included in the *HaMotzi* since it is not a main part of the meal. The fruit does not, however, require a blessing after eating it. Since it was eaten within the meal, *Birkat HaMazon* includes it.[418]

Alternative Positions — Many *Aharonim* hold that if the fruit is on the table at the time one recites *HaMotzi*, and even if it is cooked, it is still not counted as part of the meal. Moreover, even if the fruit is cooked with meat, many *Aharonim* still require a person to recite a blessing on the fruit since it is not subordinate to the meat; therefore, it is still considered separate from the meal. The *Hayye Adam*, however, rules that fruit in this case does become subordinate to the meat. The *Yad HaKettana* writes that one does not recite a blessing on the fruit, yet he gives a different ruling than that of the *Hayye Adam*. According to the *Yad HaKettana*, when a person cooks a dish of fruit and meat, or a fruit dish that is made with fat or honey, the dish is not made for the purpose of cleaning one's palate. Rather, it is made for the sake of being part of the meal.

Discussion — When eating *tsimis*, a fruit dish not made with meat but usually considered part of a meal, there is a doubt as to whether a person must recite a blessing over it or if the blessing would be superfluous.

The *Mishna Berura*'s Position — In the *Sha'ar HaTziyun*, the *Mishna Berura* distinguishes between cooked vegetable dishes and fruit dishes. The former do not require a blessing since they are considered part of a meal, yet the latter do since they are generally used as a means to clean one's palate. For a dish such as apple-*tsimis*, however, difficulty arises since it may, like a vegetable dish, be considered part of the meal.[419] In order to balance between having an obligation to recite a blessing and possibly transgressing by saying a superfluous blessing, the *Mishna Berura* writes that one should take a raw piece of the type of fruit of which the *tsimis* is made and recite a blessing on it with the intention to also include the *tsimis*. If he does not have a piece of raw fruit, the *Mishna Berura*

---

418 *Shulhan Arukh, Orah Hayyim* 177:1.
419 *Sha'ar HaTziyun* 177:7.

advises that one follow the suggestion in the *Shulhan Arukh*, that he should eat the *tsimis* at the beginning and at the end of the meal with bread in order to demonstrate that it is a part of the meal.[420] This is not an isolated ruling for the *Mishna Berura*; rather, it commonly uses this technique to resolve doubt in relation to reciting blessings during a meal.

Halakhic Principles — 4

138.

Shulhan Arukh — If a person remembers after finishing his meal that he has not said *Birkat HaMotzi*, he may no longer say the blessing.[421]

Alternative Position — The *Raavad* rules that one should recite *Birkat HaMazon* even when he has finished his meal.

The *Mishna Berura*'s Position — The *Mishna Berura* recommends that if he can still eat a little, it would be good to say *HaMotzi* over bread, eat a bit, and then recite *Birkat HaMazon*.[422] In the *Sha'ar HaTziyun*, he explains that not only would this allow the person to have in mind that the *Birkat HaMotzi* also includes that which he ate previously, it would allow him to also be in accord with the *Raavad*, who, in opposition to Rabbi Karo, holds that one should recite *Birkat HaMazon* even when he has finished his meal.[423]

Halakhic Principles — 4

139.

Position of the *Poskim* — The *Mishna Berura* writes that, according to the *poskim*, the obligation to say the *Birkat Kohanim* is annulled in a place that is impure. Therefore, if a person dies immediately after the Kohanim are called up to recite the blessings the Kohanim must leave the synagogue and not say the *Birkat Kohanim*. If, however, the impurity arises in a house connected to the synagogue, and if it

---

420 *Mishna Berura* 177:4; *Biur Halakha* 177: s.v. *k'gon te'enim.*
421 *Shulhan Arukh, Orah Hayyim* 167:8.
422 *Mishna Berura* 167:47.
423 *Sha'ar HaTziyun* 167:46.

is possible to close the doors and windows of the house or of the synagogue so that the impurity cannot enter the synagogue, then the Kohanim do not need to leave until after reciting the *Birkat Kohanim*. The reason for this is that such impurity is only of a rabbinic level, yet saying *Birkat Kohanim* is a Torah obligation, and the Torah obligation trumps the rabbinic obligation that a *Kohen* must refrain from contracting impurity.

The *Mishna Berura*'s Position — The *Mishna Berura* writes, however, that if the Kohanim knew about the impurity that arose in the connected house before they washed their hands, it would be better if they immediately left the synagogue.[424]

Discussion — The *Mishna Berura* recommends that the Kohanim leave the synagogue before they become obligated to recite the *Birkat Kohanim* in order to avoid having to annul a rabbinic decree, even though its annulment is legitimate, since it is trumped by the Torah obligation of *Birkat Kohanim*. The *Mishna Berura*'s intention to avoid negotiating between conflicting obligations, rather than choosing between them, is further demonstrated in the *Sha'ar HaTziyun*, wherein the *Mishna Berura* explains why it only advises that the Kohanim leave and does not insist that they do so.[425] Elsewhere, the *Shulhan Arukh* rules that a *Kohen* may subject himself to impurity of a rabbinic level in order to marry or learn Torah.[426] Regarding this ruling, the *Pithei Teshuva* cites the *Havat Ya'ir*, who says that he has seen in many communities that the Kohanim leave the synagogue, without saying the *Birkat Kohanim*, if they hear that a child has passed away in an adjacent house. The *Havat Ya'ir* justifies their leaving by claiming that they have not transgressed a positive commandment if they leave before the *Hazan* calls them to recite the blessings; if, on the other hand, the *Hazan* has already called them it is more difficult to justify leaving.[427] Because the practice of the Kohanim to leave the synagogue seems to contradict

---

424 *Mishna Berura* 128:8.
425 *Sha'ar HaTziyun* 128:7.
426 *Shulhan Arukh, Yoreh Deah* 372:1.
427 *Pithei Teshuva, Yoreh Deah* 372:1.

the ruling in the *Shulhan Arukh* which allows them to contract impurity of a rabbinic level in order to perform a Torah obligation, and the *Havat Ya'ir* searches for a justification for the practice rather than claiming that it is legitimate, the *Mishna Berura* can only support the justification as a suggestion and not as an obligation.

Halakhic Principles — 4

140.

Position of the *Poskim* — The *Mishna Berura* writes that almost all of the *poskim* contend that incorrect performance of any one of the components of *Birkat Kohanim* will render the blessings invalid.

The *Mishna Berura's* Position — In light of this high standard, the *Mishna Berura* recommends, though does not require, that one who is unable to properly perform all of the necessary components leave the synagogue before the *Hazan* recites "*Retzei*."[428]

Discussion — Because it is difficult to say that a *Kohen* should not fulfill his obligation to say *Birkat Kohanim*, or that he should incur a transgression by refraining from saying the *Birkat Kohanim* since he does not know how to say it correctly, the *Mishna Berura* suggests that he leave the synagogue before becoming obligated. By leaving the synagogue, the *Kohen* does not have the obligation to say the *Birkat Kohanim*, and the other Kohanim need not worry that their blessings will be invalid.

Halakhic Principles — 4

141.

***Rema* —** Someone who is not a male *Kohen* should not recite the *Birkat Kohanim*.[429]

The *Mishna Berura*'s Position — In the *Biur Halakha*, the *Mishna Berura* writes that an *androgynous* person or a *tumtum* should not

---

428 *Mishna Berura* 128:50.
429 *Shulhan Arukh, Orah Hayyim* 128:1.

recite the *Birkat Kohanim*. Rather, they should leave the synagogue before the *Hazan* recites *"Retzei."*[430]

Discussion — An *androgynous* person is someone who has both male and female genitalia. A *tumtum* is a person with no visible genitalia. Regarding the former, there is a disagreement among the *poskim* as to whether such people should be considered as neither gender but rather as a category unto themselves or whether they should be considered people whose gender is in doubt. If the *androgynous* type is a wholly different gender, then such people should not recite the *Birkat Kohanim*. If there is a doubt that they may be male, then *androgynous* people would have an obligation to recite the *Birkat Kohanim*, since the Halakha inclines toward obligation rather than exemption in the case of doubt regarding a Torah obligation. Furthermore, there, a disagreement among the *Aharonim* as to whether there is a prohibition for someone who is not a *Kohen* to recite the *Birkat Kohanim* or not. With respect to a *tumtum*, on the other hand, all consider such a person to be of doubtful gender, either a male or a female. Therefore, the obligation, or prohibition, for a *tumtum* to recite the *Birkat Kohanim* rests solely on the disagreement among the *Aharonim* over whether there is a prohibition for someone who is not a *Kohen* to recite the *Birkat Kohanim* or not. Nevertheless, the *Mishna Berura* advises indiscriminately that both the *androgynous* person and the *tumtum* leave the synagogue. The assiduousness of the *Mishna Berura*'s recommendation becomes clear in light of the ruling in the *Shulhan Arukh* which states that if a *Kohen* does not move when the *Hazan* recites *"Retzei,"* he is no longer allowed to go up to recite the *Birkat Kohanim* in any case.[431] If a *Kohen* does not move his feet in a way that would indicate a refusal to say *Birkat Kohanim*, he can afterwards rely on the rabbinic precept of *"shev v'al taaseh."* Nevertheless, the *Mishna Berura* recommends that the *androgynous* person and the *tumtum* leave the synagogue. His reasons why a *Kohen* should not rely on this principle in general are twofold: because *ab*

---

430 *Biur Halakha* 128: s.v. *v'ein l'zar.*
431 *Shulhan Arukh, Orah Hayyim* 128:8.

initio a person should not rely on this rabbinic principle if he can help it,[432] and because people may think that he has a blemish that makes him unfit to recite the blessings.[433] Since an *androgynous* person or a *tumtum* need not worry about the second reason, the *Mishna Berura*'s suggestion that they leave the synagogue rests solely on his discomfort in relying on a valid rabbinic principle in a situation when it is not essential to do so.

Halakhic Principles — 4

142.

Shulhan Arukh — An *androgynous* person should only make a *zimun* with other similar people, and not for either men or women.[434] A *tumtum* should not make a *zimun* at all.[435]

The *Mishna Berura*'s Position — With respect to the ruling regarding *androgynous* people, the *Mishna Berura* first explains the reason to *be because they make* up their own category,[436] yet also includes the reason that there is a possibility that they may be of the opposite gender.[437] Therefore, they cannot join with men, for fear that they may be women, nor can they join with women, for fear that they may be men. In the *Sha'ar HaTziyun*, it is stated that when three *androgynous* people eat together, but not to satiety, they may voluntarily make a *zimun*. This is permissible because the obligation to make a *zimun* would be of a rabbinic level, so that the doubt as to what gender to consider an *androgynous* person can be dealt with leniently. If, however, they have eaten to satiety, ideally they should not make a *zimun*. The reason for this is because there is a doubt as to the gender of each person, and since the obligation upon men to make a *zimun* is not the same as for women, the varying levels of obligation precludes the three of them joining together. Nevertheless, *ex post facto* it may be permissible since

---

432 *Sha'ar HaTziyun* 128:14.
433 *Mishna Berura* 128:9.
434 *Shulhan Arukh, Orah Hayyim* 199:8.
435 *Shulhan Arukh, Orah Hayyim* 199:9.
436 *Mishna Berura* 199:20.
437 *Mishna Berura* 199:21.

they may all have the same obligation by virtue of making up their own gender category.[438] In contradistinction, the *Mishna Berura* writes that even if three *tumtumim* eat together, they cannot make a *zimun*, since for each one there is a doubt as to its gender. The same distinctions are made with respect to blowing *Shofar* for others on Rosh Hashanah[439] and for reading the *Megilla* for others on Purim.[440] Moreover, the *Mishna Berura* explains that an *androgynous* person may not be circumcised on Shabbat since there is a doubt if the person is a male, and one does not suspend the laws of Shabbat due to doubtful fulfillment.[441]

Halakhic Principles — 2, 8

143.

Shulhan Arukh — If a person is drinking one type of wine and another wine is brought to the table, he should say the blessing "*HaTov v'HaMeitiv*" on the second wine.[442]

The *Mishna Berura*'s Position — The *Mishna Berura* writes that at the Passover *Seder*, it is good *ab initio* if a person does not drink a second type of wine so that he is not required to say the blessing "*HaTov v'HaMeitiv*," since it may seem as if he is adding to the number of required cups of wine.[443] The *Sha'ar HaTziyun* adds that if he brings the second wine to drink as one of the required cups of the *Seder*, he should say both "*Boreh Pri HaGafen*" and "*HaTov v'HaMeitiv*."[444]

Halakhic Principles — 2

144.

Shulhan Arukh — If two wines are brought to the table simultaneously, a person should bless "*Boreh Pri HaGafen*" on the better wine

438 *Sha'ar HaTziyun* 199:11.
439 *Mishna Berura* 589:5-6.
440 *Mishna Berura* 689:9-12.
441 *Mishna Berura* 331:18.
442 *Shulhan Arukh, Orah Hayyim* 175:1.
443 *Mishna Berura* 175:2.
444 *Sha'ar HaTziyun* 175:3.

and include the inferior wine in his intention. He should not first recite "*Boreh Pri HaGafen*" on the inferior wine and then "*HaTov v'HaMeitiv*" on the better wine, since it is customary to recite a blessing on the main or the more beloved object first.[445]

The *Mishna Berura*'s Position — The *Mishna Berura* writes that if one is in doubt as to which wine is better, it is permissible *ab initio* for him to say "*Boreh Pri HaGafen*" on one and "*HaTov v'HaMeitiv*" on the second according to the law. Nevertheless, it is better if one would first remove one of the wines from the table, say "*Boreh Pri HaGafen*" and then bring the second wine back and say "*HaTov v'HaMeitiv*" in order to avoid any doubts.[446]

Halakhic Principles — 4, 5

Doubling One's Efforts

When the *poskim* give a number of possible alternatives that do not contradict each other, the *Mishna Berura*, at times, recommends that a person act in accord with more than one position.

145.

Shulhan Arukh — If a Gentile deposits his *hametz* with a Jew, if the Jew would be liable for its theft or loss, whether the *hametz* is in his house or in another domain, the Jew is obligated to destroy it.

Rema — This is the case even if he then deposits it with another Gentile.

Continuation of *Shulhan Arukh* — Some say that even if he is only a *shomer hinam*, who would be liable only for gross negligence, he must still destroy it. If he is not liable according to law but knows that the Gentile is violent and will force him to pay for what is lost, he must also destroy the *hametz*. There are, however, those who disagree.[447]

---

445 *Shulhan Arukh, Orah Hayyim* 175:3.
446 *Mishna Berura* 175:14.
447 *Shulhan Arukh, Orah Hayyim* 440:1.

Alternative Positions — If the Jew would be obligated to destroy it, it is a matter of dispute among the *Aharonim* if he could nullify it or sell it instead, as he could with his own *hametz*. According to the *Magen Avraham*, he should deposit the *hametz* with a different Gentile or he should sell his house with the Gentile's *hametz* inside it.

The *Mishna Berura*'s position — The *Mishna Berura* proffers that it is correct to follow both of the suggestions presented by the *Magen Avraham*. The person should sell the house and sell the *hametz*.[448] *Ab initio*, the *Mishna Berura* suggests that one should defer to the opinion that holds that this applies even for a *shomer hinam*, yet, *ex post facto*, if the sixth hour has already passed and he cannot sell the *hametz* to another Gentile, he may rely on the first opinion that does not include him.[449] In the *Sha'ar HaTziyun*, the *Mishna Berura* writes that if the Jew would be liable based on secular law, even if he would not be liable according to the Torah, he would still be obligated to destroy the *hametz* according to everyone.[450]

Halakhic Principles — 3

146.

Shulhan Arukh — If a Jew gives his *hametz* to a Gentile on the day before Passover before the sixth hour, he does not need to burn it.[451]

Discussion — According to some opinions, there is an independent commandment to physically destroy one's *hametz* and not only to not possess any *hametz* on the holiday.

The *Mishna Berura*'s position — The *Mishna Berura* writes that even if he gives his *hametz* to a Gentile, it is correct to perform the burning if the Jew would not remove all of his *hametz*. Rather, he should take at least a *kazayit* of *hametz* and fulfill the

---

448 *Mishna Berura* 440:4.
449 *Mishna Berura* 440:8.
450 *Sha'ar HaTziyun* 440:22.
451 *Shulhan Arukh, Orah Hayyim* 445:2.

commandment "to put away the leaven from one's house" properly through burning it.[452]

Halakhic Principles — 3, 4

147.

Shulhan Arukh — In order to prepare for Passover, one should pour boiling water on tables and drawers in which one usually puts food, since sometimes hot soup from a pot spills on them.[453]

Alternative Positions — The *Magen Avraham* writes that one should also put something down on top of the tables or drawers, for it is possible that visible *hametz* may remain. The *Elya Rabba* writes that it is appropriate to cover cupboards as well, since it is impossible that they would not have something left in the cracks, yet one need not be stringent with respect to flat tables.[454]

The *Mishna Berura*'s position — The *Mishna Berura* cites both opinions. With respect to flat tables, the *Mishna Berura* details elsewhere how one must *kasher* the table top, and does not explicitly mention that they need to be covered, but it does refer back to the disagreement between the *Magen Avraham* and the *Elya Rabba*.[455]

Halakhic Principles — 3

148.

Shulhan Arukh — After finishing the Seder meal, everyone should eat a *kazayit* of *matzah* in remembrance of the Passover offering that was eaten when satisfied.[456]

The *Mishna Berura*'s position — Citing the Aharonim, the *Mishna Berura* writes that *ab initio* it is good to take two *zaytim*, one to remember the Passover offering and one to remember the *matzah* with which it was eaten.[457]

Halakhic Principles — 2, 5

---

452 *Mishna Berura* 445:10.
453 *Shulhan Arukh, Orah Hayyim* 451:20.
454 *Mishna Berura* 451:115.
455 *Mishna Berura* 452:20.
456 *Shulhan Arukh, Orah Hayyim* 477:1.
457 *Mishna Berura* 477:1.

149.

Shulhan Arukh — If a person rents his house in a way that transfers legal possession during the lease to a friend starting on the fourteenth of *Nissan* but did not give him the key so that the renter did not have access the night before, the landlord must search the house for *hametz*. If he did give him the key before the fourteenth, then the renter must perform the search.[458]

Discussion — The *Mishna Berura* explains that Rabbi Karo rules according to the opinion of the *Ran*, that a renter is not obligated to search for the *hametz* unless two factors have been fulfilled: the renter has gained possession of the house and has been given the key before the fourteenth. According to *Tosafot*, however, giving the key to the renter is sufficient to cause the renter to be obligated to search for the *hametz*, since the landlord is unable to enter the house without the key.

The *Mishna Berura*'s position — The *Mishna Berura* notes that there are *Aharonim* who write that it is correct to be stringent for both opinions; therefore, both the renter and landlord would be obligated to search when only the key was transferred. It adds that though the *Pri Hadash* writes that the view of the *Shulhan Arukh* is the main one, if one of them becomes the representative of the other, one can account for all the positions.[459]

Halakhic Principles — 2, 3, 4 5, 8

150.

Shulhan Arukh — It is a fitting *minhag* not to eat meat or drink wine on the night before and the day of the tenth of *Av*.

Rema — There are those who are stringent until noon but not afterwards.[460]

Alternative Positions — Some *poskim* apply the restraint to the other aspects of the fast as well, such as not washing in a bathhouse, getting a haircut, or laundering. The *Ma'amar Mordekhai* writes that

---

458 *Shulhan Arukh, Orah Hayyim* 437:1.
459 *Mishna Berura* 437:2.
460 *Shulhan Arukh, Orah Hayyim* 558:1.

we are not stringent with respect to washing in a bathhouse, getting a haircut, or laundering.

The *Mishna Berura*'s position — The *Mishna Berura* writes that the statement of the *Shulhan Arukh* also applies to washing in a bathhouse, getting a haircut, and laundering.[461] In the *Biur Halakha*, it cites the *Ma'amar Mordekhai*, yet writes that it is difficult to be lenient since many of the *Aharonim* of our time uphold the stringency as the rule in practice.[462]

Halakhic Principles — 5, 8

151.

Shulhan Arukh — A person must say *Vidui* at *Minha* before eating the *Seuda Ha'Mafseket* before Yom Kippur.[463]

Alternative Position — There are *poskim* who hold that one must also say *Vidui* after eating before it gets dark.

The *Mishna Berura*'s Position — The *Mishna Berura* suggests that it is appropriate to be stringent like the latter opinion, and supports his suggestion with the fact that there is the custom of saying *Tefilla Zakka* after the meal and before it gets dark.[464]

Halakhic Principles — 2, 5

Requiring Something Additional For Public Benefit

The *Mishna Berura* may demand that a person do something in addition to the requirement set forth by the *Shulhan Arukh* in order to avoid public confusion, which may result in potentially negative consequences. The *Mishna Berura* suggests that a person take an additional measure to avoid the misconception that one is acting erroneously, or so that people do not draw improper conclusions that are contrary to the Halakha.

---

461 *Mishna Berura* 558:3.
462 *Biur Halakha* 558: s.v. *ad hatzot hayom.*
463 *Shulhan Arukh, Orah Hayyim* 607:1.
464 *Mishna Berura* 607:1.

152.

Shulhan Arukh — If a person is publicly reading from the Torah and makes a mistake, he must return to the place where he made the error.[465]

The *Mishna Berura*'s Position — The *Mishna Berura* writes that if the one who errs has already finished and recited the blessings after reading, the following person should start at the verse in which the mistake was made, continue until the end of the section, and then continue for three verses in the following section.[466] In the *Sha'ar HaTziyun*, the *Mishna Berura* admits that this suggestion is a superfluous gesture. According to the law, the second person may read the verse in which the mistake was made and the following two verses. He may then skip to the end of the section and begin the section for which he was called up. It is even possible that, according to the law, only the verse in question must be read before continuing on to the succeeding section. The *Mishna Berura* nevertheless recommends doing more than is required so that the congregation does not recognize the changes that were made in the order of reading the verses of the Torah portion,[467] which may potentially cause them to draw conclusions contrary to the Halakha.

Halakhic Principles — 5

153.

Shulhan Arukh — In a community that has a congregation in which no one can read the Torah properly with the correct accentuation and cantillation as according to the law, they should read the Torah with its accompanying blessings (without the proper accentuation) as according to the law.[468]

Alternative Positions — The *Mishna Berura* notes that according to a number of *Aharonim*, if no one knows how to read at all and if someone would read, he would certainly make mistakes which

---

465 *Shulhan Arukh, Orah Hayyim* 142:1.
466 *Mishna Berura* 142:2.
467 *Sha'ar HaTziyun* 142:3.
468 *Shulhan Arukh, Orah Hayyim* 142:2.

would change the meaning of the passage, the congregation should still read from the Torah with its accompanying blessings in order that the public reading of the Torah not be completely abrogated. The *Mishna Berura* adds, however, that the *Pri Hadash* and the *Pri Megadim* object to this leniency, yet do allow such communities to read the Torah without its blessings.[469]

The *Mishna Berura*'s Position — The *Mishna Berura* suggests that if someone in the *Minyan* can read with proper accentuation from a *Humash*, he should read quietly in front of the person called to the Torah as he reads in order that he hear how to recite the passage properly.[470] By doing this, the congregation can uphold the custom of reading the Torah with its accompanying blessings while avoiding improper performance as much as possible.

Halakhic Principles — 4, 5

154.

Shulhan Arukh — If a person delays praying *Minha* until the community has already accepted Shabbat, he should not pray *Minha* in the synagogue but rather should step outside and pray. If he goes to the synagogue close to the time the community accepts Shabbat and begins to pray *Minha*, even though he will still be praying when the community accepts Shabbat, it is of no concern since he began his prayer in a permitted manner.[471]

Discussion — Based on the language of the *Shulhan Arukh*, it seems that the latecomer who started to pray *Minha* in a permitted way does not need to worry about praying a weekday prayer beside others who are praying a Shabbat prayer, since it is only prohibited by a general stringency and not according to the law. This may, however, cause confusion and negate the general stringency.

The *Mishna Berura*'s Position — The *Mishna Berura* adds that it is better if the latecomer exits the synagogue and prays outside in order

---

469 *Mishna Berura* 142:7.
470 *Mishna Berura* 142:8.
471 *Shulhan Arukh, Orah Hayyim* 263:15-16.

to distinguish between his weekday prayer and the Shabbat prayer of the community.[472]

Halakhic Principles — 4, 5

155.

Shulhan Arukh — If a person is compelled to do so, he may pray *Maariv* Saturday night from *Plag HaMinha* onwards and make *Havdala* immediately, yet he may not recite the blessing over a candle nor may he do any prohibited activity until *Tzeit HaKokhavim.*[473]

Discussion — *Plag HaMinha* is one and a quarter *shaot zmaniyot* (proportional hours) before sunset. To determine a proportional hour, one takes the total daylight hours and divides it by twelve. *Tzeit HaKokhavim* is the time when three stars are visible in the sky.

The *Mishna Berura*'s Position — The *Mishna Berura* writes that even if permissible, the *Aharonim* write that one should not act in such a manner since it may confuse the populace; also the person may come to do a prohibited activity. The *Mishna Berura* adds that especially today where we have the custom to pray *Maariv* after sunset, certainly according to the law one may not pray earlier on Saturday night.[474]

Halakhic Principles — 1, 4, 5

Giving an Alternative to Avoid Transgression

The *Mishna Berura* introduces alternative practices when necessary to avoid potential transgression.

156.

Shulhan Arukh — A solid food item that has not been cooked before Shabbat may not be immersed in hot water on Shabbat, but one may pour hot water over it on Shabbat, with the exception of aged salted food and fish called *"kulias ha'ispenin,"* which do not require much

---

472 *Mishna Berura* 263:63.
473 *Shulhan Arukh, Orah Hayyim* 293:3.
474 *Mishna Berura* 293:9.

cooking, and it is possible for them to be completely cooked by only pouring hot water over them.[475]

Discussion — A *kli rishon* ("first vessel") is a vessel that was heated directly on a flame or other source of heat. Even when it is removed from the heat source, it maintains its status as a *kli rishon*, and possesses the capacity to cook any type of food placed within it. This capacity remains until the pot and its contents cool below the temperature of *yad soledet bo* (the degree of heat "from which the hand recoils"). *Irui kli rishon* is when hot liquid is poured from a *kli rishon*; since the liquid is being poured from a *kli rishon*, it still has some cooking power. A *kli sheni* ("second vessel") is a vessel once removed from the vessel that was on the fire in that contents from a *kli rishon* are then poured into it. The walls of a *kli sheni* are cold and constantly lose heat, so that it does not have the same ability to cook as a *kli rishon*, yet it does have the ability to cook somewhat under certain circumstances.

Coffee and tea are similar to aged salted food and fish called "*kulias ha'ispenin*," in that they can be completely cooked if one only pours hot water over them. The *Mishna Berura* writes that to make tea in the normal manner on Shabbat would therefore be a Torah transgression, since making tea is considered to be cooking. Because many people get it wrong since they rely on erroneous leniencies, he writes that he feels obliged to explain how one can permissibly make tea on Shabbat, but first must delineate what is prohibited. To pour hot water from a *kli rishon* onto tea leaves would possibly be considered as actually cooking. Putting tea leaves into a cup after hot water was poured into it so that the cup is a *kli sheni* is also prohibited based on the ruling in the *Shulhan Arukh* that one may not put something in a *kli sheni* on Shabbat if it was not soaked in hot water beforehand. Additionally, it is prohibited to put something that easily cooks, such as tea leaves, in a *kli sheni*.

Alternative Positions — The *Mishna Berura* cites *Aharonim* who conclude that in order to make tea, a person should pour boiling

---

475 *Shulhan Arukh, Orah Hayyim* 318:4.

water on the leaves before Shabbat from a *kli rishon*, stirring the leaves while pouring the water. Afterwards, he should remove the tea essence into another cup in order to let the leaves dry. It would then be permissible on Shabbat to pour hot water from a *kli rishon* on the leaves since they have already been cooked beforehand.

The *Mishna Berura*'s Position — The *Mishna Berura* writes that even though one should not protest against a person who follows the above procedure of the *Aharonim*, there is a better suggestion. A person should make tea essence before Shabbat that needs nothing else to make the tea except adding water. If he would then want to drink tea on Shabbat, he should put the essence into a cup which already has hot water poured into it. It would be even better if the tea essence never lost its temperature. The person would then be in accord with all opinions.[476] In the *Sha'ar HaTziyun*, the *Mishna Berura* notes that the opinion to which he refers in his last suggestion is the one that suspects that the tea colors water, thus causing the person to transgress "coloring" on Shabbat. If the tea essence is still warm, the person could then pour the water into the essence, rather than vice versa, avoiding the problem of "coloring."[477]

Halakhic Principles — 4, 5, 6

157.

Shulhan Arukh — It is permitted on Shabbat for a person to slowly pour liquid from one cup that contains both liquid and sediment to another as long as he stops pouring when he notices that the liquid stops flowing and begins to trickle from within the sediment. If he does not stop, the trickling would be a sign that he is separating.[478]

The *Mishna Berura*'s Position — The *Mishna Berura* provides a lenient alternative if the person is not able to stop before the liquid

---

476 *Mishna Berura* 318:39.
477 *Sha'ar HaTziyun* 318:65.
478 *Shulhan Arukh, Orah Hayyim* 319:14.

starts to trickle. He should continue pouring so that a little refuse will go into the second cup with the liquid.[479]

Halakhic Principles — 4, 6

158.

Rema — [The area beneath] a roof that protrudes past the front of a house has the same status as the domain in front of it.[480]

Alternative Position — The *Taz* writes that many people make the mistake of thinking that one may carry under the awning of a house that faces that street. This contradicts the *Rema*'s position, which would consider the area to be either a public domain or a *Karmelit*.

The *Mishna Berura*'s Position — The *Mishna Berura* offers a way to allow a person to carry under his awning. If the awning has poles at its end near the street, the person should erect poles opposite them against the house. The roof above the four poles will create a *Tzurat HaPetah* on each of the three open sides, with the house serving as a wall for the fourth side. The person would then be able to carry within this area. If there are a number of houses connected, like row-houses, it is permissible to connect all of the awnings together in this fashion, as long as the inhabitants make an *Eruv Hatzerot*.[481] In the *Biur Halakha*, the *Mishna Berura* writes that even though, according to the *Taz*, a *Tzurat HaPetah* would not be effective in this case, since the *Taz* defers to the *Rambam*'s opinion, all of the *Aharonim* rule leniently.[482] It warns, however, that the *Gra* holds that this would not work with slanted roofs, even if one would make proper partitions around the edge of the awning.[483]

Halakhic Principles — 4, 10

---

479 *Mishna Berura* 319:55.
480 *Shulhan Arukh, Orah Hayyim* 346:3.
481 *Mishna Berura* 346:31.
482 *Biur Halakha* 346: s.v. *ha'boltin lifnei ha'batim*.
483 *Biur Halakha* 346: s.v *v'khen b'gagi*.

159.

Shulhan Arukh — The required measure of wine that a person must drink for the four cups on Passover is a *revi'it*, and he should drink all or most of it. If he has many *revi'yot* in his cup, the requirement is to drink only one *revi'it* of the cup's contents. There are those who say that he must drink the majority of the cup even if it contains many *revi'yot*.[484]

The *Mishna Berura*'s Position — The *Mishna Berura* writes that when a person's cup holds a *revi'it*, *ab initio* he must drink all of it and only *ex post facto* does drinking most of it suffice.[485] With respect to the two opinions brought by Rabbi Karo, the *Mishna Berura* writes that even though the law is according to the first opinion, if a person does not wish to drink a lot he should take a cup that only holds one *revi'it* in order to defer to the more stringent opinion.[486]

Halakhic Principles — 2, 4, 5

160.

Shulhan Arukh — Some say that the measure of a *kazayit* is about half the size of an egg.[487]

Alternative Positions — The *Rambam* holds that it is one-third the size of an egg. There are *Aharonim* who argue that the eggs we find today are much smaller, up to half the size of eggs found in the times in which the Sages calculated measurements. According to this, every place where the Halakha demands the size of half an egg would today necessitate a whole egg. The *Sha'are Teshuva* distinguishes between Torah and rabbinic obligations in terms of whether to demand the larger measure or not.[488]

The *Mishna Berura*'s Position — Due to the doubt regarding which position to follow, for a Torah obligation, the *Mishna Berura* states that we rule stringently to require the size of half an egg. For

---

484 *Shulhan Arukh, Orah Hayyim* 472:9.
485 *Mishna Berura* 472:30.
486 *Mishna Berura* 472:33.
487 *Shulhan Arukh, Orah Hayyim* 486:1.
488 *Mishna Berura* 486:1.

rabbinic obligations, we rely *ex post facto* on the lenient opinion to require one-third the size of an egg, yet *ab initio* we require half of an egg. However, in general, it is correct *ab initio* to avoid finding oneself in doubt regarding the obligation to say a blessing. Therefore, it seems correct *ab initio* to eat the size of a whole egg of bread so as not to put the obligation of washing one's hands before eating into doubt.

The *Mishna Berura* also writes that, based on the position of the *Aharonim*, Rabbi Karo's ruling that a *kazayit* is the size of half an egg is not decisive today and that a whole egg is required wherever the Halakha demands the size of half an egg. The *Mishna Berura* nevertheless also refers to the *Sha'are Teshuva*, who distinguishes between Torah and rabbinic obligations in terms of whether to demand the larger measure or not.[489]

Halakhic Principles — 1, 2, 4, 5

Clarifies in Order to Add

When the language of a ruling in the *Shulhan Arukh* is ambiguous and may draw a person to an erroneous inference, the *Mishna Berura* clarifies its scope in order to save the reader from making what he believes are false assumptions. When the language of a ruling in the *Shulhan Arukh* is ambiguous and a lenient practice has developed which can be interpreted as being in line with the wording of the *Shulhan Arukh*, the *Mishna Berura* attempts to clarify the language in order to legitimate the lenient practice.

161.

Shulhan Arukh — If a person rents a house on the fourteenth of *Nissan* and does not know if it has been checked for *hametz*, he should ask the landlord. If the landlord is not available, there is a presumption that it has been checked and therefore it is enough just to nullify the *hametz* in one's heart.[490]

---

489 Ibid.
490 *Shulhan Arukh, Orah Hayyim* 437:2.

Discussion — If the landlord is available, the renter must inquire whether the landlord has checked for *hametz* because the presumption that he checked is not strong enough, when there is a possibility that one can find out for sure, to counter the presumption that there is *hametz* in the house, since a person has *hametz* in his house for the rest of the year. From the wording of the ruling in the *Shulhan Arukh*, it would seem that if the landlord says that he checked for *hametz*, the renter would not need to make a declaration to nullify the *hametz*. He can assume that if the landlord checked for *hametz* he also nullified it. Since, however, the renter may acquire the abandoned *hametz* by virtue of renting the house, he must nullify in his heart the possible remnants as a precaution. However, just as the renter could find out whether the landlord checked the house, he can also find out if he nullified the *hametz*; therefore, it should not seem correct to rely on the presumption that he did.

The *Mishna Berura*'s Position — The *Mishna Berura* writes that Rabbi Karo's wording is not exact; *ab initio* the renter must ask the landlord if he had also nullified the *hametz*, in case the landlord did not act completely according to the law. *Ex post facto*, if the renter did not ask about nullification and there is not enough time to do so before the onset of the holiday, he may rely on the assumption that his question about checking included nullification as well.[491]

Discussion — The *Mishna Berura* is lenient *ex post facto* since nullification is only a rabbinic requirement after one has already checked; therefore, in the case of doubt, one can be lenient. The *Mishna Berura* explains that the *Shulhan Arukh* does not mention the additional requirement *ab initio* of asking the landlord if he nullified the *hametz* since the doubt does not hinder the efficacy of removing the *hametz* from one's possession through the landlord's checking and the renter's nullification.[492]

Halakhic Principles — 2, 8

---

491 *Biur Halakha* 437: s.v. *sho'alo im badku.*
492 Ibid.

162.

Shulhan Arukh — A person should not light Hanukah candles before sunset but rather should light at the end of sunset, and he should not delay nor should he light beforehand. There is an opinion which states that if a person is preoccupied, he may light earlier, from *Plag HaMinha* onwards, as long as he has enough oil to last until there is no one left in the marketplace.[493]

Alternative Positions — The *Tur* rules that a person should light Hanukah candles at *tzeit ha'kokhavim*. Yet many *Rishonim* assert that the intention of the Talmud is that the time to light is the beginning of the second *Shkia*, when the light in the sky begins to completely disappear (the beginning of the first *Shkia* is when the sun begins to set), which is about fifteen minutes earlier than *tzeit ha'kokhavim*. The *Mor U'Ketzia* and the *Gra* write that for those who pray *Maariv* on time, which is after *tzeit ha'kokhavim*, it is correct *ab initio* to light candles before *Maariv*.

The *Mishna Berura*'s Position — The *Mishna Berura* explains that even though he says explicitly "the end of sunset," Rabbi Karo actually means *tzeit ha'kokhavim*, since he rules according to the *Tur*.[494] The *Mishna Berura*, however, writes that it is correct to light before *Maariv* for two reasons. First, many *Rishonim* hold that *ab initio* one should do so. Second, even according to the *Tur* who writes "at the end of sunset," he immediately adds that one is able to light up to almost half an hour earlier. Also, the *Mishna Berura* interprets the ruling of the *Rambam* that one should light during sunset to mean exactly at the time when the sun is no longer visible. Moreover, since the *Rambam* holds that the mitzvah to light Hanukah candles lasts only half an hour or a little more after sunset, after which one may no longer light, then if a person lights at *tzeit ha'kokhavim*, according to the *Rambam* he does not fulfill his obligation at all. The *Mishna Berura* further explains that those who allow a person to light candles a little later are lenient only because there is a doubt among the *poskim*. Therefore, he concludes that it is good and

---

493 *Shulhan Arukh, Orah Hayyim* 672:1.
494 *Mishna Berura* 672:1.

correct *ab initio* to light before *Maariv*, which would be before *tzeit ha'kokhavim*.[495]

Halakhic Principles — 5, 8, 10

163.

Shulhan Arukh — A wall is still considered a valid partition even when its gaps make up as much of the wall as the material of the wall itself, whether vertically or horizontally, as long as none of the gaps is wider than ten *amot*.[496]

Discussion — The difficulty in interpreting this ruling is that if the breaches are in certain places in the wall, then the wall would not be considered a valid partition. Whether or not the breaches in the wall are discounted depends on whether they are enveloped by the material of the wall or not. (The *Mishna Berura*'s position will make this clear.)

The *Mishna Berura*'s Position — The *Mishna Berura* writes that to be considered valid a partition may not contain a hole in the bottom three *tefahim* of the wall, since then it would be considered as if the wall was not rooted in the ground. Also, the wall cannot be six *tefahim* high with a three *tefahim* breach and a final *tefach* on the top of the wall, for even though the amount of wall is more than its breach, the hole joins to the air above the wall to nullify the one *tefach* strip. This is also the case when a wall is three *tefahim* high, then has a breach of four *tefahim*, and finally the top of the wall is three *tefahim* high, since in this scenario the top three *tefahim* are nullified by the breach and the air above the wall. Due to the many constraints, the *Mishna Berura* admits that one can never find a legitimate partition where the wall has horizontal gaps and the amount of gap space is equal to the amount of wall, despite the ruling of the *Shulhan Arukh*. The *Mishna Berura* therefore explains that Rabbi Karo's language is inexact. It is based on the language

---

495 *Biur Halakha* 672: s.v. *lo m'aharim*.
496 *Shulhan Arukh, Orah Hayyim* 362:9.

used by the *Tur*, but the *Tur* had only intended to discuss vertical breaches and not horizontal ones.[497]

Halakhic Principles — 8, 5

164.

Shulhan Arukh — While it is permitted to do work on *Rosh Hodesh*, those women who have the custom not to work have a good custom.

Rema — If the custom is that she does some work but also refrains from some work, she should follow her custom.[498]

Discussion — The *Shulhan Arukh* is ambiguous. It could mean that all women are obligated to refrain from working by virtue of an old custom which was accepted by women of previous generations. It would be similar to other customs which the daughters of Israel accepted upon themselves to forbid something. Alternatively, it could mean that it is a good custom for women to refrain from working, but even *ab initio* they are not obligated to do so even by virtue of an existing custom.

Alternative Positions — According to Rabbenu Yeruham, it seems that women are not obligated by virtue of an ancient custom. Rather, only those who have already accepted the custom are held to it. The *Mishna Berura* writes, however, that, in truth, even if one were to think that Rabbenu Yeruham intends to be lenient, one should not follow this conclusion, since the majority of the *Rishonim* hold that the matter does not depend on a woman's choice of whether she wants to keep the custom or not. Rather, all women are obligated to refrain from working by virtue of an established custom. The only difference is that in some places, women partially refrained from work, and in some places women completely refrained from working.

The *Mishna Berura*'s Position — Interpreting the *Rema*'s comment as an elucidation of Rabbi Karo's ruling, the *Mishna Berura* explains that the custom to refrain from work does not entail the same obligation everywhere. There are some places

---

497 *Mishna Berura* 362:50.
498 *Shulhan Arukh, Orah Hayyim* 417:1.

where some women would do a bit of work while other women would refrain completely. Nonetheless, he does mention that those women who do a bit of work should refrain somewhat so that it does not look like a regular day.[499]
Halakhic Principles — 8, 5

165.

Shulhan Arukh — If one finds *hametz* in his house on *Hol Hamoed*, he should remove it and destroy it immediately. If he finds it on Yom Tov, he should cover it until nighttime and then destroy it.

Rema — This is so because it is prohibited to move *hametz* on Yom Tov and burning it in its place is also prohibited.[500]

Discussion — From Rabbi Karo's wording, one can infer that it means both *hametz* that has been nullified and that which he has not, such as, for example, if something has leavened on the Yom Tov. According to the plain understanding of the ruling, it would be impossible to immediately nullify the new *hametz*, and the person would thereby transgress the prohibition of "*bal yira'eh*." Nevertheless, there would be no remedy to the situation except to cover it.

Alternative Positions — Many *poskim* hold that this ruling only applies to *hametz* that has been nullified and through which one does not transgress "*bal yira'eh*" if it is found. The reason one must cover it, yet cannot burn it, is that once *hametz* has been nullified, a person must destroy it only by virtue of rabbinic decree, so that he will not come to eat it. Therefore, there is no necessity to destroy the *hametz*. *Hametz* that has not been nullified, on the other hand, which will cause a person to transgress the prohibition of "*bal yira'eh*," pushes aside the rabbinic proscription against moving it. Therefore, he would be permitted to throw it in a river or into the toilet. According to some *poskim*, it is even permitted to burn it since there is some need to do so.

The *Mishna Berura*'s Position — The *Mishna Berura* cites the *Aharonim* who write that the world has the custom to follow Rabbi

---

499 *Biur Halakha* 417; s.v. *ve'ha'nashim she'nohagot*.
500 *Shulhan Arukh, Orah Hayyim* 446:1.

Karo, who states that in all cases one should cover the *hametz*. Nevertheless, it writes that those who are accustomed to following the lenient opinion which differentiates between the two types of *hametz* should not refrain from doing so.[501]

Halakhic Principles — 5, 6

166.

Shulhan Arukh — With respect to fasts which begin at sunrise, one may eat and drink up until the point when the fast begins if he has not fallen asleep. If he does fall asleep, he may no longer eat or drink unless he made a stipulation before going to bed that he may do so.

Rema — There are those who say that one need not make a stipulation to drink, since in general a person has in mind to drink after he wakes up and thus it is as if he has made a stipulation.[502]

Discussion — From Rabbi Karo's wording it seems that even if one falls asleep in the middle of a meal he may not return to eat when he awakens.

Alternative Positions — Many *Aharonim* write that if a person falls asleep in the middle of a meal, he may finish his meal when he wakes up since he initially intended to continue eating.

The *Mishna Berura*'s Position — The *Mishna Berura* cites the opinion of the *Aharonim*, yet adds that, nevertheless, one who is stringent upon himself will be called holy.[503] Also, with respect to drinking before the fast, the *Mishna Berura* cites the *Aharonim* who write that *ab initio* it is appropriate to be stringent to make a stipulation, as ruled by Rabbi Karo, but if one regularly drinks upon awaking he need not make a stipulation.[504]

Halakhic Principles — 5, 6

---

501 *Mishna Berura* 446:6.
502 *Shulhan Arukh, Orah Hayyim* 564:1.
503 *Mishna Berura* 564:3.
504 *Mishna Berura* 564:6.

167.

Shulhan Arukh — A *Karmelit* is a place where many people do not walk, such as outside the stores where sellers conduct business in front of the pillars demarking the public domain.[505]

Discussion — From the fact that Rabbi Karo did not mention the space between the pillars, it is reasonable to assume that he would consider it a public domain. This understanding is consistent with the opinion of the *Rambam*. The majority of *poskim*, however, rule that the space between the pillars, even though there are times when many people walk there, would nonetheless be considered a *Karmelit* since walking there is difficult.

The *Mishna Berura*'s Position — Because both opinions have strong halakhic support, the *Mishna Berura* cites both opinions without giving a strong indication of which position it fully supports.[506] In this case, the *Mishna Berura* must negotiate between incorporating conflicting positions and maintaining consistency with the language in the *Shulhan Arukh*. However, because it mentions that the lenient opinion is held by the majority of *poskim*, even though the more stringent opinion is held by more than just the *Rambam*, it seems as if the *Mishna Berura* implies that the lenient opinion is fully legitimate.

Halakhic Principles — 5, 6, 10

Provide Alternative Explanation so That the Halakha Remains Relevant:

In order to uphold the consistency of the *Shulhan Arukh*, the *Mishna Berura* provides alternative explanations for a particular ruling in order for it to maintain its relevance. The *Mishna Berura* provides an alternative explanation to rulings in order to maintain the legitimacy of a lenient practice which previously rested on faulty reasoning.

---

505 *Shulhan Arukh, Orah Hayyim* 345:14.
506 *Mishna Berura* 345:50.

168.

Shulhan Arukh — It is forbidden to lend a tool to a Gentile on Shabbat; one may not even lend it on Friday evening close to dark when there is not enough time to remove it from the house before it becomes dark, because an onlooker may think that the Jew commanded the Gentile to remove the tool from the house.[507]

Discussion — The concern behind the ruling is that there would be a suspicion that the Jew told the Gentile to remove the object from a private domain and take it to a public domain. In many places, however, communities follow the halakhic opinion that there is no such thing as a public domain today. Therefore, it would seem that the ruling is no longer relevant.

The *Mishna Berura*'s position — The *Mishna Berura* explains that, despite the fact that the original reason for the ruling may no longer apply, the ruling is still relevant since a Jew is not allowed to tell a Gentile to do something that is prohibited, even if only by virtue of rabbinic decree. Therefore, there may still be a suspicion that the Jew told the Gentile to remove the object from a private domain and take it to a *Karmelit*.[508] In the situation where Jews live with Gentiles in an area enclosed such that it is considered a private domain, on the other hand, it would be permitted to lend tools to a Gentile, since there would not be a suspicion of telling a Gentile to carry from one domain to another. The Jew may still not, however, lend tools that may be used to perform prohibited activities on Shabbat, even if the Gentile removes them before Shabbat, since there may be a suspicion that the Gentile is acting on the Jew's behalf when performing the prohibited activities.[509]

Discussion — The *Mishna Berura* attempts to maintain the relevance of Rabbi Karo's ruling in two different ways. First, it explains its

---

507 *Shulhan Arukh, Orah Hayyim* 246:2.
508 A *Karmelit* is a domain that is rabbinically defined. It is not a private domain because it has no walls, nor is it a public domain. Carrying from a private domain to a *Karmelit* thus transgresses the rabbinic prohibition of carrying on Shabbat.
509 *Mishna Berura* 246:9.

applicability despite the lesser degree of violation involved. Second, it explains its relevance regarding the type of tool that may or may not be lent.

Halakhic Principles — 1, 5, 8

169.

Shulhan Arukh — One who does creative activity on *Erev Pesach* from noon onwards should be banned. The activity is prohibited even if he does it for free.[510]

Discussion — The original force behind this ruling was that this is the time when people were involved with the Passover sacrifice. It was considered like a Yom Tov, where work is forbidden. The rabbis, therefore, prohibited people from performing creative activity during this time. Today, however, people do not perform the Passover sacrifice, so it seems as if the reason for the ruling is no longer relevant.

The *Mishna Berura*'s position — The *Mishna Berura* writes that the rule applies even today, despite the fact that we no longer offer sacrifices.[511] It cites *Rashi*, who provides a reason for the continued prohibition: it is so that people can focus on removing *hametz* from their homes, on making *matzah*, and on preparing for the night.[512]

Halakhic Principles — 1, 5

170.

Shulhan Arukh — A person transgresses a Torah prohibition when trapping a species on Shabbat that is usually hunted, and a rabbinic prohibition when trapping a species that is not usually hunted. Therefore, it is forbidden to trap flies even though they are a species that is not usually hunted.

Rema — One must be careful not to shut a small box when there are flies around on Shabbat, because it is a *psik reishei* that they will be trapped. There are those, however, who are lenient in

---

510 *Shulhan Arukh, Orah Hayyim* 468:1.
511 *Mishna Berura* 468:1.
512 *Biur Halakha* 468: s.v. *me'hatzot*.

circumstances where upon opening the box to remove them, they would escape.[513]

Discussion — A *psik reishei* is a Talmudic expression which indicates an action which has a known, inevitable consequence. The expression is derived from a case in the Talmud where a man wants to cut the head off of a chicken so as to give it to his child as a toy. His intention was not to kill the chicken, but rather to give the child a toy. However, the Talmud asks, "Can you cut the head off a chicken and the chicken won't die?" Because the consequence is known and inevitable, one must say that the person had the intention for that consequence as well. Because the forbidden consequence is inevitable, even if the action itself is permitted per se, it becomes forbidden to perform on Shabbat.

Alternative Positions — The *Bach* and the *Magen Avraham* are stringent with respect to closing the box. The *Taz* writes that if one has shooed away the flies that he saw, he need not search or check to see if there are any more around since it is a case of a doubtful *psik reishei* relating to a rabbinic prohibition. Thus, one need not be stringent. [514]

The *Mishna Berura*'s Position — The *Mishna Berura* explains the *Taz*'s reasoning for leniency, calls it an innovation, and questions its validity. The *Taz* draws an analogy from the position of Rabbi Shimon, that in the case wherein there is a doubt as to whether one has performed a prohibited action or not, one can say that he did not commit a transgression due to the fact that he acted unintentionally, and applies it to a case where the person does not care for the unintended forbidden consequences. As an illustration, just as dragging a bench over sand is permitted if one does not intend to make a groove, and it is not a *psik reishei* that it will create a groove, so too should it be permitted to close the box if one doubts that there are flies around that may be trapped. The *Mishna Berura*, however, argues that the two cases are not comparable since shutting the box involves performing a direct action, whereas making a groove while dragging a bench is an indirect one. The doubt in the former case is

---

513 *Shulhan Arukh, Orah Hayyim* 316:3.
514 *Mishna Berura* 316:16.

whether the action per se will involve a transgression. Although it rejects the *Taz*'s reasoning, as a practical matter, the *Mishna Berura* admits that the *Taz* is correct, albeit for a different reason. It explains the reason for leniency to be simply that since trapping flies is only a rabbinic transgression, in doubtful cases of potential rabbinic transgression one may be lenient.[515]

Halakhic Principles — 6, 8

Typographical Errors and *Girsa* Changes

At times, the *Mishna Berura* justifies changing the language of a ruling so that it will support what it believes should be the law. The *Mishna Berura* assumes that there are scribal errors when the language of a ruling or to whom it is attributed differs from what it believes should be the ruling or the attribution.

171.

Shulhan Arukh — It is permissible for a person who entered the synagogue through one door to exit through another.[516]

Discussion - Rabbi Karo bases his ruling on the *Rif* and the *Rambam*, who give as the source for this ruling the statement in Tractate *Megilla* (29a) which states, "Rabbi Helbo said in the name of Rabbi Huna: If one enters a synagogue to pray, he may afterwards use it as a short cut." The *Rosh* and the *Tur*, however, write that it is a *mitzvah* to exit through a different door, and not that it is just permissible, based upon having a different version of the Talmudic text.

The *Mishna Berura*'s Position — The *Mishna Berura* changes the language to say "It is a *mitzvah* for a person who entered."[517]

Discussion — Although Rabbi Karo's ruling is in line with his general methodology of ruling in accord with the majority when the *Rif*, the *Rambam*, and the *Rosh* are not unanimous, the *Mishna Berura* changes the language of the ruling to be in line with the *Rosh*, basing

---

515 *Biur Halakha* 316: s.v. *v'lakhen yesh lizaher*.
516 *Shulhan Arukh, Orah Hayyim* 151:5.
517 *Mishna Berura* 151:21.

its decision on the *Magen Avraham* and other *Aharonim* who question the version of the *Rif* that Rabbi Karo possessed.
Halakhic Principles — 5, 8

172.

Rema — There are those who are stringent even when it comes to *Okhel Nefesh* on a holiday with respect to food that would not lose any taste if prepared beforehand; however, if a person did not prepare it before and there is a need for it on the holiday, he may prepare the food in an abnormal manner.[518]

Discussion — In the *Biur Halakha*, the *Mishna Berura* writes that the attribution of the *Rema*'s ruling to the *Smag* and the *Ran* is a scribal error, since according to the *Ran* it is even permitted to prepare the food without having to be in an abnormal manner, as explained by the *Gra*. Similarly, Rabbi Karo makes no mention of the need to prepare the food in an abnormal manner, which implies that he holds that since that he is permitted to cook he may cook normally. The *Mishna Berura* subsequently raises two difficulties with the *Rema*'s ruling. First, it seems that the opinion of those who are stringent is to forbid cooking even in an abnormal way. Furthermore, the *Smag* is among those who are lenient in allowing cooking. According to the *Rema*'s attribution, it seems that the *Smag* is stringent, yet he is not in line with the opinion which prohibits it even if done in an abnormal manner. Second, it seems from his attribution that the *Smag* and the *Ran* share the same opinion, but in truth this is not so.

The *Mishna Berura*'s Position — The *Mishna Berura* attempts to answer these challenges by saying that actually, the *Rema* holds that even cooking in an abnormal manner would not be permitted, and that the opinion of Rabbi Karo is to permit cooking, but only in an abnormal way. This is why the *Rema* first writes "There are those who are stringent," to mean that even in an abnormal manner cooking is not permitted. Only after does he add, "however, if he …

---

518 *Shulhan Arukh, Orah Hayyim* 495:1.

in an abnormal manner," by which he means to say that *ex post facto* one may rely on the *Smag* that an abnormal manner is permitted. According to this interpretation, the *Mishna Berura* offers that one should not be lenient *ab initio* to leave food to be cooked on the holiday in an abnormal manner.[519]

In the main commentary, the *Mishna Berura* writes that if a person was not able to cook before the holiday due to an unforeseen circumstance, he may rely on the *Ran* and cook even in the normal manner. This justification is based on the fact that the *Magen Avraham* writes that one may even *ab initio* wait to cook on the holiday in an abnormal manner, but notes that the *Sefer Bigdei Yesha* challenges this. Therefore, it concludes, if one did not have enough time before the holiday, he may certainly rely on the leniency.[520] The reason for leniency is that if one were unable to prepare food he would be unable to fulfill his obligation of *Simhat Yom Tov.*

Halakhic Principles — 2, 8

173.

Shulhan Arukh — If there is a roof that is both part of a private domain and next to a public domain, and is less than ten *tefahim* high from the perspective of the public domain but more than ten *tefahim* from the perspective of the private domain, its status depends on how it is used. If many people make use of it, it is considered a public domain. Therefore, the owner of the roof may not use the roof unless he affixes a permanent ladder to it.[521]

Discussion — If the roof was less than ten *tefahim* from the ground of the courtyard, then affixing a permanent ladder would not be of any effect. Since, however, it is more than ten *tefahim* above the ground of the courtyard, affixing a ladder will make the roof a private domain since it is known that it is not for public use.

Alternative Positions — The *Magen Avraham* writes that if the roof is less than ten *tefahim* high from the outside, yet from the inside of

---

519 *Biur Halakha* 495: s.v. *im lo asa'hu.*
520 *Mishna Berura* 495:10.
521 *Shulhan Arukh, Orah Hayyim* 361:1.

the house it is ten *tefahim* above the floor, one would not need to affix a ladder, since the roof would be a private domain. Many *Aharonim* disagree and hold that the roof would be considered a *Karmelit* if the owner does not affix a ladder, and possibly even a public domain if people regularly made use of the roof.[522]

The *Mishna Berura*'s Position — The *Mishna Berura* dismisses the *Magen Avraham*'s position and cites the *Tosefet Shabbat* and the *Mahatzit HaShekel*, who write that the *Magen Avraham*'s words contain a typographical error, and that in reality his opinion is that the person would need to affix a ladder in such a situation.[523]

Halakhic Principles — 5, 8

174.

Shulhan Arukh — If a person is traveling and cannot reach water up to four miles in front of him or by backtracking one mile behind him, he may "wash" his hands in a tablecloth and eat bread.[524]

The *Mishna Berura*'s Position — Recognizing the awkward language of the *Shulhan Arukh*, the *Mishna Berura* quickly changes the word "wash" to "wrap."[525] It supports the change with the fact that Rabbi Karo quotes *Rishonim* who use the word "wrap" instead of "wash" and that the *Tur* gives a synonymous expression in his ruling.

Halakhic Principles — 8

175.

Shulhan Arukh — After a person leaves the synagogue, he should go to the *bet midrash* to learn, and the time must be fixed, so that he will not dismiss it even if he thinks that he may profit [if he does business during the time he has designated for learning].

Rema — Those who are unable to learn should still go to the *bet midrash* and they will receive a reward for going, or should designate

---

522 *Mishna Berura* 361:1.
523 *Sha'ar HaTziyun* 361:4.
524 *Shulhan Arukh, Orah Hayyim* 163:1.
525 *Mishna Berura* 163:4.

a place and learn a little of what they can and think about the issues and let *yirat shamayim* enter their hearts.[526]

The *Mishna Berura*'s Position — The *Mishna Berura* changes the *Rema*'s last words to apply to those who can learn rather than those who cannot, thereby demanding that those in the *bet midrash* find a regular seat for their daily studies. To justify the change in reference, the *Mishna Berura* asserts that the *Rema* meant to write "and he should designate" and not "or he should designate."[527]

Halakhic Principles — 8

Gra as the Deciding Factor

Many times when the *Mishna Berura* confronts a disagreement in which it cannot find a compromise that can successfully include opposing positions, it grounds its ultimate suggestion on the opinion of the *Gra*. The *Mishna Berura* also relies on the *Gra* to further support the ruling of the *Shulhan Arukh* when there are others who rule contrarily. The *Mishna Berura* cites the *Gra* to support its opposition to a custom endorsed by the *Rema*. There are times when the *Mishna Berura* defers to the *Gra* despite the fact that its general methodology would have it rule to the contrary. If the *Mishna Berura* does not suggest following the *Gra*'s opinion in practice, it may still defer to his position intellectually.

176.

Shulhan Arukh — The blessing "*Elokai Neshama*" is a blessing of thanksgiving and therefore need not be said immediately after "*Asher Yatzar*."[528]

Alternative Positions — The *Shulhan Arukh* follows the opinion of the *Tur*.[529] The *Mishna Berura* states that there are some, the *Gra*

---

526 *Shulhan Arukh, Orah Hayyim* 155:1.
527 *Mishna Berura* 155:7.
528 *Shulhan Arukh, Orah Hayyim* 6:3.
529 *Tur, Orah Hayyim* 6.

among them, who disagree and hold that one must say *"Elokai Neshama"* immediately after *"Asher Yatzar"* since they necessarily go together.

The *Mishna Berura*'s Position — After explaining that there is a disagreement, the *Mishna Berura* writes that the opinion of the *Gra* is that *"Elokai Neshama"* should be said immediately after *"Asher Yatzar"*; therefore, it is proper to be careful to do so *ab initio*.

Discussion — The *Mishna Berura*'s methodological priorities in resolving this disagreement are pronounced when compared with its solution for the disagreement related to washing one's hands in the morning. In a disagreement between the *Rashba* and the *Rosh* regarding why one must wash his hands in the morning, the *Mishna Berura* recognized that the Halakha was according to the *Rashba*, but suggested a practice that would cover all the opinions so to remove oneself from doubt. In this case, one would expect the *Mishna Berura* to act likewise, yet the *Mishna Berura* does no such thing. After explaining that there is a disagreement, it does not look for a synthesis between opinions; it rules according to the *Gra*. The difference between this case and the case of the disagreement between the *Rosh* and the *Rashba* is that, in this situation, the conclusion of when to say the blessing will define the blessing's character one way or the other. The *Mishna Berura* is therefore forced to pick sides. The disagreement over the blessing of washing one's hands in the morning does not have a similar consequence at stake; therefore, the *Mishna Berura* has more leeway to incorporate opposing positions.

Halakhic Principles — 5, 10

177.

Rema — If a community skips the public recital of the Torah portion on Shabbat, then it should recite the skipped portion the following Shabbat along with the portion ascribed to that week.[530]

Alternative Positions — Regarding the case where the Torah portion was omitted for a number of weeks, the *Mishna Berura* gives two

---

530 *Shulhan Arukh, Orah Hayyim* 135:2.

opinions. One opinion states that one should only recite the portion immediately before the one ascribed to the current Shabbat; the other states that the community is required to recite all the portions omitted.

The *Mishna Berura*'s Position — Although it does not say definitively which decision to follow, the *Mishna Berura* does state that it seems that the *Gra* rules according to the first opinion.[531] The *Gra* does not actually give a ruling, but rather compares the case to that of not reciting the correct prayer.[532] The *Mishna Berura* interprets the *Gra* in order to provide his opinion in the main commentary. The *Mishna Berura* recognizes that it is doing this, however, and the *Sha'ar HaTziyun* explains explicitly that the *Gra* compares this case to that of making up missed prayers, where he rules that one can only make up the prayer immediately missed.[533] In the *Biur Halakha*, the *Mishna Berura* similarly explains the opinion of the *Gra*, and expands on the *Gra*'s comparison of missed Torah portions to missed prayers in order to clarify that the permission to recite the missed portions is only applicable if they were missed accidently or via compulsion.[534]

Halakhic Principles — 10

178.

Rema — We do not say *Kiddush Levana* until after Yom Kippur.[535]

Discussion — *Kiddush Levana* (literally: Sanctification [of the] Moon) is a ritual in which observant Jews recite a series of prayers shortly after the beginning of the new month; they may be said until the moon is full.

The *Mishna Berura*'s Position — The *Mishna Berura* explains that it is best for a person to say *Kiddush Levana* when he is in a state of joy, and a person is certainly in a state of joy after Yom Kippur. It notes, however, that many *Aharonim* conclude that it is better to say

---

531 *Mishna Berura* 135:6.
532 *Biur HaGra* 135:2: s.v *im bitlu*.
533 *Sha'ar HaTziyun* 135:8.
534 *Biur Halakha* 135: s.v. *im bitul*.
535 *Shulhan Arukh, Orah Hayyim* 602:1.

Kiddush Levana before Yom Kippur in order that the person's merit for fulfilling the *mitzvah* is included in the Divine judgment.[536] In the *Sha'ar HaTziyun*, the *Mishna Berura* refers us to the *Biur HaGra*, who explains that the latter opinion is the main one.[537]

Halakhic Principles — 10

179.

Shulhan Arukh — If a person forgets and leaves a pot of food that is already fully cooked on [an uncovered flame on] the stove on Shabbat, he may eat it, even though the food will be improved through sitting on the stove. On the other hand, if the food was not yet fully cooked, he may not eat it until the night after Shabbat.[538]

Discussion — The Talmud (BT *Ketubot* 34a) states: "If someone has cooked on Sabbath, [if] by mistake, he may eat it, [and if] willfully, he may not eat it—this is the view of Rabbi Meir. Rabbi Yehuda says— [if] by mistake, he may eat it after the Shabbat ends, [if] willfully, he may never eat it. Rabbi Yohanan Hasandalar says: [if] willfully, others may eat it after the outgoing of the Sabbath, but not he, [if] willfully, neither he nor others may eat it."

The Talmud (BT *Shabbat* 38a) further states: "[i]f one forgot a pot on the stove and [thus] cooked it on Shabbat: unwittingly, he may eat [thereof]; if deliberately, he may not eat. When is that said? In the case of hot water insufficiently heated or a dish insufficiently cooked; but as for hot water sufficiently heated or a dish sufficiently cooked, whether unwitting or deliberate, he may eat [thereof]: thus said Rabbi Meir. Rabbi Yehuda said: hot water sufficiently heated is permitted, because it boils away and is thus harmed; a dish sufficiently cooked is forbidden, because it shrinks and is thereby improved, and whatever shrinks and is thereby improved, e.g., cabbage, beans, and mincemeat, is forbidden; but whatever shrinks and thereby deteriorates, is permitted."

---

536 *Mishna Berura* 602:10.
537 *Sha'ar HaTziyun* 602:7.
538 *Shulhan Arukh, Orah Hayyim* 253:1.

Alternative Positions — The *Magen Avraham* writes that if a person were to say that the Halakha is in accord with Rabbi Meir's opinion, then if he did it unintentionally (*b'shogeg*), he should be able to eat it. Also, the *Haga'ot Mordekhai* does consider the Halakha to be in accord with Rabbi Meir's opinion. The *Gra*, on the other hand, argues that the food is forbidden to everyone, as opposed to the *Haga'ot Mordekhai*, who permits it.[539]

The *Mishna Berura*'s Position — The *Mishna Berura* explains that the food is forbidden for everyone, especially the members of one's own household, since the person who forgot the pot on the stove originally intended to cook the food for them as well.[540]

Halakhic Principles — 5, 10

180.

Shulhan Arukh — One may not place food upon a stove which is fired with the refuse of olives or wood before sunset with the intention of leaving it there, unless the food has already been fully cooked, in which case there is no suspicion that the person will stoke the coals. He is also permitted to place the pot on the stove if the food is completely raw, since he will not pay attention to it until the next morning.[541]

Alternative Positions — In the *Biur Halakha*, the *Mishna Berura* explains that when Rabbi Karo writes not to place food on a stove with the intention of leaving it, he means food that is meant to be served for dinner. If he intends for the food to be served the following day, some *poskim* permit him to put it on the stove since they do not suspect that he will stoke the coals, just as in the case when the food is raw. The *Mishna Berura* cites the *Gra*, the *Magen Avraham*, and the *Elya Rabba*, who rule that, nevertheless, one cannot rely on this opinion. It is only when the food is raw and inedible that we do not have a suspicion. In the case where the food is not completely raw but is still intended for the following day, since it can become

---

539 *Sha'ar HaTziyun* 253:33.
540 *Mishna Berura* 253:31.
541 *Shulhan Arukh, Orah Hayyim* 253:1.

edible in time to eat that night, one must still suspect that he may stoke the coals.

The *Mishna Berura*'s Position — The *Mishna Berura* writes that *ex post facto*, one may rely on the lenient opinion of the *Shulhan Arukh*, as long as he does not regularly do so.[542]

Halakhic Principles — 2, 8, 10

181.

Shulhan Arukh — When Shabbat falls on the fourteenth of *Nissan*, which is the eve of Passover, one should have his third meal before the tenth hour with *matzah ashira*.

Rema — In these lands, the custom is not to eat *matzah ashira*. Instead, one should have his third meal with various fruits and meat and fish.[543]

Discussion — *Matzah* that was kneaded only with fruit juice, wine, or oil without any water is called *matzah ashira* (rich *matzah*). According to the *Shulhan Arukh*, it does not become *hametz* even if it sits all day. Therefore, it is permitted to be eaten on Passover, or on the eve of Passover in the afternoon when the prohibition to eat *hametz* begins, but one cannot fulfill his obligation of eating *matzah* with it. According to the *Rema*, *matzah ashira* is not baked or eaten unless there are extenuating circumstances, such as that it is needed for an ill or elderly person. Even then, one should bake the dough immediately and not let it sit, out of consideration for the opinions that fruit juice does becomes *hametz*, even quicker than water, or that some water may have gotten mixed into the juice.

The *Mishna Berura*'s Position — The *Mishna Berura*, after noting the numerous opinions on when to eat the third meal and what should be eaten, concludes by saying that one should look toward the *Aharonim* who write that it is good to split the morning meal into two, since there are those who say that doing this would count as having a third meal. He ultimately justifies this suggestion with the fact that the *Gra* writes that it is correct to do this. However, the

---

542 *Biur Halakha* 253: s.v. *le'hash'hoto aleiha*.
543 *Shulhan Arukh, Orah Hayyim* 444:1.

Mishna Berura warns that the person should leave enough time between the two meals in order to prevent saying a superfluous blessing.[544]

Halakhic Principles — 4, 10

182.

Shulhan Arukh — A doubtful *Eruv*, such as when there is a doubt as to whether it existed during twilight (*ben ha'shmashot*) or not, is permitted on the condition that it had a presumption of being kosher, such as if it were already in place and then the doubt arose. If it did not have a presumption of being kosher, such as in a case where there is a doubt if the bread was ever in place, then the *Eruv* is not permitted.[545]

Alternative Position — In the *Biur Halakha*, the *Mishna Berura* refers to the *Gra*, who explains that the source of this ruling is BT *Eruvin* 36a, which starts, "An *Eruv* of *terumah* about which there is doubt whether it was clean." The *Gra* argues that even though the matter being discussed is an *Eruv* to establish a *Tehum* (boundary for Shabbat travel), the law applies for an *Eruv Hatzerot* (a unification of domains for the purpose of carrying within them) as well. The *Mishna Berura* does note, however, that this ruling is not clear, and that many *Rishonim* disagree and believe that the discussion only applies to an *Eruv* for a *Tehum* and not for an *Eruv Hatzerot*. According to them, even an *Eruv Hatzerot* that has a doubt with respect to the purity of the bread is still kosher, and so it would be kosher if there was a doubt regarding whether it was in place during *ben ha'shmashot*.[546]

The *Mishna Berura*'s Position — In the main commentary, the *Mishna Berura* does not mention the lenient opinion of the *Rishonim* who disagree with the *Gra*, implying that the normative Halakha is in accordance with the *Shulhan Arukh*'s and the *Gra*'s opinion. However, by mentioning the lenient opinion in the *Biur Halakha*, the

---

544 *Mishna Berura* 444:8.
545 *Shulhan Arukh, Orah Hayyim* 394:1.
546 *Biur Halakha* 394: s.v. *aval im lo hayah hezkat kashrut*.

Mishna Berura expands the realm of acceptability to include those who follow the position of the *Rishonim*.

Halakhic Principles — 5, 6, 10

183.

Shulhan Arukh — There are those who say that regarding the *Kedusha* within "*Yotzer*" (the first blessing before the morning recital of the *Shema*, within which the angelic expressions that make up the *Kedusha* are said), an individual praying alone may say the *Kedusha*, and there are those who say that an individual praying alone must skip the *Kedusha* since it may only be said in a quorum. We take the second position into consideration and are careful that an individual says the verses in a melody as if reading them from the Torah.

Rema — The custom is according to the first opinion; therefore, an individual praying alone need not worry about saying the *Kedusha* and he should say it aloud.[547]

Discussion — Though the *Shulhan Arukh* states that we defer to the latter opinion, it does not say that the Halakha is according to the second opinion. One can infer, therefore, that the deference to the latter opinion is for the purpose of covering one's bases and not because it is the essential ruling. Support for this assumption is that an individual still recites the *Kedusha*, only reciting it in tune.

The *Mishna Berura*'s Position — The *Mishna Berura* notes that the *Gra* rules that the Halakha is according to the second opinion, which is that a person praying alone should not say it at all. However, because the *minhag* is so strong, the *Mishna Berura* says not to budge from it. Rather, he advises that one take the suggestion of Rabbi Karo and say the verses in tune so as not to contradict the ruling of the *Gra*.[548]

Halakhic Principles — 4, 10

---

547 *Shulhan Arukh, Orah Hayyim* 59:3.
548 *Mishna Berura* 59:11.

184.

Shulhan Arukh — If a person eats less than the volume of an olive (*kazayit*) of bread, there is an opinion which holds that he does not need to wash his hands before eating.[549]

Alternative Positions — The *Mishna Berura* adds that when a person eats a small amount of bread in order to remove the sharpness of a drink, he would not need to say "*HaMotzi*" since the bread is subordinate to the drink. He also notes that there are *poskim* who say that the person does not need to wash his hands even if he eats the volume of an egg (*kabeitza*) of bread. The *Mishna Berura* writes, however, that other *poskim* disagree and believe that the person must wash his hands before eating a *kabeitza* amount of bread.

The *Mishna Berura*'s Position — The *Mishna Berura* suggests that when a person eats less than a *kazayit* of bread to remove the sharpness of a drink, he does not need to wash his hands. If he eats a *kazayit* or more he must wash his hands, though he should not say the blessing since there is a doubt as to whether the blessing is required or not.[550] In the *Sha'ar HaTziyun*, the *Mishna Berura* explains why it rules stringently for the size of a *kazayit* when there are *poskim* who are lenient even when a person eats a *kabeitza*. He infers that the *Gra* holds that a person is required to wash his hands and say the blessing whenever he eats a *kazayit* of bread.[551] Therefore, in order to defer to the position of the *Gra*, the *Mishna Berura* rules that a person must wash his hands, yet, because the omission of a blessing does not impede upon the fulfillment of an obligation, it is lenient due to the doubt of its necessity.

Halakhic Principles — 3, 10

185.

Shulhan Arukh — It is a *mitzvah* to shave on the day before Yom Tov.[552]

---

549 *Shulhan Arukh, Orah Hayyim* 158:3.
550 *Mishna Berura* 158:10.
551 *Sha'ar HaTziyun* 158:11.
552 *Shulhan Arukh, Orah Hayyim* 531:1.

Rema — *Ex post facto* one may shave at any time of the day.

Alternative Positions — The *Pri Megadim* writes that *ab initio* one should shave before noon, because the *Ari* writes that one should not shave after *Minha*, by which he means after the arrival of *Minha Gedola*. Other *Aharonim*, however, hold that one can rely on the *poskim* who understand *Minha* to mean *Minha Ketana*.

Discussion — *Minha* is the afternoon prayer service. There are two time periods during the day in which one is permitted to pray the *Minha* prayer. The earliest time is six and a half hours after sunrise. This time is known as *Minha Gedola*. The second time period, known as *Minha Ketana*, begins three hours later, nine and a half hours after sunrise.

The *Mishna Berura*'s Position — Taking into consideration the more lenient opinion, the *Mishna Berura* writes that if time is pressing, a person may rely upon the *poskim* even *ab initio* to shave up until *Minha Ketana*. The *Mishna Berura* concludes by saying that the entire discussion refers to an *ab initio* situation, since *ex post facto* the *Rema* rules that one may shave at any time of the day.

Discussion — The *Mishna Berura* explains that its last comment does not contradict its ruling that one can rely on the *poskim ab initio* if time is pressing, since it makes a distinction between a situation in which a person perceives that time will be pressing and a situation in which time just ran away from the person. Also, to justify his permitting a person to shave all day, the *Mishna Berura* does not rely solely on the *Rema*'s ruling. As a final justificatory remark, he writes that even the *Gra* challenges limiting the permission to shave until *Minha*, and so that one will not enter the Yom Tov looking ugly we should not be stringent.[553]

Halakhic Principles — 2, 10

186.

Shulhan Arukh — The person called up to the Torah must read the portion quietly along with the cantor (*Hazan*), yet not so loudly that

---

553 *Sha'ar HaTziyun* 531:2.

he can hear himself, so that his blessing over reading from the Torah is not made in vain.

Rema — It is not a problem if he reads loud enough that he can hear himself.[554]

Alternative Positions — The *Mishna Berura* writes that the source for Rabbi Karo's ruling not to read aloud is the *Zohar*.[555] The *Sha'ar HaTziyun* adds that according to the *Gra*, *ab initio* it would be better to read audibly, and that the *Gra* maintains that even the *Zohar* does not contradict this.

The *Mishna Berura*'s Position — The *Mishna Berura* rewords the *Rema*'s statement to say that although it is better if a person reads at an inaudible volume, it is not a problem if he can hear himself.[556] The *Sha'ar HaTziyun*, basing itself on the *Gra*, states that a person should not worry at all about hearing himself. Nevertheless, it leaves its practical ruling undecided.[557]

Discussion — The *Mishna Berura* tries to find a compromise between the position of the *Shulhan Arukh*, which warns a person against reading audibly, and the position of the *Gra* and the *Rema*, which is that one need not worry about reading audibly. Due to the difficulty of such a compromise, the *Mishna Berura* vacillates and finally does not come to a conclusive decision. It does maintain greater fidelity to the *Shulhan Arukh*, since that is the only opinion which has a potential negative consequence.

Halakhic Principles — 3, 9, 10

187.

Shulhan Arukh — A roof that protrudes over the walls of a house in such a way that the walls cannot be seen when standing on the roof would be considered a *Karmelit*, even if the roof is very wide and high off the ground. If, however, a window is open to the roof from the house, the roof would be considered a private domain. Similarly,

---

554 *Shulhan Arukh, Orah Hayyim* 141:2.
555 *Mishna Berura* 141:1.
556 *Mishna Berura* 141:13.
557 *Sha'ar HaTziyun* 141:12.

a ledge that has the dimensions of four by four *tefahim* (a halakhic measurement) which protrudes from a wall would be considered a *Karmelit* unless a window from the house opens to it.[558]

Discussion — The *Mishna Berura* explains that according to Rabbi Karo, when we say that a *Karmelit* extends only up to the height of ten *tefahim*, this is only when the *Karmelit* begins on the ground so that it does not extend past ten *tefahim* in the air. When an area is considered to be a *Karmelit* because it lacks partitions, the area may even be ten *tefahim* above the ground. Wherever its floor, the status of *Karmelit* will apply up to ten *tefahim*, as the example of the roof demonstrates.

Alternative Positions — The *Mishna Berura* notes, however, that the *Elya Rabba* questions this ruling, and that the *Gra* cites many *Rishonim* who disagree and hold that an area ten *tefahim* above the ground is never considered to be a *Karmelit*. The *Gra* also rules in accordance with this opinion.[559] In the *Biur Halakha*, the *Mishna Berura* cites the *Magen Avraham*, who brings the opinion of *Tosafot* that only when a roof extends four *tefahim* past the walls would it be considered a *Karmelit*, whereas if the roof extends less than four *tefahim* it would be permitted to carry on the roof and its protrusions. The *Mishna Berura* challenges this distinction and says that, in truth, one can infer from the language of the *poskim* that they seem to agree with *Tosafot* that even if the roof protrudes only a little bit it would be forbidden to carry on it.

The *Mishna Berura*'s Position — The *Mishna Berura* writes that because the *Gra* and the *Elya Rabba* allow a person to carry in any event, if the roof does not protrude four *tefahim* from the walls, one may certainly rely on their opinion to permit a person to carry.[560]

Discussion — The *Mishna Berura* only applies the leniency of the *Gra* and the *Elya Rabba* to a situation wherein the roof does not protrude four *tefahim* from the walls, rather than applying the leniency regardless of the protrusion, in order to defer to the more

---

558 *Shulhan Arukh, Orah Hayyim* 345:16.
559 *Mishna Berura* 345:66.
560 *Biur Halakha* 345: s.v. *gag ha'bolet*.

stringent opinion, even if it disagrees with it, when it does not contradict what it believes to be the essential Halakha. Because the *Gra* allows the entire roof, regardless of protrusion, *Tosafot* allows the roof whenever the protrusion is less than four *tefahim*, and the other *Rishonim* (according to the *Mishna Berura* and not the *Magen Avraham*) forbid the roof if there is any protrusion, the *Mishna Berura* can incorporate the position of *Tosafot* without contradicting the position of the *Gra*.

Halakhic Principles — 3, 4, 10

188.

Rema — It is the custom to read the *Haggadah* after *Minha* on *Shabbat HaGadol*.[561]

Discussion — The *Haggadah* is a Jewish text that sets forth the order of the Passover Seder. *Shabbat HaGadol* (Great Shabbat) is the Shabbat immediately before Passover.

The *Mishna Berura*'s Position — In his main commentary, the *Mishna Berura* explains the reason for the custom.[562] However, in the *Biur Halakha*, the *Mishna Berura* cites the *Gra*, who writes that one should not follow this custom, since it says in the Haggadah, "'On that day,' however, could mean while it is yet daytime; the Torah therefore says, 'It is because of this.' The expression 'because of this' can only be said when the *matzah* and *marror* are placed before you."[563]

Halakhic Principles — 7, 10

189.

Rema — It is a custom to spread out grasses on *Shavuot* both in the synagogue and at home as a remembrance of the joy of the giving of the Torah (*Matan Torah*).[564]

---

561 *Shulhan Arukh, Orah Hayyim* 430:1.
562 *Mishna Berura* 430:2.
563 *Biur Halakha* 430: s.v. *b'minha ha'haggadah*.
564 *Shulhan Arukh, Orah Hayyim* 494:3.

The *Mishna Berura*'s Position — The *Mishna Berura* notes that the custom has developed to place trees in the synagogues and in people's homes as a way to remember that we are judged at this time regarding how abundant the fruit trees will be over the next year, but writes that the *Gra* discontinued this custom because it is a contemporary practice of the Gentiles to put up a tree during their holiday.[565]
Halakhic Principles — 7, 10

190.

Rema — On the Shabbat preceding *Tisha b'Av*, one should not wear Shabbat clothes, yet he may change his shirt.[566]
The *Mishna Berura*'s Position — The *Mishna Berura* writes that the communities of Vilna follow the custom established by the *Gra* to wear Shabbat clothes on this Shabbat.[567]
Halakhic Principles — 7, 10

191.

Shulhan Arukh — If the three people called to read from the Torah read less than nine verses cumulatively, then the one who reads less than three verses must repeat his *Aliyah*.[568]
Alternative Positions — The *Mishna Berura* writes that if each person read three verses, yet one of the verses was repeated so that only eight verses were read in total, then it is as if the reader who repeated the verse only read two verses and must repeat his *Aliyah*. He does mention, however, that there are *poskim* who state that *ex post facto* the requirement to read from the Torah is fulfilled, since each person, in any case, did recite three verses.[569]
The *Mishna Berura*'s Position — In the *Sha'ar HaTziyun*, the *Mishna Berura* writes that as a practical matter one should not teach this

---

565 *Mishna Berura* 494:10.
566 *Shulhan Arukh, Orah Hayyim* 551:1.
567 *Mishna Berura* 551:6.
568 *Shulhan Arukh, Orah Hayyim* 137:4.
569 *Mishna Berura* 137:15.

leniency, since the *Gra* and the *Panim Meirot* hold that even when the three people read nine verses cumulatively it is insufficient.[570]
Halakhic Principles — 5, 10

192.

Shulhan Arukh — It is prohibited to grind salt in a wooden grinder on Shabbat, but a person may grind salt with a knife's handle or with a wooden spoon without concern.[571]
The *Mishna Berura*'s Position — The *Mishna Berura* writes that the person should grind the salt on a plate or on the table, and should not use a mortar and pestle, as is the case with pepper.[572] The *Sha'ar HaTziyun* adds that even though the *Gra* is lenient to crush salt with a knife's handle even in a mortar, it is difficult to be lenient in practice since all of the *Aharonim* who prohibit using a mortar to grind pepper also prohibit it to grind salt.[573]
Halakhic Principles — 5, 10

193.

Shulhan Arukh — If a Gentile is going of his own accord to a place where a Jew happens to have a letter to send, it is permissible for the Jew to give the Gentile the letter.[574]
The *Mishna Berura*'s Position — The *Mishna Berura* writes that this applies only if there is enough time for the Gentile to reach the destination of the letter before Shabbat. If he does not have enough time, the Jew is forbidden to send the letter with the Gentile; for even though the Gentile travels of his own accord, he nevertheless carries the letter on behalf of the Jew.[575]
Discussion — In the *Sha'ar HaTziyun*, the *Mishna Berura* explains that this comment is based on the opinion of the *Magen Avraham*, yet the *Elya Rabba* as well as other *Aharonim* also agree. It continues

---

570 *Sha'ar HaTziyun* 137:24.
571 *Shulhan Arukh, Orah Hayyim* 321:8.
572 *Mishna Berura* 321:27.
573 *Sha'ar HaTziyun* 321:32.
574 *Shulhan Arukh, Orah Hayyim* 247:5.
575 *Mishna Berura* 247:18.

to say that even though the *Gra* rules leniently in accordance with Rabbi Karo, and though the *Magen Avraham*'s challenge to Rabbi Karo's ruling can be answered, it is nevertheless difficult to be lenient since the *Aharonim* bring in support of the *Magen Avraham*'s opinion the fact that he rules like the *Maharam*. The *Mishna Berura* concludes by saying that one should therefore act according to the *Magen Avraham*'s understanding, even though it is difficult to comprehend the *Shulhan Arukh* through the interpretation the *Magen Avraham* gives it. What stops the *Mishna Berura* from ruling like the *Gra* is that the *Gra* is in the minority and, due to the fact that he is lenient, acting stringently does not necessarily contradict his position. [576]

Halakhic Principles — 5, 10

Gra as Basis for Interpretation

The *Mishna Berura* utilizes the *Gra*'s writings as a means to reinterpret or explain the *Shulhan Arukh* when he thinks that either Rabbi Karo or the *Rema* contradicts himself. The *Mishna Berura* also utilizes the *Gra*'s writings as a means to reinterpret or explain a *Rishon* when he thinks that the *Rishon* seemingly contradicts himself. The *Mishna Berura* relies on the *Gra* to give an alternate justification for a position whose initial justification has been rejected. The *Mishna Berura* reinterprets the *Shulhan Arukh*'s or the *Rema*'s rulings so that they accord with the *Gra*'s position. The *Mishna Berura*, at times, writes that the simple reading of a ruling is misleading and should mean something different, i.e. as the *Gra* understands it, or will simply rewrite a ruling to conform to the *Gra*'s understanding. The *Mishna Berura*'s veneration to the *Gra* is so substantial that it even reinterprets the *Gra*'s writings in order to let him remain a consistent foundation upon which to rely.

---

576 *Sha'ar HaTziyun* 247:17.

194.

Shulhan Arukh — A *Kohen* who killed someone, even accidently, may not say *Birkat Kohanim*, even if he repents.

Rema — There are those who disagree and allow him to say *Birkat Kohanim*. The custom is to be lenient with penitents (*Ba'alei Teshuva*) so as not to close the door in the face of those who repent.[577]

Alternative Position — Regarding the *Rema*'s comment that we have the custom to be lenient, the *Mishna Berura* writes that there are *Aharonim* who disagree with the *Rema* in a situation in which a *Kohen* killed another person intentionally.[578]

Seeming Contradiction — In the *Biur Halakha*, the *Mishna Berura* writes that though Rabbi Karo gives an undisputed ruling in this case with respect to prohibiting a *Kohen* who became an apostate to say *Birkat Kohanim*, Rabbi Karo mentions that there is another opinion which allows a *Kohen* to say *Birkat Kohanim* if he repents.[579]

The *Mishna Berura*'s Position — The *Mishna Berura* first provides a means to reconcile the difference by simply saying that Rabbi Karo is strict regarding a murderer because of the halakhic idea that a prosecutor cannot be made into the defense lawyer, that is, that the hands which killed a person are no longer a suitable instrument to seek mercy for the Jewish people. It also gives this as the reason for Rabbi Karo's ruling in the main commentary.[580] In the *Biur Halakha*, however, the *Mishna Berura* writes that the *Olat Tamid* and the *Gra* show that, in truth, Rabbi Karo rules that the murderer, like the apostate, may say *Birkat Kohanim* if he repents. Its reading of Rabbi Karo through the eyes of the *Gra* also allows it to interpret the *Rema*'s custom of leniency more expansively and apply it both to those who kill accidentally and to those who kill intentionally, since the *Rema* permits an apostate *Kohen* who repents to say *Birkat Kohanim*, and the *Mishna Berura* has equated the two rulings as the same without any distinction. With respect to offering a practical legal decision,

---

577 *Shulhan Arukh, Orah Hayyim* 128:35.
578 *Mishna Berura* 128:131.
579 *Biur Halakha* 128: s.v. *afilu aseh teshuva*; *Shulhan Arukh, Orah Hayyim* 128:37.
580 *Mishna Berura* 128:129.

the *Mishna Berura* still writes that the matter requires further investigation, yet remarks that if a penitent went to say *Birkat Kohanim* we need not force him to remove himself.

Discussion — The *Mishna Berura*'s reliance upon the *Gra* clearly challenges its general inclination to be strict in order to avoid transgression, yet allows it to find coherence within a seeming contradiction due to a lack of distinctions in the *Shulhan Arukh* and the *Rema*.

Halakhic Principles — 4, 6, 8, 10

195.

Rema — There should be no interruption in the morning prayers from the time the *Hazan* starts to say the *Kaddish* after *Pesukei d'Zimra* until after saying *Barkhu.*[581]

Discussion — An interruption during the prayer service would consist of any activity that is not directly related to the part of the prayer service being said.

Seeming Contradiction — The *Mishna Berura* explains that this period of time has the same legal status as the time between sections during the recital of the *Shema* and its blessings.[582] In the *Biur Halakha*, the *Mishna Berura* notes that the *Rema* seems to contradict himself, since his refusal to allow any interruption once the *Kaddish* has started contradicts his statement that one may don phylacteries

---

581 *Shulhan Arukh, Orah Hayyim* 54:3. The parts of the morning prayer are as follows: The service starts with the "morning blessings" (*birkot ha-shachar*), including blessings for the Torah. This is followed by a series of readings from biblical and rabbinic writings recalling the Temple Sacrifices. The section concludes with the "Rabbis' Kaddish" (*kaddish de-rabbanan*). The next section of morning prayers is called *Pesukei D'Zimrah* ("verses of praise"), and contains several psalms and prayers, followed by the Song at the Sea (Exod., chapters 14-15). The section concludes with the "Half Kaddish" (*hatzi kaddish*). Then *Barkhu*, the formal public call to prayer, introduces a series of expanded blessings embracing the recitation of the Shema. This is followed by the core of the prayer service, the *Amida* or *Shemoneh Esreh*. The next part of the service is *Tahanun* (supplications), which is omitted on days with a festive character. On Mondays and Thursdays a Torah reading service is inserted, and a longer version of *Tahanun* takes place. Concluding prayers and *Aleinu* then follow, with the *Kaddish* of the mourners generally after *Aleinu*.

582 *Mishna Berura* 54:13.

during the recital of the *Shema* and its blessings, even if he cannot recite the blessing over the phylacteries before he prays the *Amida*.[583]

The *Mishna Berura*'s Position — To resolve this contradiction, the *Mishna Berura* could have reevaluated its assumption that the *Rema* considers the time between *Pesukei d'Zimra* until after saying *Barkhu* as having the same legal status as the breaks during the recital of the *Shema* and its blessings. Instead it says that the *Rema* is not giving his own opinion in this case, but rather is just citing another position.

Discussion — The *Mishna Berura*'s justification for suggesting this is the *Gra*'s statement that the beginning of the morning blessings starts after *Barkhu*; therefore, the *Rema* must consider everything from the beginning of *Kaddish* to the end of *Barkhu* as being in between parts of prayer. The *Mishna Berura*'s confidence that the *Rema* allows interruption for the sake of donning phylacteries even within a section and not just at the breaks between sections during the recital of the Shema and its blessings, which is the cause for the contradiction in the first place, is also based on the *Gra*'s reading of the two *Halakhot*.[584] Because the *Mishna Berura* believes the *Gra*, as the foundation for its halakhic analysis, is coherent, the only reasonable conclusion that it can make is that the *Rema* is not, and in this case does not hold by his own comment.

Halakhic Principles — 5, 8, 10

196.

Shulhan Arukh — It is prohibited to leave the synagogue while the Torah scroll is open, yet one may leave in between *Aliyot*. Once the public reading begins, however, it is forbidden to converse, even about Torah and even between *Aliyot*.[585]

Alternative Positions — The *Mishna Berura* cites the *Magen Avraham*, who is stringent and forbids a person to speak even when

---

583 *Shulhan Arukh, Orah Hayyim* 66:2; 66:8.
584 *Biur Halakha* 54: s.v. *ben kaddish*.
585 *Shulhan Arukh, Orah Hayyim* 146:1-2.

the Torah scroll is open, yet before the reader begins. The *Gra* rules likewise.[586]

Seeming Contradiction — In the *Biur Halakha*, the *Mishna Berura* notes that Rabbi Karo's ruling is in accord with the *Rambam*'s with respect to forbidding a person to speak once the public reading begins, yet seems to diverge from the *Rambam*'s opinion with respect to leaving the sanctuary. The *Rambam* prohibits leaving only once the reader begins; Rabbi Karo, on the other hand, forbids it once the scroll is first opened.

The *Mishna Berura*'s Position — The *Mishna Berura* writes that during the time when the Torah scroll is open but the reader has not yet begun, one certainly cannot be lenient and permit leaving, since the *Magen Avraham* and the *Gra* are stringent to prohibit people speaking. It follows the *Magen Avraham* and the *Gra* in their stringent rulings, even though the *Rambam* is lenient and allows people to leave.[587]

Discussion — The *Mishna Berura* does not even accept the *Rambam*'s leniency to allow people to leave when the scroll is open yet before the reading begins *ex post facto*. Once it accepts the position of the *Magen Avraham* and the *Gra* regarding speaking, no longer is there any room for the *Rambam*'s position.

Halakhic Principles — 5, 10

197.

Shulhan Arukh — On the first night of the holiday of Hanukah, a person should light one candle, and on each subsequent night he should add a candle until the last night, when he lights eight candles. Even if his household consists of many people, he should not light more than the number of candles suggested.

Rema — There are those who say that each person in the household should light, and this is a widely accepted custom.[588]

---

586 *Mishna Berura* 146:4.
587 *Biur Halakha* 54: s.v. *k'shehu patuah*.
588 *Shulhan Arukh, Orah Hayyim* 671:2.

Seeming Contradiction — In the *Biur Halakha*, the *Mishna Berura* refers to the *Gra* who writes that the *Rema*'s ruling seems to be the ruling of the *Rif* since the *Rif* quotes the following statement from the Talmud: Rabbah bar Bar Hana said: "There were two old men in Sidon: one did as *Bet Shammai* and the other as *Bet Hillel*: the former gave the reason of his action that it should correspond to the bullocks of the Festival, while the latter stated his reason because we promote in [matters of] sanctity but do not reduce."[589] The *Mishna Berura* is troubled by the fact that the *Rif* quotes this Talmudic statement, since it may imply that the *Rif* permits one to act in accord with either position.

The *Mishna Berura*'s Position — The *Mishna Berura* writes that because of the *Gra*'s statement, one need not infer that the *Rif* does not hold that the Halakha is according to *Bet Hillel*; rather, it is possible to understand the discussion to be over the notion of *hiddur mitzvah* (going over and above what is ritually required). Both of the elders agreed that the base Halakha was according to *Bet Hillel*, and it was only with respect to *hiddur mitzvah* that one of them acted according to *Bet Shammai*. With such an understanding, the *Mishna Berura* concludes, saying that it did not present this analysis for the purpose of making a practical ruling and that one should not include this analysis as part of the Halakha at all. Rather, it is presented only as an academic analysis to awaken the hearts of those who investigate such matters.[590]

Discussion — In this case, the *Mishna Berura* did not intend to incorporate an important *Rishon* into its practical halakhic decision. Nevertheless, it still endeavored to avoid misinterpretation and thus incorporate his position into the greater halakhic framework.

Halakhic Principles — 8, 10

---

589 BT *Shabbat* 21b.
590 *Biur Halakha* 671: s.v. *ve'yesh omrim de'khol ehad*.

198.

Shulhan Arukh — Anything is kosher to use as walls of a *Sukkah*, even if more sunshine passes through the material than is blocked by the material.[591]

Initial Justification — In the *Biur Halakha*, the *Mishna Berura* cites the *Bach*, who writes that a *Ba'al Nefesh* should defer to that which the *Rema* writes in the *Darkhei Moshe*, which suggests that one be stringent regarding what he considers acceptable to use for the walls of a *Sukkah* in the same way as one is regarding what he deems acceptable to use as the *Sekhakh* (the material that forms the roof of the *Sukkah*). The *Mishna Berura* then cites the *Elya Rabba* and the *Birkei Yosef*, who write that one need not defer to the *Rema*'s stringency since the support the *Rema* brings from the Jerusalem Talmud is not found in our editions. Moreover, the *Gra* dismisses the *Rema*'s proof in any case.

The *Mishna Berura*'s Position — The *Mishna Berura* does, however, refer to the *Biur HaGra*, who gives a different reason for a *Ba'al Nefesh* to be stringent *ab initio*. The *Sekhakh* will lean on the walls, and many *Aharonim* believe that *ab initio* a person should not place the *Sekhakh* on something that is disqualified to be used as *Sekhakh*, as a decree to prevent him from using it as such. Though there is an exception for the poles at the corners of the *Sukkah* under the *Sekhakh*, regarding the walls one should be stringent.[592]

Halakhic Principles — 5, 6, 10

199.

Shulhan Arukh — For the purpose of *Mayim Aharonim* (the hand washing at the end of a meal), one need only wash one's fingers up to the second joint.[593]

The *Mishna Berura*'s Position — The *Mishna Berura* comments that its author has seen people who have been careful with respect to always washing *Mayim Aharonim*, yet do not fulfill their

---

591 *Shulhan Arukh, Orah Hayyim* 630:1.
592 *Biur Halakha* 630: s.v. *kol ha'devarim kesherim la'dafanot.*
593 *Shulhan Arukh, Orah Hayyim* 181:4.

obligation at all, since they only put the tips of the fingers in water, and because the water does not even reach the first joint, their fingers remain dirty with food. In truth, according to the law a person must wash at least up to the second joint.[594]

The *Mishna Berura*'s Position II — In the *Biur Halakha*,[595] however, there is a reference to the *Biur HaGra*, where the *Gra* proves that the ruling regarding *Mayim Aharonim* is contingent on the debate regarding washing one's hands before a meal. Rabbi Karo writes with respect to washing before a meal that one must wash his whole hand until the wrist, and then adds that there are those who say that he may wash up to where his fingers connect to the palm.[596] The *Gra* explains that the *posek* (halakhic authority) who holds that one must wash his hands until the wrist before a meal also rules that he must wash his fingers up to the palm for *Mayim Aharonim*. Therefore, because Rabbi Karo rules according to the opinion that a person must wash his hands up to the wrist before a meal, it is good *ab initio* for a person to wash his fingers up to where they connect to the palm for *Mayim Aharonim*.

Discussion — This interpretation, consequently, turns Rabbi Karo's ruling into a statement of *ex post facto* acceptability instead of an *ab initio* requirement. To further support the *Gra*'s comparison between the two types of washing, the *Mishna Berura* cites the *Gra*'s statement that the required measure of water for *Mayim Aharonim* is a *revi'it*, the same minimum amount required to wash one's hands before eating bread.[597]

Halakhic Principles — 2, 8, 10

200.

Shulhan Arukh — One should not go out on Friday close to dark with a needle or a pen in his hand lest he forget and go out holding them on Shabbat.[598]

---

594 *Mishna Berura* 181:10.
595 *Biur Halakha* 161: s.v. *ad perek sheni.*
596 *Shulhan Arukh, Orah Hayyim* 161:4.
597 *Mishna Berura* 181:19.
598 *Shulhan Arukh, Orah Hayyim* 252:6.

Discussion — The *Mishna Berura* writes that those actions which are prohibited on Shabbat only by rabbinic decree should not be prohibited Friday close to dark, since the rabbis do not make decrees to safeguard the rabbinic decrees that have been previously instituted. Today, since there are no public domains, and since public places have the status of *Karmelit*, it would be permitted to go out carrying an object on Friday close to dark, i.e., before sunset.

The *Mishna Berura*'s Position — The *Mishna Berura* does note that many *poskim*, Rabbi Karo among them, hold that public domains still exist today, and so his ruling would still be relevant, but in order to maintain the Halakha's applicability even for those *poskim* who consider all public spaces to have the status of *Karmelit*, the *Mishna Berura* cites the *Gra*, who forbids a person to carry immediately close to dark even in a *Karmelit*.[599] In the *Biur Halakha*, the *Mishna Berura* explains the *Gra*'s reasoning. According to the *Gra*, the discussion in the Talmud over whether the rabbis may make a decree on a decree is only in the context of when it is close to dark, but when it is immediately close to dark, almost sunset, the rabbis may decree something to be prohibited even when if done on Shabbat it would only entail a rabbinic transgression.[600]

Halakhic Principles — 5, 8, 10

201.

Shulhan Arukh — It is a *mitzvah* to examine one's clothing on Friday close to dark so as to avoid carrying on Shabbat.[601]

Discussion — In the *Biur Halakha*, the *Mishna Berura* notes that the *Tur* also uses this language, yet the Talmud does not say that it is a *mitzvah*, but rather that a person is obligated.

The *Mishna Berura*'s Position — The *Mishna Berura* first tries to resolve this discrepancy by saying that the *Tur* and Rabbi Karo changed their wording because the original language did not

---

599 *Mishna Berura* 252:52.
600 *Biur Halakha* 252: s.v. *b'yado*.
601 *Shulhan Arukh, Orah Hayyim* 252:7.

properly convey the statement's true meaning. The Mishna only prohibits going out close to dark when one is holding an object in his hand, but does not require a person to examine his clothing lest he go out with something in his pockets. Also, the rabbis only made the decree for the case where a person wants to leave his house. To use the wording that a person is obligated to examine his clothing, on the other hand, would indicate that even when he is staying at home he must examine his clothing close to dark. Therefore, they changed the language to "it is a *mitzvah*," to make it clear that one does not commit a transgression if he does not do it.

The *Mishna Berura*'s Position II — The *Mishna Berura* then challenges its own explanation, and the leniency that it entails, by giving the *Gra*'s distinction between the wording in the Mishna of "at dark" and Hanania's wording in the Talmud of "close to dark" as it relates to this ruling. According to the *Gra*, Hanania and the Mishna are referring to two different situations. Thus, "at dark" there is an obligation to examine one's clothing even when one is staying in the house, while "close to dark" there would only be a *mitzvah* to examine one's clothing.[602]

Halakhic Principles — 3, 4, 8, 10

202.

Shulhan Arukh — It is permitted to read a letter delivered on Shabbat if one does not know its contents, but he should not read it aloud. If, however, the letter came from outside the *Tehum*, it is good to be careful not to touch it.[603]

Discussion — The *Mishna Berura* first explains that the reason to be careful is because the letter is *muktze* since it came from outside the *Tehum*. By stating that it is good to be careful not to touch it, the *Mishna Berura* infers that the *Shulhan Arukh* still allows a person to read the letter. The *Mishna Berura* then asks: if we rule in general that the intended recipient of something brought from outside the

---

602 *Biur Halakha* 252: s.v. *mitzvah*.
603 *Shulhan Arukh, Orah Hayyim* 307:14.

Tehum on Shabbat may not benefit from the object brought, how can Rabbi Karo allow the person to read the contents of the letter?

The *Mishna Berura*'s Position — The *Mishna Berura* answers this question, basing its opinion on the *Gra*, by stating that the reason why something brought from outside the *Tehum* is considered to be *muktze* is to prevent people from asking Gentiles to retrieve things for them on Shabbat. This reason, however, would not be applicable to receiving a letter, since one does not know who brought it. Furthermore, according to some *poskim*, when reading the letter the person is not benefitting from the prohibited activity itself.[604] Based on this explanation, the *Mishna Berura* writes that the *Aharonim* conclude that, in truth, the letter is not *muktze* at all. Therefore, the warning not to touch the letter must be for fear of participating in a forbidden activity, such as carrying the letter from the public domain into one's private domain or opening it if it is sealed.[605] The *Biur Halakha* confirms that one need not worry at all about touching the letter, but, nevertheless, the intended recipient should not read or examine the letter if possible.[606]

Discussion — In essence, the *Mishna Berura* changes the ruling to be the exact opposite of what Rabbi Karo wrote, yet still defers to the position that one should not benefit from something brought from outside the *Tehum* when it is possible to do so.

Halakhic Principles — 6, 8, 10

203.

Shulhan Arukh — If a person intentionally cooks food on Shabbat, he is forbidden to eat the food forever, but others may eat it immediately after Shabbat. If he cooks accidentally, the food may be eaten by everyone, including him, immediately after Shabbat.[607]

Discussion — In this example, the *Mishna Berura*'s commentary at first seems contradictory, yet gains clarity as soon as one realizes

---

604 *Mishna Berura* 307:55.
605 *Mishna Berura* 307:56.
606 *Biur Halakha* 307: s.v. *tov lizaher*.
607 *Shulhan Arukh, Orah Hayyim* 318:1.

that the *Mishna Berura* is reinterpreting *Shulhan Arukh*'s ruling to fit with the *Gra*'s understanding of the issue. The *Shulhan Arukh* rules in a general manner, without making any distinction between Torah and rabbinic prohibitions.

The *Mishna Berura*'s Position — The *Mishna Berura* interjects and writes that with respect to rabbinic prohibitions, the *Gra* writes at length that according to everyone, if a person performed the act accidentally, it is not prohibited *ex post facto* to benefit from it even on Shabbat.[608]

Discussion — In the *Biur Halakha*, the *Mishna Berura* explains that the *Gra* asserts that even though Rabbi Karo rules according to Rabbi Yehuda[609] with respect to Torah transgressions, for rabbinic transgressions he did not penalize the person who transgresses accidentally as a means to prevent him from acting intentionally.[610] Therefore, Rabbi Karo would agree that for rabbinic transgressions that are done accidently, one may benefit from the forbidden activity. Based upon the *Gra*'s analysis, the *Mishna Berura* assumes that Rabbi Karo makes a distinction between Torah prohibitions and rabbinic prohibitions, even if this is not explicitly stated in the ruling of the *Shulhan Arukh*.

Halakhic Principles — 6, 8, 10

204.

Shulhan Arukh — A partition that was erected on Shabbat is kosher, provided it was erected unintentionally. If erected deliberately, it has a status of a partition with respect to making someone liable for throwing something from a public domain into the partitioned space, but a person may still not carry within that space. This is true when the partition was not previously erected, but if the partition was in place, then taken down, and then re-erected, even deliberately, it reverts to its original status. For example, two or three people enclose themselves within partitions in a public domain and erect

---

608 *Mishna Berura* 318:3.

609 See Example 179 for the disagreement between Rabbi Meir and Rabbi Yehuda on this matter.

610 *Biur Halakha* 318: s.v. *ha'mevashel b'Shabbat oh she'assah.*

partitions between them, and also make an *Eruv* so that they may carry from one partitioned space into another. If they remove the partitions they may not carry, yet when they put them back, even deliberately, they are permitted to carry as they were originally.[611]

Discussion — The example presented in the *Shulhan Arukh* has two different interpretations which are presented as follows:

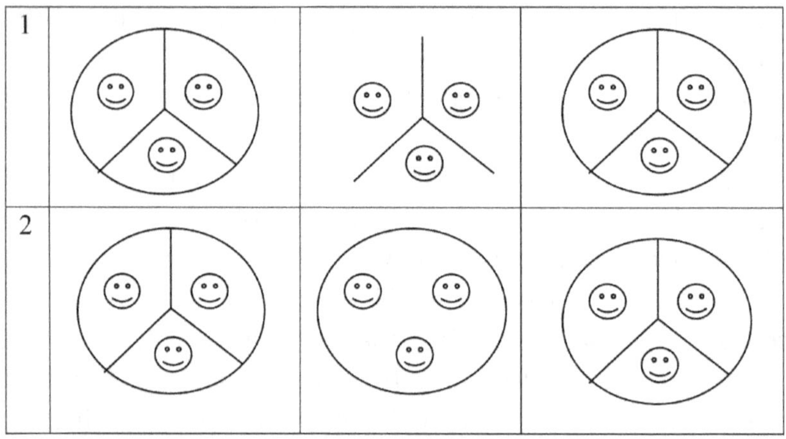

The first interpretation is that of the *Ran*, who rules that even if they deliberately return the outer partitions after they have been removed, then the people may carry within the area, since the partitions originally created a private domain. The second interpretation is that of the *Rosh*, who rules that only if the inner partitions have been removed and then returned may the people carry within the area. If the outer partitions have been removed, then the original private domain has been annulled; therefore, the partitions' return would not allow the people to resume carrying. Also, the *Ran* rules that it is prohibited to erect partitions (outer or inner) for the first time on Shabbat. The *Rosh*, on the other hand, rules that one may erect inner partitions for the first time on Shabbat, and they become valid partitions, which prohibit people to carry from one subsection to another. In the *Sha'ar HaTziyun*, the *Mishna Berura* explains that many *Aharonim* understand that

611 *Shulhan Arukh, Orah Hayyim* 362:3.

Rabbi Karo's ruling is in accord with the position of the *Ran*. He notes, however, that many *Rishonim* side with the *Rosh*.

The *Mishna Berura*'s Position — The *Mishna Berura* incorporates both stringencies, and says that the *Gra* understands that this is the opinion of the *Tur*.[612] In the main commentary, it also suggests that this is the correct understanding of Rabbi Karo's ruling.[613] Because Rabbi Karo basically copies the wording of the *Tur*, albeit with slight variations, the *Mishna Berura* is providing an alternative explanation for Rabbi Karo's ruling, based upon the *Gra*'s understanding of the *Tur*. This interpretation is in stark contrast to those who explain that both the *Tur* and the *Shulhan Arukh* refer to the removal of the outer partitions and not to the dividing partitions which demarcate individual dwelling places.[614]

Halakhic Principles — 3, 5, 8, 10

205.

Shulhan Arukh — It is prohibited to rent or to lend one's animal to a Gentile in order for him to perform prohibited activity on Shabbat, since he is commanded to have his animals rest.[615]

The *Mishna Berura*'s Position — The *Mishna Berura*, basing his view on the *Gra*, changes Rabbi Karo's ruling for "in order to perform" to "for he might perform" to forbid renting or lending one's animal to a Gentile in general, to prevent the possibility of him using the animal to perform prohibited activity on Shabbat. He also inserts that it is prohibited to rent even on Sunday and even *b'havla'ah*.[616]

Discussion — Following the *Gra*, the *Mishna Berura* expands the ruling of the *Shulhan Arukh* to never permit a Jew to rent out his animal to a Gentile.

---

612 *Sha'ar HaTziyun* 362:14-17.

613 *Mishna Berura* 362:25.

614 *Mishna Berura* 362:25; *Sha'ar HaTziyun* 362:15.

615 *Shulhan Arukh, Orah Hayyim* 246:3.

616 *Mishna Berura* 246:10-11. The leniency of *havla'ah* is that it is permitted to receive a single lump sum as compensation for use that was both during the week and on Shabbat. *Havla'ah* means that the payment for use on Shabbat is mixed in with the payment for use on a weekday.

Halakhic Principles — 5, 10

206.

Shulhan Arukh — One may not wipe up with a sponge on Shabbat lest he come to squeeze it, unless the sponge has a handle.[617]

The *Mishna Berura*'s Position — The *Mishna Berura* cites the *Gra* who writes that Rabbi Karo's ruling has a typographical error and should say "because of squeezing," instead of "lest he come to squeeze," since it is not a preventative decree. Rather, if the sponge has no handle, it would be a *psik reishei* (a relationship of certain causality).[618]

Halakhic Principles — 5, 10

Note: The strictness of principle 5 is from a certain perspective. Of course, if the sponge has a handle, it would be permitted to use since the worry of squeezing is no longer present. The stringency here is that when the sponge does not have a handle, using it is no longer a transgression of a rabbinic decree meant to avoid the prohibition of squeezing. It would be considered as a fact that one had actually squeezed it, even if he did not want to do so.

207.

Shulhan Arukh — Holes that are in the walls bordering a private domain that face the private domain are considered a private domain.

Rema — If they face out and do not pass through to the inside, they are judged according to their height and width.[619]

The *Mishna Berura*'s Position — The *Mishna Berura* explains Rabbi Karo's ruling to mean that even if the holes also face a public domain, since they pass completely through, they are judged as a private domain. Therefore, it is prohibited to remove anything from them to bring into a public domain, or to place something into one of the holes from a public domain. He notes, however, that according to

---

617 *Shulhan Arukh, Orah Hayyim* 320:17.
618 *Mishna Berura* 320:48.
619 *Shulhan Arukh, Orah Hayyim* 345:4.

Tosafot this would not entail a transgression unless the hole is four by four *tefahim*, yet the *Rashba* and the *Meiri* hold that holes of a private domain need not be four *tefahim* wide, since they have the ruling of a private domain in any case.[620]

The *Mishna Berura*'s Position II — The *Mishna Berura* also notes that it seems from Rabbi Karo's wording that this applies even to holes that are below ten *tefahim* high, since he writes in general that holes facing a private domain are considered part of the private domain. It also seems, according to the *Mishna Berura*, that the *Rema* holds this to be true as well, since he writes only about holes that do not pass through. The *Mishna Berura* cites the *Elya Rabba*, however, who writes that this is actually a matter of disagreement among the *Rishonim*. There are those who hold that since they are below ten *tefahim*, people of a private domain would not use them due to their short height, but people in a public domain would use them. Thus, the holes should be judged as part of a public domain. The *Mishna Berura* concludes by saying that this is also the opinion of the *Gra*, and thereby limits Rabbi Karo's ruling to apply only to holes above ten *tefahim* high.[621]

Halakhic Principles — 8, 10

208.

Shulhan Arukh — A person is allowed to carry within four cubits in a public domain, which actually means the diagonal of a four-by-four cubit square, which is, in truth, five and three-fifths cubits. There is an opinion that holds that a person is forbidden to carry rabbinically from four cubits to five and three-fifths cubits.

Rema — He refers us to his comments in *Siman* 396.[622]

Discussion — The *Mishna Berura* explains that the *Rema*, in *Siman* 396, writes that the limit of four cubits is not an expression that is in truth a measure of its diagonal but rather means only four cubits.

---

620 *Mishna Berura* 345:9.
621 *Mishna Berura* 345:10.
622 *Shulhan Arukh, Orah Hayyim* 349:1-2.

Also, there, it notes that there are those who are stringent to limit the permitted distance to this shorter measure.[623]

The *Mishna Berura*'s Position — The *Mishna Berura* writes that the *Aharonim* concur that the Halakha is according to the second opinion brought by Rabbi Karo,[624] but cites the *Gra*, who explains that the *Rambam*, who is the second opinion that Rabbi Karo cites, would allow a person to carry five and three-fifths cubits if it was clear that it was the diagonal of a predetermined four-by-four cubit area. The *Rambam* only disagrees with the first opinion to prohibit the extra distance when the five and three-fifths cubits demarcates the length of the side of a square area or when the intended four by four area has not been clearly designated so that the diagonal can be mistaken for the length of a side.[625]

Halakhic Principles — 8, 10

209.

Shulhan Arukh — If a person offers a Gentile a job for a fixed fee and the Gentile acts of his own accord, even on Shabbat, he is permitted to benefit from the product of his labor. This is the case, however, only when people are unable to recognize that the work done on Shabbat is for a Jew. If, on the other hand, this is not the case, one may not benefit from the Gentile's labor since onlookers may not know that a fixed fee was determined and will say that the Jew hired the Gentile to do the work on Shabbat. Consequently, if a Jew hires a Gentile to build a courtyard or a wall, or to reap his fields, and the work is either in the city or within the *Tehum*, it is forbidden to allow the Gentile to work on Shabbat. If the work takes place outside the *Tehum*, and no other city is within the *Tehum* in which the work is being performed, it is permitted to benefit from the Gentile's work on Shabbat. With respect to carving stones or fixing beams, even if done in the Gentile's house, it is forbidden for the Gentile to do the work on Shabbat because they are needed for immovable property. If he

---

623 *Mishna Berura* 349:5.
624 *Mishna Berura* 349:7.
625 *Mishna Berura* 349:9.

does the work, the stones or beams should not be installed in the Jew's building.

Rema — There are those who say that if it is not publicized that the work was done for a Jew, it is permitted.[626]

Seeming Contradiction — In the *Biur Halakha*, the *Mishna Berura* quotes the *Gra*, who writes, commenting on the ruling in the *Shulhan Arukh*, "'*Privately*'—The Jerusalem Talmud stated that it is with moveable property certainly in the Gentile's house," from which it initially infers that the *Gra* is stringent to forbid the Gentile to work publicly, even with movable property, even if people will not recognize that he is working for a Jew. The *Mishna Berura* notes that this contradicts both the general understanding of the *Shulhan Arukh* and the *Gra*'s own comment on the *Rema*'s opinion, where the *Gra* explains that the difference between Rabbi Karo and the *Rema* is with respect to whether the distinction of publicity which applies to movable property should also apply to immovable property.

The *Mishna Berura*'s Position — To resolve this contradiction, the *Mishna Berura* attempts to show that the *Gra*'s statement quoted above regarding movable property does not in fact contradict its own understanding of the difference between Rabbi Karo and the *Rema*. The *Mishna Berura* explains that the difficulty in comprehending the *Gra*'s comment lies in the fact that it starts with "*Privately*—." In truth, the *Mishna Berura* writes that it should actually be written as "*Privately, etc.*—" since the source to which the *Gra* refers in the Jerusalem Talmud discusses the idea of not being recognized in general, and does not specifically imply that the Gentile must work in his own house.[627]

Halakhic Principles — 6, 8, 10

Custom When the Law is Debated

Although the *Mishna Berura*'s attempt to incorporate as many opinions as viable may result in advocating a change of practice, it

---

626 *Shulhan Arukh, Orah Hayyim* 244:1-2.
627 *Biur Halakha* 244: s.v. *b'tzina.*

does not recommend a change if the law itself is debated. In such cases, it will accept and further support the current custom in practice. The strength of an established custom may even supersede other halakhic methodological principles due to its social influence. The *Mishna Berura* will maintain an established custom while, at the same time, forbid its introduction into a different community. The *Mishna Berura* also uses the existence of a custom to measure the validity of a written norm. When a legal dispute exists and there is no established custom in a particular area, the *Mishna Berura* considers the existence of a custom in the same way as the various textual opinions.

210.

Shulhan Arukh — If while a *Kohen* is reciting the Shema he is called to the Torah, there is an opinion which holds that he should interrupt his recital, and there is an opinion which states that he should not, and the Halakha is according to his words.

Alternative Positions — The *Aharonim* rule according to the first opinion, which allows a *Kohen* to interrupt his recitation, and they even extend the permission to a case in which the person is not a *Kohen* and another could take his place for the *Aliyah*.

Discussion — According to the opinion that allows the interruption, the reason for allowing a person to interrupt his recitation of the *Shema* in order to have an *Aliyah* is for the sake of honor and respecting the community, as well as giving honor to the Torah. According to the opinion that does not allow interruption, the reasoning is that continuing to recite the *Shema* instead of having the *Aliyah* would not be considered a disparaging of the Torah, nor would it imply that the *Kohen* is not fit for the *Aliyah*, since he is engaged in a *mitzvah*.

Issue — Though the *Shulhan Arukh* gives both opinions, it clearly rules according to the latter, while the *Aharonim* rule according to the former. How can the *Mishna Berura* reconcile the practice endorsed by the *Aharonim* with the ruling of the *Shulhan Arukh* in a way that does not challenge the authority of the *Shulhan Arukh*?

The *Mishna Berura*'s Position — The *Mishna Berura* writes that the world has the custom to follow the latter opinion, and that one should not change the custom since the ruling is subject to dispute. Therefore, with the exception of the situation of when a person is in the middle of reciting the first verse of the *Shema* and "*Barukh Shem,*" the *Mishna Berura* sides with the *Aharonim*, saying that their position has become common practice and we do not change a custom when there is a disagreement in the law. Despite accepting the legitimacy of the custom in opposition to a ruling in the *Shulhan Arukh*, it is compelled to find a position which can better accommodate the conflicting views. The *Mishna Berura* continues to say that when there is only one *Kohen* in the synagogue, it is better for him to walk out before the first person is called to the Torah, yet if the Torah is already lying on the table and no one is able to read except for him, everyone would agree that he should interrupt his recitation for the sake of honoring the Torah. The *Mishna Berura*, still trying to refine its position so that it does not run up against any opposition, adds that if the person can easily finish until a section break, he should do so before going up to read. In the end, however, the *Mishna Berura* ultimately advises that the person remove himself from any potential doubt of transgression as a consequence of complying with a contested opinion.[628]

Halakhic Principles — 4, 5, 6

211.

Shulhan Arukh — A left-handed person dons his phylactery on his right arm, and an ambidextrous person dons his phylactery on his left arm, like a right-handed person. With respect to a person who writes with one hand but does all other work with his other hand, there are those who say that he should don his phylactery upon the arm with which he writes, yet others say that the arm with which he writes is considered the stronger arm and he should, therefore, don on his other arm.

---

628 *Mishna Berura* 66:26.

Rema — The custom is to follow the second opinion.[629]

The *Mishna Berura*'s Position — After discussing the various opinions on the subject, the *Mishna Berura* writes that it seems that the current practice is in fact the Halakha according to everyone and that the custom of Israel is Torah.

Discussion — The *Mishna Berura* does not defend this position by justifying the custom textually. Rather, it considers the custom as one of the sources, along with the other textual sources, to consider as part of its general approach of trying to incorporate as many positions as possible. According to the *Mishna Berura*, the first of the two opinions brought by Rabbi Karo refers to a situation in which a person's writing hand is unable to do anything else. If the person can also do other things with his writing hand, but it is just easier to use his other one, then the *Mishna Berura* claims that it is obvious according to everyone that the writing arm is the stronger one. Disagreement exists only with respect to the situation where a person cannot do anything else with the hand with which he writes and cannot write at all with his other hand, since then each hand demonstrates a superior capability, thus creating doubt as to which is the stronger arm. Therefore, except for the situation in which a person's writing hand is incapable of doing anything else, which is an unlikely occurrence, everyone should unequivocally don his phylactery on the arm opposite the one with which he writes.[630]

Halakhic Principles — 3, 8

212.

Shulhan Arukh — When saying *Tahanun*, one should lean to the left.

Rema — There are those who say that one should lean to the right, and the main practice is to lean to the right in the morning, since one is wearing his phylactery on his left arm, and to lean to the left in the afternoon.[631]

---

629 *Shulhan Arukh, Orah Hayyim* 27:6.
630 *Biur Halakha* 27: s.v. *v'hakhi nahug.*
631 *Shulhan Arukh, Orah Hayyim* 131:1.

Alternative Positions — The *Taz* and the *Magen Avraham* state that one should not change the custom. The *Gra* holds that one should always lean to the left.

Discussion — *Tahanun*, meaning "supplication," is a prayer that is recited following the weekday prayer in the morning and in the afternoon.

The *Mishna Berura*'s Position — The *Mishna Berura* writes that one should maintain the current custom and, in synagogues where the custom of the *Rema* is followed, it is prohibited to act differently due to "*lo titgodedu* (do not create factions)."[632]

Discussion — If the *Mishna Berura* were to only rely on textual justification, it would either have affirmed Rabbi Karo's ruling out of deference to the *Gra* or would at least have suggested that a person should *ab initio* lean to the left but accept the alternative *ex post facto*. It might even have said that one should not protest against those who always lean to the left, since they have legal support upon which to rely. However, its reason for supporting the established practice described by the *Rema* is not based upon its acceptance by the later *poskim*. Rather, the *Mishna Berura* writes that in a synagogue where the custom of the *Rema* is followed, it is prohibited to act differently due to "*lo titgodedu*."[633] Even though the *Mishna Berura* relies heavily on the rulings of the *Gra* as the basis for its own recommendations, it dismisses what it perceives to be the halakhically correct opinion for the purpose of maintaining social unity.

Halakhic Principles — 10

213.

Shulhan Arukh — The conclusion of the blessing "*Borei Nefashot*" is "*Barukh hei ha'olamim*."[634]

Alternative Position — According to the *Gra*, God's name should be mentioned in the concluding phrase, as stated in the Jerusalem Talmud.

---

632 *Mishna Berura* 131:6.
633 *Mishna Berura* 131:6.
634 *Shulhan Arukh, Orah Hayyim* 207:1.

The *Mishna Berura*'s Position — The *Mishna Berura* dismisses the *Gra*'s position by saying that the world does not recite it that way.[635]

Halakhic Principles — 10, 6

214.

Rema — We do not create suspicion based upon *hashma'at kol*, saying that so-and-so's mill is being used on Shabbat, yet there are those who do prohibit the use of a mill because of *hashma'at kol*. It is the custom *ab initio* to accept the principle of *hashma'at kol* to create suspicion of prohibited activity on Shabbat, yet in a situation of loss, there are those who are lenient.[636]

Alternative Position — The *Gra* brings support to follow the stringent position, saying that we follow *Rabbah* in the Talmudic discussion, who holds that there is a rabbinic prohibition of *hashma'at kol*. The *Rashba* also follows this position.

Discussion — *Hashma'at kol* is making noise which comes from something forbidden to use on Shabbat.

The *Mishna Berura*'s Position — The *Mishna Berura* writes that, nevertheless, one can infer from the *Rema* in the *Darkhei Moshe* that where the practice is to allow it, one should not protest.[637]

Halakhic Principles — 2, 5, 6

215.

Shulhan Arukh — In a place where it is difficult to find wine, one may recite *Kiddush* on Shabbat day with a different alcoholic drink.[638]

The *Mishna Berura*'s Position — The *Mishna Berura* writes that this implies that in a place where wine is available one should recite *Kiddush* on wine and not another alcoholic beverage. Nevertheless,

---

635 *Mishna Berura* 207:5.
636 *Shulhan Arukh, Orah Hayyim* 252:5.
637 *Biur Halakha* 252: s.v. *ve'hakhi nahug*.
638 *Shulhan Arukh, Orah Hayyim* 289:2.

he writes, we have the custom to be lenient. It does admit, however, that the ideal performance of the *mitzvah* uses wine.[639]
Halakhic Principles — 2, 5, 6

216.

The *Mishna Berura* writes that in those communities where the synagogue's custom is to give the first *Aliyah* on Shabbat Bereshit to a donor, yet a particular *Kohen* does not want to set aside his honor of receiving the first *Aliyah*, the community may still call up the donor instead of the *Kohen*, since it is the established custom and it is for the sake of honoring the Torah. However, this is only the case when the custom has been agreed to by all, and is practiced with the general acquiescence of the Kohanim. Communities that want to institute the custom of selling the first *Aliyah* without the acquiescence of the Kohanim on the condition that the Kohanim will leave the synagogue during the Torah reading, do not have the permission to do so.[640]
Halakhic Principles — 5, 6

217.

Magen Avraham — At the Passover Seder, if one uses horseradish for *marror*, he should not recite a blessing of benefit (*birkat ha'nehenin*) upon it at all; rather, he should only say *"al akhilat marror"* before eating it. The reason is that horseradish is not fit to eat and because it is not eaten in any substantial amount.

Hok Ya'akov — One does recite a blessing of benefit upon eating horseradish, since it is fit to eat with vinegar, and in his opinion one should recite *"boreh pri ha'adamah"* and not *"she'hakol"* upon eating it.

The *Mishna Berura*'s Position — In analyzing the two contradicting opinions, the *Mishna Berura* states two reasons why the *Magen Avraham*'s opinion is difficult to accept. The first, based on textual analysis, reveals a contradiction in the argument itself,

---

639 *Mishna Berura* 289:8.
640 *Mishna Berura* 135:18.

namely, since if it is not fit to eat, how can it then be fit to fulfill the obligation of eating *marror*, since the *poskim* rule that what is used for *marror* must be something that is fit to eat? The second reason for finding the *Magen Avraham*'s position difficult is that current custom does not support his premise that horseradish is not fit to eat. Because, according to Ashkenazi custom, people eat grated horseradish, and many dip their bread into it throughout the year, surely it must be considered fit to eat. To further support the custom of using horseradish for *marror*, and for saying a blessing of benefit upon eating it, the *Mishna Berura* also attempts to give a reasoned, yet not textual, defense. It offers that since the Torah obligates us to eat *marror* on this night, it is considered important even if a person eats only the tiniest amount. Therefore, he should make the appropriate blessing of "*boreh pri ha'adamah*" since, as shown above, horseradish is an edible vegetable even when raw. To be more inclusive, however, it adds that in any case saying "*she'hakol*" would certainly fulfill one's obligation.[641]

Halakhic Principles — 3, 8

218.

Shulhan Arukh — Regarding the permissibility of a mixture of prohibited and permitted foods, *noten taam lifgam* is a reason to permit leniency even on Passover.

Rema — It is the custom to be stringent, and even the smallest amount will still prohibit the mixture.[642]

Discussion — *Noten taam lifgam* literally means "it gives a spoiled taste." After twenty-four hours, the absorbed tastes in the pot are spoiled, and that which is expelled from the pot during cooking is no longer considered to prohibit the mixture.

The *Mishna Berura*'s Position — The *Mishna Berura* writes that in a place where the custom is not known, one should teach that a

---

641 *Biur Halakha* 475: s.v. *b'tibul rishon.*
642 *Shulhan Arukh, Orah Hayyim* 447:10.

person who is lenient will not lose, yet he who is stringent will come to blessing.[643]

Discussion — The *Mishna Berura* prioritizes the two opinions in a way that legitimates both according to its acceptance in a given location. In a place where a position is not firmly rooted, the *Mishna Berura* does not choose between positions. Rather, it offers both as acceptable alternatives, albeit preferring the more stringent opinion due to its overall goals of incorporating as many legitimate opinions as it can in one ruling in order to endorse a more systematic and coherent Halakha.

Halakhic Principles — 5, 6

219.

Regarding whether a first-born may partake in a *Seudat Mitzvah* or not during the Fast of the First Born, the *Mishna Berura* writes that in communities where the custom is to be stringent, if a first-born wants to eat at a meal for a *Pidyon HaBen* or *Brit Milah* he needs *Hatarah*, since the custom is considered to create an implied *neder*, and he must also make up the fast after Passover. In places where the custom is to be lenient and allow a first-born to join a meal in celebration of a *mitzvah*, he may do so. The *Mishna Berura* approvingly notes that in its time, many places had the custom to be lenient for a first-born to even partake in a meal celebrating a *siyyum*, even when the first-born did not learn the tractate himself.[644]

Halakhic Principles — 5, 6

220.

Shulhan Arukh — There is an opinion which holds that a person should recite a blessing over lighting candles for Yom Kippur.

Rema — Such is the custom where he lives.[645]

---

643 *Mishna Berura* 447:98.
644 *Mishna Berura* 470:10.
645 *Shulhan Arukh, Orah Hayyim* 610:2.

Alternative Positions — The *Pri Hadash* and the *Gra* agree with those *poskim* who rule that one should not recite a blessing.

The *Mishna Berura*'s Position — Because omission of the blessing does not detract from fulfillment of the obligation to light candles, the *Mishna Berura* concludes that although many *Aharonim* consider the *Rema*'s words to be the law, in those places where the custom is not established, it is certainly better not to recite the blessing.[646]

Halakhic Principles — 5, 6, 10

Custom Contrary to the Written Halakha

When a prevalent custom contradicts the *Shulhan Arukh*, the *Mishna Berura* still may defend its acceptability as an *ab initio* manner of fulfillment. One way in which it supports such a custom is through applying or elevating legal principles not previously attributed to it in order to bolster its legitimacy. The legal principle used to support a custom may sometimes be simply a reprioritization of conflicting values. When there is a common practice that explicitly contradicts the ruling of the *poskim*, and where the *Mishna Berura* cannot add other principles to tilt the scales definitively in the custom's favor, it will explain the rationale behind the custom and leave the final ruling open ended.

221.

Shulhan Arukh — Neither a blind person nor one who is unable to read from the Torah may be called for an *Aliyah*. If a person who is unable to read from the Torah wants to be called, one must protest; however, if the person is a *Kohen* or a Levi, and there is no one else who can replace him, and he can recite along with the *Hazan* word for word, he may be called to the Torah.[647]

Rema — Today we call blind people as well as those unable to read from the Torah for an *Aliyah*.[648]

---

646 *Sha'ar HaTziyun* 610:5.
647 *Shulhan Arukh, Orah Hayyim* 135:4; 139:2-3.
648 *Shulhan Arukh, Orah Hayyim* 139:3.

Discussion — The *Mishna Berura* writes that Rabbi Karo's leniency for giving an *Aliyah* to a *Kohen* or a Levi unable to read by himself is based on his ability to read the Torah along with the *Hazan*. Therefore, it only permits him to be called as a last resort; if there are other people who can be called to the Torah, one should not call a person unable to read.[649]

The *Mishna Berura*'s Position — The *Mishna Berura* legitimizes the contemporary custom of calling up a blind person and one unable to read, even when there are others who can be called in their place, by emphasizing the idea that reciting with the *Hazan* is like reading the text oneself.[650] Moreover, the *Mishna Berura* supports the common practice of not checking to see if people can actually read with the *Hazan* through emphasizing the notion that listening is equivalent to reading and by saying that there is a general presumption that people are able to repeat the words.[651]

Discussion — Although the *Mishna Berura* remarks that its position is in accord with various *Aharonim*, its acceptance of this lenient custom is not solely based on textual analysis. This is evident from the fact that the *Mishna Berura* does not allow this leniency *ab initio* for *Parshat Para* or *Parshat Zakhor*, since some contend that *Parshat Para* is a Torah obligation and *Parshat Zakhor* is unanimously considered so.[652] Its disapproval of this custom when it comes to *Parshat Para* and *Parshat Zakhor* reveals that it recognizes that the prevalent custom is not ideally in accord with the Halakha, yet also shows its willingness to acquiesce to contemporary practice when it contradicts the codes.

Halakhic Principles — 1, 6

222.

Rema — Some say that a person must abide by the conditions of returning a pot to the stove only when it is removed before Shabbat.

---

649 *Mishna Berura* 139:4.
650 *Mishna Berura* 139:12-13.
651 *Mishna Berura* 135:15.
652 *Sha'ar HaTziyun* 139:6.

If the pot is removed after dark, it is permitted to return it even if placed on the ground. This leniency is the practice for our type of ovens [those of the time of the *Rema* which are similar to contemporary ovens in terms of size and the amount of heat produced], but it is nevertheless good to be stringent.[653]

Discussion — The *Mishna Berura* explains that the lenient opinion is that of the *Ran*, and many *poskim* disagree with him, and even Rabbi Karo in the *Bet Yosef* believes that the *Ran* refers only to returning a pot to the top of a stove and not inside an oven. Based upon textual analysis alone, the *Mishna Berura* should advise that a person not follow this practice.

The *Mishna Berura*'s Position — The *Mishna Berura* writes that there is some merit to the custom, since the *poskim* do not prohibit returning the pot unless the oven is hot enough to cause the food to re-boil. (In the *Sha'ar HaTziyun*, he changes "re-boil" to "*yad soledet bo*.")[654] Since this is not common with our ovens, one need not challenge the custom.[655]

Halakhic Principles — 1, 6

223.

Rema — A person should not *ab initio* build his *Sukkah* in the public domain.[656]

Alternative Position — The *Magen Avraham* and others write that some have the custom to build their *Sukkah* in the public domain.[657]

The *Mishna Berura*'s Position — The *Mishna Berura* writes that one should not protest against those who build their *Sukkah* in the public domain since many rule leniently. Furthermore, it writes, it seems that to be stringent and forbid a person to build a *Sukkah* in the public domain even if it is next to the entrance of the person's

---

653 *Shulhan Arukh, Orah Hayyim* 253:2.
654 *Sha'ar HaTziyun* 253:59. *Yad soledet bo* (the degree of heat "from which the hand recoils") is the temperature at which Jewish law considers food to be cooked. It is between 110°F (43°C) and 160°F (71°C).
655 *Mishna Berura* 253:67.
656 *Shulhan Arukh, Orah Hayyim* 637:3.
657 *Mishna Berura* 637:10.

house would cause a great problem. Many people would make their *Sukkot* behind their houses. In small cities where it is not common for each house to have its own bathroom, the back of the house becomes the designated place for children, and sometimes even adults, to relieve themselves. Therefore, it is not a clean place, and even if one wanted to clean it, it may still not be permitted according to the law, since it is a well-established "bathroom." Therefore, even though the *Rema* writes that one should not do so *ab initio*, it is better to make a *Sukkah* in a public domain than behind a person's house.[658]

Halakhic Principles — 6, 8

224.

Shulhan Arukh — It is permissible to give one's clothes to a Gentile to wash, or his leather to tan, on Friday close to dark if the two have determined a fixed price for his services. However, if the work will be done publicly and it will be known that it is being done for a Jew, it is preferable to be stringent and prohibit it.[659]

Discussion — The *Mishna Berura* explains that the ruling of the *Shulhan Arukh* would apply to the situation wherein a Gentile publicly washes clothes that are distinctly Jewish,[660] yet notes that the custom has arisen to give one's clothes to a Gentile on Friday close to dark even if the exact price is not stipulated before-hand.[661] The *Mishna Berura* brings two grounds to support the existence of this custom. First, it cites the *Tosefet Shabbat*, who writes that since one does not know exactly whose clothes are being washed, one need not protest. Second, it cites the *Hayye Adam*, who gives another leniency, namely that today it is a known custom that washing clothes is done on a contract basis and not on a wage basis. Therefore, even when a Gentile publicly

---

658 *Biur Halakha* 637: s.v. *v'khen b'karka she'hi shel rabim.*
659 *Shulhan Arukh, Orah Hayyim* 252:2-3.
660 *Mishna Berura* 252:25.
661 *Mishna Berura* 252:14.

washes clothes on Shabbat, the suspicion that he is a day-wage earner need not arise.[662]

The *Mishna Berura*'s Position — In the *Biur Halakha*, the *Mishna Berura* writes that all of the *Rishonim* write explicitly that if the Gentile does not know exactly how much he will be paid, it is as if he is working for a wage and thus, his work would not be for his own benefit but rather for the Jew who employed him. However, it remarks that perhaps since the price to have clothes laundered is generally known, even when there is no mention of payment, the Gentile relies on an implied agreement based upon the known price and thus does the work of his own accord. The *Mishna Berura* reserves final judgment, however, saying that further investigation is needed to find a resolution on which one can rely in practice, since full support of the custom would contradict its greater methodological priorities.[663]

Halakhic Principles — 6, 8

225.

Shulhan Arukh — If a person eats something that is dipped in wine, honey, oil, dew, blood, or water, and is not dried, he must wash his hands without saying a blessing before he eats, even if he will not touch the wet part of the food.[664]

Discussion — The halakhic literature provides two possible reasons for why a person must wash his hands before dipping his food which are explicitly mentioned in the Talmud.[665] The first is that it is an extension of the rabbinic requirement to wash when a person eats bread, and therefore, when dipping his food he should even recite the blessing when he washes his hands. The second reason, which is found in *Tosafot*, is that the requirement is intended so that a person avoids rendering himself impure through possible contact with the liquid; therefore, because washing one's hands is not a *mitzvah*

---

662 *Mishna Berura* 252:25.
663 *Biur Halakha* 252: s.v. *im katzatz*.
664 *Shulhan Arukh, Orah Hayyim* 158:4.
665 BT *Pesahim* 115a.

per se, and since we do not currently worry about contracting impurity, one should not recite the blessing.[666] Despite their disagreement regarding the recital of the blessing, according to both opinions the obligation to wash one's hands before dipping food into liquid still applies.

Alternative Position — The *Magen Avraham* cites the *Lehem Hamudot*, who writes that the prevalent custom is not to wash one's hands, and notes that there are opinions on which to rely in justifying this custom even if it opposes the ruling of the *Shulhan Arukh*. Nevertheless, many of the *Aharonim* are very stringent and write that the essential ruling is according to those *poskim* who believe that a person must wash his hands according to law even today. The *Gra* even requires that a person say a blessing over washing his hands.

The *Mishna Berura*'s Position — The *Mishna Berura* writes that based upon the *poskim* one cannot be lenient in eating without washing one's hands beforehand in any case, even if the prevalent custom were that one need not say the blessing.[667]

Halakhic Principles — 3, 5

An Erroneous Custom Does Not Uproot Halakha

The *Mishna Berura* will not endorse a custom that has developed if the custom contradicts, or cannot be incorporated into, its greater halakhic methodology. This is the case even if the custom is practiced by those considered to be scrupulous in fulfilling the commandments. Even if a custom is erroneous, the *Mishna Berura* often first searches for means to legitimate it and will only disallow it when it clearly has no support. One should not infer that this demonstrates that the *Mishna Berura* considers the legitimacy of custom to be subordinate to written texts; rather, it shows that it recognizes that not all customs are similar and that some practices develop outside of the four cubits of the Halakha. The *Mishna Berura* also takes into account the reason for the development of a

---

666 *Tosafot*, BT *Pesahim* 115a.
667 *Mishna Berura* 158:20.

particular erroneous custom in determining how adamantly to oppose it.

226.

Shulhan Arukh — In the morning, one must wash his hands.[668]

Alternative Positions — The *Mishna Berura* records the practice of some of the *Ba'ale Nefesh* who, upon rising from their bed, walk less than four cubits at a time towards the water with which they will wash their hands if there is no one who can bring it to them. Their reasoning is based upon the fact that the *Shlah* prohibits walking four cubits without washing one's hands.

Discussion — The suggestion not to walk more than four cubits is meant as a total distance in order to reduce the amount of time that a person would not have his hands washed in the morning. This alternative explanation of walking four cubits at a time stems from people making an erroneous analogy to the prohibition of carrying four cubits in a public domain on Shabbat.

The *Mishna Berura*'s Position — The *Mishna Berura* cites the words of the *Sha'are Teshuva*, who does not see the benefit in such a custom and advises that running toward the water would be more effective, implying that it is not the walking of four cubits that is essential but rather the length of time the *Ruah HaTumah* remains on a person's fingers.[669]

Halakhic Principles — 7

227.

Shulhan Arukh — A person should not say "amen" after "*Ga'al Israel*," the concluding words of the blessing after the recital of the *Shema* which is said immediately before the recital of the *Amida*, since it would be an interruption between "*Geula*" and "*Tefilla*."[670]

---

668 *Shulhan Arukh, Orah Hayyim* 4:1.
669 *Mishna Berura* 1:2.
670 *Shulhan Arukh, Orah Hayyim* 66:7-8; 111:1.

Rema — Some say that one should answer "amen" after the *Hazan* recites the blessing, and that such is the custom.[671] However, he writes that there are those who are of the opinion that the necessity of juxtaposition only applies to weekdays and holidays; on Shabbat, on the other hand, it is not required. He concludes, however, by saying that it is good to be stringent and not interrupt if it is not necessary to do so.[672]

Discussion — The *Rema*'s advice to be strict may seem like he is conceding to the opinion of Rabbi Karo; however, when one takes his suggestion in light of what he writes in his *Darkhei Moshe*, it becomes clear that he does not retract his position that saying "amen" is permissible. In the *Darkhei Moshe*, the *Rema*'s concern is that since Shabbat does not require "*Tefilla*" to immediately follow "*Geula*," one may think it permissible to engage in any type of interruption, even those that have nothing to do with the prayer service. Therefore, he specifically remarks that things not associated with the service would be considered a prohibited interruption, but for those necessary interruptions, such as responding for *Kaddish* or *Kedusha*, one may rely on the *Or Zarua* and not consider an interjection to be prohibited.[673] The reason that the *Rema* does not consider "amen" to be an interruption is that it is part of the conclusion of the blessing. Rabbi Karo, on the other hand, bases his decision that "amen" is considered an interruption on the *Zohar*.

Alternative Positions — The *Mishna Berura* notes that there are those who are scrupulous and try during the week to fulfill their obligation according to all opinions by pausing at "*Tzur Israel*" or "*Shira Hadasha*," in order to answer "amen" after the *Hazan* finishes the blessing.

The *Mishna Berura*'s Position — The *Mishna Berura* interprets the *Rema*'s statement that it is good to be stringent in a different way than the *Darkhei Moshe* does. Where the *Darkhei Moshe*'s stringency relates to superfluous interruptions, the *Mishna Berura* attributes it

---

671 *Shulhan Arukh, Orah Hayyim* 66:7.
672 *Shulhan Arukh, Orah Hayyim* 111:1.
673 *Darkhei Moshe, Orah Hayyim* 111.

to a doubt in interpreting the justification for Shabbat's exclusion from the prescription. According to the *Mishna Berura*, the *Rema*'s comment now refers to the fact that Rabbi Karo disagrees with making any distinction between Shabbat and other days, and due to the negative consequences of interrupting, "it is good to be stringent."[674] The *Mishna Berura* does, however, maintain that it is legitimate to be lenient regarding necessary interruptions on Shabbat, since the opinion is a legally valid one.[675] With respect to the practice of the scrupulous, the *Mishna Berura* disapproves of their strategy, writing that all the *Aharonim* agree that this is not a good practice, since one should not say an additional "amen" within the recital of a blessing, nor should a person refrain from starting the *Amida* with the congregation. To correctly fulfill the obligation according to all opinions, the *Mishna Berura* gives different alternatives. A person should intend to finish the blessing at the same time as the *Hazan*, whereby he would not have the obligation to say "amen." Likewise, he could say the introductory verse of the *Amida* slightly before the *Hazan* finishes, which would uproot the obligation to say "amen," while it would still be considered as if he started the *Amida* with the congregation.[676]

Halakhic Principles — 4, 7, 8

228.

Shulhan Arukh — It is prohibited to play with a ball on Shabbat and Yom Tov.[677]

Rema — There are those who permit it, and we have the custom to be lenient.[678]

Alternative Position — The *Rashal* questions the validity of permitting it since it is not something that one needs to do at all. Moreover,

---

674 *Mishna Berura* 111:8.
675 *Mishna Berura* 111:9; *Biur Halakha* 111: s.v. *tov l'hahmir*.
676 *Mishna Berura* 66:35.
677 *Shulhan Arukh, Orah Hayyim* 308:45.
678 *Shulhan Arukh, Orah Hayyim* 308:45; 518:1.

it is child's play. Therefore, the *Rashal* writes that adults who have the custom to play ball have a bad custom.

The *Mishna Berura*'s Position — The *Mishna Berura* cites the *Rashal* that it is a bad custom and also cites Rabbi Karo who prohibits it.[679]

Halakhic Principles — 5, 7

229.

Shulhan Arukh — If a Gentile lights a candle for a Jew, everyone is forbidden to make use of the candle, even a person for whom it was not intended.

Rema — There is no difference whether the Jew allotted the Gentile a wage or not, or he if acted under a contract or a wage, since the Jew is benefiting from prohibited activity itself.[680]

Alternative Position — The *Korban Netanel* writes that he desired to find a justification for those people who have the custom to permit this by stipulating a price, but he notes that in truth this is not correct. Even those who rely on the *Rosh* to permit the custom do so erroneously. The *Be'er Heitiv* also attempts to justify the contemporary custom to have a Gentile light a candle on Shabbat after *Minha* when the following day is Yom Tov, noting that many *Aharonim* have already objected to it.

The *Mishna Berura*'s Position — The *Mishna Berura* supports the *Korban Netaniel*'s conclusion that there is no justification for the leniency of stipulating a price by citing Rabbi Karo and the *Rema* that stipulating a price is not effective, and, therefore, it is forbidden to benefit from a Gentile lighting a candle for a Jew on Shabbat.[681] The *Mishna Berura* also writes that it cannot understand the *Be'er Heitiv*'s leniency when one is permitted to light candles on Yom Tov. Trying to find some reason to legitimate the practice, the *Mishna Berura* proposes that it may be because people think that during *ben ha'shmashot* there should be light in the synagogue so

---

679 *Mishna Berura* 518:9.
680 *Shulhan Arukh, Orah Hayyim* 276:1.
681 *Biur Halakha* 476: s.v. *b'kablanut.*

that we enter the Yom Tov joyfully. However, it challenges that assumption since if it were the case, it would be better to tell the Gentile to light during *ben ha'shmashot* rather than after *Minha*, which a few *poskim* actually allow for the sake of a *mitzvah*. Unable to find any logical justification, it concludes by saying that in truth, it is difficult to be lenient.[682]

Halakhic Principles — 5, 7

230.

Rema — On *Tisha b'Av*, when it is normally required that Jews be barefoot to demonstrate that they are in mourning, in places where Jews live amongst Gentiles, they need not remove their shoes except when walking on the Jewish streets.[683]

The *Mishna Berura*'s Position — The *Mishna Berura* remarks that due to our many sins, many people are lenient with the prohibition to wear shoes, and wear them all day even when they sit in their own houses. This is a grave sin, since even when a person is allowed to be lenient, such as when walking among Gentiles, when he gets home he is immediately obligated to remove his shoes.[684] The *Mishna Berura* also quotes the *Hayye Adam*, who discusses the custom of wearing shoes when walking among Gentiles, saying that even though we do not protest, since great ones permit it, there is no reason for it. Lack of justification stems from the fact that the fear of being heckled cannot serve as a reason, since the Gentiles would make fun anyway. Furthermore, those who sit in their stores are certainly forbidden to wear shoes, since the Gentiles would not be able to know if they were wearing them or not.[685]

Halakhic Principles — 5, 7

---

682 *Biur Halakha* 514: s.v. *she'hari b'hadlakato*.
683 *Shulhan Arukh, Orah Hayyim* 554:17.
684 *Mishna Berura* 554:35.
685 *Mishna Berura* 554:36.

231.

Rema — We place the *Bima* in the middle of the synagogue, so that the one who reads from the Torah may be heard by everyone.[686]

Alternative Position — The custom has developed in some synagogues to place the *Bima* in the front.

The *Mishna Berura*'s Position — The *Mishna Berura* writes that having the *Bima* in the middle of the synagogue is an early custom whose source is in the Babylonian Talmud.[687] It continues to write that due to our great sins, there are places that have ignored this early custom and have begun to place the *Bima* next to the *Aron Kodesh*, out of a desire to run after the ways of the Gentiles who arrange their temples in like fashion. To those who change the location of the *Bima* the *Mishna Berura* applies the verse, "Israel will forget, they will make and they will build Temples," and refers to the responsa of the *Hatam Sofer*, the *Maholat HaMahanaim*, and the *Imre Esh*, who are even more inflammatory in their protest against this new custom.[688]

Halakhic Principles — 5, 7

Contemporary Changes

The *Mishna Berura* considers social changes in order to adapt practices so that they concur with the principle of the law given new circumstances. The *Mishna Berura* does not always broaden the scope of acceptability when a general trend of laxity in observance develops; there are times when it takes a hard line in order to uphold what it thinks is the correct practice.

232.

Shulhan Arukh — The Kohanim may return to the congregation after *Birkat Kohanim*, either during "*sim shalom*" or after the congregation says "*amen*" after "*sim shalom*."

---

686 *Shulhan Arukh, Orah Hayyim* 150:5.
687 BT *Sukkah* 51b.
688 *Biur Halakha* 150: s.v. *b'emtza bet ha'knesset*.

Rema — The second opinion is the custom.[689]

The *Mishna Berura*'s Position — The *Mishna Berura* writes that since today congregants commend the Kohanim on their recital, it is proper that they not return to their seats until after the *Hazan* finishes the *Kaddish*, so that people will not fail to respond, as it was common in his day for this to occur.[690]

Halakhic Principles — 1, 4

233.

Shulhan Arukh — A person who is unable to properly pronounce the Hebrew letters—for example, he confuses the sound of an *aleph* with an *ayin*—should not recite *Birkat Kohanim*.[691]

The *Mishna Berura*'s Position — The *Mishna Berura* writes that if everyone in the city equally mispronounces the letters, then the *Kohen* may recite the blessings. The reason for this leniency is because the majority of people in its author's time (and today) are unable to distinguish between an *aleph* and an *ayin*. It also notes that there are those who say that in Russia, where many people regularly call *Shibolet* "*Sibolet*" even though the general populace knows the difference between a "*shin*" and a "*sin*," those people may still recite *Birkat Kohanim*.[692]

Halakhic Principles — 1, 6

234.

Shulhan Arukh — The ability for one person to exempt another through his blessing over foods other than bread only applies to blessings that precede eating. For the blessing said after people eat, each person must recite the blessing for himself. The people cannot become a group in order to make a collective after-blessing on food such as fruit, for example.[693]

---

689 *Shulhan Arukh, Orah Hayyim* 128:16.
690 *Mishna Berura* 128:60.
691 *Shulhan Arukh, Orah Hayyim* 128:33.
692 *Mishna Berura* 128:120.
693 *Shulhan Arukh, Orah Hayyim* 213:1.

Discussion — In the time of the *Mishna Berura*, many people did not know how to recite the blessings after eating, and had to rely on others to say the blessings for them.

The *Mishna Berura*'s Position — The *Mishna Berura* writes that *ex post facto* if the person reciting the blessing intends to exempt the others and they intend to become exempt through his blessing, then it is effective. If a person does not know how to recite the blessing for himself, then even *ab initio* he may be exempted by another person's recitation. The *Mishna Berura* concludes by citing the *Taz* and other *Aharonim*, who write that in their time the masses are disrespectful towards reciting concluding blessings; therefore, a person may exempt others even *ab initio* by having one person recite the blessing aloud so that the others, even those who can recite themselves, may be exempt through it. This is especially so regarding the "Three-faceted Blessing" (*Berakha M'ain Shalosh*) since few can properly recite it by memory. Nevertheless, it concludes, consistent with its greater methodology, that it is better if each says the blessing along with the one reciting it aloud.[694]

Halakhic Principles — 1, 2, 6, 8

235.

Shulhan Arukh — A person must say the blessings over food eaten after the meal but before reciting *Birkat HaMazon*, but this rule is not commonly applied since we do not usually stop eating bread until we say the *Birkat HaMazon*.[695]

The *Mishna Berura*'s Position — The *Mishna Berura* discusses whether the ruling should still apply today or not. In the *Biur Halakha*, it writes that for large meals at which it is customary to stop eating bread and to set the table with all sorts of fruits and drinks, the *Tur* and the *Levush* still hold that the ruling is still relevant. The *Bach*, the *Magen Avraham*, the *Elya Rabba*, and the *Hayye Adam*, on the other hand, believe that the ruling applied specifically in the times of the Talmud, when the tables were actually removed before reciting the

---

694 *Mishna Berura* 213:9.
695 *Shulhan Arukh, Orah Hayyim* 177:2.

Birkat HaMazon, so that when dessert was brought it looked as if it were a different meal. Today, since we do not remove the table, even when we have finished eating and do not intend to eat more bread, it is still considered the same meal as long as the *Birkat HaMazon* has not been said. Therefore, a person should not recite blessings over the food eaten after the meal but before reciting the *Birkat HaMazon.* The *Mishna Berura* also notes that the *Elya Rabbah* cites the *Kol Bo,* the *Rashba,* and the students of *Rabbenu Yona,* who specifically mention the removal of tables in their explanation of this ruling. However, it also points out that the remainder of the *poskim* seem to hold like the *Tur.* Even though it justifies the custom of not saying the blessings, in deference to its greater methodology, it does not conclude with any recommendation as to which opinion to follow.[696]

Halakhic Principles — 1, 3

236.

Shulhan Arukh — If the *Hazan* is a *Kohen* and there are other Kohanim in the synagogue, the *Hazan* should not say *Birkat Kohanim.* Even if there are no other Kohanim present, the *Hazan* should still not say *Birkat Kohanim* unless he is sure that he can return to the repetition of the *Amida* without any trouble.[697]

The *Mishna Berura*'s Position — The *Mishna Berura* notes that since today people pray from a *Siddur,* we can have the presumption that the *Hazan* will return without any trouble; nevertheless, since Rabbi Karo mentions this exception only for the situation where other Kohanim are not present, if others are present in the synagogue, the *Hazan* should not say *Birkat Kohanim.*[698] In the *Sha'ar HaTziyun,* however, the *Mishna Berura* cites the *Pri Hadash,* who disagrees with Rabbi Karo and allows the *Hazan* to say *Birkat Kohanim* even if other Kohanim are present. The *Mishna Berura* states that in places that have the custom to allow the *Hazan* to say *Birkat Kohanim* in accordance with the ruling of the *Pri Hadash,* even

---

696 *Biur HaLakha* 177: s.v. *she'ain anu regilin.*
697 *Shulhan Arukh, Orah Hayyim* 128:20.
698 *Mishna Berura* 128:76.

though it contradicts the *Shulhan Arukh*, it is possible that one should not protest against them.[699]

Halakhic Principles — 1, 5, 6

237.

Shulhan Arukh — It is prohibited for a person to rent or to lend his animal to a Gentile in order for it to perform prohibited activity on Shabbat, since he is commanded to allow his animals to rest.[700]

Discussion — The *Rambam* writes, "It is permitted to sell a Gentile a horse, since a horse is used only for human transportation and not for transporting burdens. [Hence, there is no forbidden labor involved, because] 'A living entity carries itself.'"[701] A Jew is only prohibited from riding a horse on Shabbat as a rabbinic decree to prevent him from pulling a reed in order to hit the animal to make it move.[702] Previously, horses were not used for any activity that was prohibited on Shabbat; however, in the time of the *Mishna Berura* horses were used to carry loads, a Shabbat prohibition, and not only for riding. Therefore, the worry arose as to whether the Gentile will work the horse on Shabbat or not.

The *Mishna Berura*'s Position — In the *Biur Halakha*, the *Mishna Berura* explains that the *Shulhan Arukh* is discussing a large animal. A small animal, on the other hand, which does not usually perform work, does not fall under this prohibition. The *Mishna Berura* also explains that the distinction that the *Rambam* makes between selling horses and selling other large animals to a Gentile is due to the custom that horses were only used for riding, whereas other animals were used to carry things, and the rabbinic prohibition to not sell the animals to a Gentile is in order to prevent lending or renting them to perform prohibited actions on Shabbat. Therefore, notes the *Mishna*

---

699 *Sha'ar HaTziyun* 128:64.
700 *Shulhan Arukh, Orah Hayyim* 246:3.
701 *Hilkhot Shabbat* 20:4.
702 BT *Beitsah* 36b; *Shulhan Arukh, Orah Hayyim* 305:18; *Mishna Berura* 305:61.

Berura, today, since horses are specifically used to carry things, it is certainly obvious that one may not rent out his horse.[703]
Halakhic Principles — 1, 8

238.

Shulhan Arukh — From *Rosh Hodesh Av* until the fast, people should reduce their business activity.[704]

Discussion — Due to economic circumstances and social changes, Jews were not reducing their business activity in the time of the *Mishna Berura*.

The *Mishna Berura*'s Position — The *Mishna Berura* writes that there are some *poskim* who hold that this is with respect to business activities that give a person happiness, such as buying silver objects or what is needed for a wedding, but a person does not need to reduce his regular business activity at all. Others hold that all business activity must be reduced; only that which a person needs to do in order to make a living is permitted. Based on this last opinion, the *Mishna Berura* remarks that today we have the custom to be lenient, since we consider everything today as being needed to make a living.[705] In the *Sha'ar HaTziyun*, it is stated that there are communities which have the custom not to conduct any business at all, but that this is a stringency that is not according to the law. It indicated that it is possible that the custom was made as a protective measure, and, therefore, if a person wants to conduct business in such a place he must receive permission to do so.[706] Also, with respect to our lenient custom, it is written in the *Sha'ar HaTziyun* that it seems from the *Magen Avraham* that a person should nevertheless refrain from conducting those business activities which make him happy, but the *Taz* and the *Elya Rabba* seem to be lenient even in this type of activity, since a person might not be able to

---

703 *Biur Halakha* 246: s.v. *behemto l'aino yehudi*.
704 *Shulhan Arukh, Orah Hayyim* 551:2.
705 *Mishna Berura* 551:11.
706 *Sha'ar HaTziyun* 551:11.

procure what he wants afterwards. The *Mishna Berura* concludes by saying that even so, it is good to be stringent.[707]
Halakhic Principles — 1, 5, 6

239.

Shulhan Arukh — It is forbidden to squeeze olives and grapes on Shabbat, and if the juice seeped out by itself it is forbidden to drink the juice, even if the fruit was intended for eating. It is also forbidden to squeeze berries and pomegranates, but if the juice seeped out by itself, it depends; if they are intended for eating the juice is permitted, and if intended for squeezing the juice is forbidden. It is permitted to squeeze all other fruit.

Rema — In a place where certain fruits are squeezed to drink their juice, either to quench one's thirst or for pleasure, they share the status of berries and pomegranates. If, however, they are only squeezed for medicinal purposes, it is permitted to drink their juice.[708]

Discussion — Given the changes in international trade, the determination of which fruits are primarily used for the juice and which are not could no longer depend on local custom.

The *Mishna Berura*'s Position —Regarding the *Rema*'s opinion, the *Mishna Berura* adds that if a certain fruit is exported from one place to another, then it is classified as one squeezed for its juice and it is forbidden worldwide.[709] For example, today apples are classified with berries and pomegranates.[710]

Halakhic Principles — 1, 5

240.

Shulhan Arukh — If a person kneads more than an *isaron* of dough to make *matzah*, the *matzah* will still be permitted *ex post facto*.[711]

---

707 *Sha'ar HaTziyun* 551:13.
708 *Shulhan Arukh, Orah Hayyim* 320:1.
709 *Mishna Berura* 320:8.
710 *Mishna Berura* 320:9.
711 *Shulhan Arukh, Orah Hayyim* 456:2.

Discussion — The concern over kneading more than an *isaron* of dough is that it may become *hametz,* since a person cannot handle so much dough at one time. He will therefore let it sit still and leaven. This is especially the case when ovens are small and only a small portion of dough can fit at a time. By the time of the *Mishna Berura,* however, people no longer made *matzah* by themselves in small ovens. Rather, many people began to work together to knead dough, and they used large ovens to bake a lot of *matzot* at a time. Therefore, it seemed as if more than an *isaron* of dough could be handled without fear of its becoming *hametz.*

The *Mishna Berura*'s Position — Regarding the ruling in the *Shulhan Arukh,* the *Mishna Berura* adds that the permission is so even if he does so purposely. He notes that many *Aharonim* prohibit it even *ex post facto,* since it is impossible for a person to properly handle so much dough at one time, yet some *poskim* are lenient today since they believe that the suspicion that a person could not handle so much dough was only at the time of the Sages when a person would knead his dough alone and used small ovens. Today, when many people work together and ovens are large enough to accommodate many *matzot* at one time, one need not be strict, and the world has the custom to be lenient *ab initio* according to this opinion and one should not protest against it. The *Mishna Berura* adds that nevertheless, all those who fear Heaven will seek to be stringent, even in our time, and particularly in small communities where many people are not engaged in making *matzot* together.[712]

Halakhic Principles — 1, 5, 6

241.

Shulhan Arukh — On Yom Kippur, if a doctor who is an expert, even if he is a Gentile, says that if a sick person does not eat it is possible that his illness will get worse and he will be in danger, he should be fed, and it is not necessary for the doctor to say that he may die if he

---

712 *Mishna Berura* 456:7.

does not eat. Even if the sick person says he does not need to eat, one must still listen to the doctor.[713]

Discussion — By the time of the *Mishna Berura*, doctors were not as sensitive to religious demands and were more prone to dismiss them in the medical considerations, even when it was not absolutely necessary to do so.

The *Mishna Berura*'s Position — In the *Biur Halakha*, the *Mishna Berura* cites the *Sefer Tiferet Israel*, which states that today it seems that we should not be as trusting of Gentile doctors in this matter, since they always say that if a sick person would fast, even if he has only a minor illness, it will be dangerous for him. The *Mishna Berura* also cites the responsa, *Ruah Hayyim*, which expands the suspicion to include Jewish doctors who are suspect of transgressing the Torah and profaning the Shabbat and who do not fast out of contempt for the Torah. The *Mishna Berura*, however, recognizes that it cannot make a comprehensive legal judgment due to the fact that the social context is so variable and writes that, in truth, the matter rests on how the local rabbi perceives the matter.[714]

Halakhic Principles — 1, 5

242.

Shulhan Arukh — It is a good custom to bring one's children to hear the *Megilla*.[715]

The *Mishna Berura*'s Position — The *Mishna Berura* writes that today, due to our many sins, the opposite is the case, since the children not only do not listen to the reading but also upset the reading so that the adults cannot hear. They come only to make noise when they hear "Haman," and because of this behavior fathers do not fulfill their obligation to teach their children at all. The *Mishna Berura* concludes by saying that, in truth, to fulfill the commandment to teach his child, every father should keep his small children by him and make sure that they hear the *Megilla*, and when "Haman"

---

713 *Shulhan Arukh, Orah Hayyim* 618:1.
714 *Biur Halakha* 618: s.v. *holeh she'tzarikh l'ekhol.*
715 *Shulhan Arukh, Orah Hayyim* 689:6.

is mentioned they may make noise as is the custom, but it should not be the main reason for coming.[716]

Halakhic Principles — 1, 5, 8

Limmud Zekhut[717]

Even when the *Mishna Berura* cannot find a way to accept as legitimate a practice which has developed in a way that it perceives as contrary to the Halakha, in order to incorporate those who have such a practice into the realm of halakhic acceptability, it still tries to find some justification for their actions. In its attempt to justify a common practice, the *Mishna Berura* at times tries to dissect a general practice into a number of possible variations in order to validate at least some of the permutations rather than be forced to reject the entire gamut. The *Mishna Berura* attempts to justify many practices even if it does not support them. When the *Mishna Berura* cannot validate a customary practice at all, it attempts to give its adherents some other form of support.

243.

Shulhan Arukh — If a person designates a bag to always be used for his phylacteries and uses it in such a way at least once, he may no longer use it to hold money.

Rema — If he initially made a stipulation that he will also use the bag to hold money, then he would be permitted to do so.[718]

The *Mishna Berura*'s Position — The *Mishna Berura* writes that with respect to those people who use their phylactery bags to hold

---

716 *Mishna Berura* 689:18.

717 A *limmud zekhut* is a method of defending a current practice that seems to be at odds with the normative Halakha as represented in the textual sources. One need not necessarily be convinced that the suggested defense is the correct reading of the classical sources—it is enough for one to be convinced that it is a *plausible* reading. This conviction can come from the individual's own insight into the texts, from a single precedent (*da'at yahid*), or from a collection of precedents, none of which represents the consensus. See "Hair Covering and Jewish Law: A Response," *Tradition* 42:3 (2009): 95-179.

718 *Shulhan Arukh, Orah Hayyim* 42:3.

mundane objects, even though it is prohibited by law, one may attempt to justify their actions by saying that since they regularly do this it is as if they initially made a stipulation. However, *ab initio* it is not correct to do this.[719]

Discussion — Even though the *Rema*'s leniency applies to an explicit stipulation, the *Mishna Berura* attempts to extend it to include implied stipulations as well.

Halakhic Principles — 2, 8

244.

Shulhan Arukh — People may not eat or drink in the synagogue.[720]

Discussion — The custom has arisen of people eating and drinking in the synagogue.

The *Mishna Berura*'s Position — With respect to the custom of people eating and drinking in the synagogue, the *Mishna Berura* writes that it is possible that they rely on the idea that synagogues in the Diaspora are built with the condition that if destroyed the location may be used for any other purpose, and therefore they may likewise be used for any purpose even when they are intact. Recognizing the weakness of this justification, the *Mishna Berura* admits that this reasoning cannot apply universally and that there is no justification for eating and drinking in synagogues in the land of Israel, where such stipulations do not take effect.[721]

Halakhic Principles — 3, 8

245.

Sefer Ma'amar Mordekhai — The customary practice at large meals, where one tears the flesh of a cooked fish from its back and removes the spine in the middle, seems to be *borer*, and one should be careful not to do it on Shabbat, since it is removing refuse from food, which is prohibited even if done for immediate consumption. Rather, one should leave the spine and not throw it away. Also,

---

719 *Mishna Berura* 42:11.
720 *Shulhan Arukh, Orah Hayyim* 151:1.
721 *Biur Halakha* 151: s.v. *v'ein okhlin v'shotin ba'hem.*

people should not remove meat bones unless it is via the normal eating process, meaning that one chews on the bone to remove the meat on it and then throws it away after finishing with it. Bones that do not have meat on them should not be touched; rather, they should be left on the plate and only afterward thrown away if desired.

Discussion — The *Mishna Berura* notes that the world is not careful to be scrupulous about this at all, neither during nor even before meals, and when people prepare food and remove the bones from the meat they are stumbling into a prohibition that obligates a *Hatat* offering.

The *Mishna Berura*'s Position — Nevertheless, the *Mishna Berura* attempts to save people from transgressing *borer* by saying that one cannot protest if people separate bones from meat when eating since there are opinions which permit one to do so. Also, one cannot protest against people who are lenient and remove bones from the meat when preparing food before the meal, since the *Rema* and the *Maharshal* consider this to be like eating if a person's intention is to eat immediately thereafter. One can further support this decision with the opinion of those *Rishonim* who hold that one is permitted to remove refuse from food if it is for immediate consumption. Even though many prohibit this and the *Shulhan Arukh* rules against it, in this case, where there are many lenient opinions, one cannot protest against those who are lenient. The *Mishna Berura* warns, however, that a person must be careful not to prepare food long before eating as is done for large meals. Moreover, it limits its leniency to bones that have meat on them, but for those bones that do not have meat on them one must be careful not to separate them from the rest of the food and remove them from one's plate before eating, since it would constitute *borer* even if for immediate consumption. The *Mishna Berura* suggests that he should instead take the meat and leave the bones on the plate, yet if it is difficult to be scrupulous about this, he should suck on the

bones before removing them, since sucking on them would demonstrate that they are not considered refuse.[722]
Halakhic Principles — 5, 8

246.

Shulhan Arukh — Clay pots that were used for *hametz* all year round should be scrubbed well so that no more *hametz* can be seen in them. Then a person may leave them until after Passover, as long as he hides them during Passover in a place that he normally does not go in order to prevent him from using them.[723]

The *Mishna Berura*'s Position — The *Mishna Berura* notes that there are those who have the custom to put clay dishes in a high place that a person could not reach but to still have them displayed during the holiday. Although it disapproves of this custom, it says that one should not protest against it. The reason is that even though the rabbis made decrees to prevent a person from forgetting and using something prohibited and did not differentiate between types of dishes, since the dishes are not *ben-yoma*, and since they are primarily used as a *kli sheni* or with cold food, we do not suspect them of transgressing.[724] It concludes, however, that a person who is stringent will come to blessing.[725]
Halakhic Principles — 5, 6, 7, 8

247.

Shulhan Arukh — One should be careful to do *Hagala* before the fifth hour on the day preceding Passover, so that one need not worry about whether the water was boiling or not.

---

722 *Biur Halakha* 319: s.v. *mitokh okhel*.
723 *Shulhan Arukh, Orah Hayyim* 451:1.
724 When a dish is not *ben-yoma*, whatever is absorbed into it is *noten taam lifgam*, which literally means, "it gives a spoiled taste." Therefore, that which is expelled from the dish is no longer considered to prohibit a mixture. Also, a *kli sheni* cannot transfer tastes that are absorbed into it, and a cold plate does not absorb anything from the food that is placed on it.
725 *Mishna Berura* 451:7.

Rema — *Hagala* is not effective if the water is not boiling.[726]

Discussion — *Hagala* is the process of *kashering* a kitchen utensil by completely submersing it in boiling water. *Hagala* is only one process of *kashering* a utensil and only works under certain circumstances. For a utensil that is put directly on a burner, *Hagala* will work only if the water is boiling. The reason is that, according to the Halakha, food is emitted from a utensil in the same way that it was absorbed. Because the utensil was on a burner, the fire heats the mixture of food continuously, causing it to be absorbed; therefore, one must immerse the entire pot into the boiling water on a burner in order to reach the same temperatures. For a utensil that is not placed on a burner, food will still be absorbed into the utensil, but since it does so at a lower temperature, emission of the food from the utensil does not need to be via a pot of boiling water on the burner. It is sufficient to place it in a larger utensil of hot water that is no longer on the burner. The *Mishna Berura* recognizes that there are those who are careless and do *Hagala* quickly, without making sure that the water is still boiling. Therefore, all the utensils which have undergone *Hagala* while the water may have not been boiling are in doubt as to their kosher status.

The *Mishna Berura*'s Position — The *Mishna Berura* attempts to justify their actions, so that they may avoid transgressing the prohibition against having and consuming *hametz* on Passover. Normally a person does *Hagala* on plates and utensils that are not directly put on the fire, so the water would only need to be *Yad Soledet Bo* and not boiling to kosher the dishes. This would not be true, however, for copper pots and other things that are used directly on a burner, even *ex post facto*.[727]

Halakhic Principles — 6, 8

---

726 *Shulhan Arukh, Orah Hayyim* 452:1.
727 *Mishna Berura* 452:8.

248.

Shulhan Arukh — On *Sukkot,* one must eat, drink, and sleep in a *Sukkah* the entire week, whether daytime or night, and one must not even sleep in an *ad hoc* manner outside the *Sukkah.*

Rema — Regarding the custom to be lenient and not sleep in a *Sukkah* today, except by those who are scrupulous in the fulfillment of *mitzvot,* there are those who say that it is due to the cold, that it is painful to sleep outside in cold weather. It seems to him, however, that it is because the commandment to sleep in the *Sukkah* is meant to be for a man to sleep with his wife as he does all year round, and when he cannot do that in the *Sukkah* he would be exempt.[728]

Alternative Positions — The *Gra* and the *Magen Avraham* disagree with the *Rema'*s reason for leniency.

The *Mishna Berura'*s Position — In order to validate the current practice, the *Mishna Berura* provides a different reason to exempt a man from sleeping in the *Sukkah,* writing that it is because a man is usually troubled when he is unable to sleep with his wife. Recognizing that this reason is not all-inclusive, it adds that according to this reason, if a man would not be troubled, for example during a time when they cannot sleep together, he would not be exempt from sleeping in the *Sukkah.*[729]

Halakhic Principles — 3, 8, 10

249.

Shulhan Arukh — It is prohibited to eat *Hadash* even today, whether it is bread, parched grain, or roasted grain, until the night of the eighteenth of *Nissan,* and in the land of Israel until the night of the seventeenth of *Nissan.*[730]

Rema — All unmarked grain is permitted after Passover by virtue of a *sfeik-sfeika* (a double doubt). The first doubt is with respect to whether the grain was from the previous year or not; and if you want

---

728 *Shulhan Arukh, Orah Hayyim* 639:2.
729 *Mishna Berura* 639:18.
730 *Shulhan Arukh, Orah Hayyim* 489:10.

to say that the grain is from the current year, nevertheless, it may still have taken root before the sixteenth of *Nissan*.[731]

Alternative Positions — There are *Aharonim* who write that in Poland a person can only be lenient with wheat and rye since most of it is planted in *Heshvan*, so *Hadash* does not apply to it. The great majority of barley, oats, and spelt, however, are planted after Passover; therefore, where it is not normal to import it from elsewhere, one cannot be lenient.

Discussion — The majority of people are not careful at all regarding *Hadash*. Since it is so difficult to be careful, they rely, due to the difficulty, on those few *Rishonim* that hold that *Hadash* outside the land of Israel is only a rabbinic obligation and even that is only for those lands close to Israel, like Egypt and Bavel. They also rely on the fact that there are some *poskim* who hold that *Hadash* only applies to grain owned by Jews at the time of growing, but not to grain of Gentiles.

The *Mishna Berura*'s Position — The *Mishna Berura* states that we are unable to protest against those who are lenient; nevertheless, a *Ba'al Nefesh* will not rely on these leniencies and will be stringent upon himself as much as he can.[732] In the *Biur Halakha*, the *Mishna Berura* repeats that we should not protest against those who are lenient regarding *Hadash*. Nevertheless, it continues, saying that it seems that those who are careful to avoid the suspicion of transgression regarding other prohibitions yet are lenient with respect to *Hadash* make the exception because they think that if a person wants to be careful he must be careful regarding all stringencies of a particular matter. Therefore, they rely on the custom to be lenient completely. The *Mishna Berura* writes, however, that it is not correct to be completely lenient in everything when it is easy to fulfill one's obligation properly in at least some respects. It concludes by saying that in certain instances it is quite easy to not rely on leniency, and that people should at least make a distinction between certain and

---

731　*Shulhan Arukh, Yoreh Deah* 293:3.
732　*Mishna Berura* 489:45.

doubtful *Hadash*. It assures those who are willing to be more stringent that they will be able to acquire *Yashan* in the winter as well.[733]
Halakhic Principles — 5, 6, 7, 8

250.

Shulhan Arukh — In cold lands, it is permitted for a Gentile to make a bonfire for children on Shabbat, and even adults may warm themselves by it. The Gentile may even make a bonfire for adults if the cold is great, since all are considered as ill when it comes to the cold. One should not, however, follow those who have the custom of allowing him to make a bonfire even though it is not very cold.[734]

The *Mishna Berura*'s Position — The *Mishna Berura* writes that nevertheless, we should not protest against those who are lenient since it is better that they err unknowingly and intentionally.[735]

Discussion — Because of the difficulty of legitimating the custom, the *Mishna Berura* seeks to mitigate the severity of following it. This principle, however, can only be applied to rabbinic offenses or to a Torah prohibition that is not written explicitly in the Torah.[736]

Halakhic Principles — 5, 7, 8

---

733 *Biur Halakha* 489: s.v. *af bazman ha'zeh.*
734 *Shulhan Arukh, Orah Hayyim* 276:5.
735 *Mishna Berura* 276:44.
736 *Shulhan Arukh, Orah Hayyim* 608:2.

Appendix A:
A Summary Index of the Examples

Example 1: If a Jew ties *tzitzit* on a garment without the proper intention.

Example 2: Working on Friday from *Minha* onward.

Example 3: Learning books of wisdom on Shabbat or Yom Tov.

Example 4: Which garments need *tzitzit*.

Example 5: Immersing a new dish in a *mikveh* on Shabbat.

Example 6: If the community prays the evening prayer (*Maariv*) while it is still daytime.

Example 7: Making an *Eruv* that contains a public domain.

Example 8: Fast days due to tragedy.

Example 9: Walking outside on Shabbat wearing gloves.

Example 10: When the day before Passover falls on Shabbat, what one does with his remaining bread.

Example 11: Prohibitions on fast days.

Example 12: Squeezing grapes into a pot on Shabbat.

Example 13: Buying meat on Yom Tov.

Example 14: Putting salt in a *kli rishon* that is no longer on the fire.

Example 15: *Hametz*-based adhesive.

Example 16: Relighting a torch left over from the first day of Yom Tov, that had gone out on the second day of Yom Tov.

Example 17: *Rosh Hodesh* meals.

Example 18: "Amen" after "*Ga'al Israel*."

Example 19: Washing one's hands with soap on Shabbat.

Example 20: *Kohanim* turning toward the congregation to say the *Birkat Kohanim*.

Example 21: Saying the passage "The Incense Mixture."

Example 22: Clothes washed in wheat-water and paper that has a *hametz*-based adhesive on Passover.

Example 23: Folding an article of clothing on Shabbat.

Example 24: Using a prayer book when Rosh Hashanah falls on Saturday night.

Example 25: Making the blessing over spices for *Havdala* if Yom Kippur fell on Shabbat.

Example 26: Writing salutary letters on *Hol HaMoed*.

Example 27: Asking one's servant to walk with him and light a candle on Shabbat.

Example 28: Making a hole for the *tzitzit*.

Example 29: A father purchasing phylacteries for his child in order to teach him how to don them.

Example 30: When to say *Kiddush Levana*.

Example 31: Squeezing unripe grapes into food on Shabbat.

Example 32: Cutting vegetables finely on Shabbat.

Example 33: Learning on the day before *Tisha b'Av*.

Example 34: Searching for *hametz*.

Example 35: Repeating the phrase "Hashem, your God, is true."

Example 36: A mourner who desires to recite the *Shema* and to pray.

Example 37: Drying one's hands after washing *mayim aharonim*.

Example 38: Assembling a detachable bed on Shabbat.

Example 39: Finding *hametz* within one's possession on Passover.

Example 40: Insulating food on Erev Shabbat with something that adds heat.

Example 41: If a monkey washes a person's hands before his meal.

Example 42: Having the intention that one's washing of his hands permits him to eat.

Example 43: Sealing the opening of a hot oven that contains food for Shabbat.

Example 44: Baking bread on Yom Tov.

Example 45: Eating legumes on Passover.

Example 46: Praying *Maariv* for Shabbat on a cloudy day.

Example 47: Nullifying *hametz* through a representative.

Example 48: Marrying on the eve of a holiday and having a celebratory meal on the holiday.

Example 49: Making a tent on Shabbat or on Yom Tov.

Example 50: If a Gentile ties *tzitzit* on a garment while a Jew is standing over him.

Example 51: Having sexual relations in the room where one's phylacteries are lying.

Example 52: Reciting the *Shema* at dawn.

Example 53: If a doubt arises as to whether something was prepared on the first day of Yom Tov or the day before.

Example 54: Buying something in exchange for their *hametz* on the day before Passover after the sixth hour of the day.

Example 55: Mixture of *hametz* on Passover.

Example 56: Selling something to a Gentile and having him pick it up close to dark before Shabbat.

Example 57: Praying in a synagogue with the community.

Example 58: Rabbinic decrees are permitted during *ben-ha'shmashot* (the time between sunset and nightfall).

Example 59: A doubt as to whether something is considered *nolad* on a Yom Tov which is preceded by a weekday.

Example 60: Sitting a hen on her eggs to hatch chicks on *Hol HaMoed*.

Example 61: If a Hanukah candle becomes mixed with other candles.

Example 62: Going to guard one's fruit on Shabbat.

Example 63: If a fire breaks out on Shabbat.

Example 64: Making an *Eruv Tehumin*.

Example 65: Reciting the *Shema* if one has a doubt that there is urine in the litter.

Example 66: If a Gentile bakes bread in a Jew's oven on Shabbat.

Example 67: If a person takes a cup of beer or water and makes the blessing for wine.

Example 68: If one interrupts his recitation of *Hallel*.

Example 69: If a groom, his best men, and all the members of the wedding party are exempt from sitting in a *Sukkah* for the seven days after the wedding.

Example 70: A person with a stomach illness donning phylacteries.

Example 71: One who is watching a corpse is exempt from all other commandments.

Example 72: Pregnant and nursing women fasting.

Example 73: Washing one's hands and reciting the blessing *al netilat yadaim*.

Example 74: Where to put on *tallit* and *tefillin*.

Example 75: Saying *Tahanun*.

Example 76: Bending one's head while praying.

Example 77: Praying silently.

Example 78: How to perform *Hagba*.

Example 79: Staying awake throughout the night of the holiday of *Shavuot* to study Torah.

Example 80: Investigating one's actions during the Ten Days of Repentance.

Example 81: Obligation to form a *zimun*.

Example 82: Calling a *Kohen* for an *Aliyah* after a *Kohen*.

Example 83: Carrying on Yom Tov for unnecessary purpose or for a Gentile.

Example 84: Reciting the *Birkat HaMazon* for others.

Example 85: Leaving a meal before saying the *Birkat HaMazon*.

Example 86: If a community collects money for a certain purpose.

Example 87: If alleyways are considered public domains.

Example 88: If a hole in a wall bordering a *Karmelit* is considered a *Karmelit*.

Example 89: Preparing something for Shabbat in order to honor it.

Example 90: Saying the *Birkat HaMazon* silently.

Example 91: If, due to sickness or conditions out of his control, a person recites the *Shema* without moving his lips.

Example 92: Touching one's foreleg or thigh in the middle of a meal.

Example 93: How much *matzah* one must eat at the Seder.

Example 94: Carrying on Yom Tov.

Example 95: Selling a sanctified object to buy another object of similar sanctity.

Example 96: The blessing over *Hallel*.

Example 97: How much of the hand one must wash when washing before eating bread.

Example 98: Doing something in a regular manner on *Hol HaMoed*.

Example 99: Making partitions of a *Sukkah* from linen sheets.

Example 100: Entering through one door of a synagogue and exiting through another to take a short cut.

Example 101: Giving a Gentile a letter to send before Shabbat.

Example 102: Giving a Gentile money on Friday to buy something.

Example 103: Setting sail before Shabbat.

Example 104: Giving food to a person who does not know how to make a blessing over it.

Example 105: Discussion during a meal.

Example 106: Picking up one's son who is holding a stone on Shabbat.

Example 107: Moving a tool on Shabbat that has on it both prohibited and permitted objects.

Example 108: Making a tent on Shabbat with books.

Example 109: Watering vegetables on Shabbat.

Example 110: If a person is alone on the road as Shabbat begins.

Example 111: If a person rents a house for Passover with the presumption that it has been checked for *hametz* and it is found not to have been checked.

Example 112: Washing dishes on Shabbat.

Example 113: Extinguishing a candle for a sick person on Shabbat.

Example 114: Reducing happiness during the month of *Av*.

Example 115: "Seeking one's needs" on Shabbat.

Example 116: Receiving *hametz* from a Gentile as payment on Passover.

Example 117: If one forgot to say a blessing before taking a drink.

Example 118: Spooning out food from a cooking utensil or pot on Shabbat.

Example 119: Definition of a private domain.

Example 120: If the bread for the *Eruv* became moldy and is inedible.

Example 121: Standing during Torah reading.

Example 122: Two *Hatanim* or two *Ba'alei Brit* in the synagogue on Monday or Thursday.

Example 123: If one has a doubt as to whether he mentioned "*Ya'ale ve'Yavo.*"

Example 124: Speaking before hearing *HaMotzi.*

Example 125: Telling a Gentile to light a candle for the Shabbat meal.

Example 126: Chewing cinnamon sticks during a fast.

Example 127: Until when a person can pray in the morning.

Example 128: Wearing phylacteries on *Hol HaMoed.*

Example 129: Wearing phylacteries of *Rashi* and of *Rabbenu Tam.*

Example 130: Hiring a *Hazan* to pray on Shabbat.

Example 131: Eating stolen *matzah* on Passover.

Example 132: When the Yom Kippur fast begins.

Example 133: If sleep is considered an interruption in learning Torah.

Example 134: Accepting Shabbat by candle-lighting.

Example 135: The blessings over wearing phylacteries.

Example 136: Saying the wrong blessing.

Example 137: Eating fruit with a meal.

Example 138: Forgetting to say *Birkat HaMazon.*

Example 139: Saying the *Birkat Kohanim* in an impure place.

Example 140: Incorrect performance of a component of *Birkat Kohanim.*

Example 141: Who can recite the *Birkat Kohanim.*

Example 142: An *androgynous* person or a *tumtum* making a *zimun.*

Example 143: Bringing a second wine to the table at a meal.

Example 144: If two wines are brought to the table simultaneously.

Example 145: If a Gentile deposits his *hametz* with a Jew on Passover.

Example 146: If a Jew gives his *hametz* to a Gentile on the day before Passover.

Example 147: Preparing tables and drawers for Passover.

Example 148: Eating *matzah* in remembrance of the Passover offering.

Example 173: When a roof is both part of a private domain and next to a public domain.

Example 174: What to do regarding eating bread when a person is traveling and cannot reach water.

Example 175: Fixing time to learn Torah.

Example 176: When to say the blessing "*Elokai Neshama*."

Example 177: If a community skips the public recital of the Torah portion on Shabbat.

Example 178: Saying *Kiddush Levana* after Yom Kippur.

Example 179: If a person forgets and leaves a pot of food that is already fully cooked on the stove on Shabbat.

Example 180: Placing food upon a stove before Shabbat.

Example 181: The third meal when Shabbat falls on the fourteenth of *Nissan*.

Example 182: The status of a doubtful *Eruv*.

Example 183: Saying the *Kedusha* within "*Yotzer*" when praying alone.

Example 184: Washing for less than the volume of an olive (*kazayit*) of bread.

Example 185: Shaving on the day before Yom Tov.

Example 186: The person called up to the Torah reading along with the *Hazan*.

Example 187: The status of a protruding roof when the walls cannot be seen.

Example 188: Reading the *Haggadah* after *Minha* on *Shabbat HaGadol*.

Example 189: Spreading out grasses on *Shavuot* both in the synagogue and at home.

Example 190: What to wear on the Shabbat preceding *Tisha b'Av*.

Example 191: If the three people called to read from the Torah read less than nine verses cumulatively.

Example 192: Grinding salt on Shabbat.

Example 193: If a Gentile is going of his own accord to a place where a Jew happens to have a letter to send.

Example 194: A *Kohen* who killed someone saying *Birkat Kohanim*.

Example 195: Interruptions between *Kaddish* after *Pesukei d'Zimra* and *Barkhu.*

Example 196: Leaving the synagogue and talking while the Torah scroll is open.

Example 197: Lighting Hanukah candles.

Example 198: Materials to use as walls of a *Sukkah.*

Example 199: How much one needs to wash for *mayim aharonim.*

Example 200: Going out Friday close to dark with a needle or a pen in one's hand.

Example 201: Examining one's clothing on Friday close to dark.

Example 202: Reading a letter delivered on Shabbat.

Example 203: If a person intentionally cooks food on Shabbat.

Example 204: Status of a partition that was erected on Shabbat.

Example 205: Renting or lending one's animal to a Gentile in order for him to perform prohibited activity on Shabbat.

Example 206: Wiping up with a sponge on Shabbat.

Example 207: Status of holes that are in the walls facing a private domain.

Example 208: Carrying within four cubits in a public domain on Shabbat.

Example 209: If a person offers a Gentile a job and he works on Shabbat.

Example 210: If while a *Kohen* is reciting the *Shema* he is called to the Torah.

Example 211: How a left-handed person dons his phylactery.

Example 212: How to lean when saying *Tahanun.*

Example 213: The conclusion of the blessing "*She'hakol.*"

Example 214: *Hashma'at kol* on Shabbat.

Example 215: *Kiddush* on Shabbat day with a different alcoholic drink.

Example 216: When a synagogue's custom is to give the first *Aliyah* on Shabbat Bereshit to a donor, yet a particular *Kohen* does not want to set aside his honor.

Example 217: The blessing if one uses horseradish for *marror.*

Example 218: Using *noten taam lifgam* to permit mixtures on Passover.

Example 219: Whether a first-born may partake in a *Seudat Mitzvah* during the Fast of the First Born.

Example 220: Reciting a blessing over lighting candles for Yom Kippur.

Example 221: Calling a blind person or one who is unable to read from the Torah for an *Aliyah*.

Example 222: Returning a pot into the oven on Shabbat.

Example 223: Building a *Sukkah* in a public domain.

Example 224: Giving one's clothes to a Gentile to wash, or one's leather to tan, on Friday close to dark.

Example 225: Washing one's hands, if eating something that is dipped in wine, honey, oil, dew, blood, or water, and is not dried.

Example 226: Washing one's hands in the morning.

Example 227: Saying "amen" after "*Ga'al Israel*."

Example 228: Playing with a ball on Shabbat and Yom Tov.

Example 229: If a Gentile lights a candle for a Jew on Shabbat.

Example 230: Going barefoot on *Tisha b'Av*.

Example 231: Placing the *Bima* in the middle of the synagogue.

Example 232: When Kohanim may return to the congregation after *Birkat Kohanim*.

Example 233: Reciting *Birkat Kohanim* when unable to properly pronounce the Hebrew letters.

Example 234: The ability for one person to exempt another through his blessing over foods.

Example 235: Saying the blessings over food eaten after the meal but before reciting *Birkat HaMazon*.

Example 236: A *Hazan* who is a *Kohen* saying *Birkat Kohanim*.

Example 237: Renting or lending one's animal to a Gentile.

Example 238: Reducing one's business activity from *Rosh Hodesh Av* until the fast.

Example 239: Squeezing fruits on Shabbat.

Example 240: Kneading dough to make *matzah*.

Example 241: Listening to a doctor who tells a person to eat on Yom Kippur.

Example 242: Bringing one's children to hear the *Megilla*.

Example 243: Designating a bag to always be used for one's phylacteries.

Example 244: Eating and drinking in the synagogue.

Example 245: Eating fish on Shabbat.

Example 246: What to do with clay pots used for *hametz* on Passover.

Example 247: Kashering utensils through *Hagala*.

Example 248: Eating, drinking, and sleeping in a *Sukkah*.

Example 249: Eating *Hadash*.

Example 250: Having a Gentile make a bonfire on Shabbat in cold lands.

Appendix B:
A Brief Note on the History of Halakha

"Jewish law," or Halakha, is used herein to denote the entire subject matter of the Jewish legal system, including public, private, and ritual law. A brief historical review will familiarize the new reader of Jewish law with its history and development. The Pentateuch (the five books of Moses, also referred to as the Torah) is the touchstone document of Jewish law and, according to Jewish legal theory, was revealed to Moses at Mount Sinai. The Prophets and Writings, the other two parts of the Hebrew Bible, were written over the next seven hundred years, and the Jewish canon was closed around the year 200 before the Common Era (BCE). The time from the close of the canon until 250 of the Common Era (CE) is referred to as the era of the *Tannaim*, the redactors of Jewish law, whose period closed with the editing of the *Mishna* by Rabbi Judah the Patriarch. The next five centuries were the epoch in which the two Talmuds (Babylonian and Jerusalem) were written and edited by scholars called *Amoraim* ("those who recount" Jewish law) and *Savoraim* ("those who ponder" Jewish law). The Babylonian Talmud is of greater legal significance than the Jerusalem Talmud and is a more complete work, other than in the area of agricultural law.

The post-Talmudic era is conventionally divided into three periods: (1) the era of the *Geonim*, scholars who lived in Babylonia until the mid-eleventh century; (2) the era of the *Rishonim* (the early authorities), who lived in North Africa, Spain, Franco-Germany, and Egypt until the end of the fourteenth century; and (3) the period of the *Aharonim* (the latter authorities), which encompasses all scholars of Jewish law from the fifteenth century up to the current era. From the period of the mid-fourteenth century until the early seventeenth century, Jewish law underwent a period of codification, which led to the acceptance of the law code format of Rabbi Joseph Karo (1488–1575), called the *Shulhan Arukh,* as the basis for modern Jewish law. Many consider this to be its own era, the period of the codifiers (*"mekhokikim"*). The *Shulhan Arukh* (and the *Arba'ah Turim* of Rabbi Jacob ben Asher, which preceded it) divided Jewish law into four separate areas: *Orah Hayyim* is devoted to daily, Sabbath, and holiday laws; *Even Ha-Ezer* addresses family law, including financial aspects; *Hoshen Mishpat* codifies financial law; and *Yoreh Deah* contains dietary laws as well as other miscellaneous legal matters. Many significant scholars—themselves as important as Rabbi Karo in status and authority—wrote annotations to his code, which solidified the place of the work and its surrounding comments as the modern touchstone of Jewish law. The most recent complete edition of the *Shulhan Arukh* (Vilna: *Ha-Almanah veha-Ahim Rom,* 1896) contains no less than 113 separate commentaries on the text of Rabbi Karo. In addition, hundreds of other volumes of commentary have been published as self-standing works, a process that continues to this very day. Aside from the law codes and commentaries, for the last twelve hundred years, Jewish law authorities have addressed specific questions of Jewish law in written responsa (in epistolary, question-and-answer form). Collections of such responsa have been published, providing guidance not only to later authorities but also to the community at large. Finally, since the establishment of the State of Israel in 1948, the rabbinical courts of Israel have published their written opinions (*Piske Din*) deciding cases on a variety of matters.

This book focuses on matters discussed in *Orah Hayyim,* which is the most widely studied of the four areas of Jewish law in that it addresses matters of daily life. It opens with the laws related to arising in the morning and then proceeds to discuss the laws of daily prayer, daily blessings, and evening prayers. It then discusses Sabbath laws, new month laws, festival laws, and fast days, and then discusses each of the festivals as they appear in the Jewish calendar: Passover, Shavuot, Rosh Hashanah, Yom Kippur, Sukkot, Hanukah, and Purim. Since the writing of the *Mishna Berura* and the *Arukh HaShulhan* a century ago, no additional complete commentary on this area of Jewish law has been published.

Appendix C:
Biography of Selected Rabbis Mentioned in Mishna Berura

Rif — Rabbi Yitzchak Ben Yaakov HaKohen Alfasi
Born: Kila Chamad, Algeria, 1013
Died: Lucena, Spain, 1103
Talmudist and first halakhic codifier as well as the author of hundreds of responsa in Arabic, author of _Sefer HaHalakhot_, a Talmudic code representing the early rulings on the discussions of the Talmud which was a primary source for the _Rambam_ and the focus of great rabbinical studies in the following centuries.

Bach — Rabbi Yoel Ben Shmuel Sirkes
Born: Lublin, Poland, 1561
Died: Cracow, Poland, 1640
Author of the _Beit Hadash/The Bach_, a major commentary on the _Tur_, where he establishes the source of the laws in the Talmud and traces their developments through the interpretations of the different generations. He also wrote _HaGahot HaBach_, emendations on the Talmud included in the traditional versions of the Talmud. Two major volumes of his responsa were published after his death: _Shealot v'Teshuvot Beit Hadash_, and _Shealot v'Teshuvot Beit Hadash HaHadashot_.

Be'er Heitiv — Rabbi Yehuda Ben Shimon Ashkenazi
Born: Frankfurt, Germany, 1730
Died: Frankfurt, Germany, 1770
Be'er Heitiv is a commentary on _Shulhan Arukh Orakh Hayyim_ and _Even HaEzer_.

Beit Shmuel — **Rabbi Shmuel Ben Uri Shraga Faivish**
Born: c. 1630
Died: Lemberg, c. 1700
Author of *Beit Shmuel*, a commentary on the *Shulhan Arukh, Even HaEzer.*

Hayye Adam — **Rabbi Avraham Danzig**
Born: Poland, 1747 or 1748
Died: Vilna, 1820
A major halakhic authority and codifier; famous for the books *Hayye Adam* and *Hokhmat Adam.*

Rabbi Akiva Ben Moshe Eiger
Born: Eisenstadt, Austria, 1761
Died: Posen, Poland, 1837
Wrote *Tosefot Rabbi Akiva*, a commentary on the Mishneh, as well as *Gilyon HaShas*, comments on the Talmud, *Rashi*, and *Tosefot*, which is included in the traditional editions of the Talmud; also wrote *Chidushei Rabbi Akiva Eiger*, a commentary on the Talmud and *Teshuvas R' Akiva*, a three-volume compendium of Responsa.

Elya Rabba — **Rav Eliyahu ben Binyamin Wolf Shapiro**
Born: Prague, 1660
Died: Prague, 1712
Director of a large Talmudic academy in Prague, published *Eliyahu Zuṭa*, a commentary on the *Levush's* comments on the *Shulhan Arukh*; most important work, *Elya Rabba* or *Eliyahu Rabba*, discusses the *Shulhan Arukh's Orakh Hayyim* section, printed posthumously by his son.

Gra — **Rabbi Eliyahu Ben Shlomo Zalman of Vilna**
Born: Vilna, Lithuania, 1720
Died: Vilna, Lithuania, 1797
Author of countless seforim, many recorded and published by his students. Wrote *Aderet Eliyahu*, a commentary on the Torah; *Divrei*

Eliyahu, a commentary on Ecclesiastes; *Shenos Eliyahu,* a commentary on Neviim. Wrote a commentary on the Mishneh, as well as a commentary on the *Mishneh Torah, Beyur HaGra,* which glosses on the *Shulhan Arukh.* Wrote *Hagahot HaGra,* emendations on the Talmud included in all the traditional editions. Author of a commentary on *Sefer Yetzirah,* one of the main books in Kabbala.

Rema — **Rabbi Moshe Isserles**
Born: Cracow, Poland, 1525
Died: Cracow, Poland, 1572
Author of commentaries on the Torah and tractates of Talmud, the author of the *Darkhei Moshe,* which is a gloss on the *Bet Yosef* and the *Tur*; a compendium of responsa; the *Torat Hatat,* a compendium on the dietary laws; the *Torat Ha-Olah,* a work on the philosophical concepts of Judaism; as well as several works on Kabbala, including *Yesod Sifrei HaKaballa* and a commentary on the *Zohar.* Most famous work is the *Mapah,* which is a gloss on the *Shulhan Arukh,* where he brings the Ashkenazi views into what is otherwise mostly a Sephardic work, thereby making it into a universal code of Jewish law.

Rabbi Yosef Karo
Born: Toledo, Spain, 1488
Died: Safed, Israel, 1575
Author of the *Kesef Mishne,* a commentary on Maimonides' *Mishneh Torah*; the *Bet Yosef,* a commentary on the *Tur*; the *Bedek HaBayit,* his own proofreading of the *Bet Yosef*; and the *Shulhan Arukh.*

Lehem Mishne — **Rabbi Avraham Ben Moshe Di Boton**
Born: Salonika, c. 1545
Died: Salonika, 1588
Notes: Author of *Lehem Mishne,* a commentary on *Rambam* and its early commentaries.

Magen Avraham — **Rabbi Avraham Abeli Gombiner Halevi**
Born: Gumblin, Poland, 1637

Died: Kalish, Poland, 1683

Talmudic scholar, was brought to prominence by the *Shach*.

Rambam/Maimonides — Rabbi Moshe Ben Maimon

Born: Cordova, Spain, 1135

Died: Cairo, Egypt, 1204

Author of *Peirush HaMishnayos*, commentary on the Mishna; *Sefer HaMitzvot*, an enumeration of the 613 commandments and an introduction to *Mishneh Torah*; a monumental and original code of Jewish law also known as *Yad Chazakah*; and *Moreh Nevuchim* (Guide for the Perplexed), a philosophical work.

Maharil — Rabbi Yaakov Ben Moshe Halevi Molln

Born: Mainz, Germany, c. 1365

Died: Worms, Germany, 1427

Leading Ashkenazic halakhic authority of his time. Active in Austria and Germany. Author of *Minhagim*, where he reports on the customs of the German Jews, in particular in rituals, which are often incorporated by the *Rema* in his glosses to the *Shulhan Arukh*.

Ramban/Nachmanides — Rabbi Moshe Ben Nachman

Born: Gerona, Spain, c. 1194

Died: Israel, c. 1270

Great Biblical and Talmudic commentator, Kabbalist, and Jewish leader, and a physician and linguist by trade. Opposed the rationalism of the Rambam while not opposing his halakhic rulings. Author of a major commentary on Chumash, printed in the *Mikraot Gedolot*, which integrates midrashic and kabbalistic elements; a commentary on the Talmud; *Milchamot Hashem*, a halakhic work in defense of the views of the *Rif*; and *Torat HaAdam*, on the laws of the sick and dead.

Ohr Zarua — Rabbi Yitzchak Ben Moshe of Vienna

Born: Bohemia, Germany, c. 1180

Died: Vienna, Austria, c. 1250

Halakhic codifier. Student of *Rabbi Yehuda HaHasid, Raavyah,* and the *Rokeach.* Author of *Ohr Zarua* (*Light is Sown*), a halakhic guide on religious but not civil and criminal law, which includes extensive quotations of sources as well as information about Jewish life at the time.

Pitchei Teshuva — Rabbi Avraham Tzvi Hirsch Ben Yaakov Eisenstadt

Born: Grodno, Russia, 1813
Died: Kovno, Russia, 1868
Rav of Utian. Author of *Pirhei Teshuva,* a running commentary on the *Shulhan Arukh. Pithei Teshuvah (Opportunities for Repentance/ Responsa)* follows the same approach and format of *Shaarei Teshuva* as it provides a digest of responsa as a supplement to the *Shulhan Arukh,* including the responsa composed after the publication of the *Shulhan Arukh.*

Pri Hadash — Rabbi Chizkiyah Ben David Da Silva

Born: Livorno, Italy, 1659
Died: Israel, 1698
Author of *Pri Hadash,* a commentary on the *Shulhan Arukh, Orakh Hayyim, Yoreh Deah,* and *Even HaEzer.* It contains sharp criticisms of the *Shulhan Arukh* as well as earlier codes, with the seeming exception of the *Mishneh Torah.* This commentary seems at times to attempt to undermine the *Shulhan Arukh* as the source of halakhic decisions, and the current version is said to be a somewhat toned-down version of the strongly worded original. It often seems to favor more lenient positions.

Pri Megadim — Rabbi Yossef Ben Meir Teomim

Born: Lemberg, Poland, c. 1727
Died: Frankfurt, Germany, 1792
Author of *Pri Megadim,* a two-part commentary including *Mishbetzos Zahav,* commentary to the Taz, and *Eshel Avraham,* commentary to the *Magen Avraham.* He wrote *Rosh Yossef,* novella on several Talmud treatises.

Radbaz — **Rabbi David Ben Shlomo Ibn Avi Zimra**

Born: Spain, 1480

Died: Safed, Israel, 1574

Chief Rabbi of Egypt for 40 years. Wrote extensive responsa, about 2400, which are compiled under the name *Radbaz*. He tended to favor leniencies in halakhic interpretation. Author of a commentary on the Rambam's *Mishne Torah*.

Ran — **Rabbi Nissim Ben Reuven of Gerona**

Born: Gerona, Spain, c. 1290

Died: Barcelona, Spain, c. 1380

Author of *HaRan*, a commentary on the *Rif* which is printed in the back of many Talmudic tractates; *Hidushei Ha-Ran*, a commentary to the Talmud (many question his authorship on Shabbat, which is the *Ritva*). Also wrote *Drashot HaRan* on the basis of faith and philosophy, and his responsa, of which only 77 are known, are collected in *Teshuvot HaRan*.

Rashba — **Rabbi Shlomo Ben Avraham Ibn Aderet**

Born: Barcelona, Spain, c. 1235

Died: Barcelona, Spain, c. 1310

Wrote *Hidushei HaRashba*, a commentary on the Talmud; and *Hidushei Aggadot HaShas* a commentary on rabbinical legends. Author of *Teshuvot HaRashba*, 8 volumes containing about 16,000 responsa, the most extensive of any *Rishon*, which are of great importance to *p'sak halakha* and lay the foundation of the later codes like the *Tur* and *Shulhan Arukh*.

Rashi — **Rabbi Shlomo Yitzchaki**

Born: Troyes, France, c. 1040

Died: Troyes, France, c. 1105

Wrote famous commentaries on *Tanakh* and the Talmud. After his death, students in France and Germany, called *Tosafists*, elaborated on his commentaries, creating another famous commentary of the

Talmud, entitled *Tosafot* (additions). People rarely study Talmud without referencing the Rashi and Tosafot commentaries, which surround the Talmud's text.

Rosh — Rabbi Ashe Ben Yechiel

Born: Germany, c. 1250
Died: Toledo, Spain, 1327

Wrote a commentary on the Mishna, *Perush HaRosh*, a commentary on the Talmud patterned after the Rif, *Hilkhot HaRosh* (also known as *Piskei HaRosh*, and *Sefer Asheri*); a compilation of *halakhot* which are the basis for subsequent compilation including the Tur, and which are included in the end of the corresponding Talmud tractate, *Tosafot HaRosh*, where he clarifies the *Tosafot*. He also wrote *Teshuvot Ha Rosh*, a compilation of over a thousand of his responsa, and *Orkhot Hayyim*, on ethics, which includes 131 principles organized in six parts, one for each workday.

Shach — Rabbi Shabbetai Ben Meir Hakohen

Born: Amstibov, Lithuania, 1621
Died: Hollischau, Bohemia, c. 1663

Wrote *Siftei HaKohen/Shakh* (*Lips of a Kohen*), a major commentary on the *Shulhan Arukh Yoreh Deah* and *Hoshen Mishpat*, which includes attempts to rule on issues where Rabbi Karo and the *Rema* differed. Author of *Nekudot HaKesef*, a response to the Taz, with whom he conducted a sharp controversy.

Sma — Rabbi Yehoshua Ben Alexander Hakohen Falk

Born: Lublin, Poland, c. 1550
Died: Lemberg, Germany, 1614

Rosh Yeshiva in Lemberg. Author of *D'risha uPrisha*, twin commentaries on the *Tur*. He also wrote *Sefer Me'iras Einayim/SMA* (*The Book that Enlightens the Eyes*), a commentary on *Shulhan Arukh Chosen Mishpat*, which is included in the standard editions of the *Shulhan Arukh*.

Smag — **Rabbi Moshe Ben Yaakov of Couchy**

Born: France, early 1200s
Died: Spain, middle/late 1200s

Author of *Tosafot Yeshanim* to Yoma. He wrote the *Sefer Mitzvot Gadol/SMAG*, an enumeration of the 613 *mitzvot* based on Rambam's *Mishne Torah*, which marks the penetration of the *Rambam* in France. The importance of the *Smag* was only surpassed by the publication of the *Shulhan Arukh*, and its author is regarded as one of the major *poskim* of all generations.

Taz — **Rabbi David Ben Shmuel Halevi**

Born: Ludmir, Volhynia, 1586
Died: Lemberg, Poland, 1667

Author of *Turei Zahav/Taz* (*Golden Rows*), a major commentary on all sections of the *Shulhan Arukh*, of which the ones on *Orakh Hayyim* and *Yoreh Deah* gained greatest acclaim. He attempts to re-establish the original decisions of the *Bet Yosef*, refuting subsequent criticisms and bringing order to the commentaries on the *Shulhan Arukh*. He often disagreed with the *Shakh*.

Tur — **Rabbi Yaakov Ben Asher**

Born: Cologne, Germany, c. 1275
Died: Toledo, Spain c. 1349

Torah commentator, Talmudist and Halakhic codifier. He wrote *Kitzur Piskei HaRosh*, compiling halakhic conclusions of the Rosh. Author of *Arba Turim* (*The Four Rows*), the code of Jewish law that bridged the gap between the French and Spanish schools and formed the basis for the *Shulhan Arukh*. Unlike the Rambam in *Mishne Torah*, he includes all sources. Also, he only deals with the laws that are still applicable in the post-Temple period. He introduces the division in four parts—*Orakh Hayyim*, on the laws of daily practice throughout the year, including Shabbat and holidays; *Yoreh Deah*, on the laws of kashrut and purity, mourning and *niddah, Chosen Mishpat*, on civil and monetary issues; and *Even HaEzer*, on marriage and divorce.

Appendix D:
A Brief Note on the Names of Jewish Books

A note on the names of Jewish books is needed, if for no other reason than to explain why the single most significant work of Jewish law written in the last 500 years, the *Shulhan Arukh*, should have a name which translates into English as "*The Set Table.*" Unlike the tradition of most Western law, in which the titles to scholarly publications reflect the topics of the works,[1] the tradition in Jewish legal literature is that a title rarely names the relevant subject. Instead, the title usually consists either of a pun based on the title of an earlier work on which the current writing comments, or of a literary phrase into which the authors' names have been worked (sometimes in reliance on literary license).

A few examples demonstrate each phenomenon. Rabbi Jacob ben Asher's classical treatise on Jewish law was entitled "*The Four Pillars*" (*Arba Turim*) because it classified all of Jewish law into one of four areas. A major commentary on this work that, to a great extent, supersedes the work itself is called "*The House of Joseph*" (*Beit Yosef*), since it was written by Rabbi Joseph Karo. Once Karo's commentary (i.e., the house) was completed, one could hardly see "*The Four Pillars*" on which it rested. A reply commentary by Rabbi Joel Sirkes, designed to defend "*The Four Pillars*" from Karo's criticisms, is called "*The New House*" (*Bayit Hadash*). Sirkes proposed his work (i.e., the new house) as a replacement for Karo's prior house.

---

1   Consider John T. Noonan, Jr. and Edward McGlynn Gaffney, *Religious Freedom: History, Cases and Other Material on the Interaction of Religion and Government* (New York: Foundation Press, 2001).

When Rabbi Karo wrote his own treatise on Jewish law, he called it *"The Set Table"* (*Shulhan Arukh*), which was based on (i.e., located in) *"The House of Joseph,"* his previous commentary on Jewish law. Rabbi Moses Isserles's glosses on *"The Set Table"*—which were really intended vastly to expand *"The Set Table"*—are called *"The Tablecloth,"* because no matter how nice the table is, once the tablecloth is on it, one hardly notices the table. Rabbi David Halevi's commentary on the *Shulhan Arukh* was named the *"Golden Pillars"* (*Turai Zahav*), denoting an embellishment on the *"legs"* of the *"Set Table."* This type of humorous interaction continues to this day in terms of titles of commentaries on the classical Jewish law work, the *Shulhan Arukh.*

Additionally, there are book titles that are mixed literary puns and biblical verses. For example, Rabbi Shabtai ben Meir HaKohen wrote a very sharp critique on the above-mentioned *Turai Zahav* (*Golden Pillars*), which he entitled *Nekudat Hakesef*, "Spots of Silver," a veiled misquote of the verse in Song of Songs 1:11, which states "we will add bands of gold to your spots of silver" (*turai zahav al nekudat hakesef*, with the word *turia* misspelled). Thus, HaKohen's work is really *"The Silver Spots on the Golden Pillars,"* with the understanding that it is the silver that appears majestic when placed against an entirely gold background.

Other works follow the model of incorporating the name of the scholar into the work. For example, the above-mentioned Rabbi Shabtai ben Meir HaKohen's commentary on the *Shulhan Arukh* itself is entitled *Seftai Kohen*, *"The Words of the Kohen,"* (a literary embellishment of "Shabtai HaKohen," the author's name). Rabbi Moses Feinstein's collection of responsa is called *Iggerot Moshe*, "Letters from Moses." Hundreds of normative works of Jewish law follow this model. Consider for example, the works of Rabbi Moshe Schreiber (Moses Sofer), whose primary work of Jewish law is an acronym of his name, ChaTaM Sofer, (translated as *Seal of the Scribe* and acronym for *Chidushei Toras Moshe Sofer*). His son, Rabbi Avrohom Shmuel Binyamin Sofer (born in 1815 and died in 1872) also wrote a volume of Jewish law, entitled *Ktav Sofer* (translated as

Writing of the Scribe), and a grandson named Rabbi Akiva Sofer authored writings titled *Daas Sofer*, *"The Insights of the Scribe."* Indeed, many of the descendants of Rabbi Sofer write in Jewish law using the word Sofer within their works.

Of course, a few leading works of Jewish law are titled in a manner that informs the reader of their content. Thus, the fourteenth-century Spanish sage Nahmanides (*Ramban*) wrote a work on issues in causation entitled "Indirect Causation in [Jewish] Tort Law" (*Grama Benezikin*), and the modern Jewish law scholar Eliav Schochatman's classical work on civil procedure in Jewish law is called "Arranging the Case," a modern Hebrew synonym for civil procedure.

INDEX

www.ingramcontent.com/pod-product-compliance
Lightning Source LLC
Chambersburg PA
CBHW051434050726
47593CB00005B/1777